D0778774

# The Representative of the People?

## Voters and Voting in England under the Early Stuarts

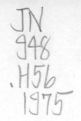

# The Representative of the People?

Voters and Voting in England under
the Early Stuarts

DEREK HIRST

*Fellow and Director of Studies in History*
*Trinity Hall, Cambridge*

CAMBRIDGE UNIVERSITY PRESS

CAMBRIDGE

LONDON · NEW YORK · MELBOURNE

Published by the Syndics of the Cambridge University Press
The Pitt Building, Trumpington Street, Cambridge CB2 IRP
Bentley House, 200 Euston Road, London NW1 2DB
32 East 57th Street, New York, NY 10022, USA
296 Beaconsfield Parade, Middle Park, Melbourne 3206, Australia

Library of Congress Catalogue Card Number: 75-9283

ISBN: 0 521 20810 6

First published 1975

Printed in Great Britain by
Western Printing Services Ltd
Bristol

*For my parents*

# Contents

# Acknowledgements

The number of notes and appendices to this book will indicate that it began its life as a Ph.D. thesis, and while they had to be retained in order to support what could be a rather contentious case, it is hoped that the scale of the problem discussed will lessen their deterrent effect to the general reader. The research for that thesis was financed by a research studentship from the Department of Education and Science and the Master and Fellows of Gonville and Caius College, and latterly by a Research Fellowship from the Master and Fellows of Trinity Hall, Cambridge. To all of these bodies, and particularly the last, in whose pleasant company this book was written, I am indebted.

It is often suggested that any product of academic research is a co-operative enterprise: this can be nowhere more true than of work which attempts to study aspects both of parliamentary politics and local developments through the country, as this one does. Because the scope of the enquiry is so broad, a deep investigation is precluded, and the consequence is that authorities on particular fields are drawn by the kindness of their hearts to set right some of the more egregious errors. The debts incurred in the compilation of this work are too many to acknowledge in full here, and it is hoped that the notes provide some redress for this omission. I am happy, however, to be able to thank those to whom my obligations are greatest.

The Marquess of Bath, the Marquess of Salisbury, the Marquess Townshend of Raynham, the Earl Fitzwilliam and the Trustees of the Wentworth Woodhouse Estate, Sir Robert Throckmorton, Bt, and Capt. C. B. Fetherstone-Dilke, all kindly permitted the consultation of documents in their ownership. My thanks also extend to the staffs of libraries, record offices and town halls, whose help and kindness made my research possible. A glance at the bibliography will indicate just how many have been my benefactors, but I would like to single out for especial thanks the staffs of Cambridge University Library, and of the Bedfordshire, Essex, Kent, Norfolk, Northamptonshire and Somerset County Record Offices.

Contrary to some popular belief, academic historians are not normally hyper-competitive and suspicious individuals, and I have benefited from discussions with many, particularly Vivienne Millenson, whose forthcoming Columbia University Ph.D. thesis on patronage and elections should fill the large gap left in this work, to John Morrill, Charles Phythian-Adams, Jack Pole, Roger Schofield, Hassell Smith, Joan Thirsk, Prof. David Underdown, John Walter and Keith Wrightson. My Ph.D. examiners, Profs G. E. Aylmer and J. R. Jones, also have my thanks for their valuable criticism and advice. But the sometimes frustrating process of research and writing is not sustained by detailed scholarly criticism alone, and debts for their encouragement are owed to many, to Rosemary Delbridge most of all, Prof. G. R. Elton, Clive Holmes, Neil McKendrick, Roy and Sue Porter, Quentin Skinner, Jonathan Steinberg, Richard Tuck and Prof. John Wallace.

My greatest debts are fewer, and I cannot thank them sufficiently: Valerie Pearl, who supervised part of my research, John Cooper and Conrad Russell who unstintingly read through drafts of the text, have over a long period never ceased to stimulate and challenge. They saved me from many, though I fear not all, of my errors. But still more do I owe to Jack Plumb. He it was who first appreciated the significance of the electorate in the early modern period, who unselfishly guided the early stages of my research, and criticised the draft of this text. He has never failed in his encouragement and his friendship.

D.H.

# Abbreviations and notes

| | |
|---|---|
| A.O. | Archive Office. |
| *A.P.C.* | *Acts of the Privy Council.* |
| B.M. | British Museum classmark. |
| Bodl. | Bodleian Library, Oxford, classmark. |
| *C.D. 1621.* | *Commons Debates in 1621*, ed. W. Notestein, F. H. Relf and H. Simpson (New Haven, 1935). |
| *C.J.* | *Journals of the House of Commons.* |
| *C.S.P.D.* | *Calendar of State Papers, Domestic.* |
| C.U.L. | Cambridge University Library classmark. |
| *D'Ewes* (C). | *The Journal of Sir Simonds D'Ewes from the first recess of the Long Parliament to the withdrawal of King Charles from London*, ed. W. H. Coates (New Haven, 1942). |
| *D'Ewes* (N). | *The Journal of Sir Simonds D'Ewes from the beginning of the Long Parliament to the trial of the Earl of Strafford*, ed. W. Notestein (New Haven, 1923). |
| *E.H.R.* | *English Historical Review.* |
| Harvard | Houghton Library, Harvard, classmark. |
| *H.M.C.* | *Historical Manuscripts Commission, Report.* |
| M.A. | Unpublished M.A. thesis. |
| N.N.R.O. | Norfolk and Norwich Record Office. |
| N.R.O. | Northamptonshire Record Office. |
| Ph.D. | Unpublished Ph.D. thesis. |
| P.R.O. | Public Record Office classmark. |
| R.O. | Record Office. |
| U.L. | University Library. |
| *V.C.H.* | *Victoria County History.* |

Contemporary abbreviations have been expanded throughout, although spelling and punctuation have been retained.

Dates are given in Old Style, although the year is taken as beginning on 1 January. The place of all 17th-century publications is London, unless otherwise stated.

'... we are the Representative of the people of England.'
> – Thomas Hobbes, describing Parliament's justification of
> its decision to fortify Hull against the King in 1642.
> *Behemoth*, ed. F. Tonnies (London, 1969), 120.

'... in Parliament, ... the Lords and Commons represent the whole
Kingdome.'
'The vertue of representation hath beene denyed to the Commons, ...
and so that great Priviledges [sic] of all Priviledges, that unmoveable
Basis of all honour and power, whereby the House of Commons
claimes the entire rite of all the Gentry and Commonalty of England,
has beene attempted to bee shaken and disturbed.'
> – Henry Parker, *Observations upon some of his Majesties
> late Answers and Expresses* (1642), 9, 15.

'.... both Houses of Parliament containing all the Peeres, and representing all the Commons, of England.'
> – *A Remonstrance or Declaration of Parliament* (1642)
> B.M., E148/23, p.2.

'... this House representing the whole Body Politicke of this Kingdome.'
> – *Mr St John his Speech in Parliament ... Concerning the
> Charge of Treason then exhibited to the Bishops* (1641),
> 1–2.

# Introduction

## The Context

In the years which Prof. Plumb has suggestively termed those of 'the rage of party' at the end of the 17th century, the political impact of the electorate was obvious. Whig electoral successes in the Exclusion Crisis and 1689, the inroads of Tack and anti-Tack propaganda in 1704, the Tory landslide of 1710 borne in on Sacheverellite excitement and war-weariness, all reflect intense arousal and involvement on the part of very large numbers of ordinary voters. But this had just as clearly not been the case a century earlier. The Elizabethan studies of Sir John Neale reveal a political scene where the wishes of the bulk of the population counted for little, and where the alignments that mattered were those of the patrons and the gentry.[1] Political consensus and the more or less effective workings of the patronage system averted both elections and the open agitation of issues.

The intervening century must therefore have been one of rapid electoral development. The attitudes and awareness of those active in the troubled 1640s and 1650s suggest that the first half of that period may have witnessed the decisive change. Sophisticated calculations were being made in the revolutionary years about the likely behaviour of the electorate: the timing of the issue of writs for new elections was subject to political manipulation in the 1640s, in the disputes on when, or even whether, to hold Recruiter elections to fill vacant seats in the Long Parliament. It was on a similar rock to this that the Rump Parliament foundered, for the glaringly unrepresentative image of that body contri-buted to the fatal alienation of the Army. Both conservative Rumpers and Army radicals had clear views on the potentially major political and social consequences of certain courses of electoral action (holding, or not holding, new elections on the old, or a new, franchise), and all parties were playing a recognisable game of electoral politics in consequence. The Army Grandees, Lambert and Cromwell, presumably had certain immediate political expectations in mind when concocting the franchise and constituency redistribution provisions of the Instrument of Govern-ment. Politicians at mid-century considered that the loyalties of voters or potential voters were of enormous national significance, but such a conclu-sion would hardly have been reached two generations earlier.

Marked change had taken place in certain major areas. The financial importunity of the early Stuarts, and their inability to live with any particular parliament, occasioned the summoning of yet more parliaments to replace the ones that had failed before. The membership of these parliaments was increasingly contested as the status-hungry gentry multiplied in number, and as developing polarisation along a 'Court' versus 'Country' axis meant that a further incentive to seek a seat in the House was added to that of social climbing. Gentlemen began to see the House of Commons as a means of realising political as well as social objectives. The number of contested elections rose fast; and as the gentry were beginning to manifest novel political concerns in looking for a seat, the election campaigns which they brought about tended to borrow something from those new concerns. The anxieties of the candidates were thus communicated to a wider group.

A further, but less obvious, change was that there was a growing awareness of the fact that an electorate existed. In part, this was an inevitable consequence of the more frequent contacts with the voters occasioned by more contests. The increased activity of the electors was causally related to the greater eagerness of candidates to ply for their support. But they were also becoming more conspicuous for a quite different reason – there were more of them, and this inexorably altered their role. This expansion of the electorate was itself partly a result of gentry activity, as, in pursuit of personal aggrandisement or political goals, candidates sought to extend the franchise in many urban constituencies, thus by-passing narrower groups hostile to their campaigns. The efforts of the gentry were aided by indigenous pressures building up in many communities, which culminated in domestic challenges to unpopular urban oligarchies. But the expansion was also a result of a quite unrelated development, the impersonal devaluation of the 40s. freehold qualification for the vote in the counties as inflation took its toll. And when the size and activity of the electorate had grown considerably, as was the case by the middle of the 17th century, it became, as we shall see, more appropriate to think in terms of voters than of interests and connections.

The fact that development was taking place in this period is itself thoroughly significant. It meant that many participants in the electoral process were unfamiliar with what were by the end of the century easily recognised features of the landscape. Consequently, a certain naïveté is commonly visible. One of the most obvious instances of this is the way in which the Levellers in the later 1640s were advocating electoral reforms whose probable political effects would have been largely counter-productive when measured in terms of their other aims. As the maypoles which greeted Charles II's return from exile suggested, the freedom coveted by a majority of the population was one providing for ale-drinking and an implementation of the canons of good-neighbourliness, rather than for the rational exercise of political rights.[2] The execution of the Levellers' Agreement of the People would in all likelihood have heralded a return to a version of the old order. The Instrument's electoral reforms were equally short-sighted. An elimination of the rotten boroughs and of the poorest voters (by raising the property qualification) certainly must have made the electorate as a whole less easily influenced. But it also ensured that it became more solidly composed of those substantial people who had little cause by 1653 to love much of what Cromwell aspired towards. The removal of those boroughs where pressures, military or otherwise, could have been brought to bear (such as the influence exercised by the Lord Warden or Admiral in some of the decayed Cinque Ports before the war) meant that the government was unable to compensate for its unpopularity with the 'independent' voters. Ignorance of some of the salient facts of electoral life thus led to serious political error.

It must also be held to account for at least some of the confusion which surrounds modern treatments of some aspects of this subject, most particularly the lengthy debate of recent years over the extent to which the electoral proposals of the Levellers were 'democratic'. Clarity has been sought in a field where almost by definition it could not be, as few had yet succeeded in thinking coherently on the matter. Discoveries of apparent contradiction or uncertainty are therefore only to be expected.

Part of the purpose of this study is to examine this uncertainty, and the process of change and development which gave rise to it. Such an undertaking has, however, a wider potential, and is capable of providing more than the antiquarian's verdict that electoral politics were in their infancy. A study of the electorate in this period must also raise the question of the extent of the 'political nation', that group which had a part to play in politics. This can then tell us how 'open', socially, politics was. Political histories of the period tend to preoccupy themselves with the gentry and, sometimes, the richer townsmen, displaying an implicit assumption that the 'meaner sort' in general effectively neuters. In towns, retailers, artisans and below, in the countryside, yeomen, or perhaps husbandmen and below (for, given the traditional adulation of the English yeoman, most historians are constrained to make passing reference to him), have been tacitly dismissed as mere economic beasts of burden. It is admitted that they had what passed for a remedy for their immediate grievances, or at least a way of letting off steam, in riot. When times became too bad, they could let the local elite know they were suffering and required attention by knocking down fences or by seizing grain. But it is often thought that the more legitimate ways of demanding redress of their wrongs were closed to them. They had no vote, and so could not make their voices heard. And even if they had a vote, it is axiomatic that politics functioned without reference to them: they cast their votes at the behest of their betters, and then the parties to the transaction promptly forgot each other. The victorious candidate went off to Westminster, and operated there in in a closed world, immune to pressures from outside and below. What few voters there were went home, expecting little of a parliament which voted taxes and passed a few statutes *ex cathedra*.

Such assumptions about the political structure of pre-civil-war England are open to challenge. Political consensus and the patronage system broke down, elections and contests ensued, and a surprisingly large social group became involved in legitimate politics. This might be suspected on *prima facie* grounds alone, for the sophisticated popular activity of the 1640s is unlikely to have broken out spontaneously, fully developed, with the calling of the Long Parliament and the collapse of royal authority: some prehistory and education had surely taken place. Even before civil war temporarily submerged the old order, parliamentary politics was not limited to the few at the summit of the social pyramid. Many people in the localities participated, and had expectations that parliament might deliver political goods to them.

It is of course a truism that any lengthy period is one of transition, but thanks to the occurrence of a revolution in the middle of the 17th century, there has been a temptation for historians to borrow from Marxian analysis and to think in terms of defined social groups, whose competing fortunes produced concrete political developments. This approach makes it easy to write off the majority of the population as forming a sub-political culture, and to concentrate on those groups who provided the real political actors. But reality was neither highly stratified nor easily categorised. The aggressions of a rising middle class, of a rising gentry, a declining gentry, the concerns of the puritanical 'industrious sort of people', have all been used to explain or elucidate the events of the period, but as Prof. Hexter has demonstrated, it is not easy to talk of coherent social groups at this time.[3] This might be deduced anyway from the very high degree of social mobility which prevailed. The categories themselves present problems, for, as contemporaries were well aware, the whole question of status (for example, in its relation to wealth) was unclear. 'Gentility' meant one thing to the College of Arms, another to the perturbed gentleman commentator who might insist on four generations of respectability, and quite another to the very wealthy townsman. Urban documents characterise some men as, for example, 'gent. draper', whereas the two might strictly have been mutually exclusive; and the Crown itself was as always helping to erode the distinctions by knighting its rich merchant creditors.

Further confusion was caused by the emergence, apparently in the first half of the 17th century, of what might be called the 'functional gentle-man', the person who qualified for the distinction solely by virtue of his office. There are signs that service on a grand jury was sufficient to bring recognition of social arrival even to quite poor men in the counties; in the towns, membership of the corporation, or sometimes of the aldermanic bench (especially in smaller communities), brought the label 'Mr'.[4] More to the point of this study, the identity of the groups lower down, the 'yeomen' or the 'freeholders', was very imprecise. In the case of the latter, contemporaries were evidently unsure whether the freeholder was an economic, a status, or a legal commodity. The statistician Gregory King might think of him as someone with a certain income from land, equating him approximately with a yeoman; while to others the term meant merely someone with a certain legal estate in his land.[5] Confusion here had direct political repercussions, for freeholders of a certain level were of course the electors in county constituencies. And as Cromwell's defence of the Anabaptists in his army showed, to some people other considerations were anyway becoming more important than the social.

The imprecision of social divisions is complemented by the existence of a common social ideology amongst rich and poor. Dearth caused both groups to turn on profiteering middlemen, the 'caterpillers of the common weal': the magistrates through quarter sessions and the enforcement of the marketing regulations, the commons by less peaceful means. There was a common espousal of a philosophy of an ordered, inter-dependent commonwealth, and while on the one hand this was indeed frequently a pious cover for unrestrained capitalistic enterprise, there seems to have been less hypocrisy from the other side, for there was little direct challenge to the ideal of the common weal from the poor. It is now known that pre-industrial riots tended to be orderly, restrained affairs with very limited goals, and the better sort often knew this too. There are, it is true, abundant instances of outspoken governmental responses to disorder, of horrified statements about the 'many-headed monster', but these were not matched by reactions on the ground. When the better sort were personally confronted with real popular grievances they often responded sympathetically, by moving to alleviate those grievances through the courts or from their own pockets, or even by siding with rioters, particularly when the disturbers of the local community came from outside. Riot and popular turbulence was much more an attempt to enforce a traditional social order on those self-interested individuals seen as upsetting it, than an outright attack on that order. The local gentry, knowing this, could afford to take a less panic-stricken and more sympathetic attitude than central government or commentators in London or the pulpit. As the Earl of Exeter, ordered to co-ordinate activity against a major enclosure riot in the Fens in 1638, reported soothingly to the King, 'In my opinion you shall not need to fear a general revolt, for though divers [gentry] that look upon them do allow of their work, being glad of the reformation [of enclosures], knowing their intents to be no further, and in that respect will levy no arms against them, yet in my opinion they are otherwise touching their allegiance dutiful subjects.' And while Viscount Conway ordered one of his servants to take defensive precautions during the anti-Laudian riots in London in May 1640, he added, 'but I believe the apprentices will make but a Shrove Tuesday business of it' – that is, the rising was seen as a bacchanalia, rather than a direct assault on order and authority. Such undismayed responses on the part of superiors to illegal acts by their inferiors were common throughout the country: accusations of gentry complicity in riots were frequent and well-substantiated (most obviously when the ultimate outsider, the Crown, was the enemy with its enclosure policy in the Fens and the South-West in the 1630s), as were gentry sureties for wrong-doers. If we look away from the normative pronouncements, that the only way to keep the poor down was by terror, and consider what happened locally, the degree to which the better sort were in conflict with their inferiors, whether ideologically or in their actions, diminishes markedly.[6] The poor were not yet the social horror which the years of upheaval made them for some.

Moreover, the gap between rich and poor was not yet as wide as it was to become. There were more gradations in the social scale, for economic development and expansion had not yet produced a society where rich and poor did not shade imperceptibly into one another. London obviously had its merchant princes and its totally destitute, as did the provincial capitals. But more characteristic of the bulk of settlements was Richard Baxter's comment on the governors of Kidderminster before the war, that most of them were worth less than £40 per annum, little more than the ordinary craftsmen. Concentration of wealth into few hands was equally incomplete on the land. English agriculture in the first half of the 17th century was still mainly in the hands of a peasantry, both large and small. It was only the agricultural difficulties of later years which produced the characteristic English landed structure of landlord, tenant farmer and landless labourers.[7] When neither farming nor trade yet displayed a marked concentration of riches or resources, and when the cultural shock of the revolutionary movements of the later 1640s was still to be felt, there was possibly a greater potential open-ness inherent in the social structure than was the case in the increasingly oligarchical society of the 18th century. While pre-war society was undeniably very hierarchical, it was not rigidly stratified, for there were many points of contact up and down the social scale. It must therefore have been more difficult to say '*this* is the dividing line, people below this level shall be excluded from the realm of political action' – for there was no obvious cut-off point. It is contended below that the 40s. freehold, the qualification for the vote in the counties, was by no means a rigorous or even particularly meaningful requirement in this period. And politicians both locally and in the House of Commons displayed great readiness to allow more and more people in to vote in the towns.

This widespread lack of clarity accounts for many of the electoral developments which are considered in the course of this study. Unfamiliarity with the basics of the election process allowed more people to vote; relative absence of social conflict made the gentry for a brief period prepared to accept them. The increasing perfection, which came with increased familiarity, of the election process in the latter part of the century served to fix, and thus to limit, the electorate; gentry fears for their position, engendered by the Civil War, caused them to view with greater disquiet those popular forces challenging for the vote. The agricultural change which was diminishing the number of freeholders on the land contributed to the success of the gentry's restrictive efforts.[8] The political world which before the Civil War had seemed so open in several important respects was giving place to a rather narrower one.

Gentry readiness to tolerate the political presence of a larger number of the commons was predictably not merely the fruit of a complacent sense of unchallenged social superiority. There was also a political point to the attitude. Many members of the House of Commons in the early 17th century were becoming concerned for the survival of that institution, and of parliament as a whole, and as they prepared their defence, their eyes opened more to certain features of the House.

Mr J. P. Cooper has pointed to the peculiarity of English constitutional development at this time, emphasising that, unlike other European states, no marked trend towards absolutism was visible. Most obviously, the Crown had very circumscribed powers of taxation. Contemporaries were not unaware of that special blessing, which was further proof, if that were needed, of England's excellence. As Sir Robert Phelips, one of the opposition leaders in 1625, declaimed, 'Wee are the last monarchy in Christendome that retayne our originall rights and constitutions.'[9] Any extension by the Crown of its ability to tax was seen by the more thoughtful, or fearful, of its subjects as a move in an ominously fashionable direction. The financially-pressed Elizabethan and early Stuart governments' growing reliance upon their powers to regulate the economy as a source of revenue brought these fears to the surface. The exploitation of patents of monopoly over certain commodities aroused storms for all three monarchs, but worse than these was the Stuarts' resort to the imposition of new (and higher) customs duties. The judges' favourable decision in Bate's Case in 1606 occasioned explicit warnings in the

Commons in 1610 that parliament was endangered by this policy; the grievance was subsequently reverted to repeatedly. It helped to break the parliaments of 1614 and 1621; Phelips in the winter of 1623-4 apparently saw it as a, if not the, major ingredient in the Crown's difficulties with parliament, and a grave precedent for the future survival of representative institutions; and the Grand Remonstrance in 1641 rated it a large instrument in the campaign of the Jesuits and the prelatical party to subvert the constitution.[10]

Conscious that they were being outflanked in the field of taxation, their major function and the chief reason for their existence; made apprehensive by the fate of representative assemblies abroad; and aggravated by the privilege disputes which were inevitable with an increasingly self-conscious and (as the Crown's financial needs grew) important body of men, the Commons could no longer look unthinkingly to consensus with the Crown to preserve them. They had to seek elsewhere for a justification and a defence. Accordingly, unconsidered and relatively infrequent assertions in Elizabethan parliaments that members of the Commons were 'public men', in a special relationship to their country, rapidly developed into a stridently asserted, if incoherent, emphasis on the fact of representation. A defensive case was being made, even if often not explicitly, that the House was a peculiar institution by virtue of a special merit of its own, and no thanks to the Crown. Members more and more stressed their duty to the country, even in opposition to that to their king. A greater preoccupation with the representative nature of the House became visible: the linkage of Commons to country, rather than to Crown, was more frequently dwelt on.[11]

In part, this linkage was strengthened by the obvious unpopularity of the Stuart Court. But it also probably had earlier roots in localist reaction against increasing centralisation, which was setting the two attitudes of loyalty to Crown or Country in confused conflict. Some of the earliest avowals of responsibility to the country in opposition to royal policy appear to have been in the monopolies debates under Elizabeth, when the attentions of patentees in the localities were feared. Dr Hassell Smith's recent work on Norfolk in this period shows this local division between the local 'community' and the agents of an interventionist Court to have been the crucial factor in county politics, and it would be surprising if this did not have some effect in estranging from the Crown those sent up to Westminster.[12] Certainly, in the next parliament where patentees were most at issue, that of 1621, the patent most bitterly attacked was that for ale-houses, where central nominees were most clearly usurping the powers of the local JPs in the invigilation of those ubiquitous institutions.

Members whose agreed duty was to speak for the country to the Crown, and who now felt themselves at odds with one part of that imperative, as the Crown appeared to be undermining both their parliamentary and their local positions, inevitably aligned themselves more closely with the other, and stressed their representative role. The Commons, then, were becoming more conscious of their standing as a representative institution. They also had an interest in stressing that function, in order to justify their obstruction of what they took to be dangerous trends which the Crown was initiating. A consequence of this was that their electoral base was brought home to them. When a member protested that he served there for thousands and therefore had a duty to question a new demand for taxes or whatever, he was drawing notice to the existence and wishes of countless people outside the House. The Commons were thus becoming more alert to the subject of their electoral position. This awareness was intensified, and given political point, by governmental blunders, which served to heighten the fears of sensitive souls.

The Buckinghamshire election dispute of 1604 was interpreted by many members as being a blatant attempt on the Crown's part to assert its judicial control over elections, and hence over who should sit. It pointed down the high road to packed and muzzled parliaments. The virulence of the protests, forcing the Crown to concede, indicates that this apprehension was widespread, and it was reawakened in the next parliament, that of 1614. Some of the King's servants apparently set themselves up as 'undertakers': that is, they undertook to prepare a programme and, by dint of concessions and conciliating the opposition, to get it and supply through the House. Garbled versions of this leaked into an atmosphere poisoned by an obvious and objectionable attempt by the Chancellor of the Duchy of Lancaster to rig the election for Stockbridge, Hampshire: in that context, undertakers 'fixing' the business of parliament looked doubly dangerous. Member after member rose to denounce packing as destructive of liberty and the constitution, and the parliament never recovered from its disastrous beginning.[13]

The rapidity with which this fear of packed parliaments arose is difficult to understand. The electoral attentions of the Court do not seem to have been especially unwelcome, and if anything often the reverse, in the high Elizabethan days examined by Sir John Neale. Some of the larger boroughs did, it is true, hold out against outside interference, but the 1571 debate in the House on the election of strangers by boroughs reveals no strong current of hostility to the Court or to magnates. A member for King's Lynn proposed a £40 fine on every borough returning the nominee of a nobleman, but this probably resulted from the local problem of the Duke of Norfolk, for whom some religious as well as localist distrust may have been felt, and it does not seem to have found much of an echo in the sentiments of other members.[14] A generation later such complaisance was at an end: fears for the future were certainly present, and vehemently expressed in the Buckinghamshire dispute, at the start of James's reign. And yet the Court does not seem to have been excessively active in the 1604 election, when compared with what we know of Elizabethan interventions by the Council or the magnates. The Jacobean Court had hardly yet had time to settle itself in and confirm its unpopularity, so it would seem unwise to attribute these undoubted constitutional misgivings to James's new departure. But if Court intervention at elections was becoming more objectionable, as seems to have been the case, and if that intervention was not growing appreciably greater, then the changed reception for it must have been caused by a changing political climate. Given that James himself could not yet be blamed for the novel unpopularity of courtiers as candidates, then it seems that we must turn to the last years of Elizabeth for an explanation.

There had been some resentment at blatant and dubious royal electoral activity in the 1580s, but the protest pales beside that of 1604, and a widespread alteration in attitudes to the Court between those dates is indicated. A possible cause might be the Queen's loosening grip in her last years, which allowed the Court to become riven by the faction dispute of Essex and Cecil, and patronage to become exercised in an increasingly self-interested fashion. The Court in consequence became more isolated from, and less responsive to, feelings in the country. The case made by Essex in his rebellion to the effect that power and office was monopolised by a corrupt clique may have reinforced people's suspicions.[15] Dr Hassell Smith's work has shown us that major doubts existed in Norfolk, polarising county society into the few with material and profitable links with the Court, and the bulk of the community which found itself in diminishing agreement with it. Consciousness of this division was not limited to the magisterial rank. The increasing governmental regulation, both economic, social and military, which developed as Elizabeth's reign advanced, meant multiplication of rates, whether for the poor, for highway maintenance, or the financing of musters: some of these, besides being unpopular, were also of questionable status, and were therefore discussed as well as disliked locally. Legalist unease was heightened by the implementation of some of these new policies, for Crown concern for efficiency led to the JPs being by-passed, as when growing military activity after 1585 resulted in the establishment of a permanent Lieutenancy system and the repeated use of provosts-marshal to discipline disbanded or runaway soldiers, barely distinguishable from the wider vagrant class who were the supposed preserve of the civil magistrates. Aspects of the grain trade and of the execution of the recusancy laws were also not wholly within the purview of the justices. Political resentment grew with this constitutional disquiet when the deterioration of the Crown's financial position as the Irish and Spanish wars continued caused Elizabeth to use her economic powers for fiscal purposes, granting licences to export commodities to courtiers or to the highest bidder.[16] The widespread anxiety about the Crown's new and indirect fiscal activity is revealed by the protests against monopolies in the late 1590s and 1601, and against purveyancing in the first session of James's first parliament. These political changes must have conditioned responses when courtiers made addresses to constituencies at election time.

The fears of packing, the fear that parliament was endangered, so obviously present in 1604, in 1614 and in the 1620s, seem irrational when set against the welcome accorded to courtiers and councillors by constituencies in Sir John Neale's studies, in the context of the relatively undramatic electoral interim. All it seems possible to do is to suggest that courtiers were becoming increasingly disliked, both in their central and local manifestations (and in the latter guise were, on the Norfolk example, threatening to disrupt the local power structure), and that there were very real fears about the constitutional ramifications of the Crown's taxation policy. In the hot-house atmosphere of the Commons, blunders like those of 1604 and 1614 quickly grew into horrifying creations which certainly had not been envisaged by their perpetrators. The notorious ability of the House to construct its own mythology then did the rest.

As the existence of parliament and, a fortiori, the House of Commons was apparently challenged by the fiscal policies of the Crown, so members began to talk about the country and representation as a justification of their existence, and sometimes of their political position too. A favourable climate was being created for thinking about what and whom representation involved, and several members were found in the 1620s and 1640 making principled statements for wider democracy. But this attitude could not remain a vague intellectual predisposition. For part of the general threat to parliament was, it seemed, a more concrete undermining, especially by royal support for oligarchic borough constitutions, of the electoral system which selected the members of the House of Commons. If that were unchecked then the independence of the House would be lost. Steps had to be taken to preserve electoral purity, to resist royal influence and manipulation, and thus to hand on intact to succeeding generations those liberties which had been inherited.

To this end, the decade of the 1620s saw a series of developments in the electoral field, apparently intended initially as a counter to royal pressure, but rapidly gaining a momentum of their own. Many borough franchises were widened by the House, in the belief that the more voters there were the more difficult it would be to influence them. The number of members in the House was also increased, as long-lapsed boroughs were restored to the privilege of representation, again in the belief that this might obstruct the efforts of malignant persons. The net result was a marked increase in the totals of those capable of voting – an increase directly created by the gentry members of the House of Commons, who evidently sensed a greater danger from above than from below. It was left to the Civil War to disturb this assessment.

The 1620s was arguably the decisive period electorally. Not only were the actions of the House establishing the determining precedents that allowed more people to vote, but more people were actually voting. The repeated elections of that decade generated excitement, which was anyway increased by the political divisions taking place. A degree of populism was the predictable outcome. As alienation from the Crown progressed, politicians inclined to an opposition stand began to bid for public support. While evidence of awareness of the potential of the common people can be found earlier, the puritan organiser John Field was surely pre-cocious in asserting in 1587 that 'it is the multitude and people that must bring the discipline to pass which we desire'. In the 1620s, such con-sciousness of the political weight of the common people was less un-common: there was some pulpit agitation against the Spanish Match in James's last years, libels against the benevolence and forced loan of 1626–7 were scattered in some localities, and overtly political appeals were made on occasion at elections.[17] Inevitably, increasing numbers must have wished to participate. Furthermore, on the other side of the process, the wish to involve more people grew: the five elections of the decade focused attention on the electorate willy-nilly, and its significance began to be more fully appreciated. The rapid recurrence of parliaments created the impression (mistakenly, as it turned out) that parliament was a more permanent part of the constitution, and the potentates therefore began taking steps to perfect the means of dealing with the electorate, identi-fying the voters, and turning them out. The result of this was that increasing sophistication and definition becomes visible.

## Electoral beginnings

The corollary of an assertion that the electoral system, as politicians before 1832 might have recognised it, was forming in this period is that these were its early days. A normal accompaniment of the initial stages of any development is a measure of uncertainty and confusion, and this was not lacking here. Of course, parliament had by 1600 been in existence for centuries, and therefore there had been elections previously. But for our purposes, the important point about elections is that they should be contested, for it is only when candidates vie for votes that a maxi-mum number of people are involved, and are brought into first-hand contact with politics, and only then do they gain real political experience. And it is only a contest, or the prospect of one, that drives politicians and patrons to elaborate their methods of appealing to or controlling the voters.

Sir John Neale's work on Elizabethan elections suggests that contests were rare, and patronage and connection predominated. There might be a squabble among rival families for possession of the prestigious county seats, but as he himself indicated, there were probably few contested elections in the boroughs. And even in the counties, contests were certainly not frequent. The start of the 17th century was little different: very tentative totals of thirteen and fifteen can be advanced for all contests for the parliaments of 1604 and 1614 respectively – higher levels than appear to have prevailed in Elizabethan elections, but not inordinately so.[18] On this evidence, not many men would have had any say in their political destinies. The evidence even from very early times points similarly to a jockeying for seats, certainly, but to this often taking place behind the scenes among the magnates, with an unchallenged pair of candidates emerging to be greeted and returned 'una voce' by the shouts of the election court. An election made in such a way is not an act which necessarily has many repercussions in the local community, for not much is demanded of the few who participate in it. Magnate control over elections, destroying any possibility of free choice by the commons, was even said to have been one of the grievances of Jack Cade's followers in 1450. In this type of election, popular involvement is actually discouraged by the gentry who wish to avoid the expense, or possibly disturbance, associated with turning out the voters. Thus, Sir Maurice Berkeley accepted advice to 'spare both his owne paynes; and prevent the Attendance of his Companye', on being told that a contest was unlikely in Gloucestershire in the spring of 1640.[19] But to restrict politics to the potentates in this way was impossible once contests occurred, as they increasingly did under the early Stuarts, for then efforts had to be made to produce support.

This is not to assert that contests and excitement were unknown before Elizabeth's reign. The definitive 1430 statute that fixed various aspects of election procedure and first limited the county franchise to the 40s. freeholders did so allegedly because of the 'homicides riotes battles et divisions entre les gentils et autres gentz' – which suggests that contests happened. Some constituencies, and even boroughs, were clearly contested – Grimsby was fought repeatedly in the later 15th century – but, even in the absence of detailed archival research in many boroughs, it seems likely that contests were isolated events.[20] The majority principle as the arbiter of elections was first explicitly recognised in that same 1430 statute, and it is therefore improbable that contests were once common and then declined to the levels of the Elizabethan and 1604 elections. As late as 1555, the Court of Common Pleas was willing to accept an allegation of a majority

in a disputed election, while holding that it was unnecessary for a candidate to provide the court with numbers, for the election might have been
'by voices, or by hands, or such other way, wherein it is easy to tell who
has the majority, and yet very difficult to know the certain number'.[21] We
may surmise that experience of contests was not yet sufficient to tell the
learned judges, all of whom had themselves sat in the Commons, that it
was sometimes not easy to discover who had the majority when the election
did not go to the poll and thus provide certain numbers. When the
opposing sides were closely matched, it was essential to be able to cite
numbers, and this had still to be learnt. That it was learnt, when knowledge of contests had grown, is indicated by the strong demands made in
the Committee of Privileges in 1625 that a poll should be conducted on
every occasion of a contest.[22] This was not in order to ascertain the
majority, but in order to weed out unqualified voters. Judging by its
silence on the matter, the Committee evidently realised by this stage that
in the event of a close contest a poll would probably be held, and hence
felt no need to press for it as proof of numbers.

Acceptance of the majority principle, the essence of contested elections,
was also hampered by the belief of some gentry that status, rather than
numbers, was what counted in politics. Much election correspondence is
heavily preoccupied with the loyalties of the gentry, and this could be
attributed to the assumption that the meaner sort would follow their
betters. But estimations of relative worth, as well as considerations of
practical politics, were involved. The interrogatories administered to witnesses in the 1604 Worcestershire election dispute in Star Chamber
enquired whether one candidate's voters were 'of better sorte and qualytie
then the freeholders who then and there gave their voyces' for the other
side. Such a concern for status was even expected to move the House of
Commons: after the 1625 election for Yorkshire, Sir Thomas Wentworth
defended his challenged return by arguing that he had been supported by
the greatest number of men of quality who had appeared at such a poll in
twenty years past. Over twenty years later, in the Recruiter election for
Herefordshire, one of Edward Harley's allies informed him that support
was coming from one quarter, 'which, though they are not many', they
should be welcome, for they were all men of quality.[23] The belief that
quality counted as much as numbers could have immediate political consequences: in the Lewes election of 1628, the gentry present refused to
have themselves numbered with the meaner sort at the poll, presumably
considering that their names should not be rated on a paper on an equal
basis with those of the commons, and in consequence saw the candidate
they supported suffer. And in the 1658 Yorkshire election, various gentry
refused to be polled with some Quakers, probably for similar reasons.[24]

The poll and the establishment of a numerical majority were not universally seen as an integral part of the electoral process. An uninvolved participant in the House's debate on the disputed 1621 Norfolk election was sufficiently unconcerned with the question of numbers as to defend the waiving of the poll on grounds of convenience, so many people having been present that it would have taken a long time. But while acquaintance with the majority principle was certainly spreading (the implicit attitude of some members of the 1625 Committee of Privileges being indicative of this), the fact that contested elections were an inseparable part of a parliamentary system was not yet fully realised. It has been argued that it was only as late as 1649 that the possibility of contests in the elections for all provincial officers was fully built into the Massachusetts electoral system.[25] If, as seems indisputable, the first-generation colonists were transplanted Englishmen, that says much for the state of English thought on the matter.

An election contest, laying open divisions within the community, was something which was often viewed with displeasure by those in authority. This could be for reasons of social order: contests meant excitement and vying for place, and, in an unpoliced society, that could cause trouble. In the London shrieval elections of 1621, Sir Heneage Finch, the Recorder, felt constrained to defend the existence of the electoral process, which had apparently been jeopardised by its factiousness: he observed that a stranger, regarding 'this greate Confluence of Cittizens', might 'apprehend that the number threatned a tumultuary or factious Eleccion, which in popular eleccions is not unusuall'. But, he continued, this crowd was one of 'faier Carriage and demeanor, ... decent Order and civill habitt'. In addition to this concern at the 'tumultuary' aspect of elections, contests and the fact of a majority vote implied divisions, and local governors were sometimes reluctant to admit that these existed in their communities, for outsiders might infer from that that something was wrong with their rule. Thus, at York, after contests, the voters were often 'enjoined ... to be at the next county court to confirme the same election'; and again, the voters in the city's county court in 1604, 'hearinge that the said Mr Askwith and Christopher Brooke had the most voices did all ioyntlie together in the Countye give ther voices unto and elect' the two men. Similarly, after the Maldon contests of 1624 and 1626, the members were noted in the borough records as having been elected 'unanimis assensibus et consensis' of all involved.[26] The illusion of unanimity was being created, and the contest concealed.

Doubtless as a result of this reluctance to create or acknowledge divisions, most people professed some hostility to canvassing for votes, which might exacerbate conflicts in the localities. The Privy Council forbade it in 1604, and efforts were made in some areas to observe this ban;[27] the distaste of local governors for canvassing amongst the commons was often expressed.[28] In response to this distaste, candidates were driven to make conventional disclaimers of ambition, or of any independent initiative on their own parts, in standing: at the start of the Norfolk Short Parliament election campaign, a friend wrote to one prospective candidate that he hoped he would 'expresse ... willingnesse to undertake the worke, and not neglect such ordenary wayes as may be fayrely used by lawes of modestie'. Apart from the typical back-bench reaction of Sir Henry Poole, in the debate on the 1621 bill to regulate elections, who believed that canvassing should be banned because it pushed up the cost of a seat, it was increasingly the case that modesty and convention alone now militated against whole-hearted activity. Thus, a fairly standard disclaimer, such as Sir John Holland's after the spring 1640 Norfolk election to the effect that 'I have not tendred you my service ... out of any pryde of a self conceipt but only to meete with your kind invitations and to satisfy the importunityes of some neere and prevalent frends', should probably not be taken at its face value. Obligatory modesty was universal: a man as self-assured and assertive as Wentworth found it necessary to preface his campaign letters in Yorkshire in 1620–1 with the rider that, 'In Truth I do not desire it out of any Ambition, but rather to satisfy some of my best Friends.'[29] Nevertheless, the premium placed on the integrity of the community probably did work against intense electioneering. It was not uncommon for non-candidate gentry to insist that contending neighbours should draw lots rather than push their efforts to the hazard of a poll. On at least one occasion, at the 1625 Cheshire election, this counsel was of partial effect, cutting three candidates for one seat down to two.[30]

In several areas, then, a reluctance to come to terms with integral parts of the electoral process was visible in this period. Contests were uncommon, unpopular, and not fully accepted for what they were. Even the apparently straightforward numerical proposition of a majority was not wholly clear of doubt. This partial incomprehension extended to a more general level, and again can be explained by the relative novelty of contested elections. In many constituencies, who should vote, how they should vote, and the manner of conducting the election, were all equally uncertain.

The occurrence of so many franchise disputes in towns in the 1620s might indicate widespread urban doubts about who were the enfranchised classes, were it not that the majority of them resulted from deliberate pressure by interested groups.[31] Nevertheless, the role of novelty in generating confusion in electoral matters can be seen in the way in which at least five of the boroughs newly restored to representation before the war – Amersham, Hertford, Malton (Yorks.), Marlow, and Pontefract – experienced controversy over the extent of the franchise shortly afterwards. For here there was obviously little experience or custom available to determine the matter, and the House of Commons had refused guidance.[32] But there were other constituencies with a more continuous representative history which met difficulties. At Chichester in 1586 and Warwick in 1621, aspiring voters qualified their votes with the statement that they cast them if they had any; various inhabitants of Cirencester turned up to vote in 1624, there being no 'certain custom, or prescription ... who ought to be the electors there', but they were sent away again on being informed by the gentry and a neighbouring lawyer that they were not enfranchised.[33] Sir John Neale concluded that Gloucester late in Elizabeth's reign possessed a freeman franchise, yet when the 1604 election was disputed and taken to Star Chamber, one of the interrogatories which the court drew up to be administered to witnesses merely asked if two of the candidates were chosen 'by the greatest nomber of the Inhabitants'; and the corporation equally did not seem overly interested in what precisely the franchise was.[34] Such issues, when contests were not a fact of life, were presumably not seen as important.

A parallel process is evident in New England. The late date of a full acceptance in Massachusetts of the fact of contests has been pointed to; the similarity is emphasised by the situation in Plymouth Colony. Although a committee appointed by the General Court in 1636 reported that the members of the colony came there 'as freeborne subjects of the State of England', with all attendant rights and privileges, the committee did not feel impelled to elaborate on what these were, for not until 1658 (twenty years after a representative assembly was established) were the franchise qualifications in the colony spelt out. The Plymouth colonists claimed that they were consciously transmitting the constitutions of old England. The partial confusion which they transmitted is surely also symptomatic of the situation in England. The uncertainty in Massachusetts extended further than has been indicated above. There has been a large debate of recent years as to the nature of the colony's franchise, and the disagreement this has given rise to is important. The debate, and the disagreement, is akin to that over the Levellers' position on the same matter, and that such differences should exist seems likely to be as much the result of confusion at source as of wilful blindness on the part of the present-day protagonists. For in Massachusetts matters relating to voting became formalised only over a period of time. It was from 1635 that paper ballots came into use, and it has been argued that town elections became more fixed in their procedure in the course of the 1640s; the voting regulations underwent frequent alterations in the early decades, and initially there seems to have been little attempt to erect a firm barrier between the enfranchised and the unenfranchised[35] – a situation which is reminiscent of the Gloucester case. The continuity between the old

English experience, or lack of it, and New England, is very marked. In England, there had as yet been little occasion to distinguish voters from the rest, or to establish fixed election procedures. In New England there was by definition no local custom or prescription to guide the settlers; and they seem to have taken little across with them.

The failure of England to provide much precise help as an electoral model is understandable. The question of the franchise, or of voting arrangements, only had to be decided when there was a contest, for only then were people asked to vote. This is seen most clearly when the position of women is considered. When there were no contests, and the affair of the election was hierarchically ordered, being arranged outside the public view by the better sort, the participation of aristocratic women in an act, the election, which was itself uncontroversial, was not especially abhorrent. The widows of various peers figured in the Yorkshire return of 1437, and Sir John Neale showed the women owners of Aylesbury and Gatton making the returns for their boroughs in the later 16th century. But when women of a lower social group were involved, questions began to be asked, although the answers were not always clear. Protests were made when women turned up to shout their choice at the 1621 election for Westminster, and that for the Long Parliament for Worcestershire. Men were not always agreed that they should be excluded: politics was often argued to be the preserve of the propertied, and it could be contended that widowed property owners had a valid claim. This claim had not yet been decided on, and consequently the sectaries were not the only ones who were unwilling to exclude them entirely. In the burgage-tenure borough of Knaresborough, Sir Henry Slingsby tried to use the votes of widowed burgage holders in 1628, though the bailiff refused to admit them; fifty years later, at neighbouring Richmond, it had to be resolved before the poll that widows were to be disallowed.[36] In a more sophisticated world, such as that provided by most 18th-century burgage-tenure constituencies, the issue would never have needed such a declaration, for it would have been quietly arranged beforehand by the discreet transfer of rights (which was in fact the course decreed in Richmond).

The uncertain position of women at this time is best shown in an incident in the Suffolk election to the Long Parliament, where a number of widows, apparently spontaneously, arrived to vote for the puritan candidates, Barnardiston and Parker. These immediately disavowed them, although some of the polling clerks had evidently been ready to register their votes. Sir Simonds D'Ewes was the invigilating sheriff, and his reaction was revealing: on hearing of the women's efforts, he 'instantlie sent to forbidd the same, conceiving it a matter verie unworthie of any gentleman and most dishonourable in such an election to make use of their voices although they might in law have been allowed'. Given his tireless antiquarian labours, and his frantic enquiries of the judges beforehand as to how to conduct an election, D'Ewes of all people should have known the state of the law here. His assertion that legally there existed no barrier to their participation, and that only 'honour' and social convention told against them, is very revealing of the primitive state of electoral law and custom.[37] Again, the continuity with the undeveloped state of early New England electoral provision is clear. In the early 1620s, doubts were evidently being expressed in London as to the likely social inclusiveness of political life in Plymouth Colony, and two of the leaders of the colony wrote home in 1623 that contrary to rumour women were being excluded, 'as both reason and nature teacheth they should be' – but no reference was made to 'constant practice', or some such phrase, for there had been none.[38]

A state of franchisal innocence could have practical repercussions, for it might mean that more than those strictly qualified could vote, in the absence of any to say what the strict qualifications were. The imprecision in Gloucester in 1604 and in Massachusetts slightly later are illustrations of this, but they could be repeated many times. The problems in the counties were if anything even greater than those in the boroughs, although there was ostensibly a precise requirement, the possession of freehold land to the value of 40s. per annum. Probably a majority of contests were decided by methods other than the poll, which meant that the aspiring voter could not be asked if he met that demand. For it was only in a polled election that the choices of the individual voter were noted down, and he was thus subjected to scrutiny. The methods which still prevailed (realisation of the value of the poll dawning but slowly) were 'the cry' and 'the view'. When a faceless crowd gave vent to its feelings by roaring the names of the rival candidates, or raised its hands or divided into partisan groups to be checked for size, it was obviously nearly impossible to verify credentials. Towns were as yet predominantly small in size, few being larger than perhaps 3000–4000 inhabitants, which meant that the adult males, the potential voters, would normally be a maximum of some hundreds of men. In communities of that scale, some form of check on sight might have been possible. But in a county, with thousands of adult males, sometimes coming from a very wide area, the identification of pretenders was a forlorn hope. Only when polls and electoral lists became standard practice could there conceivably be a properly qualified electorate. In their absence the House of Commons in 1628 gave hapless sheriffs the futile counsel that they should recognise the freeholders – when the county in discussion was Yorkshire![39]

These problems caused by novelty were apparently intensified by the intermission occasioned by the Eleven Years without parliaments. Someone thought it necessary, or at least profitable, to issue a guide-book to a variety of parliamentary matters when elections were at last in view. That there was a market is suggested by the action of Oxford corporation, which made orders on how to conduct itself for the Short Parliament election of 1640. Ludlow was in similar difficulties: 'for the better informacion of their Judgments howe to proceed therein they consulted with the statutes touchinge the electinge of burgesses . . . as alsoe perused the Charteres of this Corporacion and diverse ancient orders of Comon Councill inableinge and directing them therein'.[40]

Perhaps the most complex matter was the conduct of the poll. In some constituencies, votes seem to have been given in writing (this practice probably increased under the Protectorate, in order to cope with the problems of multiple-member constituencies).[41] Elsewhere, the fact that in almost all constituencies each voter had two votes posed the question of how these were to be taken: in the event of a contest, were there to be two polls, one for the first seat and another for the second? Or were all the votes to be cast together, with the two highest totals winning? A correspondent of various prominent Nottinghamshire figures, discussing the forthcoming Nottingham election for the Long Parliament, felt driven to elaborate on the issue at some length. He concluded that 'the election if it come to the poole will not be made by first and second voyces, but those two, who have the most voyces first or second, must bee returned, . . . if one man have 200 first voyces if another come after and have 201 second voyces and a third come and have 202 he that hath 202 must be returned as first Burgesse, he that hath 201 the second, and the first who hath but 200, though they were all first voyces shall goe without it, for it must go to the common votes first and second together'. Here we see considerations of status again acting at variance with the simple majority principle, for first votes were often thought 'better' votes. The borough of Hertford seems to have differed from these conclusions, for there separate elections for the first and second seats were made in 1624 and 1628, and a similar procedure was followed in Clitheroe in 1628, although this had been altered by the time of the Long Parliament election – which emphasises the fluidity of the arrangements. Separate polling was insisted on by the mayors of Sandwich in 1621 and Barnstaple in 1640 in order to manipulate the elections, the opposition to the oligarchs demanding that both seats should be polled together.[42] The continuation of separate polling in many constituencies was ensured by respect for the status of one of the candidates, or by his total control of one of the seats: thus, at Bedford in both 1640 elections Sir Beauchamp St John went unchallenged for the first seat, as did Sir Edward Howard at Hertford in 1628, while lesser men contested for the second. But separate polling for first and second seats was really only possible where there were three candidates and relatively few voters. More than three contestants and hundreds of voters, and the duplication required increased the amount of work and of opportunity for disputes, as the bailiffs of Clitheroe and the mayors of Sandwich probably found before going over to the simpler system of totalling votes. Most counties seem to have reached the same conclusion, for there totalling of votes prevailed. Separate polling when thousands were involved would have produced immense problems: even registering first and second votes with separate clerks in Suffolk in the Long Parliament election almost provoked a riot. D'Ewes thought that by 1641 the matter required legislation to clear it up.[43]

There was no constant and uniform method of conducting an election in the early 17th century. Just as the House was still formalising its procedure, and establishing its control over elections in this period, so people were only beginning to feel their way towards an appreciation of the existence of elections and an electorate. In this context, it should not be surprising if thought and comment sometimes lagged behind practice. For it was often the case that supposedly well-informed contemporaries were relatively ill-informed on the matter of the electorate. This is further evidence that elections had not yet loomed large in the elite's consciousness, let alone the popular one.

It is extremely rare to find an accurate account of the electorate at this time, even when the outbreak of war, and Parliament's claims that it was empowered by the country to act, brought the issue of the relationship of the Commons to the country to the fore. Sir Robert Filmer examined parliament's position, and while he was clearly aware that others besides knights of the shires sat in the House of Commons, he failed to work out who put them there. In *The Freeholder's Grand Inquest* he repeatedly talked of the freeholders alone as being the electors, and conferring their powers on the members, and this was an error into which Sir John Spelman also fell. In his trenchant assault on Henry Parker's claims that the House of Commons represented the country, Spelman too saw the Commons as elected by none other than the freeholders.[44] Admittedly, both authors had much to gain by minimising the number of those enfranchised, and so it may have been convenient to forget the townsmen; but their polemical cases would have been strengthened by pointing out that the urban franchises, like those of the counties, were restrictive. But this was overlooked.

The debates in the later 1640s between Leveller and Agitator allies, and conservative opponents, are often considered the high-point of representative debate in this period. Large issues of principle and practice were aired, in a wide-ranging and lengthy argument, but the debates illustrate areas of practical confusion as much as they demonstrate intellectual acumen or nascent egalitarianism amongst the participants.

Cowling, one of the Agitators at Putney, apparently made the same mistake as Filmer and Spelman when attacking the existing franchise, which he saw as extending to the possessors of 40s. freeholds, for he too neglected to take the boroughs fully into account. Others went even further astray. Lilburne, the charismatic figure of the Leveller movement, when demanding the reform of London's government in 1646, cited in his support the argument that 'in all the Cities and Burroughs of this Realme' the election of mayors was by popular vote, thus ignoring the many oligarchic borough constitutions scattered around the country. In continuing his diatribe, he revealed a belief that the urban parliamentary franchises were limited to the 40s. freeholders.[45] But the borough franchises were a strange medley, and in scarcely any did the 40s. freehold prevail. General Ireton, ostensibly the great theorist and expert opponent of the Levellers, repeatedly referred at Putney to an urban electorate composed of the freemen of the boroughs (a mistake made earlier by the lawyer and parliament-man Geoffrey Palmer in 1640). While the largest group of the urban franchises would have borne him out, he was overlooking the many corporation, burgage-tenure and residence franchises. Likewise, Petty's belief that leaseholders for three lives had no vote accords ill with the position of the great lawyer William Prynne, who, when he was preparing material with which to argue the Tewkesbury election as counsel before the Committee of Privileges in 1641, concluded that only copyholders and lessees for years or at will were excluded from the franchise. Prynne, having worked on the matter, might be presumed to have had some greater acquaintance with the facts than did Petty. In the light of Prynne's verdict, and of the fact that an interest of one life or more in land was considered an estate, and therefore a freehold in law, Cromwell's concession at Putney that 'a very considerable part of copyholders by inheritance' might be allowed to vote under a new dispensation, seems unreliable.[46] The whole scholarly industry which bases propositions about the actual franchise on what was said at Putney seems misguided, for speakers at Putney did not always know what they were talking about.

This ignorance helps to cast light on some of the weakness of the Agitators in polemic. When Ireton forcefully urged that if the property-less were allowed the vote, then they might elect their fellow-paupers, who could then proceed to attack property, it was open to the democrats to argue from the existing electoral system against him; for there were several boroughs with very wide, or even full adult male, franchises in areas close to regions of Leveller strength in the environs of London and in the Thames Valley. The logical reply to Ireton should then have been that by this time the property-less did already vote in St Albans, Bedford, and possibly Reading, and the Armageddon had not been ushered in.[47] But the nearest approach to this kind of argument was Cowling's weak observation that a wealthy tanner in Staines was voteless while a pauperised one in Reading was not, directed against the idiosyncrasies of a 40s. freehold franchise.[48]

The lack of pertinent reference to the *status quo* is understandable in view of the uncertainty of both sides, and many other contemporaries, as to what this was. Furthermore, as Mr Thomas has recently perceptively observed, 'the pressure of debate at Putney . . . revealed internal divisions and uncertainties over a programme which had clearly not been worked out in all details'. He suggested, rightly, that the Levellers had not thought the problem through: pre-Putney statements contained blanket, but unconsidered and unargued, assertions that all should vote (the first Agreement of the People being a case in point).[49] That position then came under heavy fire from Ireton, and the Levellers revealed the confusion that Mr Thomas and others have detailed. Lack of knowledge of precedents is not so surprising here. But it is significant that their opponents at Putney appear equally ignorant. Those in power, Cromwell and Ireton, and those on the fringes of power, the Levellers and Spelman, perhaps Filmer, were unaware of some of the factual dimensions of the political context in which they were operating. Therefore the written constitutions, the Agreement and the Instrument, were full of flaws. Correspondingly, those able to gain less wide-ranging views than the men at the centre failed to cope adequately with the problems posed by the electorate.

The steps taken to deal with contested elections and an active electorate lagged as much as did abstract thought. While election to parliament was recognised as socially, or even politically, desirable, and the gentry realised that their tenantry might be a useful source of votes, very few seem yet to have realised the value, or possibility, of taking positive steps, other than merely asking for votes, to help them along the road into the House. There was some bribery and 'entertaining' of voters, and although the sums involved, and the frequency of expenditure, may have risen slightly in the later 1620s and 1640, suggesting some growing awareness of the connection between money and votes, the scope of this activity seems to have been very limited.[50]

Likewise, other indirect means of obtaining votes to be perfected in the course of the next two or three generations were in a comparatively undeveloped state. Reports of tenants being bound more or less closely by the terms of their holding to vote with their landlords are scarce in the extreme, and allegations of the creation of bogus freeholders are few, coming from Montgomeryshire in 1588, Rutland in 1601, Somerset and Hampshire in 1614, Caernarvonshire in 1621 and Essex in 1628.[51] Defeated candidates had an interest in protesting to the House, and the rarity of the practice is confirmed by the negative evidence of the silence

on this score from the bitterly-fought and well-documented counties of
Yorkshire and Norfolk. Most means that were to hand seem to have been
used here, and the fact that bogus creations were not included in subsequent petitions suggests that electioneers had not yet perfected this ploy.
Equally, the common later technique of importing non-resident freeholders from London or elsewhere had not yet emerged. But this method
of gaining votes does seem to have been used in municipal, not parliamentary, elections for Norwich and Shrewsbury in this period. Municipal
elections, unlike parliamentary ones, were held annually, and thus
provided greater opportunity for tactical development.[52]

The manipulation of parliamentary voting rights in towns seems to have
been as unsophisticated as that in counties. Lilburne in 1646 attacked the
London merchants who 'send their *agents, creatures,* and *servants,* to all
the Ports and Sea-townes of *England,* where they have an influence into
the elections of all Burgesses', but although the 1640s added a potent
new factor to electioneering with the creation of an excise machine and a
more efficient customs organisation, his criticisms still seem wide of the
mark.[53] Urban electoral rights were obviously important: perhaps most
significant here is the listing of the right to return members of parliament
as an asset when the Earl of Bedford put Amersham up for sale in the
1620s, but there is little evidence of concerted electoral exploitation in
towns.[54] Numbers of new freemen were apparently created at Haverford-
west in 1571 and East Retford and Maldon in 1624 in order to sway the
elections, but freemen lists elsewhere do not betray marked fluctuations
in the critical years.[55] The burgages of Old Sarum were evidently multiplied by the Earl of Pembroke and by his steward in the troubled years
before 1626, when the Earl of Salisbury was trying to force his way in and
there was a need for extra votes. The same may have happened in
Pontefract in 1624 and East Grinstead in 1640, but these seem rarities.[56]

Proprietary votes, and organised proprietorial control of boroughs,
appear to be a later development. Again, it is only the increased likelihood
of contests that makes the expenditure of time and money required
worthwhile. The politics of Knaresborough provide a good illustration
of the importance of chronology in the evolution of attitudes to the
electorate. The attempt of eight widows to vote in 1628 would have
been unlikely had the less risky temporary transfer of burgages been
developed, and the low turn-out for the 1628 poll (46, although 59 tried
to vote, out of a potential total of 88) is possibly accounted for by the fact
that the richest man in the town, a yeoman, Peter Benson, one of those
elected, probably held at least twelve of the burgages. But he had bought
these up for economic reasons, with a view to enclosure, rather than for
the electoral rights accruing, and there is little sign that he temporarily
transferred ownership before the poll. Not until the 1640s, after the

bitter competitions at the start of the decade, does the purchase of burgages for electoral purposes appear to have commenced.[57] Previously, Sir Henry Slingsby, owning no burgages, had been elected repeatedly. Castle Rising, judging by its tenants, seems to have been little more to the Howards in 1642 than just another manor which, incidentally, had electoral rights – gentry names in the lists of burgage tenants do not appear until considerably later. There are signs of similar developments in Downton to those in Knaresborough. Repeated contests for the Long Parliament had produced, for the first time, some movement of the gentry into the borough by 1647; but large-scale concerted attempts to buy up the burgages did not begin until the 1690s, in the electioneering fervour then prevailing.[58] In Richmond, Yorks., the magnates moved in slightly later, in the early years of the 18th century, but in the same heated atmosphere.[59]

Politicians of all sorts, whether those writing paper constitutions or those fighting local battles, had not yet fully come to terms with elections and the voters. Because contests had been, and to a degree still were, so rare, there had been little compulsion to think out the practical steps which the existence of an electorate required, or the means of controlling it. *Ad hoc* means, like occasional bribery or appeals to religious prejudices, were increasingly used, but many of those concerned did not yet think easily in terms of votes and majorities, and in consequence failed to take long-term measures to ensure the existence of those valuable commodities.

The results of this state of innocence were large. The uncertainty over what the franchise was almost certainly encouraged disputes and challenges in the boroughs. It became easier for erstwhile unqualified groups to expound plausible claims to the vote if many people were unsure precisely who should vote. And equally in the House of Commons, gentry woolliness favoured this development, for there were no clearly elaborated principles or arguments to hand which might delimit the franchise, and piecemeal extension was thus facilitated. Locally, the absence of checks on the identities of those turning out to vote, and sometimes even of knowledge of what their qualifications should be, often allowed a fairly indiscriminate group to shout their choices. Furthermore, the primitive state of the means of influence at the disposal of the better sort meant that a degree of genuine independence in voting was possible for the meaner sort. But this open-ness was a temporary phenomenon. The Grandees' attempt to restrict the political nation formally in the Instrument of Government failed, but their aim was realised in other ways. The accumulation of experience as the century progressed meant greater precision locally, and greater awareness on the part of the gentry. This tended towards the elimination of the unqualified, and a tighter control of those who were left, whose numbers were being diminished by economic and political change.

# Part I

# The Electorate

# 2

# The County Electorate

## *The forty-shilling freeholder*

By far the largest numbers of voters were contained in the county constituencies. There should have been little problem in principle, if not in practice,[1] about the identity of these people, for they were defined by statute in 1430 as the 40s. freeholders. Sir Edward Coke in his *Institutes* denied the existence of any difficulty: 'Who shall be electors, and who shall be chosen ... you may reade in the positive lawes of 7H.4 cap.15. 11H.4 cap.1 [etc. through to 8 and 23 H.VI] ... and which need not here be particularly rehearsed', and went on to complain that 'much time is spent in Parliament concerning the right of elections, etc. which might more profitably be imployed pro bono publico'. After the outbreak of war, the apparently undisputed nature of the county franchise could be used by Sir John Spelman to make an effective polemic point against the claims of Parliament to represent the people of England. He pointed out that while 'The Lords vote in respect of their Barronies derived from the Crowne, the Commons Vote in right of their electors whom they represent, at least nine parts of the Kingdome, neither doe nor may Vote in their election, the Clergie in respect of their spirituall livings, may not, nor the substantiall Coppy-holders, Farmours nor Lessees for years ... and all that have not 40s. per annum free-hold Land, which I imagine, cannot be above a tenth part of the Kingdome.'[2]

Powerful voices argued that the 40s. freeholder electorate was plain in its extent. Voices might also have argued that it was plain in its composition. The 40s. freeholder is, in legend, the independent countryman, the man of some small property, the man whose position General Ireton extolled at length at Putney, as having a permanent stake in the country. Visions of substance and worth are conjured up by the phrase: it is clear that to both Thomas Wilson and Gregory King, social commentators and statisticians at either end of the 17th century, the freeholder was akin to the yeoman in substance. Others, writing more loosely, agreed with them.[3] Yet a freehold was, strictly, merely a form of tenure, and it did not necessarily bear any relation to the amount of land requisite to support yeoman status, or anything like it.

Even in the 15th century, the 40s. level imposed by the 1430 statute was not closely linked to the archetypal yeoman. Prof. Roskell has pointed out that the qualification laid down 'stood at no more than two-fifths of what Sir John Fortescue, little more than a generation later, could describe as "a feyre lyvynge for a yeoman" ', and argued that this 'suggests that the shire electorate under the new arrangements still remained fairly comprehensive'. Another recent scholar has observed that many ordinary wage-earners, at 2*d*. a day, would have earned over 40*s*. per annum. At its inception, then, the new rubric was not an especially rigorous economic test. It was progressively undermined by the rapid inflation of the 16th and 17th centuries, to the extent that the value requirement must have become virtually meaningless.[4]

An anonymous discourse of c. 1620 on the position of the yeoman, referring to the 1430 act, stated that '40 shillings free-houlde in yearlie revenewe ... maketh (yf the iuste valewe were taken to the proportione of moneyes) above vi poundes of oure Currante Money at this presente'. Other contemporary assessments of the impact of inflation went even further. The frustrated courtier Henry Neville complained of the Short Parliament Essex election result that, significantly, the ordinary 40*s*. freeholders were anyway below the tax floor, and therefore should not have been concerned in a process whose primary purpose was evidently seen to be the granting of supply; he went on to claim that 'when the Statute [of 1430] was made Forty Shillings it was then twenty Pound in value now', with the result that 'the Multiplicity of the People [at elections] are mean conditioned, and most Factious, and few Subsidy-Men ...' Commissary Cowling at Putney saw the decline in money values as having been even more marked, believing that the 40*s*. intended by the statute was the equivalent of £40 in the 1640s.[5] The net result of this inflation must have been that far more people crept through the statutory net.

No listings of individuals, for whatever purpose, survive for any area from both ends of the inflationary period, and it is therefore impossible to calculate the extent of the multiplication of the 40*s*. freeholders. But what is clear is that by the early 17th century, an extremely small acreage of land would have given an aspiring voter an income of 40*s*. Dr Bowden has recently estimated the incomings and outgoings of a hypothetical average small farmer on arable land in this period and suggested a net profit margin of 9·64*s*. per acre. Other areas give noticeably higher returns: Ralph Josselin's holdings in an enclosed area of Essex appear to have yielded somewhere in the region of 15*s*. per acre after rent, though seed and other charges were not deducted; Robert Loder's farm in a sheep/corn area of Berkshire seems to have brought him a return of about £1 per acre after charges, although from a considerably larger unit, whose relative costs would therefore have been lower. But much smaller holdings in non-champion regions could still yield significantly high returns per acre. A report on encroachments in Windsor Forest in 1630 noted that one cottage with only a rood of land was worth 5s. per annum after rent; a Glastonbury, Somerset, petition against poor relief ratings of 1637 noted farmland values ranging from 10s. to 30–40s. per acre; the accounts of the Bankes family of Winstanley, Lancs., show several tenants of cottages and c. one acre worth 10s. per annum upwards after rent.[6] While counter-examples of lower yields can obviously be found, Dr Bowden's figures seem very likely; and the non-champion lands in many cases, at least away from the North-West, might not distort his picture too greatly for the purposes of this study. The conclusion from these values must be that in many areas of the country a holding of about four to five acres would have given a landed income of 40s. after charges. In any case, given the poverty of accounting methods, the question of before or after charges was probably an academic one: when the sheriff of Rutland insisted on the phrase when taking the poll at the 1601 election, many people did not know what he meant and were, as he had hoped, deterred from voting in consequence. No other sheriff seems subsequently to have heeded that rubric.[7]

The implications of the fact that a holding of this size should give a 40s. return are interesting. The statutory minimum for the establishment of a cottage roughly equated with it – and it is noteworthy that the Rutland sheriff in 1601 claimed he was prepared to accept cottagers and those who supplemented their incomes by wage labour as valid votes for the candidate to whom he was opposed. Bearing out this contention that some strange people were voting is the attempt of the 1621 bill regulating the conduct of elections to exclude cottagers from voting. Now there was of course already statutory provision to limit the franchise to 40s. freeholders, so those against whom this bill was directed must have been 40s. freeholders who were also cottagers. These were virtually the rural poor. If a 40s. per annum income from freehold land had been less than what might be earned from wage labour at 2d. a day in the 15th century, how much more was that the case in the 17th century when rates might stand at 8d. a day? Dr Spufford has estimated that a holding of less than a half-yardland (which might vary between 10 and 20 acres) of arable was insufficient to provide subsistence for a family.[8] The 40s. freeholder in arable regions had to be a wage-earner to keep alive; in forest or fen, the supplements to his income available from utilisation of the waste land might just support him. But in either case, the mere 40s. freeholder was more or less a pauper. Thanks to inflation, the county electorate was becoming highly socially inclusive.

The important question remains, how many such people were there left on the land? English landed society in the 18th century is best characterised as composed of landlord, tenant farmer and landless labourers. Prof. Tawney saw the peasantry as being squeezed out, or at least forced to accept capitalist leaseholds in place of customary tenures in the course of the 16th century. But the decisive factor in eliminating the peasantry was probably more the decline in grain prices than landlord pressure. The turning-point here was around the 1650s. Both Prof. Habakkuk and Dr Thirsk have argued that the later 17th century was the watershed, dividing a largely peasant from a largely capitalist agri-cultural economy, at least in the arable regions.[9] Up to that time, the conditions were far more favourable for the peasant, and the small producer could flourish, as food prices tended on a fluctuating but con-tinuous upward course. The county electorate may have been decimated by economic changes after the Restoration, but this is unlikely to have been the case earlier.[10]

Detailed studies, such as those on which Habakkuk and Thirsk drew, certainly reveal a strong and numerous peasantry up to mid-century. More to the point, such studies also reveal numerous freeholders, some of whom were very distinctly smallholders. Prof. Tawney estimated that nationally freeholders comprised about 20 per cent of all landholders in the 16th and early 17th centuries. This proportion rose towards a half in parts of East Anglia (possibly because of the relics of socage tenure), and might go even higher where gavelkind, or forms of partible inheritance, pre-vailed. Woodland areas might also have high concentrations of freehold, where men had been permitted by the lord to clear the land at their own cost, and had been granted freehold rights in return. One scholar found that there were 'innumerable' freeholders in the Forest of Arden at this time; likewise, in the parish of Myddle in woodland Shropshire, the freeholders comprised 44 per cent of the community.[11]

The suggestion was made above that freehold was merely a form of tenure, and that nothing determined that freehold land should be held in substantial units. Where individual freeholders can be identified in manorial studies, this suggestion is reinforced. In an admittedly unrepresentative sample by Tawney, nearly 50 per cent of the freeholders held five acres or less. The 1635 survey of Laxton in Nottinghamshire which was analysed by the Orwins revealed, as they concluded, that there were a number of freeholders in the village who 'owned only a few acres of land, insufficient to support them', and supplemented their meagre incomes by either renting more land, or by hiring themselves as labourers. There were 33 freeholders present, out of a total of 103 occupants of the land: in other words, the freeholders formed about a third of the whole tenantry; six of the group held under five acres, and a further three held five to nine acres. While Prof. Hoskins's study of Wigston Magna in Leicestershire is not entirely typical of champion lands in that socially it was an 'open' village, without a resident squire, and partly as a result an unusually healthy peasantry, it does, for what it is worth, reveal similar features. More significant perhaps is a study of a sample of Essex manors made by Dr Hull some years ago. He estimated that 42 per cent of manorial tenants (in a strong freehold area) held five acres or less.[12] The Earl of Salisbury's agent drew up a very detailed listing of the freeholders on some of his master's Hertfordshire manors in preparation for the Short Parliament election, and this again demonstrates the existence of very insubstantial freeholders. On one of the manors, 45 names, with the extent of many of their holdings, are given.[13] Of the 45, at least fourteen held less than six acres, with one as low as half an acre, two with one acre, two with two, and a further two possessing 'a small parcel'. The agent numbered 28 of the more propertied names, and if this is done on the same principle as elsewhere on the list, then he considered that these 28 were usable votes. But even of this 28, four are noted as having a mere four to five acres, and another one as having a freehold worth less than 40s. (implying perhaps that the four-to-five acre men did have 40s. freeholds). That is, even if we take the more conservative figure of 28, at least 18 per cent would fall below any notion, such as that held by Wilson and King, of the freeholder as a substantial figure. If we were to consider all 45 on this manor, then almost a third appear likely to have had a landed income of 40s. per annum or less. And, in the absence of detailed accounting, many men slightly below the 40s. margin could probably have claimed the vote with a fair degree of sincerity.

There were clearly freeholders around who did fall at or about the 40s. level, or even lower. The contention that the 40s. freehold franchise legitimately included near-paupers as a result of the inflation of land values is thus not merely an abstract hypothesis. In default of an infinite amount of work in manorial archives, it is impossible to establish how many such freeholders there were; nevertheless, it is possible to conclude that the much-vaunted freeholder electorate was not necessarily a respectable one. Ireton at Putney considered the 40s. freeholder to be 'the meanest man' who had any kind of real property at all, and such an assessment of the county electorate, with cottagers being capable of voting legitimately, rather than coming to the polls illicitly under some subterfuge, accords with surviving accounts of several elections. As has been seen, cottagers were accepted in the 1601 Rutland election, and were presumably to be found voting before the 1621 election bill. Neville's resentment at the Short Parliament Essex election result was occasioned not by the fact that the 'factious' and 'mean conditioned' should have been admitted by a partisan sheriff, but that they were indeed legitimate voters. In the same election, Lord Maynard's spleen against the behaviour of 'the fellowes without shirts' is well known.[14] But his attack on the property-less was not aimed at the fact that they were voting, but at the

way they voted, that they should cross his wishes. He evidently accepted
that the shirtless could be 40s. freeholders.

### Other tenures and uncertainties

Abundant freehold was apparently geographically limited, primarily to
East Anglia, perhaps to Kent (a strong gavelkind region), and to areas
of former woodland. Elsewhere, Tawney argues that other tenures,
customary or leasehold, predominated, the holders of which would
presumably have been barred from elections.

Sir John Spelman argued that only one-tenth of the population, the
freeholders, were represented in parliament, the rest, the copyholders, etc.,
being excluded.[15] While he erred in his omission of the borough franchises (and consequently in his arithmetic), he probably erred in an even
more important respect, the exclusiveness of the definition of freehold.

If most holders of land had been of sufficient income but the wrong
tenure, then the rising value of land would not have had too great an
impact. But in his important work on tenures, Dr Kerridge testified to
the abundant confusion caused by the term freehold. He observed
trenchantly that any tenure for one life or more (as opposed to a tenure
for years) conveyed an estate rather than a chattel interest in the land.
And technically this created a freehold interest.[16] Various lawyers can be
found arguing that a customary tenure (normally copyhold) for life or
lives was in law to be accounted a freehold. Sir Edward Coke, the most
influential lawyer of the period, claimed that 'In respect of the state of
the Land, so Copyholders may be Freeholders; for any that hath any
estate for his life, or any greater estate in any Land whatsoever, may in
this sense be termed a Freeholder.' William Prynne, the great parliamentary lawyer, when preparing a brief for an election case in 1641,
concluded that only copyholders and lessees for years or at will were
excluded from the franchise. William Noy, the future Attorney-General
speaking in the House on the disputed 1621 Leicestershire election, even
contended that 'An Annuitie for life is a freehold'. The House collectively
was to follow this reasoning some of the way: in a debate on the
Cricklade franchise in 1685 it recognised the greater interest of tenants
for lives when it vested the suffrage in 'the freeholders, copyholders and
leaseholders, for three lives'.[17]

If Dr Kerridge and Coke, Noy and Prynne were correct, then the
tenurial limitation, like that on value, may not have been very effective
as a barrier to potential voters. While freeholds in the conventional
sense[18] were geographically and numerically limited, interest for life or
lives in the land was much more common. While in Tawney's overall
sample, freeholders formed only c. 20 per cent of occupants of the land,

copyholders formed 50 per cent upwards, being most common where freehold was rarest. In a small sample of 142 manors which he analysed in detail, he found only three featuring copyholds for years without right of renewal (definitely a chattel interest), and a further nineteen of copyhold for years with right of renewal (again, strictly, a chattel interest). The remaining 120 manors featured copyholds of inheritance (47), and for life or lives.[19] That is, the majority of these copyholds were not mere chattel tenures. Assuming that some at least of the leaseholds were also for lives rather than years, we encounter a situation where large numbers of landholders would be included within Coke's legal definition of a freeholder.

Tawney's sample was unrepresentative, and was biased towards the 16th century, and while there does not appear to have been a massive policy of conversion to leasehold for years in the early 17th century (although this was the case later), his figures may not be especially reliable. But detailed accounts of particular areas tend to bear him out. Dr Kerridge himself suggested that while freehold was less common in the West than the East, leases for lives were more widespread there, and that even in the Midlands, where the incidence of copyhold for years was highest, copyhold for life or lives was much the commoner form of tenure. Prof. Hoskins found that in Devon by c. 1600, while the conventional freeholders formed about 20 per cent of the rural tenantry, leases for 99 years or three lives 'had become the usual method of dealing with leasehold land'; this was also true of leasehold land in the Forest of Arden, shorter leases being still rare in the early 17th century; leases for lives (usually three) predominated on the second Earl of Salisbury's western estates in the 1620s and 30s. In Myddle in Shropshire, leases for years were converted to lives in the course of Elizabeth's reign, and by 1602 only three tenants still held for a period of years. A recent scholar has concluded that, in addition to the 44 per cent conventional freeholders, 'nearly all the lord's farms and tenements were held by leases for three lives, and the peasants were now legally secure in what were in effect freehold estates'.[20]

Whether such people were aware of the political rights incidental to their legal status is an unanswerable question. The consciousness of legal security in their land, when the land was the acknowledged basis of politics, may have given some the confidence to go along to the election, or even to undergo the poll, with its risk of being challenged on their possession of freehold. They could in all honesty have responded to such a challenge affirmatively, but whether many other than the more litigious would have known that is inevitably unclear. Certainly, late 16th- and early 17th-century Star Chamber cases include complaints of many copyholders voting; similarly, the 1626 bill to regulate elections sought to debar copyholders.[21] Both of these facts suggest that their participation was recognised, even if not universally accepted.

It is arguable that neither value nor tenure requirements were much of a barrier. A supporter of Sir Robert Harley for the Short Parliament election for Herefordshire sent a circular letter requesting votes (and one of the named recipients was described as 'Thomas Turner, his workman'), with an appended note as to the necessary qualifications: 'Now leaste there should be any doubt who have alowable voices in this case let it be knowne that all freehoulders and coppyhoulders and all that hold by tearme of three lives or on life, have voices in this case, although it be but the hould of an house, a garden, an acre, or any patch of ground, as also any annuity during one life or more.'[22] Those addressed were not being told to try their luck at getting past the sheriff. They were being informed in detail as to what was thought admissible, and their informant considered that the possession of any real property by any tenure other than one for years created a qualified voter; the insertion about annuities for life indicates that he was not totally ignorant. Presumably those, if there were any in that inflationary age, falling short of the required income, might be expected, perhaps like Thomas Turner's workman, to follow another occupation too.

Even if the individual copyholders for lives were not themselves appraised of their rights, there were clearly gentry in Herefordshire who for their own ends were prepared to educate them. The same would in all probability be found to have been true of other counties, had the evidence survived.

The anomalies of the county franchise were increased by the often unclear distinction between various forms of tenure. The status of land was constantly changing, which must have confused the unhappy sheriff who, by the 1628 ruling of the House, was expected to be acquainted with his charges. Complicating this was the fact that those involved sometimes seem to have been uncertain of the exact status of a particular piece of land. The Earl of Salisbury's 1640 Hertfordshire listing is suggestive here. The agent, who was on the whole extremely painstaking, was unable to categorise exactly nineteen of the 139 freeholders on the list for the manor of Hertford, on the grounds that he was unsure of the precise tenure by which men held, or even if they were tenants at all. By the side of other names he noted that they were unknown to him. Against a further three (not included in the nineteen), he noted that they held by either copy or lease, although he continued to list them as freeholders, so their tenures may have been for lives. An additional four were listed as being under 40s., but they too were listed as freeholders. The Salisbury agent was scrupulous, and the nineteen he was unsure of were noted as 'not usefull at this election': but someone more inclined to give himself the benefit of the doubt, or less sure of his electoral strength than Salisbury, might well have been tempted to regard all 26 as valid – for even the apparently honest agent continued to list them as freeholders. In other words, the status of 26 out of 139 freeholders, or about nineteen per cent, was open to doubt, even in the eyes of the agent of, according to Prof. Stone, the most efficient estate-managing magnate in the country.[23]

The group listed on the Salisbury manor of Little Hadham illustrates another problem related to the verification of freeholders' claims to the vote. Three of the men are noted as being copyholders of Little Hadham, but freeholders of under 40s. in neighbouring manors.[24] They are nevertheless listed as freeholders of Little Hadham, and two are apparently numbered as valid votes. When men of this size held exiguous parcels in different manors, often of different lords, it must have been virtually impossible to check rigorously on their claims at the poll.

The problems of controlling the appearance and behaviour of county voters from the lower end of the socio-economic scale were magnified by the lack of any adequate method of verification of their claims. In the counties, there could be no lists of who had been admitted to the freedom, or who paid the rates, as there could in boroughs. Evidence of the yield from land must have been extremely difficult to present or to verify – especially as it presumably varied from year to year with the harvest. County lists of freeholders were indeed compiled, but, at least before the Civil War, none of them was compiled for electoral purposes. Subsidy lists, as Henry Neville observed in Essex in 1640, bore little relation to the 40s. freeholder.[25] Entry in the subsidy rolls was sometimes used as a threat by sheriffs or powerful gentry to freeholders who were proving recalcitrant, suggesting again that subsidy-men and 40s. freeholders were different persons. As Sir John Neale noted, there would be many individuals in every county regarded as 'sufficient' freeholders for purposes of an election, but as 'insufficient' for taxation or jury service, the two great local burdens.[26]

Lists of freeholders for jury service were frequently drawn up, but these were equally useless as a guide to those men who might be admitted to vote in county elections. A 1608 proposal to rectify abuses in the returns of jurors suggested that the jurors' lists be compared with the subsidy rolls, to discover omissions in the former – hardly a testimonial to the completeness of the jury lists! The 40s. freehold requirement for the county franchise had clearly grown out of the identical requirements for service on the juries of the shire courts, a level which had prevailed since 1293. But 17th-century jurors' lists were compiled for other courts, particularly the assizes, and here the qualification for service was less clear. A 1584 statute had required that jurors possess a £4 freehold, but this seems to have been directed only at the metropolis, and there does not appear to have been any obvious rubric elsewhere.[27] Reform proposals to the Jacobean Council merely suggested that lists of freeholders be drawn up, making no mention of value; likewise, a Somerset assize order of 1648 enjoined that 'a true and perfect list of the names of all the freeholders in every parish' was to be compiled, for the better supplying of the assizes. Conversely, the sheriff of Lincolnshire in 1630 ordered his bailiff to ensure that all potential jurymen had a freehold of 20s. per annum or a copyhold of four nobles, while the Hertfordshire freeholders' book of 1657–8 was used for the selection of the Grand Jury, and is thus unlikely to have included the lesser freeholders. All the evidence suggests that the jury qualification (while probably very unclear) was not identical with that for voting, and that the one could therefore have been no check on the other.[28] The Yorkshire high constables in 1621 were reported to have taken the names of all freeholders at the election, in order 'that they might retorne the names of such as were fit at the Assizes to serve the King' – a phrasing which suggests that prior to this there had been no attempt to use the jury list as an electoral roll.[29] The argument that no electoral listing of any kind existed is borne out by the allegation that the Yorkshire sheriff used Wentworth's list of supporters as a means of checking on the qualifications of voters.[30] Such a blatant tactic was unlikely to have been used if a less obtrusive one had been available.

There remains one other conceivable test: who, or whose father, had voted before? Or rather, was there an awareness of those holdings to which the vote attached, after the manner of burgage tenures in some towns? This is unlikely to have been feasible – if only because given the novelty of contests, and even more, the novelty of polls, nobody's father was likely to have voted, or even to have thought much of having the vote, previously. Moreover, an examination of wills reveals that a freehold tended not to be regarded in the same manner as later burgage tenures, as something not to be divided. Dr Spufford has discovered a few isolated early 17th-century cases in Cambridgeshire of freeholds passing intact to the eldest son, which implies that the social connotations of freeholder status may have been having a practical effect. And in areas threatened with enclosure from above, a freehold had particular attractions, in terms of conveying security.[31] But Prof. Tawney remarked that a customary tenure had several advantages over a freehold, especially in that it could be transferred more easily, and Richard Gough noted several cases of copyholders refusing to convert their tenements to freehold in mid-17th century Myddle.[32] On the whole, probate evidence suggests that freehold might be parcelled out between heirs, or disposed of in the course of consolidation of a valuable piece of copyhold or lease-hold, in the same way as any other tenure.

The invigilating sheriffs were thus without any effective test of the freeholders. Attempts to compile aids met with a cold reception. The House's attitude had been hinted at when Wentworth was closely questioned in 1621 as to his intention in keeping a list of the Yorkshire voters of that year, for undue pressure was, rightly, feared.[33] Seven years later, after a return bout in the same county, the House was driven to resolve 'that if an elector or freeholder beinge by the shereefe uppon the pole demaunded his name if he refuse it this shall not disable him from givinge his voyce in the election'. It rejected Wentworth's opponents' assertions that a list was essential to prevent perjury,[34] on the grounds that, as the Committee of Privileges put it, it was 'inconvenient, to have them set down their Names; because Notice might be taken of them, to their Prejudice'. The House preferred to rely on the fiction that 'the Sheriffe is intended to have counsens [cognisance] of all freeholders or at least his bayliffes who there attend him'. This last was a futile wish, when those talking of that election spoke in terms of 7000, 8000 or 10,000 voters being present. Even when a much lower total of 1775 was involved in an official Essex listing, possibly for jury service, of 1634, the remark 'Ign[otus]' occurs against many of the names.[35]

The only check left to the sheriff was the oath to be tendered to the freeholder, in the event of a poll, as to his qualifications. D'Ewes's worried queries of the judges as to the nature of this oath before the Long Parliament election for Suffolk suggest that it was not too precise a test. The hapless sheriff of Yorkshire, having been chastised for his conduct of the first 1625 election, and ordered to hold a new one, attempted to improve the situation and begged direction of the House whether the oath prescribed in 8 H.VI might be made more serviceable. The House refused to be drawn, resolving 'to leave the shreife to be advised by his counsell, yt not being our office ... to make or declare the lawe in cases not yet in beinge'.[36]

Undoubtedly, sheriffs and others, including even the precisianist D'Ewes, disregarded the implications of the 1628 order and kept tallies, and the incidence of poll lists increased. But the order must at least have made initiation of a perjury action more difficult. Even if the ostensible freeholder was unaware of his right to silence, an observer for the side for whom he was voting would be on hand, and he could presumably be relied upon to warn the voter not to give his name. Some time before the order, at the 1614 Hampshire election, complaint was made that when one of the candidates started trying to take the names of suspected copyholders, the opposition 'required the said Coppyholders particularly as they passed by not to declare theire names to any, saying Wallop and his freinds had nothing to doe therewithall'.[37]

The result was that little could be done. Sir John Neale cites the prosecution for perjury of 12 Huntingdonshire voters in Star Chamber after the 1584 election, but this appears to be the only extant suggestion of an action for perjury in this period. There were accusations of perjury during the 1621 Radnorshire case in Star Chamber, but the plaintiff was proceeding against the sheriff for fraud and other miscarriages, rather than against the voters. An oath was clearly of far greater significance in the 17th century than it is today, but the absence of human sanctions was perhaps an incentive for people to stretch the truth, even if not actually to controvert it. More than the mere confusion of tenures militated against the operation of a close check on the credentials of voters. Even in contested elections, the implementation of the poll, and thus the tendering of oaths, was still a rarity, most elections being decided by the cry or the view – although, as has been seen, by 1625 some of the Committee of Privileges were coming to feel that the poll was essential in *all* contests, in order to weed out the unqualified.[38]

The county franchise appears to have been a considerably more open commodity than both contemporaries and modern historians have thought it. The surviving evidence about the identity of voters at county elections confirms the impression that the county electorate was relatively socially heterogeneous.

In addition to the actual rural freeholders, urban inhabitants of the county possessing real estate were entitled to vote, thus often being doubly enfranchised, as Henry Neville complained in 1640. Urban votes were particularly valuable, being geographically concentrated and therefore easily mobilised. It was observed during the 1597 Yorkshire election that the West Riding clothing towns provided 'the greatest number of freeholders'. Towns which formed the venue for the county court were still more useful, and the inhabitants of Abingdon, Ipswich and Norwich were said to dominate the Berkshire, Suffolk and Norfolk elections respectively.[39] Urban votes were thus often unpopular with the rural squires. An attempt in 1628 to exclude them from county elections got as far as a third reading in the House, and local initiatives were sometimes more successful. The sheriff of Norfolk barred the Norwich freeholders from voting in the Long Parliament county election, and the sheriff of Worcestershire did the same for Worcester, even when the city freeholders could prove possession of freehold outside the city limits.[40]

A solitary urban listing survives, from Godmanchester for the Huntingdonshire election of 1625, and this helps to explain the rural resentment. Godmanchester is only one mile from Huntingdon, the place of election, so its inhabitants were probably strongly laboured and turned out; and the listing, of voters in the Cromwell interest, is amongst the borough records and in the same hand as many of those records, suggesting official involvement and pressure and possibly a disproportionately high turn-out. But despite the small size of the township, 107 men are noted as having given their votes for Sir Oliver Cromwell, and presumably at least a few more would have appeared for the opposition, no matter how docile the population. While the majority of the voters may have been borough-holders, more or less equivalent to freeholders, the size of the rent many of them paid, according to the borough rental of Michaelmas 1624, suggests that they were not all occupants of 40s.-worth of land. The norm of rent was somewhere between 2s. and 4s. 6d. (some paying over 30s.), but 30 were paying less than 1s. (although nine of these were also medium-sized sub-tenants paying 2–4s.), with a few as low as 1d. or 2d. Moreover, four of the voters were merely sub-tenants, while sixteen held no real property at all (although several of these were the sons of substantial men.) It seems likely that not much attention was being paid to the precise qualifications, for twenty, or just under one-fifth, certainly should not have been voting. Probate evidence is left for 56 of the 107, and while 35 of these were gentry, yeomen and husbandmen, the remainder featured a normal cross-section of country-town trades, ranging from a miller worth £730 5s., to a shearman with one acre and goods worth £14 10s., and three labourers.[41] At least some of those people whom we have come to expect were present.

Sir Edward Dering's list for Kent in the spring of 1640 is useless statistically, for it is very incomplete. In most parishes, he can only name the gentlemen and ministers, but in those nearest to his own home he is more full, giving 43 supporters from Charing, 38 from Egerton, and 33 from Smarden – itself evidence of the number of voters, if so many came from individual rural parishes for one candidate. The few identifiable voters from Charing yield such peculiarities as the labourer who made a 'welbeloved Fellowe servant' his executrix, and a kersey-maker who left £26 and apparently no real estate beyond a house and garden; one of Dering's Egerton voters was aparently a pail-maker. Against the names of four Ashford men, he noted 'these no freehold', though he does not seem to have forborne to use them.[42]

The impression derived from Godmanchester and the Kent parishes must be qualified by evidence from the West Midlands, an area where freehold was less plentiful in the regions away from old woodland. While it is probable that over 3500 came for the Herefordshire Recruiter election, neighbouring counties provided much lower figures. Less than 2000 voted in the by-election to the Long Parliament for Warwickshire, and less than 1000 polled in the Worcestershire election in the autumn of 1640, although the mustered trained bands had been canvassed. Both these elections were polled, which tended, as we shall see, to under-register the voters, and the Worcestershire poll was apparently incomplete, but nevertheless, the conclusions which can be formed from material from primarily the eastern half of the country may not hold true universally. The calculations which can be made for Gloucestershire in 1640 tend to support them, as does the high poll in Hampshire as early as 1614. It has been argued above that the landholding structure of western England was not enormously more unfavourable to the formation of a large electorate at this time than that in the East. Nevertheless, in default of further evidence, Warwickshire and Worcestershire must be set against Herefordshire, Gloucestershire and the very large number of freeholders that the Coke interest entertained in Derbyshire in 1640, and the question of the tangible effect on voters all over the country of the pervading imprecision must be left open.[43] But even if the numbers in certain areas remained low, there was little to guarantee their *quality*.

On such sparse and inconclusive evidence as this, it seems likely that while those involved were aware of the freehold requirement for voting, not a great deal of attention was paid to it, and probably even less to the value qualification, either by canvassers, electoral officers, or the House of Commons. This may have been because the value was in practice becoming impossible to check, or because in many areas most people with any land at all could make a plausible claim to vote, if they wished.

Additionally, of course, there was the issue of fraud and blatant illegality. There were certainly allegations of the creation of bogus freeholders, but often such measures would have been unnecessary. Given the reluctance to go to the poll, would-be voters normally did not have to undergo the solitary test of the oath – and there was then no way of checking whether one shout was property-less when uttered in the midst of a throng.[44] Consequently, a candidate had every incentive to bring as many people along as he could, in the hope that his opponent would not press the point, for polls were unpopular with the rest of the gentry. Often also the candidate would not have needed to resort to much incitement. Probity was not helped by gentry insistence on being attended by their servants – who then participated. An election was a free entertainment, frequently with food and drink laid on, and certainly a spectacular event in the daily round. To Sir Henry Slingsby, an election was a by-word for disorderly excitement: talking of the Yorkshire freeholders' meeting with the King in the turbulent summer of 1642, he reported that 'their meeting produc'd nothing else but a confus'd murmer and noise, as at an Election for Knights of the Parliaments'.[45] Important events in the municipal calendar were ceremonialised, and served as an attraction to people in the vicinity,[46] and the same was true of occasions in the country-side, and of parliamentary elections. Crowds came out the few miles from Maidstone fair to the Kent county election in 1625; a neighbouring minister turned up to watch the fun at the Lewes election of 1628, and was thought sufficiently non-partisan to be asked to take the poll; when the Commission of Array was executed in Shropshire in 1642, one observer described it as 'this great show'.[47]

When no effective checks operated, an already motley electorate must have swelled and become still more disreputable. A nostalgia for the unlimited freeholder franchise that obtained before the reforms of Henry VI was apparently expressed in Yorkshire in 1621,[48] but how exclusive the voting world was by the early 17th century must be doubted. The attractions of the election as spectacle must intensify these doubts.

# 3

# The Borough Franchise Disputes

## *The pressures in the towns*

The county franchise was becoming broader through the efforts of man only insofar as he fuelled the inflationary process. That was not the case in the boroughs. Here, more people were involved as a result of certain actions, the decisions to open the limited franchises in dozens of communities to freemen, inhabitants at large, or whatever group was in question.[1] The process was normally one of local pressure from an insurgent group producing a disputed return of members to parliament, and the House of Commons then deciding in favour of the popular challengers. It is tempting to think in terms of a meaner sort that had been politically aroused by the growing educational provision and by the religious and political debate of the time and which was now entering the fray to the best of its abilities; or even demanding the vote because it realised its value. But while the clashes with reactionary and entrenched oligarchy may have occurred in the heated atmosphere of national polarisation, the genesis of the disputes must be sought over a longer period of time. This might, in any case, be suggested by the outbreak of many conflicts in the early 1620s, before the national divisions were at all clear.

The most common pattern in franchise disputes was one of the particularist grievances of an under-privileged group against oligarchy gradually building up and being capitalised on by the self-interested intervention of an outside gentleman who was looking for support in his bid for a seat. It is clear that the meaner sort was becoming active: but its pressure was not always sufficient of itself to enable it to achieve its goals. The leadership, money, contacts or political *nous* of a gentleman or disaffected oligarch might be required to bring success to a campaign, at least when that campaign involved a petition to the House of Commons for the vote. But equally, gentry populism alone would not always cause a franchise dispute: there had to be fertile soil on which it could work. The existence of either factor was in many cases a necessary but not a sufficient condition for a widening of the franchise. A full analysis of the process therefore does have to take the national arena into consideration, for increasing gentry competition for seats, and the readiness of the House of Commons to view with favour those demanding the vote, were vital factors. But more important was the urban context.

In almost every borough in which a franchise dispute occurred, long-term friction between various groups is evident: the parliamentary election was one among many occasions of division. There are predictably more signs of concern with national issues and religious divisions in the largest towns, London, Norwich, Newcastle, perhaps Exeter and Bristol; but in the third-rank towns of a few thousand inhabitants which experienced the bulk of the disputes, the most evident feature is of prolonged, particularist dissension. The danger of such an assessment is its near-determinism – size broadens horizons, parochialism characterises the friction of smaller towns. There is certainly a problem caused by the selective availability of evidence: the largest towns were often sufficiently important to excite comment on their affairs, and thus non-official accounts survive. But in the third-rank town, often the only significant source available is the magisterial archives. Such records tend to be overwhelmingly concerned with urban economics, and an analysis of the grievances of the local opposition will inevitably focus on issues arising from that sphere. Nevertheless, it remains significant that the corporations did not see fit to accuse their rivals of religious fanaticism but instead pointed to concern over the oligarchy's use of the town lands, for example. This might be taken to be less flattering to the magistrates than a belief that the opposition consisted of a bunch of zealots. Most corporations appear to have believed that the major points of friction were local ones. Their verdict is confirmed by the way in which in most boroughs the parliamentary franchise was merely one more battleground on which to contest the hold of the oligarchs on the town's affairs. The struggle had often been progressing for years before the electoral issue arose, and often continued for years after that particular episode was settled. To some men the right to vote for burgesses to parliament was doubtless an important goal in itself, but the conclusion is inescapable that on the whole the franchise disputes were primarily manifestations of local rivalries, rather than evidence of a widespread concern with parliament for its own sake. It is therefore necessary to seek an explanation for the expansion of the borough franchises not just in the parliamentary process, but in the local development of oligarchy, and the challenges to it.

The roots of oligarchy are discernible long before the period when the confrontations which concern us broke out. In virtually all boroughs, a general trend towards formal oligarchy is visible from at least the 14th century. It has variously been viewed as a natural off-shoot of the growth of towns, and of the increasing concentration of wealth, as the economy became more sophisticated.[2] Mr Hibbert concluded that the growth of privilege and internal protectionism arose with the saturation of markets at the close of the 13th century: a relatively smaller cake to be cut led the more powerful members of communities to take steps to entrench their positions. Depression in the 14th century confirmed this tendency. Difficulties in the way of making trading profits caused merchants to exploit other means of making money, by unfair distribution of the tax load, by private utilisation of the town's common resources, and so on. The growth of trade thus produced a class of merchant capitalists of a different order of economic magnitude from the bulk of the small master craftsmen; trading problems then drove them to exploit their superiority by the use of non-mercantile resources to the direct detriment of other groups within the towns. Predictably this provoked a reaction from the lesser men in the crafts who were also being squeezed by the same conditions.[3] The reaction was less successful than in the rest of Europe, and the oligarchs remained in control, for reasons which Prof. Thrupp argues have to do with the smaller size of English towns and the greater efficiency and penetration of royal justice, which meant that there was less need of the guilds as an instrument of regulation.[4]

The late 16th and early 17th centuries produced in many ways a similar set of circumstances. The markets for the traditional English broadcloth were becoming saturated, and in important areas economic expansion was slowing down.[5] Protectionism again resulted. Measures to restrict the inflow of strangers, measures to strengthen control of the crafts, measures to confirm and buttress the positions of the powerful became more evident.[6] Again the tendency of the oligarchs to exploit their strength became visible. This was not necessarily an act of irresponsibility on their part: declining corporation revenues, and increasing outgoings, particularly on the poor, meant that the members of the corporations were called upon to finance deficits or respond to crises from their own pockets. There was little wonder if they sought to compensate themselves. But again, this inevitably aroused feelings of resentment in less privileged members of the community. The quest for revenue by the magistrates, in their corporate capacity or personally, often led to an effort to extract as much as possible from corporation resources.[7] Freemen who were themselves in difficulties as a result of depression in the cloth trade might find rents rising or erstwhile common lands being viewed in a new light by the local governors — at a time when rights in these commons were becoming relatively more important to the underprivileged as their other sources of income became less secure. Contention was the outcome. And just as Mr Hibbert argued that, while the sources of friction were long-term, the occasions became more frequent and the intensity greater in the economically more adverse 14th century than earlier, so the depressions of the 1590s and 1620s seem to have brought more than their share of urban troubles. Thus, in Coventry, tension over the town lands is very prominent until c. 1610, appears to diminish in the next, more favourable, decade, only to recur in the 1620s; Exeter and Sandwich similarly seem to experience peace in the second decade of the century, but disruption before and after.[8]

Developments such as these were affected and intensified by the policy of the Crown. The Tudors had supported local trends towards corporations of self-selecting members, but not coherently, and it was not until James I's reign that the legal device of self-selecting incorporation, soon the general rule, was perfected.[9] In part this was merely the logical culmination of existing trends, but a new concern is visible. Depression in the cloth industry led to manufacturing abuses in the interests of cutting costs, and this created a new governmental and mercantile determination to regulate production by incorporating those involved into companies. Resentment was predictably excited amongst those finding themselves newly-controlled by the bigger men.[10] Furthermore, Prof. Hoskins suggested that the last quarter of the 16th century was the decisive time for urban population growth, and the general demographic and economic change of the period brought waves of hungry immigrants to the towns.[11] Problems of, or at least fears for, security arose in consequence, and government became increasingly concerned to strengthen the position of its local agents. The Privy Council took pains to stress its constant care 'to mayntaine and protect the peaceable and orderly government of citties and corporacions', and this concern may have been reinforced by the orthodoxy that towns were the centres of organised puritan opposition to the ecclesiastical establishment. To this end, a Durham cleric urged the King in 1640 not to 'suffer little towns to grow big and anti-monarchy to boot; for where are all these pestilent nests of Puritans hatched, but in corporations'.[12]

The Stuart period marks a novel departure here. Prof. Stone has suggested that the opening of Charles I's years of rule without parliaments inaugurated a policy of social reaction and social restriction:[13] whatever the truth of the general assertion, Charles and his father were certainly being more restrictive than their immediate predecessor in urban affairs. The late Elizabethan Privy Council, when faced with urban disorders, had indeed sided with oligarchy, but it had been moderately open-minded in the process. James and Charles were not. A confrontation in Ludlow in 1597 over the usual issue of exploitation of the town lands by the corporation was seen by the Privy Council as almost unprecedented in its intensity: nevertheless, while it tended to uphold the magistrates, it did not take the high-flying line in support of oligarchy which its successors were to do. Similar trouble on a similar issue in Totnes the same year met an even more investigative, rather than didactic, response.[14] The next year, at the start of a long-running dispute, the Council showed itself sufficiently aware of the temptations of oligarchic power to attempt to debar partners in the grand lease of the Newcastle coal mines from the mayoralty for ten years.[15] It may be that such judiciousness resulted from the novelty of the problem, as economic adversity and population pressure hit the towns: as the Council said of the Ludlow troubles, which had produced direct action by the inferior burgesses (a common enough problem later), such disorder 'hath not allmost bin harde of in her Majestys peaceable and most gratious government'.[16] Within a short space, the novelty, if such it was, had worn off, and James and Charles showed themselves far more fixed in their attitudes.

The early Stuart position is most clearly exemplified by the vehement reaction to standard complaints about magisterial exploitation of place and powers which came from some Barnstaple petitioners in 1637. 'Forasmuch as wee hold it very unfit in any measure or manner to countenance any Inferiors in their complaints against their Governors', the assize judges were ordered to call all before them to investigate the matter. 'And if upon examinacion yow find any thing amisse in the Government of the Mayor and Aldermen to take an effectuall Order and course to redresse and reforme the same, yet soe, as may not impeach government nor give encouragement to any to oppose or impugne it. But if yow find the Complaint wholy Causles and scandalous Then wee require that some such punishment bee by yow inflicted . . . as may bee exemplary and beget obedience.'[17] That pronouncement put into practical terms a general policy which had been evident for perhaps twenty years.

Turbulence in the two leading cities of the kingdom, London and Norwich, at the end of the second decade of the century appears to have awakened the Crown to urban terrors. The last significant vestige of popular involvement in London affairs was represented by the shrieval election, and disorder there probably determined James to eliminate the popular role – which produced in the early 1620s a series of laboured defences of elections by the Recorder, one of which has been referred to above.[18] In Norwich, the Privy Council was far more active, for the corporation there was very much more open than London's, and the crucial position of alderman, which provided the governors of the city, was largely elective. In 1619, in response to reports that municipal elections were made by 'multiplicity of laboured voyces, guided often tymes by certaine factious humours', which had resulted in the thoroughly reprehensible 'employinge of diverse of the yonger sort', the Privy Council commended and commanded the more rigid exemplar of London's constitution, 'which for good usages and happy successe deserves to be propounded as an example to direct both yow and others'. After prolonged and heavy pressure on the city, the Council gradually brought it to order, leaving only shrieval elections outside the safety-net of self-selection.[19] Predictably, and as in London earlier, disorder broke out on this last remaining front in 1627, amidst charges of corporate exploitation and oppression. The Conciliar reaction was to intervene again, in an ultimately unsuccessful attempt to eliminate the popular shrieval electoral form, that the 'popular and factious humors' that troubled the city might finally be suppressed, and its government brought at last to an 'orderly' form.[20]

The 1620s and 1630s witnessed a succession of doctrinaire actions and statements, of which that over Barnstaple was perhaps merely the most intolerant, following the initial London and Norwich precedents. In the interests of centralising all powers in the oligarchy, the Council in 1620 suppressed trading sub-incorporations in Ipswich, not with the aim of benefiting the economy of the community in question, but for reasons of security: as the government's legal counsel, Edmondes, Caesar and Hobart, advised it, 'wee are of opinion in the generall that theis under corporacions in townes and inferiour citties are seldome of good use, but doe rather disturbe the generall goverment [sic] of such places'.[21] An overwhelming concern to keep government in as few hands as possible is visible. In the midst of prolonged trouble within the corporation of Chester in 1627, both sides were heavily censured by the Council, but the gravest fault had been that one had appealed for support outside the corporation Chamber; when the Crown was desperate for cash in 1639, the Lord Mayor and aldermen of London were summoned and ordered to raise money from amongst themselves and the wealthy commons, 'always provided that they did not call their Common Council, nor put it to the Commons, which his Majesty would by no means endure' (although in this case the Crown's apprehensions may have reflected awareness of what the commons' reply was likely to be). Every corporate act clearly had to accord with the government's increasingly strict hierarchical concept. Counsel, including the Attorney-General, instructed the Council in 1629 that the government of Great Yarmouth should be reduced immediately to a mayoral form, for disorder would surely continue 'as long as the head of the body consists of 2 bailiffs, which is monstrous in nature, and dangerous and inconvenient in government'; a *quo warranto* was brought against Shrewsbury in 1637 by the Attorney-General, apparently because of the extreme popularity of its forms of government. In the same year, the Council attempted to regulate affairs within the corporations themselves into a more hierarchical form by banning ballot boxes, because of 'the manifold Inconveniences that may arise' from secret voting.[22] It was still fighting this battle as the world began to tumble around its ears in late 1641, attempting to tighten up the London oligarchy still further, before all was swept away in the London revolution over the following weeks.[23]

Restrictionist sentiments such as these were not peculiar to the early

Stuarts: they were likely to appeal to any regime feeling insecure (thus, the radical Norwich magistrates in 1648 declared their dislike of 'popular elections' which experience showed to be 'continually disquiet, factious and perilous').[24] But they were extremely marked. This may testify to a consciousness of religious and political isolation – in the case of London by the end of the 1630s this was almost certainly so. But in the early 1620s, and in the provinces, this was unlikely to be the case. The intense concern to shut out the meaner sort from municipal politics testifies to an ideological stand on the part of the government, admittedly, but it also probably points to an increase in the social problems it, or the towns, were facing. The concern was not wholly unfeeling – fear for breakdown of government and poor relief in Exeter in time of plague in 1625 could bring down massive governmental intervention on the magistrates' heads, as could maladministration of Reading's chief charity in the hard times around 1630.[25] But security was clearly central even in these episodes. The sudden flaring of disputes from about 1620, and the appearance of a hard-line governmental reaction, is testimony to the difficulties caused by the economic depression setting in then, which led both privileged and under-privileged alike to dispute over a smaller cake. Both James and Charles showed that, perhaps unlike their predecessor, their sympathies were wholly with the privileged, provided that they exercised their power judiciously.

Natural tendencies towards oligarchy were thus strengthened and hastened by the early Stuart governments. What was worse was that in a period of hardship and depression, the closed bodies appeared to become tighter and even more oppressive, just when the hard-pressed town commons felt they should be more responsive to their needs. At the same time, the central government, to whom, for example, the Barnstaple petitioners looked for redress, was becoming more unsympathetic. It is against that background that the unrest which broke out in many towns in this period should be understood.

Disputes are inherent within the structure of any corporate community, as personal rivalries merge with ideological issues. As one side in the Shrewsbury troubles complained in 1638, 'if any good mocion be made by one side it will bee sure to be cried downe by the other, for noe reason but because not mooved by themselves'[26]: X proposes and Y therefore automatically opposes. But such natural friction was stimulated by the rapid social and economic change which was taking place in the 16th and early 17th centuries, for the balance of forces within an urban community might be upset. When Bristol trebled its size although its traditional textile trade failed to keep pace, or York changed from an industrial to an administrative centre, or the Cinque Ports (with the exception of Dover) entered a prolonged decline caused by silted harbours and London competition, new pressures and resentments were created. And all this was in a period of increasing educational provision for the laity, and of mounting religious excitement.

So challenges to the oligarchies developed, and one of the occasions for such challenges was provided by parliamentary elections. In her study of medieval parliamentary representation, Dr McKisack noted that in the growth of oligarchy, no special attention was paid to the parliamentary franchise: it was merely one other aspect of local power which was to be appropriated by the few. 'The parliamentary franchise was only one, and by no means the most important, of the many powers and privileges which were gradually falling into the hands of the capitalist class', and she suggested that this was no more exceptionable to those who were 'deprived' than it was particularly valuable to those who monopolised it.[27] The position was similar in the 17th century.

It is often difficult to discern the alignments present in a particular town. Prof. Zagorin perceptively observed that, in the interests of preserving the appearance of concord within their communities, urban authorities tended to exclude evidence of discord from archives.[28] But if we take one of the best-documented and most thoroughly analysed of towns, we can see the main forces in operation. Coventry was by the end of the 16th century recovering from the slump which it had passed through earlier, but that slump had had a long-term impact on the structure of the town. Dr Phythian-Adams has shown[29] that refusal of office for reasons of poverty had led to a total concentration of power in the hands of the aldermen, and while the Common Council regained some of its lost influence in the years after 1605, by 1621 and the onset of the next depression, the aldermen had effectively re-established their dominance. Other fields of urban life were becoming equally constricted. By the turn of the century, journeymen were being excluded from the freedom of trades, and as Coventry began to face increasing competition in its cloth industry, membership of the guilds became more limited generally.[30] Dynasticism was evident amongst urban office-holders, and office tended to concentrate in the hands of members of the richer guilds.[31] The guilds themselves became less meaningful as communal organs, as their ceremony was suppressed for economic as well as religious reasons, and as commensality disappeared in the early 17th century. The corollary of this was that conflict became more marked. Dr Phythian-Adams suggests that the obstreperous apprentice became more of a problem from the 1590s, and many craft fellowships made ordinances against insubordination on the part of their junior ranks in the 1590s and 1600s; this insubordination extended equally into civic affairs.[32]

This opposition to the urban elite involved violence fairly frequently in the first three decades of the century, on the subject of the corporation's apparent profiteering. Various lands had formerly been given to the town for communal use, and many of these had been, until late in the 16th century, employed for the support of the town's ceremonial. But on the suppression of this, the lands had been diverted by the corporation to private use: the magistrates would doubtless have defended this by arguing that an increase in the town's rental was essential in order to provide for the poor, but to those outside it must have looked like profiteering. There were consequently sporadic riots by the commons, whose need became more pressing as conditions worsened, and in 1608 and 1609 the county's Lieutenancy (probably influenced by memories of the Midland Rising of 1607) showed what they thought of the corporation's actions by siding with the commons.[33] Worsening troubles in the city's basic industry, cloth, in the later 1620s, and fears for employment reflected in concern about the entry of strangers, coincided with a new outbreak of disorder over the corporation's use of the town lands in the autumns of 1627 and 1628. The occurrence of a new parliamentary election in the winter of 1627–8 provided an ideal stick with which to beat the resented oligarchy, which had strengthened itself in the preceding years. What developed was not a franchise dispute, for the freemen already had the vote: but the configurations were similar, in that a clear majority of the freemen aligned against the corporation and its two aldermen candidates in order to elect two neighbouring gentry, producing 'a great Division ... in this Citty'.[34] The confrontation in this militantly puritan centre does not appear to have been related to any religious divide, for the magistrates seem to have been as puritanical as any. Rather, the parliamentary election dispute seems likely to have revolved entirely around the indigenous problems which the city was facing. The poverty and unrest continued into the 1630s, and the Long Parliament election may have presented another opportunity for discord to express itself.[35]

A closely parallel course of events to that in Coventry occurred in Warwick, Colchester and Chippenham at least, where friction also focused on the corporation's misappropriation of town lands in a period of economic hardship, and in all these boroughs, unlike Coventry, a limited franchise existed. All that was then needed was a self-interested gentleman to exploit the discontent of the commons (which in all probability is what the gentry candidates at Coventry did in the winter of 1627–8), and then to press their cause in the House of Commons, and a widening of the franchise ensued.[36] But the very detailed history of Coventry provides the best model for an understanding of such disputes: their roots were indigenous and long-lived.

The episodic nature of the typical urban dispute, and the possibly peripheral nature of the franchise issue, is revealed by the history of several towns: the alteration of the parliamentary franchise had little effect on the municipal situation. The background to the Cambridge troubles is unclear, but their long-running nature is obvious. A new code of ordinances was promulgated in 1609, amidst references to the 'many jars and troubles in the Town', and a year and a half later, the High Steward, Lord Ellesmere, was called in to settle the differences within the governing body.[37] The disputes continued, coming to a head in the early 1620s, when the four senior aldermen attempted to exploit an indirect, committee system of election to all offices and limit effective power to themselves still more completely. This provoked a general challenge to the limited form of election in all areas, and an apparent attempt by the freemen in 1624 to elect a non-alderman as mayor. The Privy Council was forced to order then, and the High Steward to repeat in 1629, that the election of aldermen and common councillors was in fact to be self-selection. The corporation record shows endemic disorder over all forms of election in the 1620s.[38] The gradual elimination, between 1621 and 1625, of the indirect voting system, dominated by the oligarchy, in parliamentary elections must be seen in this context.[39] It was replaced by a freeman franchise, and the indigenous origins of the change are emphasised by the fact that Cambridge does not appear to have been contested in 1621, 1624 or 1625: the involvement of the freemen is thus unlikely to have been engineered from outside. That this was merely an episode in a continuing and wider conflict is clear, especially in view of the need for a further intervention from above on the municipal election front in 1629. Indeed, the parliamentary issue itself may have remained alive, for it is possible that the aldermen were trying to fight back by making a separate return of members for the Long Parliament.[40]

The opening of the Hythe franchise illustrates the same gradualism, and detachment from outside manipulation (although it was closely related to outside intervention). At the 1624 election, the freemen were called in and acquainted with the governing body's choice; there is no sign of a contest here, so the freemen's entry was probably independent of any gentry agitation. The freemen were not present at the 1625 election, but when the magistrates discovered that the Duke of Buckingham was likely to be affronted by their actions, the freemen were summoned and informed, and were then persuaded one by one and 'dyd freely elect, chose, and confirme' the already-taken decision to elect other than Buckingham's nominee. Presumably the corporation was scared, and was attempting to pass the buck. After this, the freemen could not be refused, and they participated from 1626 onwards.[41]

Probably the only major counter to the prevailing trend of boroughs seeing their electorates widened in the pre-war years was the case of Great Yarmouth, and this not only indicates that alteration of the franchise was only an episode in a wider dispute, but also raises the possibility that the parliamentary franchise was of less than central importance. The freemen were apparently deprived of the vote by the corporation in 1625[42] – it is conceivable that the magistrates took advantage of the accretion to their powers which the onset of the plague epidemic at the crucial time would have brought – and did not seem to care. In 1626 and in 1628–9, amidst the normal accusations of peculation, the commons abetted by a dissident group within the corporation were demanding a greater role in the election of bailiffs and town preachers (they succeeded on the latter score), and yet there is no hint of any grievance at the corporation's actions of 1625 over the parliamentary election.[43] Tension here may have been defused by the remarkable growth in the town's prosperity in the 1620s and 30s, and by the fact that one of the lowest (proportional) totals of freemen in the country was to be found here.[44] But it is significant that the freemen were apparently more concerned with what affected them directly and immediately than with the more distant (in every sense) matter of parliament.

The issues which were of primary importance in municipal politics at this time were municipal rather than national, and it was primarily these which led to disorder and assertive activity by the meaner sort. There is a temptation to make a direct connection between the popular organisation of the 1640s and those signs of similar behaviour which are visible before the war. After all, the freemen, or even inhabitants-at-large, were banding together in various towns to demand something, the vote, which was a part of the national political process. These were years of developing polarisation, and of some excitement. Might we not suspect then that the local insurgent groups were showing true political consciousness, defined in terms of national issues? The answer here must be in the negative in virtually all cases: a connection with the events of the 1640s there may have been, but if so, it was indirect. For few actors locally, on whichever side of the urban conflict, seemed to view the parliamentary franchise *per se* as of decisive importance. In almost every town which can claim an independent economic existence, a challenge by the commons to the oligarchy over a parliamentary election coincided with a wider conflict. It is true that the parliamentary challenge was made, but it seems to have been just another point of attack, rather than the central point.

Even in the case of London, where if anywhere sophistication is to be expected, the same pattern can be observed. An attack on the corporation's choice of members of parliament in 1628 was matched by a municipal election challenge; this might be attributable to a general upsurge in democratic spirit amongst the lower levels, but equally the parliamentary trouble might represent at least in part a spill-over from the municipal upheaval.[45] And the watch was put in readiness more regularly for municipal than for parliamentary elections from 1626 onwards.[46] Like London, Newcastle politics showed traces of national alignments before the outbreak of war, with a challenge to the oligarchy's choice of parliament men in the Short Parliament election, during which the insurgents presented a petition to the successful candidates which was wholly related to the national political situation. But here again, it seems more likely that the disruption was part of a general confrontation with the local oligarchy: the city had been experiencing internal divisions for decades, culminating in a serious riot in 1633. In 1641, presumably in a continuing development from the trouble of 1640, for there had also been an outbreak in 1638, the Common Council gained a voice in the disposal of the corporation's revenue and leases, which had been one of the major demands of the 1633 agitators.[47]

The role of parliamentary affairs in disputes in other towns makes it seem even more probable that these were not normally considered of the first importance in themselves. While it is true that the corporation of Northampton, having been challenged at the Long Parliament election, tried to take steps thereafter to confirm its hold on the limited franchise (which was, unusually, fixed by statute), it may not have been averse to strengthening its powers generally on this occasion. The statute of 1489 limiting the franchises of Northampton and Leicester had been occasioned by disorders at elections, but the disturbances had clearly occurred at municipal rather than parliamentary contests, and the act was aimed most explicitly at these. It was this act which the corporation wished 'to revive and inlardge' in 1641 in the interests of regulating the 'choice of Officers', rather than specifically of burgesses – although Leicester corporation did see the attempt as directed at parliamentary elections.[48] At Shrewsbury, disillusioned members of the corporation, angered at the alleged flagrant abuses and disorders which broke out regularly at municipal elections, were in 1638 pressing for a new charter to the borough which would exclude the freemen as much as possible from the borough's affairs, and in particular from municipal elections – but there was to be no attempt to exclude them from parliamentary elections.[49]

The main trigger of urban unrest appears to have been suspicions of mishandling of the town's common resources by the magistrates. This roots the disputes firmly in the economic difficulties of the time, and it also explains of course why the municipal election was the occasion of the challenge, for only there could an unpopular oligarchy be removed. In borough after borough the same outcry against magisterial self-aggrandisement rises – even in London, in the 1640s, Lilburne focused very closely on the corporation's exploitation of the City's finances, and their use of 'hugger-mugger' to that end.[50] The final courts of appeal of urban squabbles before the war were the Privy Council and Star Chamber:

disputes which had exceeded local powers of resolution found their way there, and the records of these bodies illustrate more clearly than do Lilburne's fulminations against the City how destructive of urban community economic fears and jealousies could be. Around the turn of the century, beliefs that the corporations of Totnes and Canterbury were abusing their powers of economic regulation to their own benefit produced near-breakdown there, and this was matched by contemporaneous troubles in Lincoln, Southwark and Salisbury, which suggest the strong link between economic and political dislocation.[51] In these boroughs, accusations of corporation misappropriation of revenues which had been donated to the town for the benefit of the poor were at the centre of the storm, and this was of course a grievance most likely to appear when the problem of the poor and unemployment was particularly pressing. Thus, the later 1590s and early 1600s, and the years on either side of 1630, are the periods which appear to feature the worst troubles over the issue of urban charities (Reading, Shrewsbury and Salisbury being the major sufferers in the latter period).[52] But the most divisive issue of all was that of the use of the town's lands, probably because it was the most visible: embezzlement of charitable funds could be hidden, whereas the private enclosure of the town's common fields could not. The disturbances caused by this issue in Coventry, Colchester, Chippenham and Warwick have been touched on, and it excited similar direct action, tending towards violence, on the part of those who felt deprived in Ludlow in the 1590s, in Hull in the 1600s, Malmesbury in the 1600s and 1610s, and at Newcastle (which had also of course suffered at the turn of the century) and Hertford in the late 1620s and 1630s.[53] Leicester and Liskeard were also troubled in the years around 1600 by bitter complaints about self-seeking corporation speculation in the town lands. Reimbursement of the oligarchs through the use of their powers was by no means wholly indefensible, as corporation revenues suffered in face of rising prices, and as private marketing often replaced taxable trading in the open market, while outgoings on the poor increased. In consequence, the magistrates personally had to indulge in heavy outlays (and hence the universally growing number of refusals of office). But the role of such self-compensation in arousing popular resentment is suggested negatively by the example of Worcester, one of the least troubled of the major English towns, which was apparently blessed with one of the least self-interested and closed oligarchies.[54]

The genesis of various parliamentary franchise disputes is traced in detail in Appendix II, and, where the evidence on the context is sufficient, they can often be related to such causes of friction as these. In almost every case, a franchise dispute (other than in such lifeless 'boroughs' as Gatton or Bletchingley) was part of a general attack on the oligarchs; in several, it can be specifically linked to the question of economic exploitation. It must be emphasised that disturbance on the question of self-seeking and corruption amongst the magistrates was part of a general urban pattern at this time. This was especially the case as the oligarchies were patently growing tighter (and hence the frequent additional charge of nepotism), partly for reasons of government policy, partly for longer-term reasons. And when a limited parliamentary franchise existed, it could serve as another issue on which to attack, for an election was certainly viewed as an event of some consequence, and some elderly inhabitant could doubtless be found to argue that the electorate had once been wider than it now was.[55] Yet another blow could then be directed against the oppressors.

The pattern holds for small towns like Sandwich, for third-rank settlements like Colchester, Oxford, Warwick, and even for the second-rank cities, the provincial capitals, which might have been expected to be better able to absorb their problems of poverty. The disputes in the later 1620s at Exeter are found to coincide with a much wider attack on the irresponsibility of the magistrates;[56] the same trends can also be seen in Newcastle and Norwich, although neither of these experienced parliamentary franchise disputes. In Norwich, heavy Privy Council pressure and aldermanic effort in 1619–21 had finally implemented a thoroughly oligarchic constitution. As we have seen, only the election of sheriffs remained as a battleground, and in 1627 an alleged drunkard was put up to stand against the corporation. Significantly, his election platform was 'that none of the Citizens should be oppressed as they have bene', and that he 'would ease the poore of burdens which they had formerly borne', for 'the Commoners were made slaves by the magistrates'. A whispering campaign against rack-renting and extortion by the magistrates ('that they kept Courts for bribery') had been going on through the 1620s, and it evidently bore fruit in 1627. In response to this confrontation, the corporation was driven to plead with the Privy Council to relax the restrictive orders which it had had enforced at the start of the decade. A disputed parliamentary election would surely have occasioned the same kind of clash: but Norwich's seats went unchallenged in the 1620s, and it was more difficult, in terms of status, for a group of freemen or members of the outer ring of the corporation to put one of their own members forward for parliament than it was for the shrievalty.[57] Otherwise, a parallel dispute to that at Coventry would surely have developed, and had the franchise been other than an open one, it would have been challenged. The franchise dispute was not a peculiar species.

Although the essential parochialism of the franchise disputes has been asserted above, they did sometimes tend to merge with wider grievances and issues in 1640, as was the case at Salisbury.[58] Dr Pearl's study of the

London revolution of 1641–2 epitomises the fusion of indigenous unrest with national issues, although some of the responsibility for widening horizons must be borne by the local insurgents' parliamentary allies.[59] The same is certainly true of the parliamentary election dispute at Hastings; and it is possibly true also of Chipping Wycombe, where a long internal conflict over poor relief in the depression of post-1620 culminated in a franchise dispute in the Short Parliament election, and an election petition to the Long Parliament against one of the town's members as a furtherer of Ship Money and a profaner of the sabbath.[60]

Even in 1640, however, it is difficult to point to much in the way of informed action on national issues in urban disputes. At Salisbury and Newcastle, the long-term local goals were probably at least as important as religious feeling, and at Hastings the freemen were probably more concerned about the suppression of a popular local alehouse. While the evidence on other franchise disputes occurring in that year is unsatisfactory, that which does survive does not seem to suggest much awareness of the national situation.[61] Reading experienced trouble at both 1640 elections, and given the town's close links with its native son and benefactor Archbishop Laud, who nominated a candidate in the spring, some religious reaction might have been expected. But instead Reading fits thoroughly into the normal localist pattern. The basis of the town's prosperity, its clothing, was declining fast, being badly affected by the depression of the 1620s and 30s, and by the growth of competition.[62] Judging by the numbers of admissions to membership of the food trades, there was no compensatory transformation of the town into a provincial centre (difficult anyway given the proximity to London and Oxford), such as helped to bolster the economies of Norwich and York. A major storm broke out in these depressed conditions over the corporation's alleged mishandling of the major charity in the early 1630s, and the atmosphere may not have been improved when the aldermen attempted to buttress their position in the new charter obtained through Laud's good offices in 1638. Abnormally high mortality in the corporation during the decade, and a consequent rapid turn-over of personnel, possibly undermined its confidence, and the end result was that pressure from the commons in 1640 compelled an expansion of the franchise.[63] As in the earlier case of Cambridge, this happened gradually, and was not stimulated by agitation from outside against the corporation's choice, for in both Short and Long Parliament elections, the challengers accepted the preferences of the oligarchs, the leaders of the insurgents in October expressly admitting that 'they could not except against either of them'. The throng of the populace about the doors in March had forced the corporation to prolong the election, and eventually to announce to the people the corporation's short-list of candidates. Although the magistrates clearly conceived their votes as of greater importance, and numbered them carefully, their totals were supplemented '*et multos alios*' – more than just the presentation of a *fait accompli* to the commons was taking place. The October election similarly was 'begun in the council-chamber and ended in the open hall by a free and general consent of all, without any contradiction but with great alacrity'. By the time of the Recruiter election of 1645, the commons were being officially polled, and this would probably have been necessary in 1640 had there been any disagreement with the corporation's choice.[64] Persistent pressure from within the town slowly broke the corporation's hold, and while there is insufficient evidence to determine whether the commons were solely concerned with the parliamentary vote, the presence of very similar economic grievances to those found elsewhere suggests that there might have been a general reaction against an unstable corporation. The agreement of the two groups in October on Sir Francis Knollys, father and son, emphasises the detachment of the dispute from the wider political conflict.

Northampton would probably tell a similar story: the town was a by-word for refractoriness, allegedly a den of puritans, in the later 1630s; the political excitement of 1640 also had an impact locally, for in early May the corporation ordered that all its members 'and other persons of habilitie in this towne shalbe fourthwith provided of holbeardes bills or clubbs to be readie upon anie occasions for use theis dangerous times'. But the corporation itself was strongly hostile to government policy,[65] so the divisions which occurred in both 1640 elections, with an unsuccessful franchise dispute in October, are unlikely to have been caused by any radical religious alienation from the magistrates.[66] Just as feasible as a disruptive force was the bad plague outbreak at the end of the 1630s.[67]

In few urban divides do we find challenges to the corporation coinciding with an explicit national alignment. Salisbury as a 1640 franchise dispute is an exception, and Hastings, as a non-franchise dispute, another. The Marlow franchise dispute in the Long Parliament election is a further possibility: while not a corporate town, there was an ostensible division between the better and the meaner sorts which coincided with a political split amongst the final candidates. But while there was a pairing of politically like-minded candidates (Bulstrode Whitelocke and Peregrine Hoby) in the second election (the first having been disallowed), large numbers of those voting for that pair seem to have been able to vote for Hoby and a future political opponent, Borlace, in the first election, rather than indulge in the politically more informed act of plumping for Hoby alone.[68] The alignments may have reflected attitudes to neighbouring landowners as much as political principles.

.   .   .

The case studies given in Appendix II tend to confirm in detail the general theme outlined here. Challenges to the local governing bodies at parliamentary elections must not be seen as evidence of the impact of parliamentary affairs on local populations. An extreme view might be that the fact that the parliamentary franchise was often at issue was almost incidental: in many communities, every aspect of the magistrates' position was under attack. The occurrence of franchise disputes in the midst of periods of internal upheaval, at times when, as in Cambridge or Great Yarmouth, other forms of municipal election occasioned disorder, suggests that they must be seen in a local socio-economic context as much as in a national parliamentary one. Everywhere, certainly from late in Elizabeth's reign, freemen were feuding with corporations, or corporations dividing within themselves with members excluded from the inner ring appealing outside for support.

There were two major respects in which urban disputes were closely connected with events on the parliamentary stage. The first was that gentry were increasing their pressure for seats in the House, and were eager to exploit divisions in the boroughs for their own ends. The gentry take-over of the borough seats had clearly happened by the end of Elizabeth's reign, but the evidence of the increasing number of contests in the 17th century indicates that there were not so many determined candidates in the 1580s as, say, in the 1620s. Secondly, in the 1620s, the House of Commons appeared on the scene as arbiter, and disputes which were being lost by the commons in the localities could now go before a sympathetic House instead of an oligarchy-favouring Privy Council or judge. But to participants other than candidates or the House of Commons, it is most unlikely that the parliamentary issue was the most important one in the struggles being waged. On the government's part, concern with municipal rather than parliamentary elections was justified, for security and stability was the watchword, even before parliamentary quiescence. Municipal politics do seem to have posed a greater threat here, for municipal elections happened annually, unlike the uncertain occurrence of parliamentary elections, and the prizes must have seemed greater locally, thus generating greater excitement. All signs suggest that oligarchies and their challengers concurred in this assessment: the parliamentary franchise merely tended to intrude into clashes on the more crucial matters of municipal revenues and office. The changes in the parliamentary franchise were a means to an end of embarrassing the oligarchies, rather than an end in themselves. As Dr Pearl has said of the constitutional developments in the London revolution of 1641–2, they 'were designed to achieve practical and immediate ends ... rather than to alter the balance of popular representation', and she considered that there was little pressure in the City towards that latter goal.[69] The same was almost certainly true in the smaller worlds of the provincial boroughs.

## Gentry intervention

In some boroughs it would obviously be foolish to look too closely for autonomous pressure on the part of the commons. In Gatton and Bletchingley, for example, there were few inhabitants and the franchise disputes which occurred there in the 1620s obviously had everything to do with self-interested gentry agitation. While it was a standard oligarchic trait to blame outsiders for any disruption which took place in the towns, much in the same way as Southern whites explained the civil rights disorders of the early 1960s, in order to lessen their own responsibility, there was an element of truth in the general theme. For even in much larger settlements than Gatton or Bletchingley, the role of the gentleman outsider was often critical in bringing long-term discontent to a head, or pressing complaints in the House of Commons.[70]

Several small boroughs seem to fall into the category of Gatton and Bletchingley. A franchise dispute at places the size of Mitchell or Bossiney in Cornwall (in the Short and Long Parliament elections respectively) is unlikely to have owed much to anything more than gentry rivalries. The case of Bossiney is clear: William Coriton, the mayor, 'supports the former custome of chusing by a few, because they are mostly at his comand'. Coriton was outflanked by Sir Bevill Grenville and Lord Robartes, Grenville telling the scot and lot men that if they voted for him, he 'would try the title to put them in a right way', and would press their cause in the House.[71] The case of Mitchell was probably little different: a plurality of candidates presumably produced an appeal by one of them outside the ranks of the 24 freemen to the inhabitants.[72] Gentry competition in the erstwhile pocket borough of Downton in Wiltshire in the by-election in the second month of the Long Parliament resulted in an expansion from a select few to what was apparently all the burgage tenants.[73] But it might be a mistake to attribute all cases of disturbance in settlements of that size solely to outside interference, for small bodies can contain rivalries as well as large. The dispute at Newport, Cornwall, in 1628 may have had little specifically indigenous in its antecedents. Again, too many local gentry chasing too few seats caused an understandable split in the local officers, the vianders, who claimed the right to elect, and one of them turned to the inhabitants. But there were five, not just two, rival indentures returning the names of candidates, and claiming a variety of franchises, and two of them had not vianders as parties to them, which might suggest a measure of independence on the part of some inhabitants.[74] Bearing out the inference of some local friction is the fact that something similar had happened in 1626,[75] and probably as a result of the failure of the House to decide on the franchise in 1628, it is possible that a dispute occurred in the Short Parliament and in the by-election to the Long Parliament caused by the removal of one candidate elsewhere.[76]

The common course in larger towns is that of an outsider coming in to exploit existing divisions for his own electoral ends by appealing to the dissidents. At both Chichester and Warwick there had been trouble on various issues, amounting to a general challenge to the oligarchy, before self-interested gentry moved in in the 1586 elections and attempted to utilise that discontent in order to outweigh their unpopularity with the magistrates. Similarly, Sandwich had been sorely disturbed in the years leading up to 1640 and one candidate in the Short Parliament election not only approached the corporation for a seat but also appealed to the commons in their own right for their votes, hoping in the 'probable confusion' to pick up some of their support, and thus fomented further division in the town. Again, at the same election for Higham Ferrers, although the town was split between two dominant burgess families, and was allegedly full of nascent 'division and distemper', only Sir Christopher Hatton's intervention and agitation of the case for a freeman franchise secured the extension of the vote to that group.[77]

The particularism of many franchise disputes is emphasised by the virtual hypocrisy of gentry machinations. Frequently, candidates accepted an existing limited franchise until they found themselves losing on it. They then challenged it. The flagrant inconsistency of Bulstrode Whitelocke's behaviour in 1640 extended beyond merely standing as champion of a closed franchise at Abingdon in March and an open one at Marlow in October. He had been willing, before the Abingdon election, to accept that the vote lay in the 'Commons', but found his opponent making greater headway amongst that group, allegedly by dubious means. He therefore submitted to the prompting of his allies amongst the oligarchy (he was the borough's Recorder) and resolved to petition the House 'for vindication of the rights and priviledge of the Towne' – although those rights had not been seen as incompatible with an open franchise until the election was concluded. This contest also points to the way in which candidates related to internal divisions: Whitelocke alleged that he was pressed by the magistrates to petition against the commons' votes. Whitelocke's next constituency, Marlow, heard the same crying of sour grapes. One of his opponents in the second election for the Long Parliament, John Borlace, petitioned against the involvement of almsmen – but the polling figures he himself provided suggest that he had accepted their votes for himself, and only excepted against them when he found that he had less of them, and more of the better sort, than did the opposition.[78] Exactly the same happened at Bedford, where the corporation franchise was successively opened to the freemen and then to the inhabitants in the Short and Long Parliament elections. The corporation resisted in March, but seems to have given up the fight after that, for the protest to the House over the October election appears entirely the frustrated candidate's work. An analysis of the poll list for October shows no marked social or economic distinction between the voters on either side, and the annotations to the names on the list suggest that non-scot and lot men, and recipients of alms, were being used by both sides. Yet it was only *after* he had accepted these votes, and lost, that William Boteler began claiming that, apparently, Bedford was a scot and lot borough.[79]

The same behaviour recurs time and again: at Chippenham in 1624, a minority within the corporation supported Sir Francis Popham against John Pym, and 'the better to fortifie their Eleccion caused divers of the Towne to ioyne with them' when they found themselves losing. At Newcastle-under-Lyme in the same year, a defeat 'in an upper roome' among the select body caused John Keeling to put his head out of the window and shout for voices to those passing in the street below. At Boston in 1628, an appeal to the freemen was occasioned by a defeat by one in the Common Council, and at East Grinstead in the Short Parliament election, a tie amongst the burgage tenants provoked one candidate to insure himself doubly by an enfeoffment creating a new tenant, and by appealing to the inhabitants too. And despite Sir Bevill Grenville's hot protestations over the Long Parliament Bossiney election 'that all inhabitants being free men have voice', he was only heard to say this after mayor Coriton had rejected his advances for the favour of a seat by the votes of the limited group.[80]

Neither popular nor gentry campaigners seem especially devoted to the expansion of the parliamentary franchise as a principle. Both groups saw it as a means to other ends – the one, of hitting at the magistrates, the other, of getting themselves into the House. Although a few of the participants in the purely parliamentary aspect of the process were evidently committed to the idea of involving more people directly in representation, such an attitude is not to be met in the localities.[81] There, all parties seem to have been unconcerned with such wider questions. But however much the local developments stemmed from particularist and self-interested motives, and however little of an independent popular national political force there was in the localities, the possibly unlooked-for result of this medley of factors was the broadening of the franchise in over thirty constituencies.[82] Whether the gentlemen in question were intending it or not, the effect of their quests for seats was to help to give the vote to many people who previously had had little contact with parliamentary politics, and who possibly were not even aiming at that goal.

# 4

# The Support of the House of Commons

*The fear of influence*

While it was probably the case that the majority of early 17th-century adult males were not particularly concerned with the parliamentary franchise, a belief that more people should be involved in the electoral process was widespread by 1640–1 – and this in a period not noted for its devotion to abstract canons of social justice. General statements that a wide franchise was, or should be, the norm were being made in the country at large, sometimes coupled with the justificatory assumption that this was the legal orthodoxy. Yet as the debates at Putney in 1647 showed, the logical conclusion of the general principle was not one that could command much acceptance, even amongst ostensible radicals. The House of Commons, the guardian of that area of the law which included the franchise, might appear then to have been acting in a puzzling fashion if its actions had allowed such an orthodoxy to form, when popular pressure on the matter was of dubious coherence and reality, and when the social ramifications of an ideological proposition that more people should vote could excite horror in a variety of breasts.

At the end of Elizabeth's reign, Sir Edward Coke reported that the judges in *The Case of Corporations* had argued that corporation franchises 'were good and well warranted by their charters, and by the law also ... and God forbid that they should be now innovated or altered, for many and great inconveniences will thereupon arise'. The decision here related specifically to municipal elections, but there is every reason to suppose that the same men would have taken the same position if asked about the parliamentary franchise, and at this date there would probably have been little questioning of the pronouncement. But forty years later the consensus, both legal and political, was virtually reversed. Bulstrode White-locke's candidature in the Long Parliament election for Marlow was opposed by the corporation but supported by the inhabitants, and he cited approvingly the latter's own argument in defence of their claims, that, 'bicause it being no corporation, all the inhabitants had their votes in the election'. As far afield as Cornwall the inhabitants of Bossiney were said to be 'griev'd' at their exclusion from the vote in the same election, 'conceiving that the rest had as much right to do it', and the reporter, the future royalist Sir Bevill Grenville, affirmed that 'I well know that the opinion of the Parliament house hath ever been, that all the inhabitants being free men have voice, and so I have knowne it often adjudg'd'. He later wrote testily to an enemy, 'you know as well as I, what the opinion of the Law hath ever been in the point of election. You will finde that all which pay scott and lott and which are suitors to the towne court have voice in all elections. So I have knowne it adjudg'd many times.' His fellow future royalist, Geoffrey Palmer, consulted in his legal capacity as to the extent of the Higham Ferrers franchise before the Short Parliament election, was firmly of the opinion that 'the libertie of generall and Free Election [was] established by the Comon lawe'; and the freemen of Bristol claimed to believe in October that an open electorate was 'in conformity with statutes'.[1] Before the outbreak of war, there was evidently a body of opinion which conceived that the corporation franchise was the abnormality needing a defence, while the wider electorate was the natural, and even the legally respectable, one.

The chief factor in securing the transition from the position of Coke and his judges to that of, for example, Palmer, was purely political. The fear utilised by Coke, that a change is a change, and therefore dangerous constitutionally and socially, was a strong one. When the Southwark oligarchy was under attack for corruption in 1605, it is alleged to have defended itself by arguing that 'The government by Thirty is ancient. And it is meeter to tolerate some wants in Magistrates than by supposing to amend them to overthrow Government and Authority; for Alterations and Changes ar dangerous'. But such fears of unnamed chaos consequent upon change were outweighed in the course of the early 17th century by more specific fears about parliament's prospects for survival as an institution. The first decisions by the House of Commons to widen the franchise were in 1621; correspondingly, the major emphasis of the 1621 bill to regulate elections was on the avoiding of undue influence at elections. Shrieval tricks were to be proscribed, and 'No request [for election was] to be made by favor of great persons', in order 'that the king may [not] choose all those that may serve his turn.' Grave apprehensions were felt in that session on the subject of privileges and independence, and these were well expressed by the lawyer Edward Alford when he admonished the House that if it permitted its privileges to be encroached upon, then 'farewell Parliaments and farewell England'. For 1621 was the first parliament since the disastrous failure of 1614, an assembly bedevilled by rumours of packing and 'undertaking'. And this had itself been the abortive successor to James's first parliament, in which the Buckinghamshire dispute of 1604 had aroused grave misgivings as to the Crown's electoral intentions. The lawyer Thomas Yelverton had then argued strongly, and with considerable support, that any concession to the Crown would be 'a Quo Warranto, to seize all our Liberties', it would open 'a Gap to thrust us all into the Petty Bag' and nomination by Chancery, thus procuring packed parliaments.[2] There were sound long-term reasons for concern as to England's political future, particularly as the Crown had effectively governed without parliamentary assistance from January 1611 to January 1621.

In view of these misgivings, the Attorney-General, Francis Bacon, warned James I in 1613 against attempts at packing or other forms of electoral influence, for 'it will but increase animosities and oppositions; and besides will make whatsoever shall be done to be in evil conceit amongst your people in general afterwards'. The accuracy of his warning was thoroughly borne out. Although he himself attempted to extenuate the courtier-inspired abuses at the Stockbridge election by reminding the House that Chancellor Parry's offence was but 'Error temporum' (hardly calculated to appease fears, when the House believed exactly that), and that 'We live not in Plato his Commonwealth, but in Times wherein Abuses have got the upper Hand', the future Earl of Manchester was more in touch with opinion in the House when he acknowledged that packing was 'the only Way to bring in Servitude', and advocated an election bill with the same purpose as that of 1621, to outlaw influence. The courtier Sir George More advised that there should be 'In nothing more Care, than the Preservation of the Right of Election of the Members of this House', and the opposition-minded Sir Edwin Sandys saw free elections as the most fundamental of all liberties to be pressed for.[3]

The aim was to produce a House 'compounded of honest, religious gentlemen', and this could only be ensured by the elimination of Court or aristocratic pressure. Such a desirable end was thought by some to be attainable by the simple mechanical means of legislating against influence, and this was the recurrent intent of election bills and orders in the 17th and 18th centuries.[4] Significantly, those taking this position, over-sanguine in its assessment of the potentialities of legislation, tended to be the real 'politicians'. It has recently been argued that most participants in the Commonwealth debates on the re-apportionment of parliamentary seats were primarily concerned with undue pressure from above, rather than with electoral justice, and the major interventions of Pym, Cromwell and Strode in 1640–1 certainly occurred at this simplistic level, as, for example, in the December 1641 order intended as a warning to the Earl of Arundel against interfering in the Arundel by-election.[5]

But many members of the House realised that merely banning sin would not suffice, and it was as a response to the implied threat from the Court that the decisions to expand the electorate in the boroughs were justified. As Prof. Plumb has pointed out, the more voters there were, the more difficult they would be to terrorise or bribe. To this end, the

Committee of Privileges pronounced in 1624 that 'the general liberty of the realm ... favoureth all means tending to make the election of burgesses to be with the most indifferency; which, by common presumption, is when the same are [sic] made by the greatest number of voices that reasonably may be had, whereby there will be less danger of packing, or indirect proceedings'. Accordingly, the franchise at Chippenham was widened. It was conceivably this same desire to obtain greater independence through greater numbers that occasioned the proposal of the 1626 election bill for compulsory voting for all those qualified, and it certainly called forth the lawyer John Glynne's remark in December 1640 that 'the more generall the Eleccion was the freer'.[6] The initial parliamentary impulse in favour of a wider electorate was one stemming from the instinct for self-preservation.

Dr Christopher Hill assumed that this activity was the equivalent of partisan gerrymandering, that the parliamentary opposition was extending the vote to the likeminded group, 'the industrious sort of people', in order to make the world safe for its own supporters. Judging by the verdicts of some contemporary commentators, this assumption of the opposition's opportunism is plausible, and insofar as royal influence was defeated, then it is correct. The Venetian ambassador believed that the 'Puritans' owed their success in the Short Parliament elections to their achievements in 'Swaying the common votes', and Thomas Hobbes more or less concurred, asserting that 'tradesmen, in the cities and boroughs ... choose, as near as they can, such as are the most repugnant to the giving of subsidies'. These, taken together with Sir John Spelman's, Sir John Bramston's and Bishop Bramhall's claims that the Committee of Privileges was, by 1640 at least, politically biased, suggest that the Committee was deciding for a larger electorate from crude political considerations. But contemporaries only alleged this when war had started, implying that the whole area of electoral decision-making prior to this was viewed as fairly non-partisan: indeed, the only apparent instance of flagrant bias before war loomed was the decision in the early days of the Long Parliament to let the hero John Hampden's election for Buckinghamshire pass unchallenged.[7]

The major contemporary objection to opening the franchises was not that the additional voters would behave in a certain (anti-Court) way but that they would be uncontrollable (which was, of course, the Commons' aim). Heneage Finch's warning in London in 1621 that 'popular Eleccions' usually turned out to be 'tumultuary' is an indication of this, and he was by no means alone here. William Prynne, in his *Brevia Parliamentaria*, noted that the statute of 8 Henry VI restricting the county franchise to the 40s. freeholders had aimed to curb the widespread disorder at elections, and wished that a similar course might be taken over the newly-opened urban franchises, 'The mischiefs of popular and tumultuous Elections, now [being] more frequent in Cities and Boroughs, than they were then in Counties, Therefore fit to be redressed upon the same account.' Prynne went as far as to see the more extensive franchises as being the root cause of the Civil War, in giving the common people a taste of power: for they made all elections 'mercenary, arbitrary, tumultuous, disputable . . . the primitive foundation of all our late confusions, and alterations of Government'.[8]

Prynne was speaking after the event, but many others would have seen the force of John Glynne's equation in 1640 of open elections with the decline of effective influence. The Earl of Northampton maintained careful control of the admission of burgesses to Bishop's Castle in the early years of the century, believing that indiscriminate admission would be a 'disadvantage' to him, and this disadvantage must have been electoral. In a slightly different sphere, the Norfolk potentate Sir John Hobart advised the Privy Council in 1632 against the enfranchisement of Crown copyhold lands in the county, not only because of his own interest in them, but also because increasing the number of freeholders would be 'inconvenient in point of government in those partes'. Significantly, the Privy Council agreed, 'considering how dangerous the infranchising of Copyholds wilbe to government'.[9] Although the Council took no active part in the 1620s franchise debates, by the end of the decade it had evidently appreciated some of the consequences of the House's activity in the field, and was uneasy.

The Council's reaction over the Norfolk copyholders was of a piece with long-term royal policy. It is perhaps surprising that councillors in the House did not declare their opposition to the extension of the electorate in the 1620s, for they had not hesitated to oppose on the allied question of the restoration of the lapsed parliamentary boroughs. The statute of 8 Henry VI limiting the shire voters to substantial freeholders in the interests of avoiding electoral disorders, '*homicides riotes battles et divisions entre les gentils et autres gentz*', was matched by royal support over a long period for the development of oligarchy in the towns. The Crown aimed to produce just that situation – a limitation of the political nation – which the House of Commons believed was its goal, although possibly not for the reason the House suspected, but merely from considerations of internal stability. The House's misgivings were thus based not only on the experience of 1604 and 1614: these Court blunders seemed to reveal the purpose of a lengthy process of political contraction and centralisation. An example of what the Commons must have feared is the case of Sandwich, where the principle of municipal self-perpetuation was introduced on the orders of the Lord Warden and the Privy Council at the end of Elizabeth's reign: the numbers of freemen 'of the vulgar sort' had increased so much that they controlled municipal elections and grew 'verie wilfull and heddie'. At about the same time the Lord Warden established his control over the port's parliamentary elections, and although the developments were possibly not directly related, they must have appeared ominous to anyone considering the two together.[10]

What the Commons feared, and acted to avert, was evidently thought by the Crown to be in its own interest, especially when James could rashly remark during the debates on the restoration of the lapsed parliamentary boroughs in 1624 that he was troubled with too many parliament men already. The House's reaction is understandable. But, surprisingly, the Crown failed to respond in the way it should have done if the apparent fears about its intentions had been accurate. While it was prepared to intervene in other electoral fields in the 1620s,[11] it neglected to act over the franchise, although the movement on this issue seems to have been in large part directed against it. Activists over the franchise probably overestimated the extent to which the Crown or individual courtiers had a coherent attitude to elections. Laud's new statutes for Oxford University in 1636 made no attempt to limit and fix the electorate there. The fact that so many of the moves towards oligarchy were of local inspiration (however much the Crown approved), and that the Council was so tardy in reacting on the franchise question, indicates that the Crown was not, in the 1620s at least, the dynamic force which parliamentarians feared, and which it was to become in this area under James II.[12] Not until 1640 was a clear statement made by a royal official, and then the Queen's Solicitor and former Chief Justice, Sir Robert Heath, pronounced firmly for a wider franchise for Higham Ferrers, so cut-and-dried had the matter now become as a result of the weight of favourable opinion built up in the 1620s. Those who expressly set themselves against this widely-held opinion were isolated individuals, such as the town clerk of Warwick in 1628, who foresaw that as a result of the House's opening of the franchise, 'now the best purse and the frankest spiret is like to prevaile let the man be worthy or un[w]orthy'. No longer could 'the beter sorte beinge men of estate and generaly best affected to religion and of the discreetest sort of inhabitance' be relied upon to return the corporation's or patron's nominees.[13] The less sure methods of bribery and political appeal by the populists, the 'frank spirits', would triumph. Doubtless the House and Committee of Privileges were building on this expectation when they denied that many royal charters could have any impact in fixing the electorate, and accordingly opened the franchises which had been limited by charter.

The chief danger with the charters whose powers Coke had so extolled in the Corporations Case ('in every of their charters they have power given

them to make laws, ordinances, and constitutions, for the better government and order of their cities or boroughs ... for avoiding of popular
disorder and confusion') was their arbitrariness: they owed their terms
solely to royal letters patent. A franchise vested in a specific group by
charter could be vulnerable to royal manipulation (as was evident under
James II), and it was even arguable that a previously unchartered,
unincorporated, parliamentary borough might have its franchise altered
by a charter of incorporation making specific mention of parliamentary
elections. Thus (though he later qualified his views), Coke, in his account
of the Corporations Case, argued that a new limiting provision for
municipal elections in a charter was valid, as it aimed at promoting order,
'although it began within time of memory' and over-rode immemorial
customary rights which 17th-century conventional opinion might have
been expected to hold as more powerful. Some corporations extended this
argument to the parliamentary arena. Coke's dictum was explicitly cited
by one of the protagonists for a limited franchise in the 1621 Sandwich
dispute, in support of the restrictions imposed by the 1595 and other
related orders 'for the avoideing of tumultes which often happened'.
Similarly, in the very important Chippenham case of 1624, where the
decisive lines of argument were elaborated, William Hakewill, counsel for
John Pym and the closed corporation franchise, argued for limitations
from the charter of 1 Mary, though he admitted that this was an
innovatory rather than a confirmatory patent – that is, it contained new
provisions for regulating the borough's affairs.[14]

In response to Hakewill's case, which had such threatening potential, the
Committee of Privileges, followed by the House, took a position determined by political considerations, rather than by established constitutional
usage. The problem was novel, and the formulation of new rules of action
was essential. A tacit outcome of the 1604 Buckinghamshire election
fracas between King and Commons had been that the House was
effectively the judge of its own electoral affairs, and that the royal judges
were not concerned unless the House suffered them to be.[15] The implication of that might be that in important respects elections were not subject
to the law which was administered in the royal courts. This possibility
was seized on and elaborated by the House in the 1620s in order to
depart from the conclusion of the judges in the almost identical case of
municipal elections. There was as yet no legal confirmation for the
argument that parliamentary elections were unique, but the proposition
was stated quite unambiguously in the decision on the Chippenham case,
and it warrants detailed examination, for the political assumptions
underlying it are significant, and it formed the basis for many later
decisions.

The starting-point for the Committee's thinking was the contention that

parliament could not be guided by other bodies, which had been behind
the decision to reject the judges' advice in 1604 over the Buckinghamshire
election: 'because the commonwealth hath an interest ... this court, and
council of state and justice, is guided by peculiar, more high, and politic
rules of law and state, than the ordinary courts of justice are'. This
determined the Committee's substantive report, which argued strongly
against Hakewill, concluding:

> 'that the said Charter of Queen Mary did not, nor could, alter the
> form and right of election for burgesses to the parliament ... from
> the course there before, time out of mind, held; so as if before this
> said charter, all the burgesses, and inhabitants, called Freemen, or any
> other larger number of qualified persons, had always used, and ought
> of right to make the election; then the charter, although it may ...
> alter the name, or form of the corporation there, in matters concerning
> only themselves and their own government; ... yet it cannot alter and
> abridge the general freedom and form of elections for burgesses to the
> parliament, wherein, as aforesaid, the commonwealth is interested.
> For then ... it might be brought to a bailiff and one or two burgesses,
> or to the bailiff alone; which is against the general liberty of the
> realm.'

The political need to withstand the apprehended threat from an aggressive
Crown impelled the Commons to elaborate a new constitutional principle,
rejecting the cautions of those members who, like the Elizabethan judges,
urged that innovation was dangerous. The justification for curtailing
royal powers to manipulate boroughs by issuing letters patent was couched
solely in terms of political necessity, that if these were allowed, then the
electorate, and consequently liberty, might be whittled away. This fear
remained to the fore throughout the period: in the debate on the
Tewkesbury election in early 1641, D'Ewes reported that it was 'agreed
by all' that letters patent could not limit the electorate, lest they should
'restraine the choice to two or three', in which case, 'wee shall have such
sent as great men will command'.[16] The connection between the size of
the electorate and its vulnerability to influence was evident to many
members.

The extent to which the Commons' policy on the franchise was
determined by considerations of immediate political advantage is revealed
by the decision taken on Bletchingley in 1624 where concern to reduce
the effect of illegitimate influence produced a decision to uphold a limited
franchise. The inhabitants at large had been terrorised by the bailiff of the
borough and the parish minister into electing an alleged recusant; the
Committee and the House thereupon decided in favour of a limited
burgage-tenure franchise.[17] In order to arrive at this conclusion, a forced

construction was put on the evidence presented. The candidate elected by the inhabitants at large cited precedents of earlier returns by the burgesses '*et alii*', which he argued demonstrated that the free burgesses (i.e. burgage tenants in this case) and others had elected previously. The Committee opined that '*alii*' referred to the rest of the borough-holders (or burgage tenants) who had not signed the indentures, and that therefore the precedents told for limitation. Yet this same argument, of '*burgenses et alii*', or rather, '*liberi et Burgenses*' (for '*Burgenses*' was extremely vague), in earlier returns was used to extend the franchise in the Warwick case in the House in 1628, as implying that more than the select group had voted. Furthermore, the Bletchingley aberration became an unfortunate precedent in the Bridport case of 1628, where William Hakewill as chairman reported rather desperately from the Committee that 'the Recordes [for Bletchingley] were answered by cleare proofe that the Borougholders onely did elect though the Returne was by the Borougholders and Inhabitantes'.[18] The House in its early decisions was clearly moved by short-term political considerations of maintaining its independence and gaining the right sort of membership. This political concern justified the elaboration of a constitutional novelty, and the assertion of mutually incompatible conclusions over a very short time-span: devotion to the abstract principle of a wider franchise at first ranked low in members' lists of priorities. Indeed, concern with electoral mechanics generally yielded precedence to the determination to eliminate opportunities for electoral chicanery by the powerful. Several members of the 1625 Committee of Privileges had felt strongly that, in the event of a contest, the poll should be taken in order to weed out unqualified voters; yet in 1628 the Committee and the House concluded that the compulsory listing of voters' names was impermissible, because it would enable pressure to be brought to bear on them.[19] The listing of voters' names was of course the only reliable means of checking voters' credentials, and the House thus demonstrated that a 'free' electorate was more desirable than a 'pure' one.

This political aspect of the House of Commons' treatment of the franchise disputes remained evident throughout, and can best be seen in those decisions which, like Bletchingley, went against the prevailing grain. In the Gatton dispute of 1621, the House favoured the candidates elected by the freeholders, even if non-resident (in effect, a few gentry), against the two papists foisted on the handful of intimidated inhabitants by the recusant lord of the borough, William Copley. More significantly, given that a body of precedents for the opening of franchises had by then been accumulated, this was repeated in 1628, with only one dissentient in Committee – and the Committee had condemned the existence of freeholder franchises in boroughs in principle (saving the usual proviso of a 'certain custom ...[or]... prescription' in favour) over Cirencester and Pontefract in 1624. The decisions for limitation at Gatton were, as was that at Bletchingley, consistent with the general desire to eliminate pressure on the voters, although they were inconsistent with the normal methods taken to this end. The role of the fear of influence, as distinct from that of democratic principle, is emphasised by the unusual decision in 1621 merely to reverse the return, rather than to order a new election: the latter course was thought unsafe 'in respect of Danger from Copley'. Yet in 1641, when the immediate danger from Copley was past, the House denied the existence of the prescription in favour of a limited electorate which it had claimed to see twenty years previously, and after a long and difficult debate, reverted to its more conventional position that non-resident freeholders were disqualified, and that the franchise should lie with the inhabitants.[20] Attitudes to the franchise were, in the crucial early years, a matter of expediency, a means to an end. Whatever democratic principle was developed was politically self-serving, and was capable of being ignored if it should prove inconvenient.

The political motivation of the House's decisions was beginning to be recognised in the country by 1640 (some colour may have been given to this by a report in 1624 that Sir George Chaworth's return for Arundel had been rejected, and the inhabitants' right of election vindicated, in part because he favoured the hated treaties with Spain), and the petitions submitted to the Long Parliament against the election results and suffrage restrictions in at least two boroughs were couched in blatantly political terms. The petition against the return of the mayor, William Coriton, for Bossiney complained of his 'severall oppressions as Warden off the Steyneryes', as well as his electoral malpractices. On receipt of this, Pym demonstrated his willingness to break the rules in order to prevent the return of such an obnoxious friend to the government and backslider from his 'Country' position of the 1620s by proposing that he be excluded from participating in the new election which was ordered, thus removing the danger of another attempt at electoral perversion by Coriton. The House 'much distasted' this, but the members were sufficiently worried to take the unusual step of ordering that a week's notice be given in the borough before the new election, and (permissively, rather than peremptorily as Pym had wanted) that the mayor need not be involved in the election.[21] Similarly, when Sir Walter Earle delivered the petition against the Laudian Robert Hyde's election for Salisbury, the articles subscribed to it alleged 'that he ys a busye man agaynst dyvers goode thyngs', and D'Ewes's account maintains that the matter was decided by the House on the (rather different) political issue of placating the Earl of Pembroke, the patron of another candidate, which Moore, the other major diarist, saw as plainly 'contrary to law'.[22]

The expansion of the urban franchises then was primarily a political weapon aimed at the elimination of aristocratic or other unwanted influence. Such influence was a major bogy to Pym (despite his career as Bedford's client), Cromwell and others at the end of 1641, and the size of the bogy is indicated by the fact that the electoral reform which did manage to survive the obstruction of conservatism in the 1640s and 1650s was primarily redistributive rather than franchisal. The driving force behind the pressure for the removal of the rotten boroughs was probably as much a desire for the destruction of strongholds of influence as any belief that the more populous areas ought to be more equitably represented. Before the war, when that influence was welcome, as when Pembroke had to be propitiated over the Salisbury election, general principles apparently established in the 1620s could be conveniently forgotten. Similarly, when an increase in the number of voters seemed likely to strengthen the position of the influential, as at Gatton and Bletchingley, general views on the need to involve more people could be ignored, however inconsistent this might be with other decisions. By the time of the Long Parliament, the matter was bound up with incipient party politics as Prof. Plumb and Dr Hill suggested, although that had not been the case earlier, if only because there had then been no parties. When petitions were forwarded at the end of 1640 against opposition stalwarts elected on narrow franchises, they tended to get lost: Northampton and Peterborough are apparent examples of this. By this stage the Committee was partly justifying Spelman's and Bramston's complaints, though this had not been so previously, when political divisions were unclear, and when all members could be concerned for the future of parliaments. The intensity of the fears for parliament's survival which an apparent increase in obnoxious electoral manipulation had engendered is suggested by the absence of any conservative backlash. It was not until shortly before the outbreak of war that any voice was heard pleading the general social dangers of bringing the people into greater political prominence – and then the voice was that of the ardent lone wolf, William Prynne.[23] The threat from above seems to most people still to have been greater than that from below.

### Parliament-men and the politics of the franchise

The politically-inspired origins of decisions on the franchise are fairly clear by 1640–1. That being so, the existence of a number of committed, politically-informed individuals steadily working towards a goal which finally had majority support in the House on the eve of war might be suspected. Both recent commentators have suggested something like this,[24] and if it is the case, then some important conclusions emerge about the nature of early 17th-century politics. Most of all, it would mean that there were some people around who thought they knew where they were heading, who had long-term aims, who could work out that certain social and political developments would best conduce to the realisation of those aims, and, furthermore, who could deduce the practical steps necessary to bring those developments about. It would mean that there was something of a campaign going on, which in this period was rather unusual. Moreover, it should then provide us with another touchstone to establish a man's political position, for consistent activism for a wider electorate would on this reading indicate a degree of intelligent radicalism. But a survey of the actions of the individuals concerned belies this straightforward picture of a conscious political campaign. It is true that an examination of the pressure in the House for a wider franchise provides a useful indicator of the nature of parliamentary politics at this time, but that is because in many respects those politics are marked by incoherence. For the movement towards a wider franchise was one of drift and often of partial confusion. The guiding hands are few, and their motivation is difficult to discern.

The starting-point for any analysis of who or what was behind the decisions to open the franchises must be the activities of the Committee of Privileges, for it was this body which made the crucial recommendations on which the House decided, and which it largely followed. It is possible to argue for a degree of consciously-directed pressure on this basis. The 1621 parliament must be excluded, for the only two boroughs widened, Oxford and Sandwich, along with Gatton which was confirmed in its limitation, provide too little material on which to base conclusions; and it was also possibly too early for the issues involved to be clear to members. Charles I's first parliament in 1625 is also of little use: perhaps because of the brevity of the session, perhaps because too long was taken up with the divisive Yorkshire election, no franchise disputes were treated. In the 1620s then, we are left with a massive outburst of activity in 1624, virtually nil in 1626, and another spate in 1628. An explanation of this discrepancy cannot be found in the overall personnel of the respective Committees: over half of the members of each Committee had served earlier, and the same over-representation of lawyers can be found in each – both of which facts are inevitable, given the functions of the Committee. The sole peculiarity seems to be that the only major royal officials named to the 1624 Committee were the Chancellor of the Duchy and the Solicitor-General, which is at odds with the normal 1620s practice of naming all Councillors that were of the House. But records of proceedings show that the Committee list was not rigorously observed, and others, including Privy Councillors, besides those named, attended and participated.[25] In all, the composition of the Committees seems fairly constant.

By process of elimination, then, an explanation for the diverging records of these three Committees might lie in their chairmen. That of 1624, the lawyer John Glanville, was clearly an extraordinary personality. He does not appear to have served on a previous Committee, and in 1624 was named far down the list of precedence, while the chairman was normally taken from the top. An argument attaching importance to him personally would seem plausible. He stated his views forthrightly during the debates on the restoration to representation of three lapsed Buckinghamshire boroughs in 1624, urging the House that he 'thought in the townes which are now restored the inhabitants ought to choose. But the house refused to give direccion in it'. In these towns, no precedent for a particular franchise existed, and Glanville was thus making an explicit statement of principle. The refusal of the House to follows his lead might be taken as supporting Prof. Plumb's hypothesis that the activists were isolated at this point, but it probably relates more to a legalist reluctance to make a general pronouncement on the franchise as a mere order of the House.[26]

It was under Glanville that the Committee and the House made their first radical decisions and assertions, and amassed a substantial and decisive body of case law.[27] This might even have conduced to his removal from the chair in 1625, and the reappointment of its holder of 1621, Sir George More, a more conservative figure – and this possibly accounts for some of the inactivity of the 1625 Committee. In the following year, 1626, the chair was occupied by another conservative, Sir John Finch, and it is significant that in this parliament, the Warwick franchise, which was to be opened by the 1628 Committee, was reportedly on the point of being restricted when dissolution halted proceedings. Certainly, only one other urban contest (Ludgershall) which was referred to the Committee was dealt with, despite the rule that cases should be handled in order of priority of complaint. The Committee's activities were confined to the more socially respectable county disputes and Oxford University, and the more politically dangerous issue of Sir Edward Coke's shrievalty, favouring the major political question before it at the expense of more minor local troubles. The Oxford University dispute did admittedly involve some question of the franchise, and the Committee favoured the wider body, but this was no expansion, but merely a bar to the Vice-Chancellor's attempts that year to narrow the choice to the heads of houses from MAs.[28]

The contrast between the tardiness and incipient restrictionism of the 1626 Committee with the succession of positive pronouncements (in line with Glanville's in 1624) made by the 1628 Committee under William Hakewill is very marked. Boston, Bridport, Colchester, Exeter, Newport (Cornwall) and Warwick were opened in the most sweeping terms, without much demur. Hakewill seems to have had little compunction about laying down the law generally, as when he reported over Boston that in all boroughs, by common right, the commons (who were left undefined) ought to vote. The more radical orientation of 1628 must reflect a clearer lead being given to the Committee than had been the case in 1626, when business had been allowed to degenerate into bickering and procedural disputes.[29]

The precedents amassed in 1624 and 1628 meant that the scope for initiative on the part of the two Committees of 1640 was more circumscribed, and both parliaments saw an outpouring of decisions in favour of a wider franchise. The Great Bedwin case in the Short Parliament reveals the perfunctoriness of the Committee's procedure by this stage: 'The Committee being not satisfied, that it did belong to the ancient Burgesses by Prescription, they remitted the Election to the Inhabitants that paid Scot and Lot'.[30] Positive proof that the franchise should lie with the wider group was not required: instead, there had to be a mere absence of proof for limitation. The Short Parliament chairman, the lawyer Charles Jones, was apparently a conservative, a follower of 'a moderate way'. He opposed Pym's attempt to introduce blatant political considerations into disputes, and was more than once in conflict with the opposition leader. And yet he was sufficiently bound by the precedents laid down in the 1620s, particularly in the Boston case, that he could bring in a report on East Grinstead asserting that 'the Right of Election [is] original'.[31]

John Maynard's Committee of the Long Parliament was more confused. It had to be checked at least twice by the House when it tried to report in favour of a narrow franchise for Marlow and Gatton, and it was much less prone to sweeping pronouncements than were its predecessors. Maynard's own position illuminates its hesitation. Although he was ready to talk unthinkingly of the need for all inhabitants to have due notice of an impending election, and willing to advise his friend and fellow-lawyer Bulstrode Whitelocke on how to help his election on the inhabitants' votes at Marlow pass through the Committee, when it came to specific issues he was much less tolerant. Despite his intimations of friendship to Whitelocke, elected unchallenged by the inhabitants, such charity did not extend to Whitelocke's partner, Peregrine Hoby, who had been opposed. When discussing his election, 'Mr Maynard mooved that the poore should not have a voice', even though they had evidently participated in naming Whitelocke. Over Salisbury, Maynard was not content to join many of the opposition in giving blanket support to the official, narrow, return, thus gratifying the Earl of Pembroke, but went as far as to extenuate the abhorrent practices in the 1630s of the Laudian Recorder, Robert Hyde (the other candidate with Pembroke's secretary Oldsworth).[32] The more narrowly legalist outlook of his Committee, when compared to those of

1624 and 1628, is thus reflected in his own views. While there were those in the House, who might be termed the heirs of the position adumbrated in the Boston and East Grinstead cases, who argued that the statutes of Henry VI had provided for citizens and burgessess to elect, and that therefore there was no need to consider charters at all (in the Tewkesbury case), Maynard drew a simple and standard distinction between prescriptive and created boroughs, contending that the latter were capable of any limitation the creating charter wished to impose. He countered the majority on his committee and apparently agreed with those conservatives who argued that inhabitants at large, as opposed to freemen, were incapable of being incorporated because they had no permanent stake in a town, and that therefore a fully open franchise in a borough whose parliamentary status had been created by charter was ruled out by definition. The Committee compromised, concluding for an open but strictly resident franchise on the basis of charter, arguing that the charter had referred to the inhabitants at large, thus differing from those who denied the relevance of charter, but going further than Maynard. In view of the confusion, the matter was recommitted.[33]

Maynard's legalism also manifested itself in his attitude to technically undue returns. At the start of the session he reported from the Committee that only indentures officially returned by mayors or their equivalents were admissible, which would have completely blocked most franchise claims, featuring as they did conflicting returns by mayor and corporation and by the commons. That this resulted from his own attitude had been demonstrated shortly before, when he moved from the floor of the House that the mayorally-returned courtier Sir Charles Herbert should sit for Bossiney without further ado, merely on a view of the indentures; his proposal failed. The views of Maynard and the Committee contrast markedly with those of Glanville's Committee in 1624, which had been prepared to waive due and official forms (over Bletchingley) when these were corruptly controlled,[34] as they were in Bossiney.

The views of Glanville and Hakewill seem to have been decisive in formulating what came to be almost the official Commons' policy on the franchise. With an unsympathetic chairman, the Committee wavered and faltered. For, surprisingly, only one or two individuals seem to have had a clear idea of what they were about. Even Hakewill, who seems to have made up his mind by 1628, had pursued an erratic course prior to this. He had indeed been instrumental in the restoration of several lapsed parliamentary boroughs, thus manifesting his interest in electoral affairs, and had, unusually, received praise from the House for his activities in the Committee in 1621; but in that same year he had been employed by the House of Lords in its own privilege claims, which came into bitter conflict with those of the Commons over Floyd's case. He was a lawyer, and his services could be bought, as they may well have been in his initial researches on the score of the lapsed parliamentary boroughs.[35] Although in 1628 he led the Committee determinedly towards the creation of a larger electorate, he had in 1626 been counsel before the House for the Vice-Chancellor of Oxford when the latter was called to account for his attempt to reduce the number of University voters. And this was a pale echo of 1624, when he had been counsel for Pym and the Chippenham corporation and had used exactly those arguments from charter which his 1628 Committee was to condemn in, for example, the Boston case. Prof. Plumb sees him as one of the mainsprings of the campaign, and as probably involved locally in opening the franchise of his home town, Exeter, but it is likely that, if he was active there, he was on the opposite side for private reasons.[36]

Hakewill's career can be matched many times. Bulstrode Whitelocke was nominated by the corporation of Abingdon for the Short Parliament, but was opposed by a candidate supported by the commons. These he castigated for being swayed by 'beefe, bacon and bag-pudding', and assisted the oligarchy in their attempt to have the inhabitants disqualified by the Commons; but several months later he was prosecuting the reverse cause in the House as the candidate of the commons of neighbouring Marlow. Furthermore, he testifies that he was advised in this by several fellow-lawyers, including Maynard, who, while anxious for his professional presence in the House, were scarcely noted for their populism.[37]

Clearly, circumstances rather than principle decided the issue. But in the prevailing uncertainty, given that the problem was novel, this was perhaps understandable. Given also that the whole movement towards a wider franchise was itself determined by short-term political considerations, it was only to be expected that men's reactions should appear idiosyncratic, owing much to ephemeral political circumstances.

Sir Edward Coke's evolving attitude demonstrates how ideas formed in order to cope with a new situation and a new problem. In the Corporations Case he viewed any alteration of existing municipal franchises with disquiet, and willingly accepted restrictions placed on popular activity 'within time of memory' as conducive to the public good. Parliamentary elections were not at issue. But in his later *Institutes* he made a distinction in conformity with the orthodoxy of the 1620s and argued that neither royal charter nor municipal ordinance could affect electoral rights, 'for free elections of Members of the high Court of Parliament are *pro bono publico* and not to be compared to other cases of election of Maiors, Bailiffes, etc. of Corporations etc.' He made the same distinction, although less fully in the report, in Committee on the Chippenham contest in 1624. He had added this new dimension to his thought since 1599, and he was unhappy about it. He had in 1621 shown himself to be much less enamoured of vaguely asserted precedent than were some of the more active electoral warriors, insisting over demands for the restoration of Minehead that precedent must be shown, and not merely claimed, and this distaste over the resurrection of long-lost rights (for that is what the claims for the vote were supposed to be about)[38] continued. He confessed that Chippenham and its opposing claims was 'a doubtfull case', and it is significant that this is the only franchise debate in which he is recorded as participating, despite his loquacity elsewhere.[39] If even a man as outspoken as Coke was worried and tentative in face of novelty, there is no wonder that others failed to follow a clear line. It also makes the activities and successes of the confident few, if they existed, more remarkable.

There were some individuals, besides Glanville, who evidently knew their own minds and remained constant. Sir Edwin Sandys was an activist in the country, if not in the House: he was instrumental in the successful claim for the vote by the freemen of Sandwich in 1621, although he himself was assured of the oligarchy's votes, and was therefore not acting in a wholly self-interested way. He performed the same service at neighbouring Dover in 1624 for his son-in-law, and was said to have been responsible for the extremely wide franchise established in Virginia. Significantly, he was resisted in his alleged efforts to model the Virginia franchise after his own design by the Earl of Warwick's group, his rivals within the Virginia Company, which tells against any simple equation between opposition to the Stuart Court and an expansionist position on the franchise.[40] Strangely enough, Sandys kept silent in the House, possibly because, like Sir Edward Coke, he was more interested in the meat of politics – it is noticeable that those most involved in arguing for a wider franchise tended not to be the political leaders, perhaps because the issue was too much a lawyers' matter.

Predictably, therefore, one of those most involved was Sir Simonds D'Ewes. He evinced no surprise at the important early decisions on Chippenham and Newcastle-under-Lyme in 1624, not finding it necessary even to justify the arguments. This casual acceptance of the validity of the extended franchise was evidenced in his irritated reaction to the involved Tewkesbury debate in the Long Parliament. He found the debate 'long and unnecessarie', and argued sweepingly on the basis of Henry VI's statutes that all inhabitants in towns should vote, 'though never soe poore', and over Salisbury on the same foundation dismissed the relevance of precedents entirely, even those stretching back to the first parliament of all, for the vote was 'the hereditarie right of the subjects of England', inasmuch as they were inhabitants of boroughs. He followed the same line on Marlow, insisting that 'the poorest man' should vote, for 'it was the birthright of the subjects of England'. As Mr Thomas has observed, this was incipient Levelling, and it was certainly consistent, even if, given the reaction D'Ewes sometimes inspired, it was not too influential.[41]

More involved even than D'Ewes, and the only real politician in the forefront, was Sir Walter Earle, one of the managers at Strafford's impeachment in 1641. As early as 1624 he favoured opening Chippenham, and was sufficiently informed of the arguments to be able to accuse the Recorder of London, Heneage Finch, of irrelevance. By the Long Parliament, he was evidently known in the country for his interests, for he presented the petition against the Salisbury election, though he apparently had no major contact with that city, and he continued to oppose the official return in debate, being uninterested in the need to propitiate Pembroke. He was in favour of an inhabitant franchise at Tewkesbury, and more remarkably, the diarist John Moore credited him with responsibility for the House's decision to open the Windsor franchise.[42]

Consistent concern for a wider franchise did not only manifest itself amongst staunch opposition men. The lawyer Geoffrey Palmer, while a good commonwealth's man in 1640, was to incur the odium of the opposition for the vehemence of his protests at the tactics over the Grand Remonstrance, and yet he pronounced strongly for an open franchise at Higham Ferrers when consulted in his legal capacity before the Short Parliament election. Like D'Ewes shortly afterwards, he argued from the regulatory statutes of Henry VI's reign that no limited election, whether derived from 'use prescripcion or Charter', was valid. Presumably on this basis, in the Long Parliament he supported Whitelocke and the commons at Marlow, and also opposed the Bossiney abuses and limitations.[43]

The franchise question was not one of crude 'party' politics, as defined by 1641-2 alignments. The imminent election for the Short Parliament at Higham Ferrers occasioned the consultation of three lawyers who were subsequently shown to be of differing political persuasions: Palmer the future 'constitutional royalist', Sir Robert Heath, the Queen's Solicitor, and the great parliamentarian Oliver St John. All advised that a wider group than the capital burgesses alone should vote. By 1640 there appears to have been a general consensus on extension. There had been some murmurings of opposition in the early stages in 1624, but these had been piecemeal and tinged with self-interest: two neighbouring members to the Chippenham dispute had argued that altering ancient forms would prove dangerous, and one of the dispossessed Dover members that year thought that if he suffered, there were many others elected in the same way who should join him. More interestingly, Pym argued the consequences of the Chippenham decision in the same terms as those in which the ex-member for Dover had bewailed his lot – and this at a time when the future popular leader had chosen to sit elsewhere, and was thus no longer so directly concerned, and might even have been sincere. Many other members had been elected by chartered corporations, and might also be vulnerable: 'itt would call into confusion the election of all corporations', he urged.[44] Apart from this, there seems to have been very little opposition to the general process. There were technical objections, but nobody claimed to resist on principle, or protested that too many people were voting, at least until the onset of war, when the implications were clear. This may have been because of the determining nature of precedent: once something had happened more than once, then it was right. But it may also have been the case that just as few could see the development clearly enough to work out a coherent position in favour, so also few saw sufficiently fully where it might lead to come out strongly against it. Apart perhaps from Glanville and one or two others, there was drift rather than purposiveness everywhere. If people were railroaded into opening the franchises, then it was at first by a backlash against the Crown and subsequently by the precedents which had been laid down, rather than by a coterie of puritan politicians and lawyers.

There was little correlation between attitudes to the franchise and general political outlook. Pym stood on a closed franchise at Chippenham in 1624, and defended it both generally (by appealing to the vested interests of other members for corporation boroughs) and specifically (by arguing from its charter). The tenor of his case can be appreciated from the entry of a diarist very much opposed to any indiscriminate widening of the franchise that 'he was very longe but to very little purpose in so much as Mr Brooke sayde he had delyvered a greate deale of false doctrine'. In view of this reaction, and the House's acceptance of Glanville's far-reaching reports, Pym may have been isolated in opposing expansion even at this early stage. By 1640 he had swum with the tide sufficiently to have abandoned his strongly antagonistic position, but he was still hardly in the van of change. His only intervention on the franchise came over Tewkesbury, and here the fullest accounts have him arguing not that the inhabitants at large, but only those free of the corporation, should vote, although others, including D'Ewes, Selden, Gerrard, Fiennes, Whitelocke and Glynne, would have extended the franchise to all the inhabitants. As this would not at this stage have altered the result – that is, Pym had no immediate tactical end in view – it was probably a clear statement of his beliefs. He was more interested in the exclusion of powerful influence, and of ensuring that the right individuals were elected, than in securing the long-term freedom of elections by creating more voters. The positions he took over Chippenham and Tewkesbury suggest that if anything he was opposed to any significant expansion of the political nation, despite his alleged rabble-rousing activities in London in 1641, and despite the fact that in the crisis over

the militia in 1641–2 he was apparently interested in a semi-academic
case on Anglo-Saxon precedents for popular election to virtually all local
offices. He nowhere appealed to an almost natural rights doctrine, or to
sweeping arguments from statute, as others were doing at this time. His
utterances were conservative, focusing on vested interest in 1624, and on
the conventionalism of vested interest and charter in the Long Parliament,
for this was 'the constant opinion and course off the howse'.[45]

The confusion of alignments on the franchise can be best understood by
analysing the divisions on the most controversial cases. Those from the
1620s are of little use, as the political lines were even less clear than in
1640. Even so, it is significant that while Pym was aided over the
Chippenham affair by his fellow Bedford client Edward Alford, several
of the opposition, Earle, Sir Robert Phelips, Sir Dudley Digges, William
Mallory, were ranged against him, and that the courtier and Recorder of
London, Finch, and the Chancellor of the Duchy, Sir Humphrey May,
were themselves tending towards opposite sides.[46] Confusion, rather than
confrontation, seems evident.

Some elections in 1640 were being treated 'politically' – the angry
intervention of Pym and Haselrig in the debate on Sudbury, for which
Pym earned a 'verie hott' rebuke from the moderate Sir John Strangways,
and had to be deftly put down by his allies, Sir Robert Harley and Earle,
shows that from the start of the session politicians were anxious to admit
fellow-travellers; and by 1641, there appears to have been a virtually
straight split on the future 'William the Conqueror' Waller's return for
Andover.[47] Nevertheless, the franchise disputes were not dealt with so
rigidly. Sir Bevill Grenville in Bossiney urged the general rectitude of a
scot-and-lot franchise. The fact that future royalists like Sir John Colpepper
and Edward Bagshaw only favoured extending the vote to the freemen
rather than all the inhabitants of Tewkesbury, and one of the Whites,
presumably the courtier John, would even have allowed the corporation
to limit it to themselves, while later parliamentarians such as Nathaniel
Fiennes, Glynne, Sir Gilbert Gerrard, D'Ewes and John Selden were
prepared to envisage all inhabitants becoming involved, suggests that
here, where the victory of either would not have ensured the return of new
and sympathetic members, the two groups were enunciating their beliefs,
and that a confirmed opposition stance was more likely to produce
expansionist leanings. But while it is true that in this case no future
royalists were to be found advocating an inhabitant franchise, there was
confusion the other way. Pym joined Colpepper, as we have seen, but also
Maynard, Harbottle Grimston jr. and William Cage were outspokenly
restrictive. Most violent of all was the great William Prynne, counsel for
a contestant in the dispute consequent on the second disordered election of

1641, who bitterly attacked any idea that 'the very scum of the people' should have any say, although he was not yet as reactionary as he was to be by the Restoration, when he denied that the 'commonalty' necessarily meant freemen, let alone inhabitants, when he had specifically accepted the former definition for Tewkesbury in 1641.[48] He did have an interest in taking his 1641 position, as the freemen's candidate for whom he was counsel was opposed by another supported by the inhabitants at large, but the violence of his language suggests that he may have meant some of what he said. There was clearly no necessary link between committed parliamentarianism and devotion to popular involvement in elections, although there was an observable tendency in that direction.

Equally, the connection between future royalism and restrictions was, although evident, not absolute. Palmer's support in particular, and also Heath's, for a larger electorate has been stressed. Robert Holburne supported D'Ewes's 'hereditarie right' opposition to the Salisbury election, though this was probably on the more conventional grounds of a charter's inability to limit pre-existing custom (although there was absolutely nothing to show that such a custom had existed), very unlike D'Ewes's blanket dismissal of precedent. Surprisingly, he was also joined on the expansionist side by Colpepper. Apart from these two, the Salisbury alignment betrayed similar configurations to that over Tewkesbury. D'Ewes's statement that the 'religious and sound men' opposed the corporation's return seems supported by the role of Sir Edward Ayscough and Sir John Corbett as tellers in the division against, and the presence on the same side of Earle, Sir Arthur Haselrig, Denzil Holles and Sir John Hotham.[49] Supporting the official return were the moderate royalists Lord Falkland, Sir John Strangways and Sir Francis Seymour, with Charles's faithful servant, John Ashburnham, and another future royalist, George Fane, as tellers for the ayes. But as over Tewkesbury, there were strange additions. Maynard's support for Hyde's actions has been noted, and the other great lawyer John Selden, despite his views on Tewkesbury, supported the return, apparently using discredited arguments from charter. More singularly, and substantiating D'Ewes's complaint about the gratification of Pembroke, a strongly opposition-biased committee favoured exculpating Hyde from the accusations of misconduct.[50]

The pattern of general royalist solidarity for limitation, and of a divided parliamentarian group, is broken by the Marlow dispute. As usual, solid opposition men disagreed: Hotham, Sir Peter Heyman and John Coucher followed D'Ewes's view that 'the poorest man' ought to vote; and as usual, Maynard found this distasteful, as did John Crew and Sir Miles Fleetwood. Sir Gilbert Gerrard was evidently unhappy with the altercation and the problem that it revealed, and tried to have the matter dropped. But on the other side, the 'royalist' participants were almost solidly for opening, only Sir Francis Seymour being recorded as not having favoured the poor, and he, like Gerrard, was not explicit, and merely tried to close the debate. The other 'royalists' in one way or another supported the popular cause, Edward Hyde and Geoffrey Palmer being among the lawyers who advised Whitelocke how to proceed, and Edward Bagshaw and John Whistler openly stating that the poor should vote.[51]

The idiosyncrasies over Marlow possibly resulted from lawyer determination to have Whitelocke admitted, to which he himself pointed – Hyde, Palmer, Whistler and Bagshaw would all fit into this argument – for he was not named in either of the original returns, and thus needed the whole election to be voided if he were to stand a chance. But this is unlikely to be the answer, for Maynard and Crew, both lawyers, were opposed to a wide-open franchise, and the election was anyway voided on the technicality of lack of notice. Differing performances over the three cases of Tewkesbury, Salisbury and Marlow must reflect the differing issues involved. Marlow was a recently restored borough, not incorporate (and thus with no limiting charter), and with no definitive prescription as to who voted, the House having refused to pronounce in 1624 on what the franchise should be. It was therefore clear, in the light of the resolutions of the 1620s that where there was no limiting custom the commons should vote, that the franchise should be open. The dispute was on the question of who were the commons, scot-and-lot men, or all the inhabitants, and on this there was no guide.[52] Apart from the doubtfully-effective factor of the lawyers' desire to admit Whitelocke, participants in this debate could give free vent to their prejudices and demonstrate the extent to which they would draw out the implications of the term 'commons'. It remains a good test for an individual's attitudes: despite his sympathy for Whitelocke, chairman Maynard was opposed; and while Gerrard could support the vague proposition that the commons should vote at Tewkesbury, when Marlow made it clear just what sort of person this meant, he had misgivings. Strangely enough, the distinctly lukewarm Hotham of the war years favoured allowing a popular role to develop in 1640.[53]

The issues at Tewkesbury and Salisbury were more technical, and were effectively a lawyers' battleground. The former centred on the meaning of the word 'commonalty' in the incorporating charter, and involved much legal dispute as to whether inhabitants or merely freemen could be a perpetual body with successors – a matter for which Gerrard expressed his impatience by demanding 'If the word Communalty doe nott expresse all the Inhabitants what other word is there for it'. In a debate revolving around the basically safe issue of the terms of a charter, it was possible for a legalist like Selden, who refused to broaden his outlook over

Salisbury, to take a liberal position; and while Maynard could hide behind a discussion of the terms of the charter and succession to legal persons, over Marlow, where there was no legal screen, he had to commit himself openly. Conversely, Bagshaw's concern with the intricacies of a charter's powers and his failure to make a statement of principle over Tewkesbury suggests that his support for the poor of Marlow may even have been an inadvertent by-product of his concern for Whitelocke. The dismissal of such minutiae by Fiennes, on the other hand, with his assertion that all inhabitants were empowered by statute to vote, probably puts him in the same enthusiastic group as Palmer and D'Ewes, given the implications of the argument when used by the latter over Salisbury. In view of its legal complexity, Tewkesbury is of less use as a barometer of emotions on the popular vote than Marlow, and the Salisbury case is probably even less helpful, as a result of its political repercussions, and the confusion introduced by such questions as whether '*burgagium*', and hence, perhaps, representation, could exist before incorporation.[54]

The concurrence of the three lawyers on the Higham Ferrers case indicates that there may have been a considerable consensus on the general principle of an enlarged electorate, and this is also suggested by the, apparently widespread, unfavourable reaction to Pym's plea over Chippenham as early as 1624. After 1624 there was no resistance on principle, merely objections on specific points in individual cases. Not until the House was asked explicitly to permit the involvement of almsmen or near-almsmen *de novo* at Marlow, and later at Tewkesbury, for whose voting there was no clear precedent, did some members draw back in consternation. As to the identity of those most active in the process, the political lines are as unclear as most members' views. The matter of the franchise was a complex one, fraught with legal difficulties, and therefore tended to be the province of lawyers, or legalists like D'Ewes – and neither of these groups were renowned for their political dynamism and awareness. Future royalists did tend to be less enthusiastic than did future parliamentarians, but the latter divided, and there were few who showed themselves to be consistent activists.[55] What few of these that there were tended to have a decisive and disproportionate influence in a sea of (probably basically favourable) uncertainty. Parliamentary alignments of 1640–1 were not those of 1642 and even had they been, they wouuld not have accounted fully for members' attitudes to the franchise.

Neither does the religious character of those involved lend itself to easy categorisation in terms of 'puritan' zealousness, which is something that has also been suggested previously in order to explain the movement, on the assumption that dissatisfied puritans were appealing downwards in order to gain support.[56] Sandys, the local activist, was anything but a puritan,[57] and Glanville and Hakewill were clearly lawyers rather than puritans. If Hakewill did side with his brother in the local Exeter confrontation, then he was ranged against one of the greatest puritans of his generation.[58] Among the 1640 actors, D'Ewes, Fiennes and Earle were men of zeal, and Corbett and Ayscough may have been fired by religious determination in opposing the Salisbury return of a Laudian to the extent that they were named as tellers. But Clarendon declared that Hotham was wedded to the government of the Church,[59] and Selden is notorious for his unpuritanical nature. Heath and Palmer surely cannot even be considered. Again, the simple notion that the expansion of the franchise was the work of a puritanically-inspired, determined caucus in the House, bidding for power, will not fit. Those most active were those who were not the power-seekers, and the political leaders remained uninterested, or even opposed. The development was an unthought-out, generally-agreed drift, arising initially from the sense of a desperate need to preserve parliaments, and not from any specific political creed. Only in the gradual polarisation of 1640–1 did it begin to acquire any more specific political connotations.

The failure of members to take sides until late in the day becomes less singular when it is noted that the political loyalties of the newly-enfranchised were not always clear. The political effects of widening Tewkesbury, Bossiney, Marlow or Salisbury might be discernible, if confusedly so in the last case, in view of the coupling of the Laudian Hyde and Pembroke's secretary Oldsworth on the official return. But elsewhere delineations were uncertain. Sandwich continued to elect nominees of the Duke of Buckingham in the 1620s despite the 1621 opening, and Dover succumbed on occasion after 1624. The corporation of Reading elected the parliamentarians, Sir Francis Knollys, father and son, to the Long Parliament, independent of the freemen pressing for the vote; after the voiding of the first Windsor election to the Long Parliament, the newly-widened electorate proceeded to elect a courtier, Cornelius Holland, and a Straffordian, William Taylor. More confusingly still, an anti-Court corporation, as that of Northampton, could be challenged by apparently less militant freemen; and one wonders what construction could have been put on the actions of the town clerk of Warwick, who attempted to have the franchise extended to all inhabitants, in order to foil the more godly freemen's support of the puritan Lord Brooke's nominee for the Long Parliament.[60]

The Warwick case might have formed the basis for a working guide to parliamentary decisions on the franchise. It appears to confirm Richard Baxter's belief that the dregs of the people were thoroughly unregenerate, and Dr Hill's that the 'industrious sort', the more substantial, were the backbone of true godliness in England. If that were so, then future parliamentarians should have been relatively consistent in favour of a freeman franchise, while royalists, when disappointed in their preference for oligarchy (which might normally be tied by vested interest to the Crown),[61] should have gone unhesitatingly for as wide a franchise as possible. But Marlow can be cited to counter Warwick, for there the wider group supported Whitelocke and Hoby. The belief anyway rests upon the probably mistaken assumption that others were as acute observers of the social scene as was Baxter.

A wider electorate, moreover, by no means always favoured the opposition, for, while parliamentary politics was not a matter of two parties until 1641 if ever, in the localities politics were even less polarised. Many very particularist considerations affected individual election contests, which could result in an overbearing, but opposition-minded, oligarchy being challenged by the freemen, whose opposition was exploited by a future royalist. Political consistency at the centre over such disputes inevitably became still more difficult to attain. When the problem was very hard, as evidently at Northampton, it seems to have been ignored, and lost in Committee. And when viewing the electoral results of earlier decisions to open the franchises, members could hardly feel confident of the political consequences of any specific dispute, even if they might of the general drift. Gatton and Bletchingley were not unique, though the House's handling of them might appear so in retrospect, and consistent partisan decision-making, therefore, became impossible.[62]

# 5

# The Urban Voters

The identity of the urban electors was considered by many contemporaries to be of fundamental importance, particularly in terms of their ability to withstand blandishments of various kinds. The richest were vulnerable to considerations of vested interest, the poorest to alcohol or bribes, and election campaigns and draft election bills might be calculated accordingly. The decisions to open the franchises were partly based on the assumption that the many would behave differently from the few. The question is also of obvious interest to modern historians, for it helps to define the extent of the political nation, and hence the exclusiveness or otherwise of society – though of course the leaders of that society may have determined to increase its numbers for quite unprincipled reasons. In addition, it points to continuity or discontinuity between the political activity of the revolutionary decades and those that preceded them.

The account of the franchise disputes, and of the reactions of the House to them, has implied that the urban franchise was a very varied commodity, unlike the uniform 40s. freehold in the counties. There can therefore be no general statement about the social composition of the urban electorate, for it differed from place to place, and from type to type of franchise, which could be based on corporation membership, on freedom to trade, on residence, or even on ownership of the defunct salt pans at Droitwich. Nevertheless, it is possible to be rather more specific about the nature of the voters than it was in the case of the county constituencies, for evidence is more accessible. More poll lists, or equivalent information, survive for a range of urban constituencies than is the case in the counties, and some identification of individual voters is possible by means of these, and case studies can thus be provided. Additionally, approximate totals for the different forms of franchises can be obtained, so estimates can be made of how widespread particular features were. The accuracy of such estimates is minimised by the fact that some boroughs were never contested, and thus never had to clarify the state of their franchises, but certain broad, unchallengeable conclusions do emerge, especially that by 1641 the freeman franchises were by far the most numerous. The rough totals in the major categories (by 1641) were: 34 governing body franchises, 83 freeman, 24 burgage tenure, 11 scot and lot, 26 residence or householder.[1]

## The corporation franchises

Prior to 1621, the oligarchic franchises had been considerably more common, but their numbers were whittled away by a generation of franchise disputes. While they obviously featured an economically substantial electorate, this conclusion must be qualified by the fact that by 1641 the corporation franchises had become effectively confined to the smaller boroughs which were family preserves. Seats in the larger boroughs were more prestigious (members being elected for two constituencies invariably choosing the larger one), and they therefore tended to attract a surfeit of candidates: conflicts within the larger boroughs might themselves generate electoral disorder. The larger boroughs were thus more likely to be contested, and in consequence were more liable to suffer disputes which would require resolution by the House of Commons. Their franchises were accordingly vulnerable to inspection and alteration by that body, which was increasingly moving towards a principled dislike of oligarchic electorates. The net effect of this was that on the outbreak of war the social dimension of the corporation franchises probably conformed most closely, not to a notion of a group of merchant princes, but to Baxter's description of unrepresented Kidderminster, where 'The Magistrates of the Town were few of them worth £40 per An. and most not half so much'.[2] Although Baxter was no doubt exaggerating, he was firmly of the opinion that masters and men were socially fairly indistinct, and this would probably be true of numbers of the smallest boroughs.

The picture of what might have been anticipated is provided by Great Yarmouth, one of the few surviving (albeit with difficulty in the 1620s) large corporation franchises. All members of the oligarchy of this second-rank outport adventured at least £5 on Irish lands in 1642, and the few surviving wills show them to have been very wealthy, with even a 'roughmason' owning at least four houses.[3] An even more extreme group is, predictably, to be found at the provincial capital of Exeter, several of whose governors were worth thousands of pounds, although they lost control in 1626–8. A more typical group, although still probably rather healthier economically than the magistrates of many of the small West Country boroughs, were ruling Newcastle-under-Lyme in 1624. They included a prosperous innkeeper, grocer and haberdasher worth £200–300 each, although a shearman who died worth £62 11s. and a butcher worth £77 6s. 8d. also gained office.[4] They were certainly more like Baxter's Kidderminster worthies than they were those of Exeter. But, like Exeter's governors a couple of years later, they lost electoral control in 1624, and there lies the key to the corporation franchises. It cannot be assumed that these generally exhibited such a wealthy electorate as did Exeter until the late 1620s, or Great Yarmouth. Almost the only boroughs

of any major significance still possessing thoroughly limited franchises by
the outbreak of war were Great Yarmouth, Nottingham, Plymouth,
Northampton and Salisbury, and the last two of these only just survived
for the political reasons outlined above.[5]

## The freeman franchises

The next category down the economic scale, and the most numerous, were
the freeman boroughs. These represented the franchise which was arguably
that most favoured by the House of Commons. The Committee of
Privileges presided over by that electoral radical, Glanville, in 1624 had
made what were effectively statements of principle in advocacy of a resident householder franchise: in the cases of Cirencester and Pontefract
there was no guide available as to whom the suffrage should lie with,
Pontefract because it was newly restored to representation (in 1621), and
Cirencester because it had never been contested previously, and not being
incorporate, had no charter to provide a definition. The Committee,
doubtless following Glanville's own promptings as evidenced by his stated
preference for an open franchise for the newly-restored Buckinghamshire
boroughs in that parliament, determined that 'of common right, all the
inhabitants, householders, and residents within the borough, ought to have
voice in the election'.[6]

But not all Committees were willing to go as far as Glanville's. Sir
Bevill Grenville and an anonymous commentator at the start of the Long
Parliament considered that the House intended a scot-and-lot franchise
(rather narrower than resident householders), and this interpretation is
supported by the Short Parliament's decision in the Great Bedwin case,
where, like Cirencester and Pontefract, there was no guide to hand, but
the Committee here pronounced for scot and lot. But scot and lot as the
norm to which the House aspired can probably be ruled out: the anonymous report saw it as a maximum, rather than an optimum, and the
express pronouncements in its favour, by Grenville on Bossiney, and by
the Committee on Great Bedwin, applied to small, non-incorporate
boroughs where the concept of borough freedom was effectively meaningless. Scot and lot, then, is an unlikely challenge to an orthodoxy of
freeman franchises, but that does not affect the question of the resident
householders, as favoured in 1624. The decision on the Boston case
handed down by Hakewill's Committee in 1628, with its statement that
in all boroughs the commons should vote, is vague, and might be taken
as following the path laid down by Glanville, but this seems improbable.
More likely is the suggestion that Glanville was out on a limb, and that
relatively few, until the Tewkesbury and Marlow debates of the Long
Parliament, were ready to join him.[7]

Local campaigns for the vote, as in Bristol, Bedford, Colchester, Northampton, Sandwich or Warwick, indicate that it was the freemen who were applying the pressure, and the Commons may merely have taken this as understood, and not felt the need to be more specific.[8] Certainly, when they were asked to be specific, over Tewkesbury in the Long Parliament, it was quite clearly a new demand, and several members were most unhappy to find that what they thought was meant by the word 'commons' was not quite what others assumed. The fact that some members stood out so far for a freeman franchise when faced with the need for precision on what the 'commons' were in 1640 suggests that they thought that that was what the resolutions of the 1620s had been about. Sir Gilbert Gerrard believed that the term 'commonalty', or commons, could only mean all the inhabitants, but conversely the 1621 election bill apparently intended a freeman electorate in boroughs not restricted by charter, and Ireton at Putney in 1647 conceived that freemen were universally the urban electors. The terms used are imprecise, unfortunately for the historian, and productively for those who wanted to open the franchise still further, but it is suggestive that the word 'burgesses' was repeatedly used with 'commons' in the 1620s debates, and was sometimes (as in the Warwick argument in 1628) explicitly tied to the word '*liberi*', and this implies a freeman electorate. Prynne certainly thought as much when surveying the 1620s developments in his brief for Tewkesbury in 1641, although he was obviously capable of error.[9] In Hakewill's fairly detailed report on the Boston case, he used the words 'burgesses' and 'commonalty' for the commons, and the opinion of the bulk of the lawyers over Salisbury and Tewkesbury in 1640 seemed to be that these groups equalled the freemen. Furthermore, the number of the Boston commons that turned out to vote (about 70) was more compatible with the likely total of freemen (about 200) than with all the householders.[10] It seems likely then that apart from the aberration of 1624, and the confusion that was becoming evident in 1640, most members thought it was the freemen that they were talking about when they determined to open the franchises to that imprecise group, the 'commons'. An analysis of what a freeman electorate could mean in practice reveals much of the limits of the House's social and political tolerance, and gives an indication of what the largest part of the urban electorate was like.

Freemen have been characterised as in effect the urban middling sort by Christopher Hill, with his emphasis on the phrase 'the industrious sort of people', whom he places between the property-less and the privileged. This is surely correct, except insofar as it conceals a multitude of gradations, for freedom could be acquired by birth or marriage as well as by apprenticeship or purchase, and neither of the former methods offered any guarantee of life-long prosperity. 'Economically independent householders' they may largely have been, but there are degrees of independence, and some houses are bigger than others.[11] The size and composition of the freeman population varied greatly from town to town, with Chester in the third and fourth decades of the century admitting one freeman per annum for every hundred head of the total population, while Great Yarmouth, perhaps unbalanced by its monoculture fishing economy, only admitted at a rate of 1 : 450 over the same period. Other towns appear to have figured in between these, and to have varied over a period of time, for economic depression could bring trading restrictions. King's Lynn, for example, had an admission rate of 1 : 180 in the second half of the 16th century, but 1 : 270 in the first four decades of the 17th.[12] It is thus impossible to give a static portrait of the urban freemen as a whole group.

The difficulties in the way of obtaining an overall cross-section of the freeman electorate do not, however, preclude all attempts at assessing the validity of Dr Hill's characterisation of the type. Some towns had freeman totals so high that doubts must be raised about the economic substance of those involved. Even fairly respectable trades in London could contain surprisingly high proportions of economic small fry: of the 1427 freemen of the Drapers' Company assessed at £2 or less to the 1641 poll tax, only 835 were able to pay, and many were unable to pay their quarterly guild fees; most freemen in the Goldsmiths' Company were only able to pay 1s. poll tax, and the Company's authorities listed them quite unambiguously as the 'poore Freemen'. London's franchise was limited to a smaller group than the freemen as a whole (the voting liverymen totalling about 4000, and in the Goldsmiths' comprising about a quarter of the freemen as a whole, but below 10 per cent in the Drapers'), but the figures nevertheless serve as a warning. If even wealthy London had such high numbers of poor freemen, the situation elsewhere was probably worse. This must have been the case in York, where the rates of admission had dropped from perhaps 1 : 180 in Elizabeth's reign to 1 : c. 145 in the first half of the 17th century. In numerical terms, this was an average of 1900 freemen every 25 years, in a total population of 10,000–12,000.[13] Assuming admissions occurred at or about age 24, and that freemen experienced the same mortality as other sections of the population, then the life-expectancy of the freemen at admission would be considerably higher than the point somewhere in the 30s which is posited for the population at birth in this period. The implication of Dr Wrigley's work on mortality would seem to be that someone at age 24 could expect at least another equivalent period of life. This then suggests that at any one time in early 17th-century York, there might have been a total of at least 1900 freemen, given the prevailing rate of admission. In a total population of 10,000–12,000, this becomes of great significance, for the ratio of adult males to the population as a whole has been estimated variously at between 1 : 4 and 1 : 6.[14] The freemen would include a minimum of 75 per cent of the adult male population; in Chester, with a freemen ratio of 1 : 100, the percentage is unlikely to be less. When between one-half and three-quarters of the urban population in the early modern period, depending on harvest and trading conditions, were sunk in poverty, a large minority of freemen in some towns were thus worse than at risk economically.[15]

Other towns substantiate the claim that the freemen were socially a very extensive group, although perhaps not quite as dramatically as do York and Chester. Bristol was averaging about 100 admissions to freedom a year in the three decades before the franchise was apparently opened to them in 1640. In a total population of somewhat less than 20,000, the likelihood must be (on the basis of the very rough type of calculation outlined above), that a minimum of 50 per cent of the adult males of the city would have gained the vote as a result of the developments of 1640. Norwich probably presents a roughly similar picture, for here in excess of 2000 freemen were created in the three decades prior to 1640, when its population after the disastrous plague of the mid-1620s was probably some way under 20,000.[16] Liverpool, Hull and Newcastle manifest similar proportions;[17] in Coventry, about 600 freemen voted in 1628, when the city's population was c. 6000, and in Dover there appear to have been 252 freemen in 1624 (when the corporation franchise was broken), and a total population of perhaps slightly more than ten times that number. Tewkesbury had possibly just over 360 freemen in 1640 when the sum of its adult males was probably not much more than double that figure.[18]

Fifty per cent of the adult males (higher at York, lower at Great Yarmouth) includes more than just the 'economically independent' members of the community. At Oxford, Bedford and Wigan there were freemen who were below the scot-and-lot level, and who were therefore presumably not fully secure.[19] Many of the Bristol freemen, particularly in the cloth trades, were on relief in the crisis of the late 1620s, and the corporation of Salisbury was compelled to subsidise many of its freemen in the 1620s and 30s. There were said to be freemen who were also almsmen in Shrewsbury in the late 1630s and in Bedford in 1640, and the poverty of some of those who were free of London trades has been noted. Independence would not normally be noted as a characteristic of many of these men, but rather vulnerability.[20]

What this might mean in practice can be seen from the example of the thriving town of Dover, where 319 freemen were admitted between Michaelmas 1603 and the New Year of 1623–4, the eve of the decisive election. Below the normal cross-section of solid urban trades were ten labourers, two beer-drawers, one 'aqua-vitae man', one hemp-dresser, and nine fishermen and eighteen sailors, as distinct from the more common (in the freemen lists) and more substantial (by probate evidence) mariners; and almost all these less-prosperous freemen were admitted either by right of birth or by marriage, rather than by apprenticeship, composition or purchase of a £5 freehold.[21] Significantly, then, over 10 per cent of the electorate of this freeman borough are likely to fall within the ranks of the urban proletariat, rather than of the middling men. The same kind of picture emerges from other boroughs of this type. In Hertford in 1624, 244 freemen voted, yet according to the 1621 survey, there had only been about 300 houses, plus 'divers cottages' on waste ground, in the town. In 1641, only just over 300 people were rated for the poll tax, with a mere 138 being listed as capable of spending over £5 per annum, and 219 households of housekeepers (including widows) not receiving alms.[22] It seems probable that the freemen here included the large majority of male householders, and they included, of the 102 voters of 1624 whose occupations are known, two labourers, two gardeners, and a candle-maker. In view of the composition of the freeman electorate at Hertford, the cries of social disaster made later about the extension of the franchise to all its inhabitants in 1640 must be qualified.[23]

The conclusion to be drawn from this evidence is clear. The freeman franchise, the one most favoured by the members of the House, and much the most widespread of all the urban franchises by 1640, covering most of the larger towns, included the greater part of a town's adult male inhabitants in some instances, and probably verging on a half of them in many more. The parallels with New England developments are again marked, and tend to emphasise the continuity of political experience in the two societies, for in Massachusetts freedom was gained by similar proportions of the males.[24] On the whole, the English freemen clearly were economically independent, although individuals who gained their franchise through their fathers or their wives were fully capable of moving downwards and becoming true urban proletariat. And many even of the industrious sort succumbed to the economic pressures of the 1620s. It was to this very large and very amorphous group that majority opinion in the House agreed to extend the vote in many cases that were presented to it in the 1620s and in 1640–1.[25] Not all members may have appreciated what it was they were doing, but some did, particularly those involved locally in the franchise disputes. Even those who felt, as in the Tewkesbury debate, that the franchise should by no means be extended further than the freemen were not being as socially restrictive as they sounded to be by their vigorous arguments.

## The burgage-tenure franchises

The social composition of the voters in burgage-tenure boroughs was, if not identical, then at least very similar to freemen boroughs. They were minor boroughs, comprising a single manor, and hence the feasibility of a tenurial qualification. A factor which possibly increased the potential turn-out was the widespread uncertainty as to what exactly constituted a burgage tenure. As was suggested in Chapter 1, the election game was new, and the pressure to think out all the rules had not yet been felt everywhere. Consequently, confusion was evident at the 1614 Stockbridge election as to which tenures were the ancient burgages, and at Clitheroe there was some uncertainty about whether holders or subtenants of the burgages could vote; later still, before the 1678 and 1679 elections in Richmond, precise statements were needed of what an enfranchised tenure was. The borough records of Chippenham in the early 17th century give a fluid total of the numbers of burgages in the town.[26]

This uncertainty that was derived from novelty was not only important in maximising the potential electorate: it also helped to determine the composition of that electorate. The gentry and magnates failed to capitalise on the opportunities for exploitation presented by constituencies where voting rights were contingent on possession of certain properties until fairly late in the 17th century, which meant that the nature of the electorate had not yet been distorted. Before the outbreak of war (and even much later in several cases), the gentry or their nominees had not moved in on small townships like Castle Rising, Downton, Knaresborough or Richmond, and these thus retained their character as normal farming villages or market towns.[27] Late in the century, there were clearly burgage tenants at Richmond who were below the scot-and-lot level, and while hearth-tax data show the burgage tenants as more substantial than the population as a whole, 22 per cent of the former group in 1673 were rated at only one hearth, and were thus poor. There were in that year 336 houses in the town, while in 1696 the number of burgage tenants was fixed at 273, representing some contraction on the 1670s levels. The authority on the town's history opines that the franchise had remained constant throughout the century, and that the number of houses had only gradually crept up to the 1673 total, after a devastating plague late in Elizabeth's reign. If that is the case, then it is safe to conclude that the burgage tenants were a large majority of the householders in the town, and represented a fair cross-section of its population.[28] At Castle Rising also, the tenants of the 49 burgages seem to show no social peculiarity until late in the century. Again, the fact that in James I's reign there were 93 burgages in Marlborough, and only about 100 inhabitant householders within the town, is likely to mean that a burgage-tenure franchise there was not far from coterminous with a householder one.[29]

Marlborough and Richmond are probably at one end of the range, but it seems likely that the other extreme would not have limited the franchise especially rigorously, whatever might become the case as towns expanded in the 18th century. At Knaresborough, the 88 free burgages comprised some 44 per cent of the total households in the early 17th-century borough; at Clitheroe, 78 voted in the Long Parliament election, in a total population of some 800. Allowing for some failures to vote (only 25 polled in 1628 and about 90 in 1689), probably c. 50 per cent of the householders were burgage tenants. The proportion probably went lower, to about 1 : 3, in New Malton.[30] The 1624 House may have displayed some reservations about a burgage-tenure franchise, for in the Cirencester and Pontefract cases it refused to sanction the establishment of an electorate of freeholders, a group bearing some resemblances to burgage tenants, although it did uphold a burgage-tenure franchise at Chippenham. But if these objections, if such they were, were for reasons of the limitations imposed by burgage-tenure restrictions, they seem to have been misplaced, for in terms of their social content, the burgage-tenure franchises bore close comparison with the average freeman electorate.

## Scot and lot

Scot and lot was being suggested as the maximum and the norm by two commentators on the House's intentions in 1640, and it might be assumed to have been more socially extensive than the burgage-tenure or freeman electorates. But it would have had the effect of eliminating some of those qualified under those two forms. We have seen how in some boroughs there were freemen below the scot-and-lot line, and the same was true of some burgage tenants at Richmond. Those paying the rates and owing service in the borough court clearly did not include all householders, as becomes very clear from the Bedford material relating to the Long Parliament election, where non-scot-and-lot men were listed under the headings of both freemen and non-freemen householders.

At the end of the century, in the 1698 election for Amersham, 258 voted, and 85 of these were reported to be non-scot-and-lot men. While there were only about 200 houses in the mid-18th century, and some at least of those objected to in 1698 must have been outsiders or inmates (i.e. lodgers), the evidence suggests that some were also householders. There had been 173 manorial tenants in 1624, so there were new erections, probably cottages, in the town:[31] subtracting the 85 non-scot-and-lot men from the total 258 could well leave us with the 173 more substantial tenants, and the householders of the new erections would thus be among the 85. The potential exclusiveness of a scot-and-lot franchise is made more evident by the example of Marlow, which was not a scot-and-lot borough, but which provides valuable evidence. Here, of 245 voters in the Long Parliament election, 77 were said to have been almsmen and inmates (even though the definition of almsmen, as D'Ewes found, was questionable), and a further 96 were 'not givers' of scot, leaving allegedly a mere 72 out of a total of 245 inhabitant voters as scot-and-lot men. Even if some of the 96 are included on the grounds that they were merely temporary defaulters and were being calumnied for partisan purposes (but there was no massive disparity between the number of 'not givers' on either side, so this is not entirely likely), or that the compiler of the list was a pedant, objecting to some on a minute technicality, we are unlikely to find more than half of the adult male inhabitants as scot-and-lot men.[32]

Even if the allegations about Marlow were correct, it was probably an extreme case – the much fuller Bedford evidence shows not nearly as high a proportion of sub-scot-and-lot men. Over 600 inhabitants voted in October 1640, and a maximum of 109 of these might have been below the scot-and-lot level. Were we to subtract the 61 listed as inmates, servants and non-inhabitants from the total voters, to leave a total for householders, and assume similar failings on both sides, we would still find almost three-quarters of the householders capable of scot and lot.[33] What does emerge, though, is that scot-and-lot franchises, like others, are variable, and that there is no necessary progression, in degrees of open-ness, from freemen to burgage tenure to scot-and-lot electorates.

### Residence

Scot and lot was obviously not the most extensive of the franchises, judging by the Marlow and Bedford evidence. There were perhaps 26 inhabitant franchises, and while in some cases (probably Westminster, for one) this meant householder (as Glanville intended), in others it meant what it said. In Arundel, Bedford, Bramber, Chester, Marlow, St Albans and probably St Germans, it appears that all inhabitant adult males could vote.[34]

At Bedford in the Short Parliament election, 191 freemen had challenged the corporation franchise. In October, the process went even further, for a minimum of 600 inhabitants had voted before the poll list keeper abandoned his incomplete efforts, and the occupations of the 99 who can be identified include seven labourers, an ostler, a fellmonger, an oatmealmaker, three gardeners and a cottager.[35] Moreover, the evidence indicates that more than merely heads of houses voted. The poll list was compiled for partisan purposes by the defeated candidate, William Boteler, and most of his objections are directed against the votes of his opponent, Sir Samuel Luke. But it appears that Boteler was initially appealing to an identical constituency to Luke's, for there is no discernible social or occupational distinction between the supporters of either side, and it seems likely that it was only when he discovered that Luke was winning on the wide franchise that Boteler felt driven to challenge it. Thus, while most of the detailed objections are made against Luke's voters, there are queries set against an almost equal number of his own, and he actually lists one of his own supporters as being an inmate. His questioning of the credentials of his own voters must suggest that there was some factual basis for his objections to Luke's, and this conjecture is strengthened by the precision with which he dealt with his opponent's supporters. Eighty were certainly noted as receiving some form of charity (nearly twice that number if the very common annotation 'rec' signifies 'receives', as seems likely); only three were noted as begging from door to door — Petty's exclusion of such in the Putney debates would not have affected many of the Bedford voters. Boteler listed the parishes in which Luke's named inmate voters lodged, and gave the names of those who were the actual town almshouses' occupants, the Beadsmen, distinguishing these from those (named) who received charity from the various parishes, in turn dividing these into those who received 'monethly Collections', and those who merely 'receive out of the poore box, stocke and gifts'. He also noted two or three others as being servants.[36] Now this election was submitted to the Committee of Privileges, and judging by the material Boteler prepared, the point at issue was the character of the electorate. The election was not voided, and this must raise the whole question of almsmen voting.

### Almsmen

The contemporary orthodoxy, and one that has been largely followed by modern commentators, with the notable exception of Mr Keith Thomas, was that almsmen neither should, nor did, vote. Roger Williams in Massachusetts expressed great surprise to John Winthrop in 1636 that diverse unmarried, unestablished men should dispute 'the Freedome of the Vote' with the 'Householders of this Towne', and in Virginia in the 1650s, the franchise was given to all housekeepers. If we assume that Williams and Virginia were basing themselves on English experience, then non-householders, let alone almsmen, at the polls must have been thought an abhorrence. The 1621 election bill contained strong proposals that only householders should vote in towns, and when Chippenham was opened in 1624, and the Committee of Privileges reported that the inhabitants should vote, a neighbouring member who was present at the debate minuted angrily in his diary, 'In which noate that when Inhabytantes have voyces, it is not yntended that every hedge breaker, or Inmate or any servante showlde have voyce, but such Inhabytantes onelye as were Contributorye to all paryshe Charges, and boroughe Charges, and were properlye burgesses, Freemen of the borowe or freeholders and no other'. Similarly, a local observer reporting on the Long Paliament's opening of the Tewkesbury franchise to the fatally vague group 'the commonalty' observed that it was 'not resolved whether the election should bee by fremen only, or all the inhabitants', but added parenthetically afterwards, 'except almesmen'. And Prynne, over the same case, although prepared to accept the voting rights of the commonalty, contemplated with horror the prospect of the inclusion of almsmen, 'the very scum of the people'. It was quite possibly in this spirit that D'Ewes intended his well-known proposition 'that the poorest man ought to have a voice that it was the birth-right of the subjects of England and that all had voices in the election of Knights etc.'[37] The exclusion could have been so obvious that he did not trouble to make it, particularly given his reference to county elections, where the 40s. freeholders were known to be the ones with the vote, rather than all the freeholders.

But D'Ewes's statement was made in the context of a franchise dispute, at Marlow, where the issue was not about 40s. freeholders, but rather between the inhabitants at large and scot-and-lot voters, so perhaps his outburst was intentionally all-embracing, even if unthought-out in its implications. Mr Thomas has recently pointed to the ambivalent position of the House, and particularly certain members, on the question of the franchise in this period.[38] It is clear, as he observes, that the policy of the House was opening the door to an unprecedentedly broad section of the community. Majority opinion probably did not intend exactly that, as is suggested by the response to the Chippenham decision quoted above, or by the dilemma of many members over the Tewkesbury case in the Long Parliament. But unfortunately for the peace of mind of some members, little was made explicit.

Sandwich was opened to the commons in 1621, and by October 1640 its corporation was complaining of the refractory electoral behaviour 'of the meanest sort and such [of] them [as] are relieved by the parishes where they live'. When over 200 men voted in that election, in a total population of about 2000, the allegation that some were on relief seems plausible.[39] Warwick suffered a similar fate in 1628, which its town clerk bemoaned in terms suggestive of what he thought it would entail: 'now what election so ever folowes herein will be very costly to all: for that beggers expeckt almes and the meaner sort will doe much for a meales meat and lesse cannot be afforded to a hungry bely which in such a numerous place of peopell is no small charge'. Within twelve years he had brought about the very situation he had feared, for he used the vagueness of the House's decision of 1628 in an attempt to gain the rejection of an outside nominee. The bailiff was only prepared to accept the freemen's votes in the Long Parliament election, but he was advised by the same town clerk 'that now in this case of popular election he should alow all voates to all inhabitants how pore soever'. As Prynne perceptively observed when preparing his brief for the Tewkesbury case in 1641, the House's failure to define the commons could mean 'every servant, Almsman, Beggar-woman, and inhabitant whatsoever . . . shall have a voyce . . . and by consequence, the very scum of the people should over-rule the better sort, and those who pay the Burgesses their wages, the servants over-rule their masters, the children their parents . . . which would be absurd'. But this absurdity was not manifest to all. The boroughs restored to parliament in 1624 were deliberately left with an undefined franchise by the House, and by 1640 the inhabitants of Hertford had with a 'high hand' usurped the vote from the freemen who alone had voted previously.[40] In the case of Marlow, it was being credibly reported by 1640 that almsmen and inmates were voting. This allegation was rejected by D'Ewes after hearing the evidence,[41] but the confusion might reflect the fact that, as the Bedford evidence shows, there were different categories of almsmen, those merely receiving *ad hoc* gifts on occasion, and those in regular receipt of charity.

The House was thus at least indirectly responsible for the enfranchisement of some of 'the scum of the people', and this was not always abhorrent to members. The father of one of the members who sat on the contested return for St Germans in the Long Parliament wrote to a friend in the House to attack an attempt that was in progress in the House to limit the franchise to scot-and-lot men, 'for all of the Inhabitants of St Germans have tyme out of mynde . . . had voyces as well the poore as the rich and that only scot and lot men should have voyces (and nonne but they) ye never hard of'; and it would appear that the House allowed the votes of the inmates in the Bramber election. But the most revealing instance of all is provided by the official organ of the Commons itself in January 1662, in a debate over the recent St Albans election, where it was reported that the almsmen 'had had Voices Time out of Mind: And that the Committee was of Opinion, that they ought to have Voices'. The House resolved to agree with the Committee.[42]

It is clear then that inhabitants (male) in the fullest sense did vote in a number of cases. The attitude of members towards this was mixed. The House consciously refused to fix the franchise for restored boroughs, probably in view of the maxim that it could not legislate under the guise of mere orders of the House, rather than for any more devious political reasons. But it also persisted in using phrases such as 'of common right' when extending the franchise to the 'commons'. The results of the two tendencies can be seen at Warwick, Sandwich, Hertford and Marlow There was certainly uneasiness in the House at this: D'Ewes took pains to make clear that the supposed almsmen of Marlow had been exculpated to his satisfaction – they were at the least 'labouring men ... and tooke noe almes or towne collection'. One of the two bills to regulate elections that came before the Commons in the spring of 1641 contained the clause 'that none who tooke almes should have voices in elections' – which implies, as did the similar proposal in 1621, that some had voted until then. This proposal D'Ewes 'well allowed', though this reaction seems at odds with his defence of the 'birth-right of Englishmen' elsewhere. But another account of the bill saw its main proposals as being an unrealistic backbenchers' hotch-potch, aimed at banning spending on elections, and ensuring the payment of members, including knights of the shire, and it was possibly this, rather than opposition to its proposals on almsmen, that ensured its death in Committee.[43] Nevertheless, the fact that nothing was done on the latter front does indicate that there was no great anxiety to preserve the respectability of the political nation by the proscription of almsmen.

The adjudication of the franchise disputes demonstrates that the House was by no means averse to granting an undefinedly large body of men a voice. The Tewkesbury dispute shows the House's reluctance to decide on a question specifically excluding almsmen, even though there was no long prescription in their favour, as was alleged for the almsmen of St Albans after the Restoration. Repeatedly both House and Committee ducked the question of defining just who should be allowed to vote, with the result that the whole problem recurred in the 1641 by-election, and again the House failed to decide. Equally to the point was the Gatton case of 1641, where the Committee of Privileges concluded, with reservations, for the freeholders, rather than the inhabitants at large, and submitted several questions for the decision of the House. The doubts expressed were all specific to the case except one, where the Committee requested 'To receive the judgement of the House, whether one that receives alms of the parish, shall have a vote'. The House fell into 'long debate' on the queries, touching all the specific issues, and eventually reversed the Committee's recommendation and extended the vote to the inhabitants – but shirked any pronouncement on the problem of almsmen.[44] In keeping with their policy of upholding particular prescription against royal charters or municipal ordinances in the franchise disputes, the Commons were prepared to tolerate all inhabitants, including almsmen, voting where it could be shown (as at St Albans) that this was the custom. But even where no custom could be shown, the House appears to have been reluctant to act.

## Conclusion: totals

The tentative conclusion of this study of the electorate in county and borough must be that the House of Commons did not directly represent a social group extending merely from the knight down to the 'independent' husbandman and artisan. In the counties and in many boroughs, especially the larger ones, a considerably broader spectrum was exposed to electoral politicking, whether licitly or illicitly, particularly given the normal absence of a poll. Playing the numbers game in any meaningful way is made almost impossible by the lack of reliable figures, either for county populations (and even less for freeholders), or many urban electorates. Even where we do have figures for counties, it is difficult to derive much from them, for they are of votes cast, rather than for the actual electorate, and in counties the size of Yorkshire or Norfolk, or where a lengthy poll was in prospect, the two figures would be very different.

In the light of the evidence presented in Chapter 2, it would appear that Gregory King's published estimate of 180,000 families of freeholders at the end of the century would give too low a total for the county voters. At one point in his notes, King was prepared to contemplate the likely existence of 400,000 freeholders with incomes from land ranging from £5 to £50, with another 50,000-plus more substantial landowners above them.[45] The discrepancy must be accounted for by his uncertainty as to whether to treat the freeholder as a term denoting legal or social status – for the published estimates of freeholder incomes are far higher than the unpublished ones. An attempt at precision would be folly, but while King's unpublished estimates may err in the opposite direction to that of his published work, the widespread distribution of freehold, whether conceived of in the conventional or the technical sense, and the very high money value of land, must have put the total of 40s. freeholders at least somewhere in between the two levels. The uncertainty as to what was meant by the specification, and the lack of any effective check on those turning out, must have pushed the potential electorate even higher.

A figure for the borough electors must be added to the notional county sum. This too is irretrievable, as so many franchises and populations are unknown. Voting figures, some actual, some potential, are given for many of the non-county constituencies in Appendix V, and by 1640 the two types of total are likely to have been fairly similar, given the population density of towns, and the growing excitement. In those few where both figures are available, the correspondence does appear close – that is, a high turn-out was achieved. The sample given in the appendix is obviously unrepresentative, for a disproportionate number of the corporation boroughs are included, as a result of the greater availability of evidence from these. But bearing in mind the fact that freemen franchises, with often some hundreds of voters, were by far the most numerous, a conservative figure of 50,000 urban voters seems plausible – especially when it is remembered that no totals are known for the massive electorates of Westminster and Southwark.

A combined total for the electorate on the eve of war thus emerges well in excess of the 200,000 which Prof. Plumb advanced as a 'conservative estimate' for the end of the century, although the crucial difference would be that his figure would represent those who were likely to vote, given the many and repeated contests that took place then. While a figure of some 300,000 could be cited for the pre-war period as an equally conservative estimate, that would represent a hypothetical and potential electorate. Nevertheless, assuming a population size of some 4 ½ millions, and again taking a ratio of adult males to the rest of the population of somewhere between 1 : 4 and 1 : 6, it could be suggested that those capable of voting after the franchise decisions of the early months of the Long Parliament may have formed between 27 per cent and 40 per cent of the adult male population.[46] Such a large potential electorate would certainly help to make sense of the relatively unrestricted nature of political life in the early American colonies.

It would clearly be dangerous to make too much of such totals as those above, for by no means all exercised their rights, or rather pushed their claims (for rights had not yet been established), by voting. Many were not given the chance. But it does suggest that election candidates had to appeal not only to a wide social spectrum, but also to a very large number of men. An analysis of the breakdown of 1640-2 solely in terms of the alienation of the gentry and the middling men of the towns is unlikely to be sufficient. Those involved in the popular outbursts of the 1640s had clearly had some form of political education beforehand.

# Part II
# Elections

'When first this Parliament convened together
Who called for such as you? How came you hither?
Confess the truth, are you not some of those,
Who made the burghers drunk when you were chose?
Or bribéd them with hopes that when you die
You would bequeath their town a legacy?
Or be at least so neighbourly unto them
As none of those discourtesies to do them,
Which must undoubtedly have been expected
If they your proffered service had neglected
Though now you look upon us as if we
Your vassals and your slaves e'er long should be,
Are not you some of those who came and went
And spake and wrote and sued for our consent?
Are you not they who trotted up and down
To every inn and alehouse in the town
To gain a voice? Did not you for your ends
Crouch to your equals, importune your friends,
Court your inferiors, scrape acquaintance with
Mere strangers, feast the cobbler and the smith,
Nay more, upon the drunken tapster fawn,
And leave your word and promises in pawn
With chamberlains and ostlers, that they might
Be factors for you, being out of sight,
To move their customers who had a voice
To make you objects of their servile choice?'

George Wither, *Opobalsamum Anglicanum* (1646)
quoted in C. V. Wedgwood, *Poetry and
Politics under the Stuarts* (Cambridge,
1960), 90–1 (my thanks are due to
Conrad Russell for this reference).

# 6

# Control and Independence in Voting

The effectiveness of political education depended upon the intensity of the electoral experience gained. Had placid electors been merely trooped out to vote by their lords, then their acquisition of any sense of what a political act was would have been minimal, for they would have taken no independent initiative, and nor would they have had to think. Our task is to attempt to discover the extent to which unhindered choice on the part of the voters was possible. To conclude that many people were capable of voting, or even that many did vote, does not say much about the character of the democracy then prevailing. Recent or present-day regimes have boasted universal suffrage and 98 per cent turn-outs, and yet we would hesitate to call them democratic, by virtue of certain habits they display of channelling the popular will. Were that the case in the 17th century, the fact that a surprisingly large number of people could have voted, or sometimes did vote, would have been of little more than academic significance. We must determine the opportunities for genuine self-expression, and also the forms that self-expression took, in order to establish whether there was any wider political awareness at the lowest levels of the process. There certainly was such awareness at Westminster, more so as 1642 approached; but Westminster was not necessarily the mirror of England. If there had been an effective representative system, it should to some degree have been so.

Municipal politics, despite the efforts of magistrates and Stuart monarchs, provided a real training for many people. The Norwich shrieval election of 1627 occasioned a show of freemen solidarity, and some fairly sophisticated campaigning, with a poll list, a platform, and efforts to drum absentees back into the city for the poll; municipal elections in Shrewsbury in the 1630s evidently saw fairly similar developments. The fact that the London trained bands were out regularly on the eve of municipal elections in the late 1620s and late 30s suggests that excitement and disorder accompanied these.[1] The potential continuity between more or less conventional municipal activity and the disturbed events of later years is indicated by Dr Pearl when she points to the way in which the parliamentary puritans in London in 1640–2 adapted existing forms of ward organisation and popular involvement to their own ends. In the Shrewsbury troubles also there were suggestions that indigenous unrest on the score of the use of the town's charitable resources was beginning to merge with the rather more dangerous issues of Ship Money and the town's religion by the end of the 30s. Such occurrences were obviously atypical, and the politics of most municipalities were concerned with little more than private grievances and rivalries. But municipal politics, in those boroughs which were not completely closed, did provide a regular field of activity for the freemen (and often doubtless for more than the freemen, as other inhabitants might feel sufficiently involved to come along and heckle), in which they could gain some sense that their actions counted. This self-awareness was presumably what Lucy Hutchinson had in mind when she complained of the tribulations suffered by her husband as commander of the Nottingham garrison during the war. She attributed them partly to the fact that 'the Townsmen, being such as had liv'd free and plentifully of themselves, could not subject themselves to Government'.[2]

In the countryside there was clearly less opportunity for self-government, though in 'open' villages without a resident gentleman, such as Wigston Magna which has been so suggestively analysed by Prof. Hoskins, a capacity for communal decision-making survived. The village- and parish-meeting were certainly not unknown in the early 17th century, and while what passed there should not be categorised as simple democracy, it probably did move at least some way towards that elusive goal.[3] A further means by which the ordinary countryman could express his wishes or his grievances and assert his own worth was by rioting. This was by no means a blind and uncontrolled form of behaviour, and certain continuities between peasant protest and the organisation of the war years can be observed, for example in the collection of a common purse to fund the campaigns, in Huntingdonshire and Cambridgeshire in the 1630s, and among the regiments in the spring of 1647. Rioting was widespread in this period, as enclosure continued, and was particularly prolonged and co-ordinated in those areas – the extensive Fenland region, and the South-West – which were bearing the brunt of the royal fiscal policy of enclosure and exploitation. The assertion of a direct continuity of rural activism suffers somewhat when the major areas of peasant unrest in the South-West in Charles I's reign (the Forests of Dean, Braydon and Gillingham) are compared with the scenes of Clubmen activity in the war in the same region, for Prof. Underdown finds no exact correlation.[4] Nevertheless, the appearance of the communalistic Diggers gives concrete evidence of how the political upheaval of the war years could fuse with a long tradition of peasant protest, as does the manner in which assaults on Catholic houses in the summer and autumn of 1642 were often a pretext for forays against the manorial records.[5] Rural England before the war was not supine, and many of its inhabitants, like their urban neighbours, were presumably not totally ignorant of their own capacity for action, even if their objectives were very particularist.

Effective contact with national politics and issues primarily occurred at parliamentary elections. There had been signs of some attempt to influence the people both for and against government policy at the time of the benevolence and forced loan of 1626–7, with brief speeches defending the reasons for the expedients being made to some quite large crowds, and being countered, in parts of Nottinghamshire and Norfolk, and in London, with scattered broadsheets.[6] Allegations of a sporadic preaching campaign against the Spanish marriage attempts several years earlier, and incipient propaganda efforts by both 'sides' at the end of the 1630s through assize sermons and Scottish pamphlets, suggest that a wider audience was not left wholly untouched by politics beyond the parish pump.[7] But the most frequent, and legitimate, occasions for political expression came at election time, and only then could many people have gained any sense that they were acting on a wider stage.

A necessary condition for the acquisition of political experience through this medium is that the elections should have been contested, for otherwise, as was suggested in Chapter 1, participation, if it occurs at all, is of a very attenuated and formalised kind. While contests were few at the start of the century, some thirteen in 1604, they multiplied rapidly. A total fluctuating in the 20s and 30s was reached in the 1620s, with a temporary peak of c. 40 in 1624, which possibly testifies to the great political and religious excitement of that year. Indicative of the role of political tension in generating contests is the sudden leap that took place in 1640. There were a minimum of 60 contests in the spring, and 80 (about one-third of all constituencies) in the autumn. These are minimum figures, for the Committee of Privileges in February 1641 was said still to have about 85 cases outstanding: some of these presumably involved disputed elections as well as non-electoral privilege cases; not all contests produced petitions to the Committee (or left surviving evidence), so the sum of contests must have been higher than the 80 suggested. Furthermore, a full total of contests would not provide a maximum indicator for the generation of political excitement, for candidates sometimes canvassed extensively and then withdrew shortly before the time of the election when they found they had no chance, as happened in Oxfordshire in October 1640.[8]

A further breakdown of the totals of contested elections provides an illuminating glimpse of how many people may have had some acquaintance with politics. Only 79 constituencies appear to have gone uncontested in the generation of early Stuart rule, and the figure would undoubtedly be lower had more evidence survived. More significant is the fact that 25 of that total came from the tiny boroughs of Cornwall, Devon,

Dorset and Wiltshire, and conversely, only six counties appear to have gone uncontested. Appeals to the voters were made in the overwhelming majority of constituencies at some time, and these appeals were made in the larger and more populous constituencies. In terms of the involvement of numbers of people in the electoral process, many of the constituencies which went unfought were of minimal relevance anyway, given their minuscule populations. An examination of the constituencies which were repeatedly contested tends to confirm the suggestion that a large number of people had at least had the opportunity for gaining acquaintance with what an election was about, for it was the larger constituencies which were fought most, possibly because of the greater prestige attaching to a seat, possibly because such constituencies were more prone to develop conflicting internal pressures – although the histories of Gatton, Newport (Cornwall), Bristol and Norwich show there was no absolute correlation with size. A minimum of 44 constituencies were probably contested at least three times in the period, and fourteen of these were counties; the remainder included many of the largest towns, such as Westminster, Exeter, York, Reading, Coventry, Oxford, Gloucester and Canterbury. Eleven constituencies probably had five or more contests, and six of these were among the most populous counties, Essex, Kent, Middlesex, Norfolk, Somerset and Yorkshire. Possibly 38 constituencies, again primarily the larger ones, were fought twice in twelve months in the last elections before the war. It seems clear that there was a large and growing potential for popular participation in the basic stage of the representative process before the war. The question of the nature of that participation, and how free it was, remains.

### Influence

Election contests were becoming increasingly frequent, but as we saw in Chapter 1, they were not yet seen as a normal part of national life. The gentry had not yet fully fathomed out what elections were about, and what preparations they required, and in consequence, it seems likely that a larger measure of latitude was allowed to the ordinary voter than was later to be the case.

Many elections appear to have been almost matters of ritual, which must have diminished the number of stops that could be pulled by those concerned. Violence certainly occurred – D'Ewes during the Long Parliament complained of the frequency of 'armatae electiones', and the Council had been driven to order Welshmen to leave their swords at home when they went to the hustings in the 1620s – but this might be offset by other tendencies: the elaborate disclaimers, the formalised promises of support or reservation of votes, the belief that 'the decorum usually followed in such matters' must be observed, indicate that people were concerned to act rightly as well as to win (although of course being seen to act rightly may well have been an aid to victory).[9] No candidate, in any surviving poll list, is to be found voting for himself; Sir William Spring, who sat several times for Suffolk in the 1620s, took a peculiarly providentialist line about the whole business, refusing even to declare whether he was a candidate – God's will must be done, and Spring could therefore neither assert himself nor withdraw: God would provide, and for the individual to imply otherwise by acting would be a sin.[10] The elected member would truly be the elect of God by Spring's reckoning. The formality of arrangements could also have militated against electoral control, for the gentry, or at least the JPs, often sat separate from the crowd at elections, even apparently fenced off in an enclosure at the county election at St Albans in 1621.[11] The possibility of keeping a close check on the actions or shouts of tenants and underlings in the throng must have been drastically lessened.

Tenants were certainly expected to comply with their landlords' wishes. Instances of confidence on the part of the latter are too common, indeed almost universal, to be cited, and must be presumed to have had a basis in actuality, in that deference was forthcoming. But such loyalty was by no means guaranteed. The surviving evidence suggests that techniques of control were not yet fully developed, and would have been hindered anyway by the existence of many small independent landowners. Furthermore, the increasing political polarisation would probably have ensured that any control which was established could not have been fully effective, for as Prof. Plumb has suggested, electoral stability only obtains when issues are, if not dead, then at least quiescent.[12]

Tenurial pressure on voters was a factor to be feared, as the House's 1628 ban on compulsory listing of voters' names indicates. Lady Hobart, the wife of a participant in the Norfolk Short Parliament campaign, threatened that 'if thay revold we will turne them all out of there farms that ar our tenants',[13] and shortly afterwards royalists in Lancashire were planning to compile lists of tenants in order to evict those remaining recalcitrant. Such threats as these were evidently made, or were thought to have been made, to those who were vulnerable. It was reported that many of the burgage tenants of Whitchurch 'wer fearefull of their Landlord Mr Deane (who wrote his letter to them for Yong Mr Cheeke)' in 1614, and some of the Marlow voters in the Long Parliament election claimed that they had been intimidated by their landlords.[14] But the significant feature is the rarity of allegations of such threats, when the opposing candidates would have had much to gain from reporting them. Victimisation of dependants did take place, at Chichester in 1586 and in Norfolk in 1640, and urban authorities had measures to hand to deal with recalcitrants, whether by punitive taxation, by legal harassment, or by impressment for service in the army.[15] Nevertheless, although the House would probably have been sympathetic to complaints on this score, they were infrequent.

Most marked is the silence on the subject of tenurial pressure. It might be answered that if voters were freeholders, then they had little to fear. But the small man was quite likely to be the holder of more than one piece of ground, by a variety of tenures, and might be directly vulnerable that way; and if he was a copyholder for life or lives, thus possessed of a legal estate in his land, he might still hold with an uncertain entry fine, and so could be threatened through his heir. Even in boroughs, where some of the enfranchised may have been very insecure tenants, there were still few allegations of direct victimisation. As was suggested in Chapter 1, the art was slow in developing. Charges were made in Shrewsbury in 1638 of the municipal elections that 'Labouringe of voyces is soe frequent that Landlords tie theyre tennants that are Burgesses by theyre Leases to give theyre voyces with them, and diverse Burgesses complayne that it is a greevance to them, and they are often displaced for refusinge to give theyre voyces with theyre Landlords'. But Shrewsbury suffered from annual elections, and in the parliamentary sphere, 'labouringe of voyces' was not 'soe frequent', and there was less occasion to develop such forceful means. The ultimate sanction of eviction would anyway have been difficult, for as Dr Kerridge has demonstrated, most tenants possessed greater legal (although not necesarily economic) security than has often been thought. Richard Baxter may have been wide of the mark when he lamented that 'Gentlemen and Beggers, and Servile Tenants, are the Strength of Iniquity', for true villein tenures were hardly thick on the ground in the 17th century, and customary tenures were not so dependent on the lord's whim.[16]

Only possessors of insecure tenures were at risk to really crude pressure. It was reported of Sir John Stawell as he was raising forces for war in Somerset in late 1642 that he had said that because most of his tenants 'holdeth their lands by rack-rent . . . if they would not obey his command, he might out with them'. While he was not altogether correct in his estimate of the insecurity of leasehold tenants, the distinction he drew between the possibility of influencing various types of tenant is important. The same division between those who were vulnerable and those who were not was made by the lord of the manor of Wigan, Bishop Bridgeman of Chester, in his disgruntlement over the electoral behaviour of some of the inhabitants. He was involved in a long and hard-fought battle to exploit his manorial rights in the town, and to convert as many tenancies as possible into tenancies at will, and he tried to put this to political use after the 1628 election. He observed that 'my Tenants began to rebell against me and would doe nothing at my motion, nor would choose a Burgesse for this parliament whom I commended, and therefore, I would henceforth take all those Tenants at will into my own hand', but Lord Strange persuaded him to make an example of one only. But sadly for the strength of his influence, only a small proportion of his total tenants were tenants at will, and even they had been prepared to show a measure of independence.[17] The qualified potency of landlord influence can perhaps be estimated from the way in which one tenant at Marlow was being bribed by his landlord to vote the right way in the Long Parliament election. A further factor diminishing the impact of landlord pressure is suggested by the vagueness of the Earl of Salisbury's list of his Hertford-shire tenants in 1640: if the chain of communication was so bad, in the case of one of the most efficient great landlords in the country, that information and identification failed to get through, then the leaders of the biggest battalions may not have been completely effective electorally.[18]

Doubts about the efficacy of control are indicated by the existence of threats, for had absolute deference been displayed, these would have been unnecessary. At one stage in the Long Parliament campaign in Somerset, Edward Phelips (the son of the great Sir Robert), despite having been absent in London, talked modestly but confidently of 'having allready transferred . . . my interest in that inconsiderable number' of voters which he controlled, but he was soon driven to confess that because of the efforts being made on all sides in this contest, that control was insecure: 'this country was very well affected . . . before it was canvased but how it now stands I cannot give you a iust account'. Again later he complained that 'I scarce yet know how feirme my owne quarter stands to me they having ben soe over labored on all sides'. A contest, and canvassing, created the possibility of the erosion of traditional loyalties, and candidates in both Yorkshire and Norfolk tried to work through the constables as well as through the landlords.[19] It was doubtless this which John Potts had in mind in the spring of 1640 when he attacked the Norfolk canvassing as tending to 'defeat others' freedom' (although there was also probably the principled though naïve point that canvassing was indeed destructive of free elections, a contention of the 1626 election bill).[20]

Canvassing was itself only of qualified effect as a means of gaining votes, for its impact might wear off at the hustings. Sir Robert Phelips's rival in the 1614 Somerset election had put the matter succinctly, observing that 'we have to doe with a waveringe multitude which are apte to alter in the instant when I have done what I can leave the rest to god'. While the Salisbury listing for Hertfordshire, or abundant correspondence in Kent in 1640, shows that application was made to individual tenants, not everyone was confident of the success of this policy. Lady Hobart was largely pessimistic in Norfolk in 1640, believing that 'with them of the beter sort, Sir John Holland needs no advocat, for the factious and volgar sort, ... [they] never live out of fames false opinion, thay ar so mutch pure as thay can crye hosana and crusify with on breath, war't possible thay cold be constant, or hold on munth in on mind, I shold ... suspect Sir John Hollands losing it, but thay begin to come about'.[21]

The urban franchise disputes are evidence of independence on the part of the townsmen. The temptation might be to attribute this to the higher levels of education prevailing within towns, the stronger tensions which might build up in more compact communities, or the greater ease of mobilising opinion. The corollary would be quiescent rural populations. But independence, and not only in the extreme situation of a riot, was shown by those outside towns, if to a lesser degree. A recent study of Lancashire showed the yeomen and husbandmen frequently differing from the neighbouring gentry in their attitudes to the taking of the Protestation just before war broke out, and it has been suggested that the estate policy followed by the landlord could be decisive in determining whether he retained the loyalty of his tenants in the war. Prof. Underdown equally showed landlords in Somerset being deserted by their tenants in 1642. Although a civil war is obviously the ultimate solvent of ordinary social bonds, it was not the only occasion on which landlords found their tenants and inferiors failing them. The gentry of Cheshire were not just apprehensive of the expense of a poll when they formed a conclave in the field in 1628 to determine the result, by pressure on candidates to withdraw and by drawing lots.[22]

Outright opposition was not the only problem which the voters posed for the gentry. They often could not be counted on more generally. Sir Edward Dering's correspondence for the Short Parliament Kent election is concerned with ensuring the support of the gentry, on the assumption that they would carry the lesser men with them. Yet he was forced to record many defaulters, or failures to turn up, even among the voters from his own parishes. Thus, only three of the fifteen men from Egerton who went to Penenden Heath stayed to poll, and a further ten failed to make the journey; the figures for Bethersden, Charing and Smarden were as bad, or worse. When faced with a long poll, their loyalty could not be relied on, understandably if expenditure was low. Over a three- or four-day poll, initial excitement abated, and voters began to worry about their livelihoods. One of Secretary Windebanke's supporters in that same election for Berkshire realistically accepted the difficulty, after talking of the efforts which could be made with various tenantries: 'The election is usually made at Abingdon, and the men who come in the morning and go home at night, are those who usually carry the business. Our forest men ... will make excuses in respect of the long journey and charge.' Dering, in Kent, complained bitterly that, on hearing that a three-day poll was in prospect, 'Multitudes heereupon took their ease and went home so that of ten thousand thought to be in the field . . . there were polled on both sides but 2325'. At first sight this looks implausible, but his poll list tends to bear out his estimate, for of the 639 names he lists as having turned out for him, only 194 are endorsed as having stayed to poll and give their names – and many of the withdrawals came from parishes dominated by himself or his friends. Similarly, the Yorkshire voters in 1625, on being informed 'that the Pollinge would last three daies made as much shift to gett out of the gates unpolled as they could'. When the 1626 Cheshire election took so long that it allegedly caused a permanent increase in the price of meat in the city, reluctance on the part of the voters to stay for the duration was only too likely.[23] Mere landlords' requests were evidently insufficient to compensate.

Those actually turning out could cause problems other than those of outright disobedience. Many voters arrived at the polls uncommitted. Sir Thomas Wentworth warned one of his supporters in the campaign for Yorkshire in 1620 that several agents would be at the field early canvassing undecided freeholders; a participant in the canvassing for the Gloucestershire Long Parliament election reported that he found 'these parts as yet capable of a suspension, till they come into the field', and it was for a similar reason that Dering entered the field some time before his opponents in the spring election, in order to work on the arriving crowds. D'Ewes's account implies that Henry North did the same in Suffolk in the autumn.[24] A great deal of evidence suggests that voters often could not be controlled, and candidates' attempts to establish 'pairing' arrangements in contests, and thus profit from each other's unused second votes, seem to have been vulnerable to this. Pairing was in any case handicapped by a tendency for landlords to ask for only one vote from their tenants, and to leave the other free, but even without that added handicap, the effectiveness of pairing, when it can be observed in action, does not seem to have been total. Despite very strong pairing in Yorkshire in 1620–1, which developed into virtual internecine strife, one of the gentry present later testified to the Committee of Privileges that 'thousands' of Wentworth's supporters gave their second votes to one or other of the opposing Saviles; and although a clear opposition pairing (of Barnardiston and Parker) existed in the Suffolk election in October 1640, there was apparently considerable cross-voting for North with second votes.[25]

In order to cope with these signs of independence, electioneering techniques began to evolve, but as with other activity in the electoral field, they remained in their infancy. Some developments, most notably entertaining, were clearly essential, if people were to be persuaded to remain in the field for a long poll. In a county the size of Yorkshire, with great distances to be travelled, and thousands of voters making a long poll likely,

Wentworth's preparations in 1620–1 for treating all those involved, and not just the gentry, were thoroughly justifiable.[26] Accusations were levelled in 1640 that 'Beere and tobacco', 'inviting to alehouses', 'beefe, bacon and bag pudding', were beginning to sway too many elections, especially through the votes of the poor, suggesting that people were now awakening to the persuasive effects of drinks on the house – although getting a man drunk is not a permanent form of persuasion. Both Dering and his opponent Twysden professed to have been initially deterred from standing for Kent in the spring of that year by the likely expense, but such references to the prohibitive charge of entertainment are belied by the small scale of the expenditure involved where details are known.[27]

Rumours that £3000 were spent on the 1626 Yorkshire election by the Savile party put that so far in a class of its own, whatever the size of the county, that they must be considered doubtful, particularly as the arch-enemy, Wentworth, was not standing that year. If the Saviles were bringing in voters from the whole county, then it might have been a realistic figure for transport, compensation for loss of earnings, etc., but that would only mean that the much lower figures elsewhere betoken an even greater level of naïveté than would otherwise appear, if nobody had worked out the full techniques of management. Even when lodgings and diet were provided for, apparently, 1127 freeholders in the Derbyshire Long Parliament election by Sir John Coke, an outlay of only £256 17s. 9d. was involved. The Earl of Salisbury's expenditure in Hertfordshire in the spring was only just over £350, and while Prof. Stone points out that the candidates he was supporting would themselves have been spending, this must have been equally true in Essex, where the Earl of Warwick and his allies were involved, and yet Sir Thomas Barrington only disbursed £42 2s. 3d. in March, and this when the fathers of those concerned in the county had learned how to spend in 1604. Sir Robert Harley's expenditure of £155 9s. 6d. in Herefordshire that autumn may have been on a smaller number of voters, but the low figure is still significant: increasing excitement and experience seem to have raised the stakes, for six years later, in the Recruiter election, the Harleys spent £402 12s. 7d.[28] William Prynne's assertion that thousands of pounds were being spent on county elections in 1660 *may* have been true then (although it is unlikely), but the pre-war period was twenty years and several elections earlier, and the bills were not as large.[29] Either the voters had not yet pushed up the ante, or the candidates were not yet aware of the electoral possibilities inherent in money, or, again reflecting inexperience, few efforts were being made to bring in voters from all over the county.

The same conclusions hold for spending in the boroughs. Secretary Morton was reputed to have regaled Cambridge University with the fruits of £200–300 in 1625, and Hastings corporation alleged that one candidate laid out the incredible sum of £500 to attract the votes of the 31 freemen in March 1640; but these, and in particular the latter, are so far above the norm as to be as unlikely as the Yorkshire figure of 1626. Salisbury spent £72 7s. 2d. in entertaining all the Hertford voters in April 1640, and £47 in October; the cost of Peregrine Hoby's entertainment of Marlow in the autumn, which, with c. 250 voters, had about the same number as Hertford, was declared to have been only £14. Sir Henry Wotton spent £50 unsuccessfully on a similar number at Canterbury in 1625, and while £40 was allegedly expended on a much smaller number of voters in East Retford in 1624, many of the unenfranchised poor were also provided for, in the hope that they would apply pressure to their betters. Reports of other spending are of the same order of magnitude: £5 14s. 3d. on some 20-odd voters at Whitchurch in 1624, £10 at one of the Wigan elections of 1640 on over a hundred voters, £16 at Knaresborough at the same time though on a smaller number, £20 in the bitter 1645 Recruiter election for Grimsby to entertain perhaps some 50-odd freemen. Thus while Sir Robert Hatton may have spent £182 17s. 11¼d. in March 1640, this possibly went on Higham Ferrers and Castle Rising (both returned him), and probably included the (presumably large) fees of the three eminent lawyers who provided opinions for him on the franchise of the former borough.[30] Spending on entertaining was clearly not as developed as it was soon to become, especially if we take it that the electorate was not appreciably smaller than that of the early 18th century.

This appearance of infancy is even more obvious in the case of bribery, the 'buiing of winde and breath' as D'Ewes called it. The 1628 election bill had attempted to outlaw bribery, suggesting that it was seen as something more than a local problem, but the rarity of the accusations, and the minimal sums involved when charges were forthcoming, indicate that the abuse was small. One of the most common forms of bribery testifies to the economic climate, as well as to the novelty and relative harmlessness of the practice – candidates often offered a gratuity of a large dole to the poor, thus taking the burden off the inhabitants. As with entertainment, there are the occasional abnormally high figures – a Court official, Robert Read, was reported to have offered £20 down and £10 per annum, with quantities of powder yearly for the Hastings youth to exercise with, and £80 was mentioned in the Long Parliament campaign for tiny East Looe – but the usual figure was much lower.[31] The poor of Ludlow received 40s. in 1626, as did those of Okehampton in 1641, and Bridport had £5 in 1626; doles to the poor also featured at Bletchingley (£4 13s. 4d.) and East Retford in 1624 (although here it was the more substantial consideration of the building of a work-house). Tewkesbury appears to have been endowed with a considerable amount of land, whose rental would presumably eventually have benefited the poor, after its enfranchisement by James: it was probably in response to an extravagant gift by the financier, Sir Baptist Hickes, that a disappointed candidate in 1625 bitterly protested that 'tis not hee who brings most in his truest love, but brings most in his purse, shalbe accepted'.³² But again, this was a gift to the corporation, not to individuals (although naturally, individuals would benefit indirectly), and this was the normal form of what petty bribery, or possibly 'rewards', that there was. Bishop Williams, the former Lord Keeper, suggested that the antiquarian Sir Robert Cotton should offer some of his books to the Westminster vestry in 1628, and there are several incidents at this minor level. The only signs of a systematic attempt at bribing voters, rather than corporations, are a mere two petty allegations about the Marlow election for the Long Parliament, and the more weighty accusation that £3 per vote was offered at East Retford in 1624, although the charge was not accepted by the Committee of Privileges, partly on the ground that it was only substantiated 'singularis testis' – which must have made proof of any charge of this nature difficult.³³

Secretary Conway in 1628 saw the feasting of voters as being 'customary', 'ther being some, itt should seeme, that cann value worthe noe other waye', as Edward Pitt put it in 1640. Even if both of these were correct, and entertaining as a means of overcoming the waywardness of the voters or their propensity to go home was prevalent, the very small sums involved suggest that it was not yet an evil that had been perfected. Furthermore, the ties that treating formed could only be tenuous, for a drunken man is not always aware where his interest lies. A recent close study of a somewhat later election has emphasised that the decisive nexus of dependence was one of trade, custom and employment, rather than landlord-tenant relations or those engendered in the ale-house. Developments in this direction were probably even less advanced than the use of treating: only two clear allegations of candidates exploiting their role as major clients of tradesmen appear to survive, and at Wareham in 1640, Pitt was unsure whether a 'good debter' of his would be 'true and reall' enough to be an agent there.³⁴ If all the stops had been pulled, there should have been little doubt. But in none of the areas of 'interest' does there appear to have been any attempt to establish systematic and effective forms. This may have been because the identity of the voters on whom money was to be spent was still not entirely clear, and the need to build up connections was not yet fully felt.

To balance the positive appeal of money, the negative means of intimidation (other than tenurial) were being developed by those (by definition on the official side) with access to them. The result of Charles I's military delusions was that troops were at arms in the later 1620s and

1640, and it began to be realised that these could be used for electoral purposes. Voters were allegedly intimidated by billeting in Somerset and Lewes in 1628, and by impressment in Monmouthshire in 1625, and East Grinstead, Hastings, Sandwich, and Northamptonshire in 1640.[35] The disappointed courtier Sir John Suckling went as far as to assert that there was a semi-official Court policy of using troops to this end in 1628, but while the Court, and the local Deputy-Lieutenants, clearly were involved in the efforts in Cornwall to prevent the election of Eliot and Coriton (those accused in the Commons being rewarded by the Court), there is little evidence of a coherent resort to this expedient.[36] Nevertheless, the trained bands were useful and used, in that they provided a large and compact body of men, and one furthermore which was under orders. They therefore seem to have been the basis for spreading propaganda and even for canvassing outside the 1628 Cornwall election, in Kent and Bossiney in the spring of 1640, and in Essex, Worcestershire and Yorkshire in the autumn.[37] But again, these developments are interesting chiefly for the contrast they provide with the sophisticated methods of later years.

Much more common was an informal appeal, aimed particularly at those arriving in the field undecided. Many candidates strove to mount what must have been a cross between a circus and a para-military display of strength, in order to impress the 'floating voters'. Wentworth's plans to array his support at Tadcaster in 1621, and then to march on York in a body, are the best documented, but they could be duplicated by Sir Robert Crane's and Sir Lionel Tollemache's organisation in Suffolk that year, or by that of some of the Cornwall contestants in 1628.[38] The dramatic impact of such a cavalcade was then heightened by activities in the field itself, designed to bring the candidate home to the notice of the voters, and to provide a rallying-point for support. When Sir Robert Gawdy found himself losing the 1624 Norfolk election, he had himself carried down into Norwich market-place from the Castle, and thence to the Maid's Head tavern, attempting to attract vulgar favours; and all the candidates had been chaired into the field initially. Chairing took place in Abingdon and in Suffolk in 1640, and its tactical importance was testified to by what was possibly the survival of an earlier form in the Yorkshire election to Richard Cromwell's parliament. One candidate gained half his votes 'after hee mounted his horse', while another, 'att the First nameing of him had a generale voice for him but haveing noe horse could not manage it amongst the crowde'.[39]

The conventional practice whereby the candidates stood by the sheriff, or sat on the bench with him, was being superseded through a new concern for persuasion. The presence, and importance, of wavering voters was newly appreciated. The candidate must be seen, must show himself to as many as possible. The fact that means were being made for votes, not only before the election on a tenurial basis, but also in the field on a non-tenurial, and often doubtless on a counter-tenurial, basis emphasises that the disposition of votes was not always assumed by gentry alignments. While the employment of such popular tactics was becoming noticeable, they were still in their infancy: the first report of the wearing of party favours does not occur until early 1642, in Yorkshire, when blue ribbons were worn by a party of anti-iconoclast vigilantes; for most candidates, purely personal appeals sufficed.[40] The means indicated above were still oddities. The independent voter was clearly a problem at this date, but one which most candidates had not yet discovered how to exploit. This relative innocence on the part of those who were bidding for votes could only increase the possibilities for independence amongst the voters.

### Voting behaviour

The failure of pairing in Yorkshire and Suffolk, absenteeism in Kent and Berkshire, Lady Hobart's apprehensions in Norfolk, have been cited to indicate that voters did on occasion cause problems for their superiors. Sometimes defections could be explained by *force majeure*: the voters in Berealston in the Long Parliament election were said to have been torn from their proper loyalties by bribes and threats.[41] But this is of little help in determining whether those proper loyalties would normally have been sufficient. The major barrier of the lack of evidence obstructs any attempt to answer such questions, for they require either more than one poll list, or a poll list and allied background evidence. While poll lists are more common than was once thought, it is extremely difficult to find the necessary series, or adequate supporting material for a single one.[42]

There are, however, a few constituencies for which conclusions on voting behaviour can be made. It would be folly to attempt to generalise from these, for the sample is far too small, and does not spread over all types of constituency. It is therefore much less satisfactory than the evidence available for the social composition of the electorate, for which a single poll list can provide useful data, if the size of the constituency is known, and where a wide range of the constituencies is covered. But it does at least allow insights into a subject which has previously been, for this period, completely obscure, even if it fails to provide firm foundations for statements about the subservience or otherwise of the populace. The compatibility of such insights with other electoral characteristics of the period, notably the uncertain and tentative nature of developments, suggests that they might not be altogether inaccurate.

The Kent poll list for the spring of 1640 is of limited value. It was compiled by Dering partly for self-vindication after his defeat, partly for a check on his strength beforehand, and in many parishes he can only give the names of the gentleman and minister, although for the parishes around his own residence, and that of his opponent Sir Roger Twysden, he is much fuller. Dering as we have seen could not rely on his support when it came to a long poll, and many of his lowly neighbours whom he had apparently counted on did not even trouble to make the journey to the election. While there was then a measure of disobedience, it was qualified. Although Dering noted defaulters among those around him, this only extended to absenteeism: it did not include voting for Twysden. The actual voters from his own area appear to have been solidly loyal, and equally, he did not note himself as having picked up a single vote from the parish of Yalding, near to Twysden, whose eighteen voters all went for Twysden. Very few parishes were noted as being split: of the rural parishes covered, only Eastwell divided, and there the resident gentleman was opposed by the minister. And beyond that, only among the Dover and Maidstone voters are significant instances of division recorded, and it was only to be expected here, in a more independent urban environment. Unfortunately, analysis of these towns is pointless, for only men of high status are included, and on the evidence of Godmanchester in 1625, more urban freeholders than that are to be expected. Differences among the more substantial were obviously only too likely: but it seems that when the Kent rural populace were given a clear lead by the gentry, opposition only went as far as absenteeism.[43]

But the Kent listing is also suggestive of the impact of political issues at elections. The poor may well have divided along geographical or tenurial lines, but alignments higher up the social scale, amongst the intelligentsia, were rather different. Dering lists 23 clergy as supporting him, and fifteen of these suffered in the ensuing decades of religious upheaval: all of them suffered at the hands of the Parliamentary authorities. Five clergy are given as favouring Twysden, and four of these suffered: only one under Parliament, but three at the Restoration. The rumours branding Dering as pro-Court and perhaps doubtful in religion had had a pronounced impact on the educated.[44] Voters in 1640 were capable of being moved by factors other than the ties of personal relationships.

Clear evidence to this effect is unfortunately difficult to come by. In the Long Parliament election for Bedford borough, Sir Samuel Luke, son of a man who must have been recognised as strongly anti-Court, was opposed by William Boteler, either the Ship Money sheriff of 1638, or a man of the same name probably still more distasteful to the godly. There is then the possibility of a division along national lines at the election. That it may have been seen in these terms by some of the voters is suggested by the presence among Luke's supporters of an ardent clerical nonconformist, and seven of the eight clearly identifiable future members of John Bunyan's congregation.[45]

The only other election where there is a modicum of evidence which might help to confirm such alignments is that in the autumn for Norwich. Pym intervened strongly in the House's debate on the dispute, and the candidate he seems to have favoured, Richard Cateline, had been one of the Norfolk Feoffees who aimed to provide a more godly preaching clergy. Given the normally highly political character of Pym's interventions, it would appear likely that some political divide lay at the root of this election, and the survival of very fully subscribed rival indentures for the election make it possible to test the hypothesis. Supporters of Cateline's opponent John Tooley provided the backbone of the malignant party within the city, and some of their most belligerent opponents were to be found on Cateline's side. But Tooley had also been a Norfolk Feoffee, and in 1643 was appointed to the county sequestration committee, while Cateline eventually inclined away from Parliament. While four of Tooley's supporters had been in a pro-Laudian group within the corporation in 1636, so had one of Cateline's, and another was one of those arrested as royalists in 1643.[46] The divisions were evidently not hard. But most significant is the list of subscribers to the parliamentary collection for the regaining of Newcastle in 1643: there were 33 signatories to the indenture for Cateline, and of these nine can be identified as paying and nine as refusing; of Tooley's 29 signatories, four paid and eleven refused. There was possibly some national bias in the recorded alignment in the autumn of 1640, but if so it was very slight. More likely as an explanation of the division is a rather more particularist one: the signatures to the rival indentures were of course the city notables, and the senior magistrates openly objected to the fact that Cateline, an outsider, was standing. The more substantial worthies therefore went for the local man, Tooley, even though he eventually showed himself more zealous than his rival. The high degree of malignancy amongst Tooley's supporters, and indeed its relative frequency amongst Cateline's, merely reflects the vested conservatism and malignant bias of senior and wealthy oligarchs, and was incidental to the more localist division which occurred at this level at this time.[47] There is unfortunately no evidence for the humbler voters, but at the magisterial level at least, local factors rather than the impact of national politics seem likely to have been crucial at this election. The alignments of 1642 did not determine local loyalties in 1640.

The bulk of surviving evidence of voting performance tends to argue against any assumption of the widespread existence of real political sophistication at this stage. But what is striking about the data is the evidence of lack of control of voting which it reveals. At Wigan, poll lists are extant for the 1628 and both 1640 elections. The lists are divided into categories of inhabitant and out-burgesses, and both groups show a marked increase in the numbers of those qualified to vote (of 30 per cent and 338 per cent of in- and out-burgesses respectively); they also show rising turn-out, the out-burgesses' performance rising from c. 10 per cent to 25 per cent to 32 per cent, and that of the in-burgesses from 78 per cent to 85 per cent to 90 per cent – a surprisingly high level, which is matched by that in one or two other towns in 1640.[48] These rising totals suggest a growing interest on the part of the electorate.

But the most obvious peculiarity of the voters is their volatility, and this can be seen fully in the placing of votes in the two 1640 elections, where the three candidates polling most votes stood both times. There were 119 inhabitant burgesses capable of voting in both elections, and 97 (or 82 per cent) did so. Their behaviour is best expressed in tabular form, as in Table I. Here, nearly 50 per cent changed their votes, or about 44 per cent

TABLE I

| | |
|---|---|
| Voting the same way in both elections | 49 |
| Reversing the order of preference[49] | 16 |
| Altering the second choice | 12 |
| Altering the first choice | 1 |
| Altering one choice, reversing the placing of the other | 12 |
| Casting only a single vote on one occasion | 3 |
| Voting for someone in spring who was unavailable in autumn | 4 |
| total | 97 |

if the four who voted for candidates who only stood in the spring, and who therefore had to make a change in the autumn, are omitted. Granted, the mere reversal of the order of preference is only a small change, but 30 per cent made a more significant alteration than that. A further measure of the idiosyncrasy of the voters is provided by those who did not vote. 30 of the 43 (or about two-thirds – itself a sign of great apparent interest) who were capable of voting in all three recorded elections did so; of the thirteen who failed, five voted in both 1640 elections, four voted in 1628 and for the Short Parliament, two in 1628 and for the Long Parliament, one for the Long Parliament only, and one did not vote at all. This does not provide very compelling evidence for a great increase of fervour between 1628 and 1640.

The gentry out-burgesses show a similar pattern, although one which marks a relatively greater peak of interest in 1640. Of the more than 150 out-burgesses capable of voting in both 1640 elections, only 25 (or c. 16 per cent) did so; these divided as in Table II. Here, 52 per cent voted the same way, and 28 per cent voluntarily made a major change, proportions which are virtually identical to those of the in-burgesses.

TABLE II

| | |
|---|---|
| Voting the same way | 13 |
| Reversing the order of preference | 4 |
| Altering the second choice | 4 |
| Altering the first choice | – |
| Altering one choice, reversing the placing of the other | 2 |
| Casting only a single vote on one occasion | 1 |
| Voting for someone in spring who was unavailable in autumn | 1 |
| | total 25 |

Perhaps the most significant fact was that in both cases, these changes represented volatility rather than swing. The voters altered their choices in every conceivable way: rather than going, say, just from A to B and C, they also went in similar numbers from B to C and A, and from C to A and B. There is no discernible pattern in the movement; and there is no hint in the surviving correspondence or other material of any political or personal factor which might have changed people's votes – indeed, neither of the two identified recusants in the town voted for their co-religionist candidate, Sir Anthony St John, in the spring of 1640. What strikes most about the electorate, then, is its almost random behaviour – behaviour which became more random further down the social scale, for only one of the eight aldermen or town officials voting both times voluntarily changed his vote, and only one reversed his order of pre-ference. Further down the list of precedence, which judging by the available wills has some bearing on relative substance, behaviour becomes more volatile.[50] The votes of the lower levels of the community were less ordered than were those of the more substantial.

An analysis which attributes the result to the influence of the lord of the manor cannot therefore tell the whole story, for the voting does not look controlled. As we have seen, Bishop Bridgeman thought that he had trouble with his tenants when his brother Edward was elected in 1628, and there was some basis for this. But his suspicions about his tenants-at-will seem partly unfounded, for of those who can be identified, only one failed to vote for his brother, although six made him second choice, as against a single first vote for him. Overall, however, the voting figures show a strikingly inconclusive connection with tenure. Bridgeman was landlord of some 44 per cent (40 out of 90) of the inhabitant burgesses in 1627, and of these, only 23 (57.5 per cent) voted for Edward Bridgeman, only one putting him first choice, the rest preferring Sir Anthony St John, who was probably the Duchy nominee. Four (10 per cent) voted for other candi-dates, and thirteen (32.5 per cent) failed to vote at all. This compares with the figures for *all* inhabitant burgesses, where 22 per cent (ten per cent down) failed to vote, and where 65·5 per cent gave a vote for Bridgeman. In sum, Bridgeman's tenants had a poorer voting record for his brother than did the burgesses as a whole. Thus, while Edward Bridgeman was elected, and while it is probably fair to attribute this to his brother's influence, the connection between the two facts was probably not as direct as it might appear.

The neighbouring borough of Clitheroe also illustrates this phenomenon of apparently random voting. Unfortunately, the poll lists here are not continuous, surviving only for 1628 and the Long Parliament; but they do compensate by listing the votes cast in separate elections for the first and second seats in 1628, and these reveal great peculiarities. Twenty-five polled in 1628, and the sample is therefore too small to be wholly reliable, but the conclusions it yields are compatible with those from other elections, and worth citing. The voting figures are shown in Table III.

TABLE III

| For the first seat: | Thomas Jermyn | 12 |
| | Richard Shuttleworth | 9 |
| | William Nowell | 3 |
| | Richard Aske | 1 |
| | | |
| For the second seat: | William Nowell | 11 |
| | William Fanshawe | 8 |
| | Richard Aske | 2 |
| | Ralph Assheton | 2 |
| | Richard Shuttleworth | 1 |
| | Thomas Carew | 1 |

Nowell received three votes for the first seat, but eleven for the second, which might suggest the transfer of second votes from the successful first candidate to those remaining, or of status considerations working against him for the first seat. But Shuttleworth received nine votes in the first instance, and only one in the second, and that one had not supported him for the first seat. There was more or less an exchange of votes between the two. Additionally, two of the three voters who supported Nowell for the first seat went for another for the second, as did the single voter who supported Aske for the first seat – and none of these three went for the three new candidates who stood for the second seat only. They all voted for men who had been available for the first seat. Only one voter remained loyal to his first choice in the second election.

But some patterns are visible. All those voting for Fanshawe, the Auditor of the Duchy, had earlier voted for Jermyn, also a Duchy candidate, which only left four of the latter's voters to scatter. And although there was such a strange reversal of the positions of Nowell and Shuttleworth, both local

men, the bulk of their total votes did stay with them jointly: seven of
Shuttleworth's first votes went for Nowell second, as did one of Nowell's,
which means that, as with the Duchy supporters, only four of the combined votes of these two local men scattered. But that only gives sixteen
voters (64 per cent) following a discernible pattern. The remaining nine
(36 per cent) seem thoroughly idiosyncratic. Again, the visible results
provide predictable conclusions, the victory of a Duchy nominee for the
first seat, and of a local gentleman for the second. But the way those
results were come by shows far more confusion than is visible on the
surface. And this confusion seems to have survived to 1640, when a
different system of voting was followed, all the votes being cast together,
and the two highest totals winning: 78 voted this time, and six of these
(or 8 per cent) cast only one vote.[51]

The Hertford lists of 1624 and 1628 are not of much use for establishing varying loyalties, for only one candidate stood in both elections and
there is thus no chance of discovering how much support was retained
over a period of time in face of similar competition. But as at Clitheroe,
the 1624 election featured separate polls for first and second seats, and
these reveal similar idiosyncrasies. Of the 244 polling, 23 (or almost 10
per cent) cast a vote for the second seat only, rather than the more prestigious first, even though their choices had also been available for the first
place; and conversely ten (over 4 per cent) voted only for the first place.
Three of these must be excluded as supporters of the successful first
candidate, who possibly found no attractive contender for the second seat;
but the other seven were supporters of candidates who had been defeated
for the first seat, and who were standing again. The disposition of second
votes (see Table IV) also reveals peculiarities. Again, a pattern is discernible. A linking of Salisbury and unofficial Prince's Council influence
secured victory for Ashton and Fanshawe: the transfer of 70 per cent of
Ashton's second votes to Fanshawe seems evidence of this. But beyond
that, very marked divergences set in. Eighty-three per cent of Willowes's
support stayed loyal to him; but although official pressure was probably
applied for Fanshawe (the gentry and corporation voted overwhelmingly
for Ashton and Fanshawe in that order), he held only 50 per cent of his
votes – while Harrington, the Prince's official nominee and a local
gentleman like the others, kept only 21 per cent of his, and saw the bulk of
it go to Willowes. There was not even constancy in the inconstancy of
voters for these contestants. It could be argued that such confusion must
have been atypical, for Hertford had only just been restored to representation, and this was its first election, let alone its first contest, and
people might therefore not have known what they were about. But many
other constituencies were experiencing their first contests at this time,
so Hertford may not have been so extraordinary. A simple verdict as made

TABLE IV

| 1st votes for | 2nd votes for | |
|---|---|---|
| William Ashton (103) | Thomas Fanshawe | 70 |
| | Sir William Harrington | 25 |
| | (Richard Willis?) Willowes | 5 |
| | No second vote | 3 |
| Willowes (58) | Willowes | 48 |
| | Harrington | 6 |
| | Fanshawe | 3 |
| | No second vote | 1 |
| Harrington (42) | Willowes | 27 |
| | Harrington | 9 |
| | Fanshawe | 3 |
| | No second vote | 3 |
| Fanshawe (18) | Fanshawe | 9 |
| | Willowes | 3 |
| | Harrington | 3 |
| | No second vote | 3 |

(In addition, 23 failed to vote for the first seat.)

by Prof. Stone, that the Salisbury 'ticket' won conceals as much about the electorate's behaviour as it reveals.[52]

Continuing the analysis to 1628, when there was a contest for the second seat, Fanshawe standing against a town gentleman and future Parliamentarian county committee activist, Gabriel Barbor, less firm conclusions emerge. Fanshawe carried it by 100 votes to 68 (the turn-out having declined substantially, even allowing for some single voters for the first seat), and 81 of his voters had appeared in 1624. The bulk of these, 44, had voted Ashton/Fanshawe, or for Fanshawe alone, so there was a degree of consistency; conversely of the 57 Barbor voters who had polled in 1624, 41 had not voted for either Fanshawe or Ashton, so there may have been a constant group of anti-official voters. But Barbor also received the votes of 5 Ashton/Fanshawe voters, and 2 who had gone for Fanshawe alone, implying some change of direction. But these suggested alignments are too tenuous to be of much use, for they suffer from the absence of continuity of candidates. Much more significant is the impression of uncertainty or uncontrol which emerges from the 1624 figures: only 137 out of the full 244 (about 56 per cent) voted Ashton/ Fanshawe, or were consistent in whom they wanted. This is a total remarkably similar to the level of consistency in the two Wigan elections of 1640, or to the more unreliable figure for Clitheroe.

It is impossible to establish tenurial relationships for the Hertford voters, for the borough rentals only commence in the 1630s, and the first clear Salisbury list of tenants in the town is for the county election of 1640, and to attempt to read back from then to a fairly small sample, and one therefore subject to a high margin of error, in 1624 would be too risky. Other possible causes of division are also questionable: Barbor was a faithful nonconformist after the Restoration, but his two identifiable fellow-travellers in the town split in 1628, and judging by the dubious evidence of the formulae of wills, committed puritans were as likely to vote for the future royalist, albeit anti-recusant, Fanshawe as for Barbor.[53] Occupational categories are only marginally helpful. The elite of the town voted Ashton/Fanshawe in 1624, and for Fanshawe in 1628, and the more respectable occupations tended to be more loyal to that alignment than those further down the social scale, who had a greater propensity to scatter.[54] But the divisions are by no means clear, and there was certainly no general rejection of the 'official' candidates by the artisans and craftsmen. On the whole, however, the picture confirms that derived from Wigan, of a greater degree of volatility among the lower levels.

This would be expected anyway, given the character of urban politics which is revealed by the franchise disputes, although the slight divergence between retailers and those in less respectable callings is interesting, and suggests that the stereotype of the docile retailer, bound by occupational ties to the elite, and the more obstreperous artisan may have held good even then. This is indicated also by the divisions among the freemen of Hastings in the Short Parliament election. Those opposed to the corporation included: 1 doctor, 1 baker/miller, 1 innkeeper, 3 mercers, 2 tailors, 1 yeoman, 1 butcher, 1 blacksmith, 1 shipwright, 1 tallow-chandler, 5 fishermen and 2 sailors; those going with the corporation were: 1 attorney, 1 scribe, 1 brewer, 1 innkeeper, 1 innkeeper/barber, 1 mercer, 1 baker, 1 cooper, 1 tailor, 1 fisherman.[55] While the margins in both Hertford and Hastings were very small, there does seem to have been something of a social divide.

The unpredictability of voting behaviour is suggested by two other instances. In the Long Parliament election for Oxford, 657 votes were cast for the first seat, and 759 for the second, which means that at least 100 of those present (or c. 13 per cent) did not vote for the more prestigious first seat. Furthermore, Recorder Whistler was defeated in the Short Parliament election, but he took first place in October.[56] Likewise, at Stockbridge 12 per cent cast only one vote in 1614.[57] And in the Short Parliament election for Higham Ferrers, 22 of those who had signed a 1638 petition as tenants of the Queen voted – but despite their tenurial relationship to officialdom, ten of them voted against the Queen's Council's official candidate, and against her steward Sir Robert Hatton, in favour of a local, and later Parliamentarian, gentleman, Edward Harby, who was married into one of the town's leading families.[58] As in Wigan, tenurial ties do not seem to have been all-sufficient.

The conclusions which can be derived from such sparse evidence must be very tentative. Influence obviously did count greatly, but its effect was probably more the creation of an intangible relationship of subordination, rather than of the enforcing of loyalty along directly tenurial lines. Security of tenure would have lessened any impact, and from other evidence, there does not seem to have been much systematic intimidation by landlords – although as the Salisbury efforts in Hertfordshire suggest, there clearly was some coherent pressure. But in Wigan and Higham Ferrers at least, tenure does not appear to have determined the disposition of votes unduly. And more generally, the high level of volatility which existed in all the constituencies for which there is evidence indicates that any influence was not wholly effective.

This volatility is probably the most important fact to emerge from the voting figures. The fact that so many men cast only one vote, often for the second seat, and the infidelity of voters in Hertford in 1624, in Clitheroe in 1628, and in Wigan in 1640, suggests that many of the participants were still confused.[59] Some discernible alignments did exist, and among a majority of voters, such that the 'influence' candidates won; but this majority was a small one, and nearly as many seem to have voted in almost a random manner. Just as electoral arrangements were uncertain and in their infancy, so, it appears, was the voters' knowledge of what was happening. There was clearly much need for the techniques, such as chairing of candidates, mass entertainment and campaigns on issues, which were being developed to supplement personal and tenurial appeals.

# 7

# The Electorate and Politics

## *The political impact of the wider franchises*

Contemporary commentators, especially in the war years, were firm in the belief that the meaner sort were hostile to the Court. Hobbes's statement in *Behemoth*, cited in Chapter 4 above, that the freeholders and tradesmen inevitably elected men who were likely to vote against subsidies, is the clearest instance of this, though some of the more subtle observers would have qualified it with the rider that the real and apolitical poor were only swayed by the appeal of 'beefe, bacon and bag pudding'. In general, though, an increase in the size of the electorate should have been calculated to increase the potential support for the national opposition, and to increase the frequency with which national political issues featured at the hustings. This might have been especially the case if, as we have seen, voters lower down the social scale were less secure in their allegiances, for the corollary of that could have been that they were more vulnerable to immediate and excited appeals to their political prejudices.

Where this hypothesis is most open to investigation, in an examination of what happened electorally to those boroughs which suddenly found their franchises expanded, it proves to be of only limited validity. For the local ingredient in urban politics, the tendency of insurgent groups to react against whatever the corporation might be doing, disrupts any facile equation. Even the assumption that the possibility of controlling the voters would be minimised by increasing their numbers sometimes did not hold good in face of local conditions. Examples can be found of franchises being kept closed in order to undermine the power of the local lord, in the belief that men of substance are more capable of withstanding blandishments than men of no worth (Gatton and Bletchingley are cases in point). Other instances exist of franchises being widened in the interests of closer control (albeit from a slightly later period) – the electorates of both Malton and Aldborough in Yorkshire were enlarged to this end in 1659 and the 1670s respectively. The accompaniments of an open franchise were not necessarily such as would have borne out the assumptions of its supporters in parliament. The existence of a wide franchise was clearly not incompatible with close electoral control: the domination of Arundel by the Earl, or of Amersham by the Drake family, is evidence of this – Algernon Sidney was later driven to appeal to a limited group in order to break this hold on Amersham.[1] When even the basic proposition that large numbers meant freer elections was open to some doubt, there can be little wonder that the more confused area of political alignments should not always have lived up to expectations.

Even in those boroughs where real popular pressure had played a considerable part in the extension of the franchise, there was little marked change in their electoral fortunes. This was perhaps unsurprising if freeman activity merely manifested resentment against the corporation, and not any widespread consciousness of what the vote and parliamentary burgesses were for. Thus, after the Dover electorate was expanded in 1624, a break in continuity ostensibly occurred in 1626 when the nominee of the Lord Warden (the Duke of Buckingham) failed to gain election. The pretext was that the letter of recommendation had come too late, though the Duke's Lieutenant of Dover Castle opined that there was more to it than that. But identical events had taken place in nearby Hythe in 1625, and there the decision was the corporation's, albeit the freemen were subsequently persuaded to avow the act in order to spread the burden of responsibility. It would be dangerous to attribute the Dover election result of 1626 solely to the intervention of the freemen in 1624, for the Lord Warden had a high degree of success in other years, getting both members in 1628.[2] Conditions had probably changed by the autumn of 1640, however, when two local men were elected in face of a recommendation from the Lord Warden. As in the case of Hythe's resistance in 1625, this might be attributed to the decision of the magistrates, were it not for a report later in the year that 'the Rable' were 'the best men in the repute' of the town's members, indicating that that same rabble may have had some role in their election. Nevertheless, the Lord Warden's nominee was successful in the by-election of 1641, so, in all, the extended franchise does not seem to have been of decisive impact in Dover. Likewise, Hythe, although opened, elected a nominee of the Warden to the Long Parliament, and Sandwich followed an even more idiosyncratic path than did Dover.[3]

For some years after the 1621 election, there seems to have been a high degree of continuity with the pre-1621 situation in Sandwich. The 'popular' candidate of 1621, John Boroughs, was one of Lord Chancellor Bacon's secretaries, so the popular fervour of that year does not appear to have been anti-governmental. Furthermore, the object of popular hostility in 1621, Sir Robert Hatton, was elected in 1624 on the open franchise, as was another courtier, Francis Drake; one official nominee in 1625, Sir Henry Wotton, was elected, although Buckingham's decision to try for both failed (the failure being the son of the hero of 1621, Sir Edwin Sandys, who was said to have been 'beloved of the Sanwich rabble' as recently as 1624).[4] Buckingham's first nominee in 1626, Sir John

Suckling, was elected 'with great applause', but the substitution of Sir
Henry Mildmay, when Suckling chose to sit for Norwich, failed. This
ambivalent attitude to the Lord Warden was traditional: the borough had
only succumbed in 1601, allowing the Warden to nominate one member
(and hence the rejection of Buckingham's attempt at both in 1625 is
understandable), but resistance was shown by the corporation in 1614,
and again by them in 1621, to Lord Zouch's claim to one nominee as a
right, rather than as a favour.[5] Until, and including, 1626, there was
little perceptible change in Sandwich's electoral history – the election of
Boroughs in 1621 and Hatton in 1624 being particularly significant here.
By the end of the 1620s the situation had changed somewhat, with the
tumultuousness of the commons being cited by the magistrates as the
reason for the failure of Buckingham's candidate in 1628 (this may have
been special pleading); and in both 1640 elections, the commons were a
distinctly disruptive factor, and were alleged (again by the corporation) to
have been responsible for the defeat of the Lord Warden's nominee for
the Long Parliament.[6]

Apart from the later years at Sandwich, there are few instances of
visible change. At Oxford after 1621, the Recorder and his Deputy were
normally elected, displacing the High Steward's nominee, although
surprisingly the Steward's candidate staged a come-back in 1640, the Earl
of Berkshire having his son elected in both parliaments, so the change
there was not quite so convincing. At Cambridge also, in keeping with
the gradual nature of the opening of its franchise, the Steward continued
to get his nominee elected in the 1620s and to the Short Parliament, but
failed in the following October. At Colchester, the opening of the
franchise coincided with the establishment of the Earl of Warwick's
influence over the town, but he was building this up anyway;[7] and
Chippenham continued to elect much the same men after 1624 as it had
done before. At Newcastle-under-Lyme and Chester, patchy Court and
Duchy of Lancaster influence seems to have been eliminated after their
franchise disputes,[8] and this was possibly also the case at Boston after
1628, although there the previous Court connection was weaker.[9] But
there is little to say that this would not have happened without the
franchise disputes.

The size of the borough, as much as the nature of its franchise, appears
to have been the decisive factor in this context at least. For corporation
franchise boroughs of roughly the same stature were going the same
way. Leicester was turning against Duchy influence in 1640; Evesham,
another corporation borough, and one which might have been expected
to be loyal because it had been enfranchised by James, returned Secretary
Conway a rather curt reply to his approach in 1628, and told him it
intended to elect lawyers with local connections. Bury St Edmunds was

also enfranchised by James, and yet its corporation was said to be ada-
mantly set against the election of a courtier in the 1626 county election.
Southampton equally was anti-Court in 1624, and Tewkesbury rejected
the Earl of Middlesex's son for the Long Parliament, before its franchise
dispute had occurred.[10] While there may be an overall impression that
open franchise boroughs were less likely to elect courtiers, such an
impression can probably be accounted for by the fact that by 1640, most
of the larger boroughs had open franchises, and the larger boroughs were
the ones most likely to be independent. In this context, one of a widespread reaction against outside, and even more, official, influence, the
undramatic history of Oxford and Newcastle-under-Lyme does not seem
out of the ordinary. The involvement of the freemen does not appear to
have changed the course of the representation of most boroughs radically.

Only at Sandwich, and then only in 1628 and 1640, could the participation of the freemen be said to have had a major impact on the town's
affairs. In 1640 in particular, they were to be seen to be most active for
the candidates who were not backed by the Court; the same is true of
Hastings, of Canterbury, of Westminster and of Salisbury.[11] But this was
often not for reasons of national politics. Thus, the ostensibly militant
freemen of Hastings were primarily concerned in 1640 with the municipal
position of the oligarchy, and were fired into action because a favourite
alehouse had been suppressed; their grievances were then exploited by a
politician.[12] More generally, where the magistrates were tied to the Court,
or to a Court-backed candidate, then the inevitable internal opposition
might seize on the issue which was to hand, in hostility to the Court, and
use that against the magistracy. Boroughs were rare which, in 1640,
produced an agreement on candidates between both groups (as happened
at Reading) which could be taken as evidence of the opposition sympathies
of the populace. In those boroughs where the corporation was inclining towards the national opposition, as Maidstone[13] or Northampton, opposition
from below took a more pro-Court line, and indeed, at Northampton
apparently produced a franchise dispute on such an alignment.[14] At
Windsor, thanks no doubt to extreme Crown pressure on those dependent
on the Castle, the members returned by the corporation were probably
less obnoxious to the majority in the House of Commons than were those
chosen by the inhabitants at large; and similarly at Higham Ferrers,
the voting figures show the magistrates almost solidly for a future
Parliamentarian, while the wider group went for the courtier and steward
of the borough, Sir Christopher Hatton. The second Long Parliament
election for Wallingford, on a wider franchise, replaced the Recorder, a
future Parliamentarian, with the royalist son of the town's High Steward.[15]
The Long Parliament election to Cambridge University evidenced a
division between old and young, establishment and rebels, which cut across

political lines. A number of committed young Laudians were to be found in support of the aged and doubtfully Laudian Sir Henry Spelman, and in opposition to the University's Laudian officialdom, symbolised by its Vice-Chancellor, John Cosin.[16] An explanation of the alignment of towns in the period 1640–2 should ask the question why the oligarchies were so closely linked to the Crown, as well as why the industrious sort were parliamentary puritans. For where the magistrates fell into the latter category, it sometimes happened that for presumably local reasons, their inferiors went the other way.

There were boroughs where the opposition support came from the lower ranks of the community, and Dr Pearl's study of London provides the clearest and most important case of this. It was the insurgent freemen, albeit led by past mayors, who opposed the Laudian Robert Hyde at Salisbury in October 1640, although the reasons for this were local as well as religio-political. Hastings is another obvious example of the same phenomenon; and at Newcastle-upon-Tyne there seems to have been a religious split between the corporation and a powerful group of freemen. The commons, and especially the bargemen, of Marlow were avowed by Whitelocke to have given him and his partner Hoby almost solid support against the pro-Court nominees of Lord Paget, lord of the borough – but whether this was because the commons were politically aroused, or 'bicause (they said) [Whitelocke and Hoby] had stood for the liberty of the commoners in the election' is not clear.[17] In all of these cases, there were internal reasons for hostility to the controlling group, and these may have helped to determine the wider political alignment.

In sum, an assumption of the political radicalism of the commons in the boroughs must be modified. The politically under-privileged groups were certainly becoming more active and vociferous, but this did not necessarily produce a coherent political stand. The populace of the towns seem more interested in local than in national goals, and thus the widening of the franchises did not have an immediate impact nationally. What ideological content there was in the commons' actions tended to be as much the kind analysed by Mr Thompson as what we would conventionally understand by the term. This is best exemplified by the establishment of a rival court by the Warwick commons in the troubles of 1615, or by the way in which the commons of Coventry repeatedly broke down the closes on the town lands on Lammas day, which was the day on which the lands had anciently been opened to them.[18] The frequency of disputes elsewhere on the issue of exploitation suggests that the commons had a clear notion of what their specific rights were, and would act if they considered them infringed, even if their actions on national issues seem to have been somewhat confused.

But the widening of the franchises did have an impact at a national

level, for it introduced another variable into politics, which had to be taken
into account by other participants. With a wide franchise, it was possible
for candidates to by-pass the corporation in a quest for seats – as most
obviously in Peyton's campaign at Sandwich in 1640[19] – and this meant
that other candidates had to cut their coats accordingly. Even if a popular
challenge did not occur, it might be dangerous to ignore the possibility of
one, and therefore more extensive canvassing might ensue. Likewise, the
existence of a larger, divided (along the normal borough lines), and
independent electorate might be a stimulant to more sophisticated forms
of canvassing. The short-term results of the expanded franchise might be
small, but the long-term and indirect results were much greater, for more
people were being involved in politics. And however parochial the origins
of the agitation against the Laudianism of Robert Hyde at Salisbury, or
the suspected papistry of Edward Nicholas at Sandwich, might have been,
the populace was becoming acquainted with political themes.

The franchise disputes also had a more direct effect. There seems to be
some positive correlation between a constituency's number of voters and
its liability to contests, as we have seen in Chapter 6. The franchise
disputes, while being themselves in most cases a result of competition, also
contributed to the increase of such competition. In part this relates to the
factor of size again: large boroughs had wide franchises, they were
prestigious, they were unlikely to be in anybody's pocket, and therefore
they were fought more. But the same propensity to be contested is also
evident among the smaller boroughs with wide franchises. For with more
voters, it became difficult for the magistrates to take charge of the requests
for seats, in order to ensure that nothing unseemly in the way of a contest
occurred. Not only did an increase in the size of the electorate mean that
more people became nominally involved in politics; it also seems to have
resulted in a tendency for them to become actually involved. Again, the
long-term effects of the franchise disputes may have been considerably
greater than the short-term ones, in introducing more people to politics.

### Politics in elections

The significance of the large electorate is not fully established by an
analysis of the electoral aftermath of the franchise disputes. The indirect
rather than the direct consequences of these were indeed probably more
important. But the extension of the electorate appears to have had a
further impact, in hastening the advent of appeals for votes couched in
terms of issues, and not influence.

The belief which was encapsulated by Glynne in the Long Parliament
in his remark 'the more generall the Eleccion was the freer' had another
implication, pointed to by the Warwick town clerk's 1628 prophecy that

the day of the 'frank spirit' had dawned.[20] The bribing or intimidation of large numbers of voters is difficult, but they are not immune to populist approaches. Manipulation of issues as a way of gaining votes is inevitable in a period of polarisation: the saint was likely to urge God's ordinances whether it was a sure vote-catching tactic or not. But the occurrence and distribution of such tactics suggests that polarisation of opinion amongst the candidates was not the sole determinant. For overt appeals to principle or prejudice were rare, judging by the surviving evidence, in the small boroughs and closed franchises. Candidates might be motivated to stand by their consideration of national issues: Bulstrode Whitelocke averred that he was urged to stand at Abingdon in the spring of 1640 'by my friends heer [in London] uppon the arguement of doing publique good, and chiefly by divers of the contrary faction to the Court, and who favoured the Scots Covenanters'. But no whisper of such matters was reported in the campaign itself, which was said to have centred on drunken, not political, enthusiasm.[21] The motivation of a candidate in standing is of greatly diminished significance to the electors if he nowhere refers to it in his campaign.

The explicit agitation of national political or religious issues is by and large only to be met in large and open constituencies. Instances can be found amongst closed corporations: as we shall see, in corporation discussions in Great Yarmouth in 1625 and Salisbury in the spring of 1640 wider considerations were aired. But these were big towns, which might be expected to have better information and communications at their disposal. On the evidence of their alignments in 1640 and 1642, the tendency was for oligarchies to think of vested interests or local factors: thus, in the case of Norwich in 1640 discussed in Chapter 6 above, Laudian magistrates can be found supporting a candidate whom they must have known was not in sympathy with them, because he was the local man. Because of this oligarchic preference, candidates may have been more circumspect in their approaches to closed boroughs – evidence of their political or religious position must have been available if people were interested, but they do not seem to have pressed it on the voters. In the one case, that of Norwich, where evidence exists, this can be substantiated; and the notoriously time-serving character of most corporations in subsequent years gives further support. It seems possible that it was those outside and below the oligarchies who were more likely to be stirred by external issues: they were presumably less prone to consider the stability and integrity of the local community. Conversely, in the small but open borough, such as Abingdon or Wareham, where the rout was more in evidence than reasoning, it may have been that horizons were too narrow for there to have been sufficient interest in greater problems than the size of the purse which was opening. Only in larger open constituencies may candidates have found it worth their while to try to generate religious or political excitement, whether by ale-house or market-place rumours, political speeches, sermons or ballads. For it is primarily in this type of constituency that reports of such tactics are met. A larger electorate was thus doubly important, in bringing more people into contact with the political process, and in increasing the possibility that they might come into contact with national issues.

Subjects like the patterns of patronage, the extent of Crown electioneering, the identity of the personal connections which controlled which election, lie outside the scope of this enquiry.[22] Such matters could have affected the consciousness of few people, and our interest is in the reverse of that. We are concerned here with the extent to which the electorate and issues met, in order that we might discover whether the elite saw politics as its own private matter, or whether it was prepared to accept to the full the existence of an electoral system by taking its political concerns outside its own social confines.

The most obvious feature in this respect is, predictably, a rising political excitement as war approached. The number of contests increased dramatically between 1628 and 1640, and the number in which express reference was made to national affairs also increased. The political divisions developing amongst a very limited social group could have been solely responsible for this; but it is open to us to suggest that these references were made because candidates saw in them a way of picking up votes. Gentry readiness to campaign on matters of religion or state indicates a belief that a sizeable number of people were concerned with those matters.[23] An increase in the frequency of such campaigns suggests that some gentlemen calculated that the common people were becoming more interested.

While in other electoral fields the acquisition of expertise may have been cumulative, in the contents of the campaigns this does not seem wholly to have been so. The wider concern that becomes visible in early 17th-century elections was sporadic in its development, the decisive period being not the 1620s but the 1630s: the fact that there were no elections but mounting grievances in the latter decade suggests than an awareness of oppression was more important than the growing experience of elections which came with the repeated summoning of parliament in the 1620s, in generating an appearance of political sophistication. The elections of 1640 were much more excited than those of 1628, and those of 1624 apparently more so than those of the surrounding years. The participants appear in this respect to have been responding to the political context, rather than to have been involved in an inexorable process of development from naïveté to sophistication. This is confirmed by the marked peaks in the number of contests which occurred in 1624 and 1640. If the electoral system was relatively responsive here, it is arguable that the overt presence of national issues reflects a general apprehension of what the Court was trying to do more than it does the fact that some of those involved were taking it into their heads to explore new approaches. And as concern about the Court did not become universal and fixed amongst the political nation until the end of the 1620s, so electoral politics remained confused and relatively unpolarised in those early years.

Persistent allegations are encountered throughout the period that a man's relation to the Court could greatly affect his chances of election. Gardiner considered this the crucial factor in the 1628 elections, in that objectors to the Crown's forced loan of 1627 were swept into the House on a wave of anti-Court feeling. But it was shown some time ago that this was not the case, that those elected in 1628 were little different from those who had sat in the two preceding parliaments.[24] Prior to 1640, there is little sign of this most obvious aspect of national politics having a direct electoral repercussion, except insofar as it might condition the attitude of the local gentry towards an individual, and determine whether they would ally with him or not. There is little evidence that the question of Court versus Country was agitated in the open at or before the hustings. Dr Hassell Smith has discovered a consistent division among the Norfolk gentry throughout the last two decades of Elizabeth's reign between a local 'Court' interest (being so by virtue of holding Court-issued economic patents) and a hostile 'country' group, and concludes that this alignment is visible in the elections of those years.[25] If the politics of other areas were to be reconstituted as thoroughly as those of Norfolk have been, similar delineations would no doubt be found – traces are visible in the long-drawn clash between Wentworth and the Saviles in Yorkshire. But what Dr Hassell Smith did not find was evidence that such considerations were brought to the notice of the freeholders, or were agitated as something worthy their interest and concern. Local politics in Norfolk, while manifesting suggestive divisions, were still effectively a world closed to those outside the ranks of the gentry: they were being asked to participate, but not told what it was about. Indeed, the issues were still probably too unclear for the ordinary commons to care sufficiently for it to be worth appealing on them. Other constituencies where similar anti-Court alignments were reported in the years before 1640 (as at Coventry in 1621) were doubtless in the same category.[26]

Misgivings about the Court connections of candidates in these years were largely localist in inspiration. As the Court under the early Stuarts became more isolated and introspective, feelings arose in the country that a man could not do service in parliament to both king and constituency, even if only because the courtier was increasingly likely to be an absentee and a stranger. A measure of political alienation must also have been involved, as the interests of the two were seen to conflict to some degree, but economic troubles, particularly in the 1620s, made it all the more imperative for a constituency to be represented by someone who could do it service.[27] Whereas in the 16th century, it might have turned to a Privy Councillor in order to gain favours from the Court, this was becoming no longer the case, and courtiers were shunned. Occasionally there were signs of dangerous estrangement: the governors of Bury St Edmunds in 1626 declared 'in Generall they wolde giue no voise to any Cortier espetialy at this time of all others', and a solitary oligarch of Great Yarmouth in 1625 argued against electing an official, Sir John Suckling, because 'Itt wold bee a question whither Sir John should inclyne rather to the Kynge then to the Subiect.' But on the whole this reluctance to elect courtiers was not yet made explicit in terms of real alienation, but merely of concern about their local serviceability. The Middlesex voters were alleged to have rejected Privy Councillors in the 1621 election because it was felt that access to such great men would be difficult; the Earl of Salisbury was told by St Albans corporation in 1628 that he could have the nomination to one seat provided 'you will not propose unto us any but such a one as shalbe compleatlie qualified for such ymployment, and acquainted with our Towne and sensible of our occasions, to whom we may have easie access'. That this was not merely the anxiety of the city fathers is shown by the conclusion: the nominee must be one 'whose election may passe the Common sufferages'. The economic roots of the need for an accessible, knowledgeable member are emphasised by the events in Salisbury at the 1626 election, when the nominees of the Earl of Pembroke and Sir Robert Heath were passed over in the interests of preserving the economy of the city from 'utter ruin' by electing someone who could push the city's interests, which a stranger was held incapable of doing.[28] Such instances as these are of course little different from the common corporation concern of the time to elect local men: courtiers were more objectionable because they were likely to be busier in London attending the King rather than the House.

Undoubtedly, some of the decisions to reject nominees of courtiers before 1629 were the result of the unpopularity, rather than just the isolation of the Court – as astute an observer as Sir Henry Neville thought so in 1614, and the verdict was later echoed by others[29] – but it does not seem that anti-Court feelings found much public expression at an electoral level. The overwhelming majority of decisions against courtiers were the exclusive acts of the closed circle of the elites (as in the case of the risky remark at Great Yarmouth). Anti-Court talk was sufficiently incendiary to find its way to the ears of the government (it did often enough in the 1630s and 1640), or to leave its mark in correspondence, and while the argument from silence is a dangerous one, the relative absence of such reports when some people (the slandered candidates) had a vested interest in reporting indicates that open appeals to the anti-Court prejudices of the commons were indeed rare. The fact that such appeals were more frequent in 1640, and that other forms of appeal were made before the Eleven Years, suggests that the Court, or central government, may not have become an issue of major importance to the ordinary man until the 1630s.

The secular affairs which were raised as campaign issues in the early years of the century tended to be those which were of direct relevance to the ordinary commons, and they were purely local concerns. The Crown had since 1611 been striving to enclose and improve the Honour of Knaresborough, and this evidently featured strongly as a grievance at the 1614 election, for Sir Henry Slingsby ordered his agents to tell the voters that he favoured enclosure: 'I would not have them say hereafter that they chose me to speak further and I was wholly against them.' Here was an election where the voters were clearly assessing the candidate in terms other than those of what family he belonged to, or what influence he could bring to bear. Similar concerns were manifest in the Cambridgeshire election of that year, where the fear was mooted amongst the freeholders 'that if Sir John Cutts, etc., were chosen, their Fens would be drained, and a third Part be given away to the Undertakers'. In the campaign for Sandwich in 1620-1, Sir Edwin Sandys was reported to have gained strong backing from the insurgent freemen by declaring his opposition to the monopoly London trading companies (a declaration which he lived up to in the House), in face of whose competition the trade of the port was suffering.[30] Where there was an issue which greatly concerned the ordinary voters, even in the early years of the century, they seem to have been capable of making an electoral decision on the basis of the (doubtless ill-informed) views they had of it. Candidates were willing to address them on that assumption. The franchise disputes showed the urban commons largely unconcerned with the parliamentary election *per se* – it was merely an opportunity for challenging the corporation. But when a concrete problem (other than a purely indigenous one of corporation exploitation) arose which affected the constituency and which did seem susceptible of alleviation by action in parliament, then the voters were thought to be able to draw the appropriate conclusions. The relative absence of Court-Country issues at elections may be accounted for by the fact that until the 1630s local awareness of the relevance of governmental policies was only dawning slowly.

There were a few areas where experience of contests, and the presence of an exceptionally sophisticated elite, appear to have been capable of generating a rather higher level of political awareness. The City of London voters in 1614 and 1628 were reported to have rejected candidates because of their ties to the Court, and the courtier candidates at Westminster went down amid noisy scenes in 1628. The forced loan was allegedly at the root of the Court's electoral debacles in both cities in 1628, and the placarding which had taken place against the 'Yield-alls' in the Guildhall over the loan, and the widespread and even turbulent resistance by the commons of the cities to the preceding benevolence, indicates the plausibility of that assessment.[31]

The metropolitan voters were clearly precocious in their ability to make such judgements, but they were not wholly out on their own in the degree of their political arousal. Probably the two most contested constituencies in the country were Yorkshire and Norfolk, the latter apparently being fought in 1586, 1593, 1597, 1601, 1614, 1624 and 1625; Yorkshire in 1597, 1614, and repeatedly in the 1620s, with the probable exception of 1624.[32] The two counties, without any unchallenged leaders, had some of the most divided (and politically advanced) gentry in the country, and furthermore both areas were relatively industrialised, a factor which, with the greater degree of education and independence it brought, would have increased the potential for turbulence. Norfolk was a county with abundant freeholders, as were the woollen areas of the West Riding:[33] the result was an abnormally large electorate in both cases. The combination of these circumstances produced electoral developments which almost ranked with those of London.

The 1621 Yorkshire election reportedly saw Sir John Savile agitating 'amonge the vulger sort' against Wentworth's partner Secretary Calvert as 'his Majesties servante'. He was presumably campaigning in those same 'towns of trades' which felt his anti-recusant tactics in 1625, for he was pitching his appeal as 'the Patron of the Clothiers, of all others the fittest to be relied upon'.[34] Savile was directing his propaganda to an audience which he sensed was eager to obstruct the Court's policies, for Calvert's allies were driven to point out that he would be elected for a borough anyway, and would be able to do the King's service there just as effectively as if he were knight of the shire.[35] Savile was appealing to an informed and relatively mature electorate: the cloth-working interest, for which he was obviously bidding, may have been particularly turned against the government by the recent onset of the clothing depression, and this may account for the suggestion of the unusually strong anti-Court line it was following. Savile stressed his earlier service to the woollen industry, and the fact that he was 'their Martyr, having suffered for them' (probably a reference to his defence of the clothiers over an earlier ship money demand and to his wrangling career in previous parliaments, a part cause of his removal from local office in 1617).[36] The terms of the campaign he was conducting, that he was 'fittest to be relied upon' by the clothiers, demonstrate that at least some electors may have entertained definite positive as well as destructive anti-Court intentions when they cast their votes. But despite the repeated contests later in the decade, such issues failed to surface again, and there were no other anti-governmental appeals to the voters, the disputes remaining largely personal. Here again, it was not the case that the people, once brought into political debate, stayed permanently involved.

The Norfolk election of 1624 reveals some similarities. The overwhelming majority of the gentry had agreed on Sir Thomas Holland and Sir John Corbet, but large numbers of the freeholders refused to accept this *fait accompli* (although they were possibly egged on by the ambitious Sir Robert Gawdy). They carried their discontent to the extent of nominating the absent Sir Roger Townsend, despite his declaration of support for the establishment pair, and even put somebody forward as proxy for him. The interest of the movement lies in its apparent non-gentry origins, and in the reported factors which produced it: 'the best suspecting Sir Thomas for his patrons sake, the worst Sir John for his owne sake, yet each of them constant to eyther in their conjunction'. Holland's links were with the crypto-papist courtier, the Earl of Arundel (Holland's son was later his steward), and Corbet was a well-known 'country' puritan.[37]

Virtually everything said about the social and political structure of Norfolk and Yorkshire holds true for Kent, and here in the 1624 election, Sir Edwin Sandys's supporters were said to have gained victory over Sir Dudley Digges by crying him down as 'a royalist', a rather dangerous term for a courtier. The fact that Sandys was subsequently hoist with his own petard for going over to the Court emphasises just how informed of, and involved in, Court-Country politics many of the Kent voters could have become.[38] If the accounts from Norfolk and Kent are correct, then it is possible that here too pregnant divisions were evident before 1630. But such instances are rare, both geographically, and in the electoral history of the counties in question.

Even when the elite were prepared to open politics to the people, it seems to have had little direct long-term impact. Thus, when the sheriff of Cheshire gave the assembled crowds a long harangue prior to the 1624 election, there were apparently few repercussions. The electors were told that the members they chose would have to guard against 'busie-headed workinge Politicians, attendinge opportunities and wicked Proiectors watchinge advantages', and that they should purge the corruption at Court; yet there is no evidence of any anti-Court sentiment being expressed in the subsequent contests for the county, or for the city in 1628 (the city merely witnessed a conventional outburst against outsiders). This was despite the fact that some kind of election address by the sheriff may have been customary. The 1624 sheriff's sad reflection that the people's ignorance of the national importance of parliament meant that 'any man who would put upp the finger, and sue for the place [was considered] a meete person for that imployment' was probably a more accurate reflection of the norm than was the ideal of an aware and aroused electorate that he aspired towards.[39] As Sir John Eliot complained bitterly some time in the late 1620s of the West Country, 'the ignorance of theis partes, allmoste as much divided from reason and intelligence, as our Iland from the world', was such that the issues of Buckingham or billeting (so long as it was not on them) mattered not at all, for their only worry was 'the greate resorte of Irishe dailie cominge over'.[40] Nowhere prior to 1630 was there a consistent record of political arousal on the part of the electorate: the most trenchant anti-Court warnings seem to have had no more than momentary effect. The secular policies of the central government were evidently not yet a topic of burning importance for the ordinary voters.

The one national issue which did regularly find its way into the open in election campaigns before the Eleven Years was religion, and more specifically, anti-papistry. This could signify that this, rather than secular politics, was what the commons were interested in, for the papist was a convenient bogy on whom all fears and resentments could centre. Alternatively, if political excitement was manufactured by the gentry, then it may have been they who believed that the papists were the greatest evil, or they may have thought it safe to defuse popular emotions by focusing them in this (socially and politically) harmless direction. But events in Yorkshire suggest both that the commons' anti-papist fervour may sometimes have been genuine and indigenous, and that it was not seen as altogether safe to stir up the meaner sort. Many of the leading gentry in 1628 were prepared to ally with the papists in order to beat the Saviles.[41] Furthermore, there is a hint that the gentry were solid against the Saviles in 1626 – following Sir John Savile's objectionable 1621 campaign, that of 1625 had been marked by strident anti-recusant agitation in the clothing towns, 'the towns of trades'. There had been the beginning of a gentry backlash against Savile's tactics early in 1625, with one gentleman describing what ensued as 'more like a Rebellion than an Election', and this distaste may have been solidified by that election.[42] In the eyes of some of the Yorkshire gentry, the arousal of the meaner sort was socially unacceptable. But they were capable of being aroused on religion, and some gentlemen evidently considered an appeal to them on that basis a powerful electoral gambit.

The distribution of incidents of anti-papist agitation at elections displays the widespread and lasting nature of that form of hysteria. Unlike feeling on secular issues, emotion against papists did not build up towards 1640, but broke out sporadically over a very long period: Sir John Neale found instances at Elizabethan elections,[43] and they can be matched throughout the early Stuart decades. Candidates' ability and willingness to use this form of appeal for votes long before the excited years of, perhaps 1628, certainly 1640, testifies that anti-catholicism was the one genuine religio-political conviction of ordinary people in the early 17th century. The location of outbreaks emphasises that it was a real and not just a manu-factured issue. Reports of its manipulation show a bias towards the areas where they might be expected, given the religious state of the kingdom: in a rough crescent stretching from Kent through to the West Midlands and round into Yorkshire. There were occasional reports from the more solidly protestant areas – anti-papist sermons preached against one candi-date for Suffolk in 1621, possible doubts about Holland for Norfolk in 1624 (and these doubts were, significantly, not the property of the gentry), a repeat of this popular concern on the score of his son in the Short Parliament election, rumours that one who stood for Northampton-shire that spring had the support of all the papists in the county[44] – but by and large, anti-catholic sentiment was to be met in the darker corners of the land, where there was a genuine problem.

While the issue of the danger to protestantism could move people at all times, in Worcestershire in 1604, in Hampshire in 1614 (a fear strong enough to move ordinary burgage tenants in Whitchurch away from loyalty to their landlord), in Suffolk in 1621, it did betray temporary peaks in intensity, which relate to obvious political developments.[45] Predictably, one such peak was in the Short and Long Parliament elections, when the Laudian excesses of the previous decade had convinced many that true religion was threatened. Overt manipulation of the anti-papist feelings of voters took place in Bedfordshire, Kent, Norfolk, Northamptonshire, Hastings, Sandwich, Knaresborough and Warwickshire.[46] But a more significant increase of concern took place in 1624, before the real polarisa-tion had commenced, and when no accumulation of fears such as was evident in 1640 could have been responsible. The horror caused by the proposals for the Spanish Match, and the general distrust of where James's religious convictions were heading, must have accounted for this. The main burden of the Cheshire sheriff's address in 1624 was against papists, not courtiers: it laboured the connections between James's foreign policy and internal religious changes; while Sandys's supporters at the Kent hustings had decried Digges as a royalist, they smeared Digges's partner, Sir Nicholas Tufton, as a papist; and as we have seen, Holland's links with Arundel in Norfolk were dubious. Suspicions of the protestant credentials of candidates were openly voiced in Canterbury, Ludlow, and Winchelsea, and similar issues were also possibly at stake at Pontefract and the Yorkshire county election.[47] If a peak did occur in 1624, then the electorate was capable of reacting to changing political circumstances.

The higher total of contests in 1624 than at other elections of the 1620s indicates a higher pitch of excitement amongst gentry candidates. But the fact that it should have been worth their while to use anti-recusant feeling as an election issue suggests that this excitement was not limited to the few. The question of whether the gentry created a new awareness in the voters by propaganda, or merely played on existing emotions, is rather like the riddle of the chicken and the egg. But it seems probable that there was genuine feeling for them to work on, for otherwise we might have found a relatively constant, or constantly increasing, distribution of incidents, as random gentry tried their hands, or learnt from others that it was worth trying.

A further point of major significance is the disproportionate number of county constituencies featuring anti-catholicism as an electoral factor. It would be dangerous to suggest anything more definite than that the size of a constituency helped to determine its electoral history. But not only did size and populousness affect the number of contests occurring for a seat: the character of those contests was probably also partly shaped by those factors, as the physical problems entailed in dealing with constituencies of those dimensions necessitated new forms of electioneering.

This becomes even clearer when the elections of 1640 are examined. These elections reveal a new world when compared with their immediate predecessors. Even if reports of Pym's campaign ride around the country are discounted, along with Nalson's later suspicion that a co-ordinated national conspiracy had been afoot, there was probably a degree of political cohesion at a local level. A Gloucestershire Laudian detected 'a kind of cunning underhand canvass ... the greater part of the kingdom over', on the evidence of his county's experience with a puritan clique and ministers with Scottish connections, and Whitelocke's report that he stood for Abingdon because of pressure from Scottish-sympathising friends lends the suspicion at least some credibility. People in Salisbury were aware of election results elsewhere in the spring. Such assertions of the impact of national politics were no longer the overly-schematised fictions of 'observers' isolated at London, as they had been a decade and more previously, but now had some firmer local roots. A defeated candidate at Hastings in the autumn received a letter from his uncle in Hampshire consoling him with the observation that 'the opinion is grown general that whoever is not Scottishly must be Popishly affected, the brethren of corporations especially being verily stiff in this opinion'. While such political assessments were themselves more far-reaching and more frequent than they had been in the 1620s, they are not alone in marking the new world. More significant is the fact that they were not kept hidden from the common people. In the autumn campaign for Worcestershire, a future royalist, said to be 'fitter to breake Parliaments then to serve in

Parliament', was repeatedly traduced before the mustered trained bands by one of the Deputy Lieutenants.[48] The assembled crowds were being told that the existence of parliament was at stake, and one of their candidates was on the wrong side.

Not that the break with a localist, introverted past was everywhere as complete as the Worcestershire electioneering might imply. The voting records which survive run counter to any notion of a novel political awakening. Again, while the awareness of national issues was clearly far greater in 1640 than it had been, the political cries raised normally concerned the local manifestations of Court policies, rather than those policies in general. Thus, while the doggerel circulating in Lincolnshire in the spring warned against Ship-Money sheriffs, courtiers and Laudians, it also cited fen drainers, but not monopolists and patentees in general; a reference to a portrait hanging in the Guildhall at Canterbury in March provoked a protest against Laudianism which was specifically directed against religion in the city; anti-Laudianism in Salisbury in March and the autumn equally centred on Recorder Hyde's activities, and not on the national state of the Church. Nevertheless, reports of agitation against candidates identified with aspects of governmental secular or religious policies multiplied, and a political commentator as subtle as Edward Hyde could confidently forecast in early October that Nathaniel Fiennes would have no trouble in the Oxfordshire election, for which there were several challengers, simply through being the son of the man who had been the chief petitioner for the recall of parliament.[49] Such assurance of the impact of issues on the electorate was not to be met in the 1620s.

The common people were certainly actively involved in national political affairs by this time. In London this was patently so: the riots which broke out on the dissolution of the Short Parliament, Nehemiah Wallington's testimony to the holding of prayer meetings to coincide with crucial parliamentary events throughout 1640 and 1641, illustrate this.[50] But further afield it was also partly the case, and there may have been some validity in the truism that the commons were ranged against the Court. An outraged minister, observing the autumn Suffolk election, alleged that the loyal puritan voters were 'Leathertrats, scarecrows, squirrel-hunters'; the pro-Court candidate and his friends concurred with his social analysis by attributing much of their misfortune to the 'water doggs', the sailors of Ipswich – who were much more likely to have been in religious sympathy, rather than any tenurial relationship, with outlying gentry like Barnardiston and Parker. Lord Maynard's well-known angry attribution of the Warwick candidates' victory in Essex in March to the 'fellowes without shirts' ranks with another partisan complaint that puritan ministers on preaching tours through the county had been largely responsible. We might then presume that the ministers' successes had been with the shirtless poor. The violence threatened to the gentry if the Earl of Warwick's friends lost indicates that the cause of true religion was not seen as best advanced by those high up the social scale.[51]

The political passions and interests of the populace could be a powerful factor. We have only to consider Edward Bagshaw's account of his election for Southwark in October, solely on the strength of a legal reading he had given against certain aspects of Laudianism, to realise that the famous politically-inspired approach to Whitelocke by the commons of Marlow at the same time was not unique: 'it was by that means [of the reading] ... the year following, without asking, or seeking, or stepping one foot out of my Chamber ... to that intent, I was, by the unanimous votes of the people chosen Burgess ... in the first place'. Even if we may doubt the extent of his inactivity, if he was unanimously chosen to the more prestigious first seat when he had apparently no close contacts with the borough, then the political interest of the voters must have been great. At both Kent elections of that year, similar rumours and expectations of the candidates' political characters appear to have played a large part with the voters.[52]

Qualitative evidence from other areas elaborates on this story, that the anti-Court votes came from those of more disreputable rank. Sir John Holland's fate in Norfolk in March was safe, opined Lady Hobart, with 'the wiser people, and with them of the beter sort', but it was amongst 'the factious and volgar sort' that rumours of his affection for his papist wife were making most headway. In Gloucestershire that spring, it was reported that Nathaniel Stephens's sufferings over Ship Money, and his 'Opinion of much zeale towardes the zealous' had 'much indeared [him] to the vulgar', and, more particularly, that the bulk of his support came from the weavers of the lowland area.[53] Again, we have seen that the opponents of the crypto-papist official candidate at Hastings in the spring came more from the artisan than from the retailing population, and while the primary focus of their activity was probably a local ale-house, they were ready to be manipulated into a wider concern by an outside candidate. But whatever the origin of the political issues, the important point is that they were present. Candidates trying to obtain a seat in face of corporation opposition no longer had a sole resort to the agitation of local grievances, or to the infusion of cash and ale. They also thought it worth their while to stimulate political passions.

While the standard historiographical equation of tradesmen with Parliamentarians is difficult to substantiate precisely by the surviving electoral evidence, it is clear that the populace did have an impact at elections. In the towns, it may well be that freemen and inhabitants formulated their political positions in reaction to those of the oligarchies. Nonetheless, although the political divisions may not have been entirely of popular creation, it is still significant that traditional urban rivalries were being overlaid by novel differences. The existence of two opposed particularist groups in towns gave assertive gentry the opportunity to profit, and in 1640 it was inevitable that political issues should be one of the means used. The increasingly self-conscious presence of the meaner sort was at least an indirect cause of the appearance of wider issues at elections. In the counties, intense and conflicting canvassing by ambitious gentry might produce a situation where loyalties of voters were uncertain (as in Somerset that year), and the numbers might be so great that it was cheaper and easier to turn to politics rather than to drink to sway them. The larger electorate of itself necessarily meant that national issues would no longer remain the limited preserve of the few.

The nature of the issues encountered, and their location, in the 1640 elections illustrates the role of the commons in affecting electoral developments. The majority of the 'property' grievances, patents and monopolies, forest laws, the law courts in general, distraint of knighthood, those which affected primarily the more substantial of the population, were agitated rarely at elections. They might figure prominently in petitions presented by the constituencies at the openings of either parliament, and thus might be argued to have reflected opinion at the time of the elections. But such petitions were normally the work of the grand jury, Sessions Bench or corporation, and there is often no evidence as to how widely they circulated, and how many people came into contact with them.[54] What this argument is concerned with is the direction of specific issues against candidates, when, for the purposes of vote-catching, the maximum numbers were likely to have had some acquaintance of them. The overt agitation of such issues may tell us something of what subjects were most likely to appeal to most voters.

The most common complaints against candidates all relate to what might be called the most 'popular' grievances, Ship Money, the levying of troops and money for Scotland, and above all, religion. These were the matters affecting the widest range of people, and the fact that many candidates chose to work on these, rather than on the less generalised property concerns which might have interested the gentry at least, suggests that the people were being told what they wanted to hear, rather than merely what troubled the gentry. The likelihood is that the open challenges to aspects of government policy which took place at many of the 1640 elections were genuinely backed by numbers of the ordinary voters, and were not wholly manufactured by the gentry.[55]

Unlike ordinary parliamentary taxation, which left the bulk of the population untroubled, Ship Money hit the pockets of a very extensive social group, and was correspondingly resented. Sir Roger Twysden noted

in Kent in the spring that its effect on 'the common people' was instrumental in the increase of anti-Court prejudice, and it was certainly present
in the list of rumours which Dering saw as contributing largely to his
defeat. The voters of Lincolnshire were being urged in rhyming verse
to 'choose noe shipp shreiffe', and similar care was advised at Salisbury
in the spring; and candidates in Gloucestershire and Huntingdonshire in
the spring and autumn respectively were said to have endeared themselves
to the people by their sufferings in the cause. Activities over the tax
featured in Long Parliament election petitions against their members
from Middlesex and the wide franchise borough of High Wycombe.[56]

The other major secular grievance which found expression before and
at the hustings was the actions associated with Charles's campaign against
the Scots. Involving as it did the levying of men and money, and
billeting, it was not something which pressed on the gentry alone. A
newsletter to Sir Thomas Roe in January warned that 'The raising of
troops before a parliament begets discourse and censures of several sorts',
and the accuracy of the report was borne out by the experience of several
counties. Electoral hostility to the Deputy Lieutenants for their proceedings in the service was voiced in Middlesex, Kent, Buckinghamshire,
Norfolk, and most especially Northamptonshire in March, where anti-
Lieutenancy preaching had taken place, and where chants of 'wee'l have
noe Deputy Lieutenants!' greeted the gentry from 'all quarters and
corners of the Castle yard', and brought an irate government retaliation.[57]
Agitation on secular issues seems to have been more concerned with what
touched the commons, rather than the better sort.

But the most universal outcry was over religion, another classless
grievance. Leanings towards popery or prelacy were explicitly broadcast
as election smears in taverns, market-places or at the hustings in Bedfordshire, Canterbury, Hastings, Kent, Knaresborough, Lincolnshire, Norfolk,
Northamptonshire, Salisbury, Sandwich and Warwickshire, and expressly puritan 'party' canvassing was alleged in Essex, Gloucestershire,
Lewes, Newcastle, Southwark and Kent again.[58]

The argument that the involvement of more people at elections helped
to produce more overtly political contests must be strengthened by the way
in which the most common issues were the ones most likely to gain the
widest support. The overwhelming preponderance of county constituencies
amongst those experiencing agitation on national issues again substantiates
this conclusion, as does the distribution of what might be called utilisation
of the 'media' (sermons, speeches, ballads, rumours, etc.) for electoral
purposes. Obviously these two categories, of political disturbance and
employment of the media, must overlap, for political appeals are non-
tenurial or non-treating approaches to large numbers, and these can only
be executed by such techniques as we are now considering. But the

reverse does not always hold true: not all reports of speech-making, for example, relate to national affairs. The employment of these techniques demonstrates the same bias towards the county constituencies as does the occurrence of appeals based on national issues. The evidence is not wholly reliable, for county constituencies were the most prestigious, and would attract most observers; but these techniques were themselves unusual enough to excite interest.

Speech-making, sermonising, or the use of other means of spreading propaganda, at election time was not novel in 1640. Instances can be found in constituencies as diverse as Bletchingley in 1624, Yarmouth (I.O.W.) in 1626, and Cheshire and Kent in the mid-1620s.[59] Nevertheless, there is a marked increase in the reports of such tactics when 1640 is compared with earlier years. I have evidence of some fourteen separate incidents in early Stuart elections before the Eleven Years,[60] while for the events surrounding the two elections of 1640, some evidence survives for Cornwall, Cheshire, Canterbury, Dunwich, Essex, Gloucestershire, Hastings, Kent, Lincolnshire, Norfolk, Northamptonshire, Sandwich, Worcestershire and Warwickshire.[61] The over-representation of counties in the list reveals the way in which elections, and still more, contests, in large and populous constituencies were calling forth new methods of dealing with the voters, and the way in which the existence of large numbers of voters brought about their own political education.

Such an account as this can scarcely lay claim to definitiveness, if only because of the limited nature of the evidence. But certain firm conclusions do emerge. The upsurge of anti-catholicism in the elections of 1624 demonstrates the presence of an electoral system, and of an electorate, which was capable of responding to the national political situation even before the crisis of 1640. It has been suggested that the same was true of puritan electioneering in the 1580s,[62] but little evidence can be shown for this, and it seems probable that what developed then was merely an increased concern, co-ordination and awareness on the part of the gentry and patrons. There is little sign that they actually appealed to the populace in terms of the puritan cause. Indeed, where the hypothesis can be tested, in the case of the Warwick election of 1586, apparent puritan machinations dissolve in the face of the local evidence, and we are left with typically confused intra-urban friction, and self-seeking gentry intervention.[63] The events of 1624 do seem different in that anti-catholic smears became an overt electoral tactic. Their increase then suggests greater gentry concern: it also implies a calculation that the electors echoed this.

While the evidence is sparse for the 1640 elections (showing signs of political arousal on national lines in something over 10 per cent of all constituencies), its significance is increased by the number of counties it illustrates, for these contained by far the greater part of the electorate. What we find is an electorate which was gradually coming to think in terms of national issues, and an elite which was prepared to accept this and to appeal to it (no doubt for self-interested reasons) in those terms. This development was of course qualified: the reaction was often localist resentment at the impact of national policies, and it may be that the truly novel change was the existence in the 1630s of a central government willing to intervene dynamically and one which was (unlike the interventions of the government in the economic crisis of the early 1620s) reluctant to consult the local leaders. Voters were apparently capable of a conscious response in the limited areas which directly concerned them before 1629: as a result of the 1630s, a much wider area became of direct relevance to them. But for whatever reason, the larger political nation was increasingly becoming involved. Parts of it were making decisions not just because they had been pressured by their superiors, bribed or made drunk; and the localist reaction against the government was not just that of the gentry and above. The fact that overwhelmingly it was the larger constituencies which were subject to novel forms of appeal indicates conclusively that the gentry and the corporations were not the sole force in politics even before the polarisation and propaganda campaign of 1641–2 took place.

# Part III

# After the Election

Part III

After the Election

# 8

# Local Benefits, and Taxes

The House of Commons was, in terms of numbers, directly representative of perhaps about one-third of the adult male population. There remains the question of the form this representation took. Did the voters take their turn at the hustings and then go home, forgetting and forgotten, or did the member maintain close and constructive links with his constituency? In other words, were the wishes and interests of the people outside parliament effectively represented?

Monarchical political theory would have argued that the question was unnecessary, since the King, as head of the body politic, filled the position of representative. This view found its most powerful expression with Hobbes, who contended that Parliament's claim to representation was a sham; its practical consequences can be seen in the Earl of Northampton's anger at the Commons' claim to be uniquely capable, by virtue of their representative status, of advising the King of the country's ills, which he thought implied that 'the Kinge slept oute the sobbes of his Subiectes, untill he was awaked with a thunder bolt of a parliament'. But the outbreak of the propaganda war of 1641–3 made it obvious, if it had not been so already, that such notions of the relationship of king to people were strongly challenged. The major single work of the period 1640–60, Henry Parker's *Observations*, legitimated Parliament's stand in mid-1642 by developing the concept of the derivation of power from the people, and this power was of course directly transmitted to the members of the House of Commons. The King, and even the House of Lords, were effectively excluded: when the Lords, in December 1641 tried to obstruct the bill ending the secular employment of bishops, the Commons warned them that they would proceed on their own, 'this House being the Representative Body of the whole Kingdom, and their Lordships being but as particular Persons, and coming to Parliament in a particular Capacity'.[1]

The claim to be representative of the people was central to Parliament's stand in the war, and we have seen that in electoral terms this was not a ludicrous proposition. Yet most historians persist in ignoring the implications of the claim, and treat the doings of the parliament men as if they functioned in isolation at Westminster, thus unwittingly suggesting a disjuncture between rhetoric and reality.[2] An examination of the rhetoric of the Long Parliament and of the reality which is illustrated by local archives demonstrates that the two were not so disparate, and that members of parliament were often doing something more than agitating their own opinions. The parliament men of the early 17th century were sometimes acutely aware of the political forces operating outside Westminster, and on occasion attempted to present the aspirations of those forces. More particularly, it appears that the link between the Commons and the localities was changing, and in important respects becoming closer, in these years, as the Court became isolated from the country, and as political passions intensified.

### The local role of the parliament-man

The prime functions of parliament, in the Crown's eyes, were those outlined by the writ of summons, to give counsel, and to consent to what was there propounded. The latter could mean money, or some specific matter which preoccupied the Crown, such as James I's abortive plan for a Union with Scotland. The former activity, the giving of advice, could be either solicited or unsolicited. The operating principle here appears to to have been that, if solicited, the advice could be of general import (the obvious examples are Henry VIII's query of the Reformation Parliament as to whether the clergy were but half his subjects, or James I's enquiry in 1624 about what he should do over the Palatinate and Spain); if unsolicited, the advice should concern purely local and particular problems. Thus, Northampton warned the Commons in 1607 that members were only intended to express the wants of the counties and boroughs for which they sat: they had 'only a local and private wisdom', and were 'not fit to examine or determine secrets of state'. Not surprisingly, Charles I subscribed to the same doctrine, and when justifying the 1629 dissolution, he looked back longingly to the better days 'where in former times the Knights and Burgesses were wont to communicate to the House such business as they brought from their countries'.[3]

The role of the Commons in informing the Crown of the state of the kingdom was often defined as, or likened to, that of a grand jury in a county.[4] By this reading, the members were an assembly of individuals who presented to higher authority their sense of what was amiss in their localities. The independent assessments which members could give were valuable, and Prof. Barnes has testified to the predicament in which the Crown found itself when it was deprived of this channel of information in the 1630s. But the grand jury comparison was not entirely apposite, for in some respects the members were not independent agents, able to present what grievances they liked to the consideration of the government. Members were often subject to close pressures from their constituencies when they acted as local spokesmen. Dr McKisack, in her work on later medieval boroughs, established the existence of a long tradition in which the parliamentary burgess was seen as an agent from the constituency to the central government, entrusted with petitions for redress of local grievances or for local benefits. Often, borough corporations set up committees to inform their members of what they should seek, and the members set off for parliament with detailed instructions.[5] This practice continued in the early modern period.

Elizabethan parliament men had shown their determination to treat the most important national matters as well as minor local ones. By doing this, they were asserting that the House of Commons was greater than the sum of its parts, that its members possessed a special capacity once assembled, and that they were no longer 'private men' bound by normal conventions. There was perhaps a fatal ambiguity in the word 'country': members could claim justifiably that they personally served for their 'countries', meaning by that their localities. But 'country' also had a wider significance, and a member who asserted that he served for his country and therefore must speak for its needs could move onto a new stage while still apparently speaking in a language that everybody could accept. It is true that exceptional state interference in the localities, as in the case of Laudianism in the 1630s, caused the two fields to overlap, localist protests merging into general attacks, but even in more normal times it was only too easy for members to cross the boundary. Under the guise of speaking for his country, he might talk of religious or foreign policy, which was a very different matter from what speaking for his *local* country might entail. It was this development, or perhaps return to the troublesome practices of Lancastrian parliaments, which Elizabeth and James resisted so strongly whenever they could, striving to keep the House's initiatives limited to matters of the economy and justice, issues which affected the subjects directly, and on which they might have some genuine cause for concern. It is this process which we are most conscious of, for the attempts of the House of Commons to expand its sphere of competence by claiming to represent the nation, and the Crown's efforts to limit such expansion, gave rise to the constitutional difficulties which are so obvious in the late 16th and early 17th centuries. But though Sir Edward Coke could assert that 'though one be chosen for one particular County or Borough, yet when he is returned ... he serveth for the whole Realm, for the end of his coming thither ... is generall', this does not give a full account of the activity of the House at this time.[6] Constituencies were probably more interested in their local problems, and members hoping for future re-election, or to stand in good stead with their neighbours, had to take account of this fact.

A contributor to a 1571 debate on abolition of residence qualifications for borough members argued that the greatest statesman was worth less as a member than a local man, and this attitude survived well into the 17th century, with the election bill introduced into the Short Parliament attempting drastic re-invigoration of the moribund requirement that members should be residents of their constituencies. The strength of this localism is best indicated by the resentment of Great Yarmouth in the 1590s at the fact that Lowestoft, which was not represented, was canvassing for support at Westminster for its herring industry: the benefits of parliamentary consideration were evidently thought (albeit by Lowestoft's economic rival) to be limited to those with their own members.[7] The corollary of such intense parochialism was the idea that only a local man could be sufficiently informed of the constituency's affairs to be able to push its needs adequately at Westminster. Sir John Neale has described the eagerness of Elizabethan boroughs to elect Privy Councillors and their clients, in the hope that they might gain some *quid pro quo* for the favour, and instances of this eagerness can be found in the later period. But the increasing isolation and introspection of a selfish Court undermined the hopes of the localities, and as was suggested in Chapter 7, they turned elsewhere. As one of the activists against the Court official Edward Nicholas's candidature for Sandwich in the spring of 1640 pointed out, Nicholas 'lived at London and it would be no help' to the local inhabitants.[8]

The emphasis placed by those looking for a representative was on the whole not on some prominent figure who would do great things, but on someone who would bring home local goods. A member for Richmond in 1628 felt bound to reassure the corporation (after his election – he was not plying for votes) that he would only look to their private welfare, for that he considered 'to be the true duty of a parliamentary burgess, without roving at random to generals'. There are accordingly abundant instances of men appealing for seats in terms implying that the only service the constituency was interested in was a purely local one. Even shire knights, with much more variegated constituencies, were viewed in this localist context. The prospective local service Edward Coke would do for the Norfolk freeholders was what was laboured to them by canvassers in 1593; county members can be found reassuring boroughs within their shires that 'their particular included in the general', their individual interests would be looked after, and various knights can be seen agitating, or being pressed to agitate, on local matters.[9] The several members for Norfolk constituencies met before or during session to co-ordinate local business in the 1620s, and there is a hint of similar local cohesion for Devon, Kent and Suffolk at other times in our period.[10]

What the interests of the constituency were was often not left to its members to determine, as Dr McKisack showed for earlier years. The parliament man survived as the delegated agent seeking after strongly-desired local goods, long after the propensity of the House for playing high politics, and the propensity of status-seeking gentry to move in on the most introverted of petty boroughs, might have been thought to have undermined this notion. Directions and instructions for action in the House continued to be sent to members, and seem almost to have been the norm. Indeed, it is even possible that they increased, in consequence of the take-over of borough representation by gentry strangers, who might not be expected to know what was required.[11] But the fact that instructions to members from the major cities, which were not flooded with outsiders, also multiplied suggests that this is not a sufficient explanation. Many urban instructions and petitions concerned economic worries, impositions and monopolies of one kind or another, and it seems possible that the consciousness of a greater potential for governmental interference in the economy, at a time when many sectors of that economy were anyway under pressure, if not actually depressed, may have produced a greater tendency to look to the centre for redress or aid. And the apparently uncaring nature of the early Stuart Court ensured that this would be sought through parliament, rather than through direct approaches to the government.

In the 1571 debate on borough representation, a speaker urged that instructions were inadequate to give even the wisest man a full sense of the place for which he served, and he must therefore be local; but the assumption of his statement was that instructions were normally forthcoming. They seem to have been widely expected. An aspiring member for Rye in 1624, speaking to the corporation of those who had sat in the previous, fruitless, assembly pointed out that they were best qualified to serve again, for 'the very remembrance (besides the papers in their hands) of every theire instructions is still fresh and perfect'. York's members in 1624 anxiously awaited the receipt of 'all such instructions as shall concerne the good of the Cittie in any kind'; and a candidate at Sandwich for the Short Parliament promised to 'advance what ever you shall let me knowe may be for the good of your Towne', and cited in particular the repair of the decaying harbour.[12] Instructions were apparently taken for granted by both parties to the process: they were freely offered by constituencies, and there is no record of any protest being made by a recipient (until the political polarisation of 1641) at an infringement of their parliamentary privilege. Evidence of instructions, often whole series of them for successive parliaments, can be found in the assembly books and records of Berwick, Bristol, Cambridge, Exeter, Gloucester, Great Yarmouth, Hastings, Hull, King's Lynn, London, Newcastle, Norwich, Oxford, Rye, Sandwich and York.[13]

Such instructions were entirely and solely of local significance. York wanted the river deepened, Rye wanted a light set on Dungeness, Berwick was concerned about the export of skins and woolfells, Sandwich sought exemption from taxation, Bristol desired local control over the castle. The tone of the letters might well be strong: Great Yarmouth in 1620 appointed a committee to instruct their burgesses 'what they shall doe this howse shall allowe of', and the Common Council of Bristol in 1626 'enacted and decreed that the Burgesses of this Citty which now serve in Parliament... shall deale for the Castle'. Sir Henry Slingsby pre-empted likely pressure from Knaresborough on enclosures in 1614 by insisting that 'my voice must go according to my heart and conscience'. But not until 1640 did constituencies generally attempt to dictate what their representatives should do at a non-local level. Indeed, although York in 1624 was manifestly very interested in 'the restoreinge of the Pallatinate' and similar major issues, it expressly disclaimed any desire to dictate to its members on such a subject. After having announced that the members must press for improvements in the navigation of the River Ouse, and that a solicitor would be sent up to assist them, the corporation advised them that as for 'weightie Causes concerning our King and the state in generall ... we pray god direct and assist yow'.[14]

It might be expected that the larger boroughs, having the most definable economic interests, and probably the greatest cultural identity, of any of the constituencies would provide the bulk of instances of pressure on members, and this is suggested by the evidence cited above. This could imply that the knights of the shires had a somewhat weaker local role, and that gentry members for the weaker or pocket boroughs could not be bothered. But again, we find a counter to this in the 1571 debate on borough representation, where one member urged that a local man as burgess was essential for a decayed borough above all others, in order that he might advance the measures which could restore it to health. In keeping with this, an unpaid member for the declining borough of Orford in 1586 was to be found requesting instructions and a solicitor to aid him. At the far from prospering Yorkshire borough of Pontefract in 1628, both knights who had recently been elected for the town came 'to know what service the Townesmen would commaund them';[15] and Rye, which has been noted as despatching instructions, was not remarkable for its economic health. Larger, independent towns were naturally more likely to send instructions, and more ready to appear to prescribe to a member: it is difficult to envisage Gatton or Castle Rising for example having any specific economic interests worth issuing instructions about. But the instances of Orford and Rye show that it was not unheard of for the smaller settlements to attempt to initiate business, and a determining factor in the impression left of activity among the larger boroughs is probably the greater likelihood of administrative continuity, and thus the preservation of evidence, in such towns.

County members, like members for lesser boroughs, were demonstrably concerned with their local functions when they made their appeals for seats. But they were also made aware of these functions when the canvassing was over. It appears to have been customary for Norfolk members to be briefed on the county's needs before they left for Westminster, and both knights in 1604–10 were receiving very sophisticated communications from their neighbours, including drafts of suggested bills. The knights for Herefordshire were requested in 1610 to secure the removal of the county from the jurisdiction of the Council at Ludlow, and all members sitting for constituencies in the county were reported to have received similar instructions in 1614. The JPs of Nottinghamshire sent up a draft bill to their knights in 1625 for the reformation of abuses committed by the clerk of the market, although with the rider that it was 'not with opinion to tye the wisdome of that house, to any ignorant forme of order, but onelye to expresse what we desire'; and Wentworth received similar detailed advice on generalised local matters when sitting for Yorkshire that year.[16] But unlike boroughs, counties had no official repositories of records, so any evidence which has survived is the result of chance retention in private hands or in central archives. The way their members received instructions was equally informal: the boroughs had clear centres of authority, in the governing bodies, but no such centre was evident in the shires. There were of course magistrates in the counties (although not so precisely in power as were the urban corporations), and the JPs of Nottinghamshire in 1625, of Cheshire in 1640, and the Deputy Lieutenants of Cornwall in 1628, can be found expressing the sense of their counties.[17] More often, and reflecting the tendency to describe the grand jury as 'the representative body' of the county, pressure originated from that quarter, or informally, in private correspondence.[18] Despite the lack of such official evidence as survives for borough members, it is clear that the shire knights were not isolated from pressure from outside the House. All types of members were made aware of public opinion.

The increasing frequency of contacts is very noticeable. Sir John Neale made passing reference to the growing amount of private business before the House under Elizabeth, but it is difficult to determine why this should have been so. In part, no doubt, it was for reasons of greater awareness of what government could do, as has been suggested above; but also those factors which Neale identified must have played a major part – the increasing education and corporate sophistication of members would give them the confidence to initiate business of their own, rather than sitting back and waiting for the Court to do so.[19] Knowledge of the capabilities of parliament men would then impel their principals at home in the localities to seek more from them.

Conclusions about the existence of more instructions based on the abundant material for the 17th century, when compared with the sparser evidence for the preceding century, are not necessarily wholly distorted by the accidents of survival. There are excellent series of communications with members in the archives of Hull and York, for example, but these archives extend back long before 1600, and mere chance is not then necessarily the sole control. This is suggested also by the increasing formalisation in the 17th century with which the records of various corporations treat the subject. There had long been a committee of the City of London corporation to instruct members as to what they should do 'for the good of this Cittye', but in 1614 there were moves to fix its composition, and in 1624 it began referring back to what had been done in earlier parliaments: two years later, regular meetings between the representatives and the committee were ordained. At Exeter, weekly meetings of the instructing committee were being ordered by 1640, that a close watch might be kept on the progress of business; again, the composition of this committee was being fixed at the same time.[20] Localities were apparently becoming aware of, and concerned with, the potentialities of parliament as an institution more than before, and were therefore more interested in the actions of their representatives. The frequent reversal, especially in the 1620s, of the 16th-century take-over of borough representation by outside gentry indicates again that boroughs were no longer content to give their members a free hand, and that they now regarded the House of Commons as fulfilling other purposes than merely providing the gentry with an education, and giving an indirect approach to the Court. The increasing alienation of the early Stuart Court from the country may have driven communities to turn elsewhere for the gratification of their wishes, and this then necessitated the application of pressure on members to produce local goods which might previously have been obtained by informal approaches.

The character and intensity of these contacts between centre and locality show some signs of change before 1640, in response to the developing religious and political tension. As early as 1604, Sir Edward Montague, sitting for Northamptonshire, averred that he could not keep silent in matters (ecclesiastical courts, the suspension of nonconformist ministers and the decay of tillage) 'so straitly enjoined me by the County for which I serve'. The sheriff of Cheshire advised the voters at the 1624 election court to consider whether the available candidates were suited to tackle the problems of monopolists and projectors, internal recusants and Arminians, and external papist threats, for these would be what they would have to face. He exhorted the electors to be conscious parties to their own actions: they were not 'to rest contented in your choice, and stay there, but to goe a little further, and commaund your knights that if there bee occasion offered they shall in the name of the Countrey make publique protestacion against a Tolleracion of Religion, or the Repealinge of the lawes formerlie made against Recusants'. The sheriff clearly hoped that not only would the knights be instructed, but that they would avow their instructions on the floor of the House, making their protest 'in the name of the Countrey'. In the aftermath of the Ile de Ré fiasco, the Somerset freeholders also entered more controversial ground, when they went as far as to 'command' Sir Robert Phelips in 1628 to secure the lifting of martial law from their shire.[21]

The cases of Northamptonshire and Somerset could be argued to have been merely developments of long and fairly respectable traditions; after all, what was complained of there were definite local grievances, although they trespassed on forbidden areas of state policy, religion and foreign affairs. The fact that central government was following lines of general policy to which the bulk of the political nation was opposed meant that when those policies impinged on the localities, a more generalised statement of grievances might ensue, although it was still the local repercussions of a policy which were directly questioned. But the Cheshire sheriff's speech was something new: the voters were being urged to attend to purely national affairs. Their old localist lethargy, they were told, which had resulted in the election of whichever of the gentry wanted it, was not what representation was about – they had to press their knights on bigger issues. The tendency of the Court to go in the opposite direction to that in which the political nation was aiming evidently risked creating a new attitude to representation in the country. The constituencies would be forced to open their eyes to what their parliament men were doing with regard to national policy, as well as to local goods, as the only way to exert pressure on the Court. The dangerous corollary of this might be that parliament men who were tending anyway, for reasons of their own views, to attack royal policy might feel doubly impelled to do so if they knew a sensitive public was watching their actions.

But such injections of overt national politics into the constituencies' instructions to members were extremely rare before 1640. It was extremely unusual for members to be asked to do anything more than see to the improvement of market regulations or of harbours. It seems likely that the few instances of wider concerns were limited to the larger, possibly more assertive (in that they had a more numerous gentry complement), county constituencies. Many borough instructions are extant, and virtually all of them are purely local; the few examples that survive for counties seem broader in outlook, although this may have been as much a result of the lack of a narrow, specific interest in the county as of the gentry presence. While such instructions were limited in their reference to the national political scene, they do nevertheless indicate that close ties existed between many members and their constituencies after the former had left for Westminster. These ties furthermore appear to have become closer as the period progressed, and to have showed signs of comprehending more contentious issues.

## The question of taxes

There was another area, besides that of purely local matters, in which the parliament men acknowledged in very practical terms the fact that they were not divorced from the public once at Westminster. As Dr McKisack realised, taxation was as important to the donor as to the recipient. The increasing, or rather recurring, tax load inflicted on the country from the middle of Elizabeth's reign was crucial in changing the relationship of member and constituency. Dr Schofield has argued that one of the peculiarities of national taxation in the first half of the 16th century was that, apart from the unhappy early 1520s, resistance to it both in parliament and the country at large actually declined. This could hardly be said to have been the case in the next periods of heavy taxation, the 1580s and 90s, and the 1620s, when yields dropped, gentry assessors shifted the burden onto their less fortunate neighbours, towns pleaded corporate exemptions, and at least in the 1620s, parliament tried to impose conditions on its grants.[22] It is significant that the first developed treatments of the role of the parliament man survive from these periods of high demands, and moreover that they were worked out in the context of fiscal debates.

As more came to be demanded of the nation by the national government, both through parliamentary subsidies and non-parliamentary imposts, the country increasingly ceased to view representation as entirely a local matter, whereby consent was accorded to what the government proposed, and the only non-governmental initiatives were purely local ones. Something came to be asked in exchange for the reluctant granting of greater supply. While the theme had strong late-medieval precedents, Dr Schofield concluded that the concept of redress of grievances in return for supply was foreign to the first half of the 16th century,[23] but it became an accepted convention in the course of the next hundred years. Obviously, the mounting grievances incurred at the hands of the Stuarts had a large part to play in this development, but the fact that the connection became evident in the later years of Elizabeth's reign, when disenchantment with government was perhaps not as great as it was soon to become, suggests that the role of taxation was a major one.

This is not to say that before Elizabeth's reign people had not tried to think out what representation was about, or how members stood in relation to the country. Sir Thomas More, as Lord Chancellor, advised that 'you of this Comen House may reporte in your countreys what you have seen and heard' of the King's uneasy conscience over the divorce;[24] Sir Thomas Smith and Richard Hooker wrote theoretically if vaguely about the notion that all Englishmen were somehow represented in parliament; and the proceedings against both Wentworth and Strickland in the 1570s were met with retorts that those involved were not private miscreants, but public men, and that care should be taken lest the country was harmed.[25] But despite a necessary proviso about the fortuitous survival of evidence, the first significant references to the House's relationship to the people seem to have come in the fiscal debates of 1593 and 1597 – and later developments occurred in similar contexts.

'Answering one that had said, we must regard them and their Estates for whom we be here', Sir George Carey defended the 1593 subsidy, 'saying, he regarded and came from them as was meet', and that their countries would thank them better for taxing them than for leaving them defenceless. Some members clearly believed that their constituents would be interested in, not to say vocal on, their liability to tax, and this point was stressed by Fulke Greville a couple of days later: 'it is said, our Countries are poor, and we must respect them that sent us hither. Why, so we must also remember who sent for us hither. This Cause is hard; for there is necessity against necessity, danger against danger, and inward discontent against outward Forces'. Although he concluded that 'if nothing will satisfy them, our doings are sufficient to bind them', his reference to 'inward discontent' and his fear that the people would not be satisfied, and another member's reported misgivings about the localities' reactions to 'these many Subsidies' if their own representatives had not voted for them, suggests that there were those in the country who did not have such a strong sense of the conclusive powers of parliament, on this issue at least, as Greville proclaimed. The monopolies debate of 1597 brought hints of the same sentiment, with members implying pressure from their constituencies when they voiced their opposition to the novel burdens with references to their localities' feelings.[26] The continuity with the actions of burgesses in the period which McKisack was treating is very marked: account apparently had to be taken of the country's views in matters of taxation.

Sir Francis Hastings testified to the strength of local resentments arising at the end of Elizabeth's reign, which made members tread warily. In June 1604 he predicted privately that a subsidy proposal would have a difficult passage in the House, 'not out of any unwilling disposition to contribute largely out of their purses to so gracious a King but the remainder of a whole subsidy lying still on his people to be paid, the continuing of them long in payments of late years without small intermission . . . cause the Commons to be loth to hear of a subsidy yet and fearful to grant any at this time, lest the people generally should distaste'. Little wonder then that Salisbury should attack those members who manipulated these fears over purveyancing as 'the Tribunes of the people', a comparison which occurred to another commentator on the debate.[27] In face of repeated demands from the Crown for supply, whether direct or indirect, members were urging their responsibility to the country and those for whom they served against the King's need for money. They did this in ways suggesting that they thought the country would hold them to that responsibility. A demand for redress of grievances, couched in terms of this being what the country wanted, was increasingly being coupled with supply.

The clearest instances of this avowal of responsibility can be found over the unprecedented matter of the Great Contract in 1610. Confronted with the need to grant unheard-of sums of money, and to do this regularly, member after member balked, and (just as some had over composition for purveyance in 1604) rose to request that they should be allowed to go and consult their countries. Sir William Twysden urged, on a precedent of Edward III's reign, 'that they may go into the country, and receive resolution and authority from them', although nobody else went quite as far as Twysden in demanding authorisation and ignoring the fact that the indentures of return of members entrusted them with full power. Another member put a rather different gloss on the need to take home something in return for the money given, when he argued that members must not, in addition to 'the great charges we put the country to, that find us our wages, return them no other news for their money than that we have given away their money'. But he also referred to the 'many projects made us which have filled our country with hope of good news':[28] the various propositions of the Contract were being aired in the country, and seen as very much a *quid pro quo* on the subsidies granted. Lord Treasurer Salisbury thought that those wishing to gain express approval for the bargain were merely temporising, hoping for their own reasons to kill the project, but shifting the blame onto absent friends. He told the House in May that 'I hear bitter and sour reports that some of you speak as if your countries were angry and discontented for that you have already offered', and warned them again in October that this was their last chance: 'If you spend the time in thinking of the security and how you may have commissions to go down to content the people before you have made your bargain perfect, you may lose your time.'[29]

Salisbury's suspicion that those with scruples about the need 'to content the people' were merely being factious seems too harsh. The Court-linked Sir George More was one of those agreeing with Sir Edwin Sandys that the articles of any agreement should be published in the country

before it was executed 'to give the People Satisfaction', and his fellow-
courtier Sir John Holles happily thought that the House had ordered a
delay in the negotiations 'that they might consult the counties thereon' in
the recess. This he assiduously proceeded to do; another member reported
that he too had felt compelled to consult his constituents by virtue of his
relationship to them: 'When I went home into my country, I did (according to the trust reposed by them in me) acquaint them with what we had
done, and withal required their advice.' An anonymous commentator
related that this was common practice in those weeks. The extent to which
all members kept one eye on the country in the Great Contract debates
was demonstrated by the House's reply to James's demand for a supplement to the original financial proposals, which expressed regret that 'we
cannot . . . in consenting to it discharge the trust which so many millions
of people have reposed in us'.[30] The House's response may merely have
been vague rhetoric, but the testimonies of individual members were more
specific, and give substance to it. Salisbury was correct in his conviction
that the Court's financial problems were creating stronger contacts
between the member and his locality. And while one of Holles's reports
of his consultations in Nottinghamshire makes it plain that he only sought
absolution from the subsidy commissioners, another referred to the 'very
uncertain temper' of the 'plebs', in contrast to that of 'the better sort'.[31]
Not only were members concerned about the reactions of the country to
subsidy proposals: it seems possible (particularly in view of references to
the poor in the 1593 debates) that the opinions of the local governors were
not the only ones to be heeded.

The fact that discussion on tax matters was not limited in its circulation
to the two Houses was something of which the government was aware.
Salisbury told the House at the start of the 1610 session that in view of
the muttering in the country against the need for granting money, he
would give it some 'observacions . . . not altogether impertinent to be by
you reported to men of inferior Judgement'. While the King himself
might resent the appeals to popular reluctance to pay made by the
Commons, he was quite ready to admit the existence of the growing
belief that redress of grievances, seen as what the country wanted, should
accompany supply. In a draft speech in 1614, James contemplated
adjourning and sending the members home before they had granted
supply, so that they could say in their localities, 'my masters come let us
consult what is good for the common wealth', which they were then to
inform him of when they returned.[32] James was quite certain that the
origins of reports of grievances lay outside the House. In March 1624,
announcing his need of a massive subsidy, he declared an intention of
proroguing until autumn, and one member observed that the House was
told, 'In the meane tyme we might goe downe, and acquaint ourselves

with the greivances of the people'.[33] The House was explicitly being told
by the Crown to go home and sound out the country in relation to supply.
The concept of the House as a channel of information between locality
and centre was uncontroversial, but there is a large gap between that and
urging the House to act as the go-between between the two main parties to
a bargain. The status of the House is derogated from, and that of the
constituencies enhanced by, the latter.

That James should have been prepared to make concessions in this
direction in 1624 is less surprising after the parliament of 1621. An
enormous outcry occurred in the early summer when it was suspected that
the King was about to attempt to gain supply and then dissolve parliament
without passing any further measures. Sir Edward Coke, at the start of
the session, had advised that grievances be treated before supply, for 'the
grievances being laid down it will be a good encouragement to us to enable
us to give a good account of our doings to our country for whom we are
intrusted': the need to give an account to the constituents, and redress
before supply, were clearly coupled in Coke's mind. Many members in the
following weeks testified graphically to their apprehension about the
country's likely reactions when they had to give an account of their
failures to produce redress for it when they went home. Coke even worried
about the dissatisfaction of 'the poore 5 li. man who beares the brunt of
the subsidy', indicating that the dimensions of the constituency were not
confined to the social elite. A speech by Sir Richard Grosvenor suggests
even more of the precise nature of the relationship between the two parties
to representation. He observed that 'The cause of our sorrow is feare of
not affecting our desyred good. We sung *placebo* and now *Lacrimae*. We
that goe home may be made subiects of the peoples fury, if not of disgrace.' A plausible reading of the statement might be that Grosvenor sang
'*placebo*' to the country on election day, or before coming up, and now
dreaded being made to answer for his promise, for the sure result was
local disgrace.[34]

A general presumption is evident among members that the localities
had very definite expectations of parliament, and these expectations centred
around the notion that a bargain would be made by their representatives
over supply. Fears in mid-1621 that James would push through his
objectives without allowing the country to obtain anything in return
caused grave misgivings amongst the people in the middle that they would
be taxed with the suggestive offence of dereliction of *duty*. That prospective charge hanging over the members' heads demonstrates how far the
constituency's role was from completion when the election court was
dissolved. The lawyer Edward Alford wept that summer, 'We cannot
(with greife I speake) doe any thing. Trafuick is gone, impossition undoes
us, all people live upon hopes, and that of this Parliament. We must not

carry them home rattles.' Sir Samuel Sandys wished 'that we may have a better satisfaction to carry into the Country then yet we have, that so we may have more hart to doe service for them by ther acceptation and our discharge of dewty', and members from all around the country took up the chorus.[35]

It could all have been a mere rhetorical device, an attempt by opponents of the Court to unload the responsibility for their actions onto those sitting safe at home. But the sheer volume of these protests, and the fact that they came from men who were not noted for their opposition as well as from people like Coke indicates that this was not entirely the case. The suggestive language of the speeches reinforces that supposition. Grosvenor's *'placebo'* to the country is matched by Samuel Sandys's consciousness that the country must accept the service the member had been able to offer, and that the member must discharge his duty: he must acknowledge his obligation, and strive to fulfil it.[36] An account was to be rendered.

As the royal demands increased in the 1620s, commensurate with the growing unpopularity of the Court, it became almost conventional for members to excuse their reluctance to supply the Crown in terms of their responsibility to their electors. The imperative to speak to the king was being balanced against that to speak for the country, and found wanting. This was almost certainly a factor in the growing rejection of courtiers at elections, for what chance was there of someone 'tyed in so partickiuler an obligation to his magesty' being able to bargain effectively in this area which was now becoming so important? Sir Peter Heyman in 1624 compared the two obligations, to king and to country, and was unable to decide between them, being reluctant to incur the odium in the country which he knew an unconsidered assent to supply would bring. In answer to the request of Buckingham, Charles and the erstwhile opposition leaders for money to break the treaties with Spain, Heyman 'would have them that heere answere for theire Countryes be carefull so toe proceede as it maye not be sayd that they drewe on the Kinge as if it came from them but lett all issue as from the Kinge himselfe and soe they satisfie them for whom they serve'. He thought some of his constituents would be as concerned about the amount of money the war would cost as they would with the orthodoxy of making the Palatinate safe for protestants and the King's daughter, and he was unhappy about the prospect of having to justify a grant. Alford confirmed his fears when he moved that members be stayed from going home before Easter, 'because the rumour of subsidies may doe hurt in the countrie'. We can only suspect who he thought that hurt might be done to, but Sir John Eliot made it quite clear when he took up the same theme in 1625. He opposed the motion to give a second war supply on the grounds of the likelihood of an adverse reaction from the country: 'that wheras last [after the 1624 subsidy] they went with praier and fasting to their Countries, then [if they were to grant another] they might take vp sackcloth and ashes in their iorney'.[37] There was, it seems, a very strong public opinion at home in many types of constituency which the member, and even the very prominent member, had to propitiate not only on the local service he did for it, but also in the justification he was able to give for granting supply. Such a justification might be couched in terms of the local goods brought home; but as taxation was a national matter, and as the national grievances mounted, so the justification might increasingly relate to these, reflecting perhaps the belief of members that the country was directly concerned in such matters.

The experiences of 1626–8, the disasters abroad and the oppressions of billeting and forced loan at home, made the reluctance to give, both in parliament and the localities, still greater. Sir Francis Seymour in 1628 agreed that members were summoned by writ to aid the king, but argued that they were expressly 'chosen by the Commons to deliver up their just grievances'. The active involvement of the commons in this process was alleged by Sir Roger North, who urged members to consider 'who have sent us hither, our cuntry, to whome wee must bee accountable'. The mere confirmation of existing laws, including Magna Carta, as a guarantee in return for supply, as the Court then proposed as an alternative to the Petition of Right, would be unacceptable to them. He considered accountability in the country (in his case Suffolk) the norm by this date: 'they ask us, when we come home, what relief we have brought them'. And that relief, and their grievances, were seen as having to do with Magna Carta and the Petition of Right, and not merely some local goods. The sphere in which an account was demanded of members for their actions was wide by now. If such an account were unsatisfactory, then the consequences which were to be feared were dangerous. Edward Kirton, coming from Wiltshire like Sir Francis Seymour, attacked the abuse of billeting and prophesied that 'If we should give supplie, and this not helpt, they would not pay in the Countrey, what we give.' Billeting was, moreover, a matter which affected primarily the meaner sort of people. If the outcry in 1628 against it was genuine, as it clearly was, given the widespread disorders, then the ordinary people did have some means of exerting pressure on parliament in a crisis.[38]

The 'taxpayers' strike' against Ship Money was not unique, as the solidly negative response to the 1626 benevolence showed. The Crown did admittedly succeed in extracting large amounts of money through the Free Gift of 1614 and the forced loan of 1627, thus strengthening the gentry's fears of the effectiveness of the Crown's prerogative, but the readiness of the country to pay levies throughout the early 17th century was always a subject of concern. This reluctance could even lead to parliament men being brought to book, and to the belief, indicated by Hastings in 1604, and by others afterwards, that the country could refuse to be bound by the actions of its representatives. By 1640, demands that redress of grievances should precede supply, justified by reference to the probable popular reaction, had become almost an orthodoxy. These demands were the cries not of the radical politicians, but of the more purely 'country' figures, and this again suggests that there may have been some factual basis to them. In the Short Parliament, Sir Ralph Hopton, Sir John Strangways, Edmund Waller, Sir Thomas Peyton and Edward Kirton all adopted this position. Sir Francis Seymour feared that 'if wee should graunt the King Subsedyes before our Greivances are debated and redressed our Judgements may very well bee questioned and it may give the Country (whom wee serve) cause to blame the men whom they have chosen as consenting to their sufferance', and Sir Harbottle Grimston predicted an even sterner reaction: 'if before reliefe in our Greivances we showld send downe a Bill for subsedyes the Countrye would not agree to it and they would give but a bad welcome to us'.[39]

While unwillingness to pay manifested itself most obviously over prerogative expedients, such as those of 1626–7 and Ship Money, it was also evident in the field of parliamentary taxation. This aversion to the payment of money apparently provoked increasing local involvement in parliamentary affairs, and increasing parliamentary concern for public opinion. This concern was the concern of men with a real public to answer to, in the counties and the independent boroughs: it was not expressed to anything like the same extent by the 'politicians', men like Pym or Sir Nathaniel Rich, who might sit for a patron's borough, and not have to worry about what the lesser men thought.[40] In that the cry that the country must be satisfied was not the rhetorical property of such men, it becomes more likely that the country did indeed have to be satisfied in some way. It seems that the Crown's financial needs were instrumental in stimulating electoral interest, and in ensuring that this interest was not merely expressed at the polls, but focused closely on the actions of the member throughout the session.

The very volume of these appeals to a duty to the people possibly indicates that they were not just empty ploys. The negotiations over composition for purveyance and the Great Contract were not the only incidents to leave evidence which indicates that this presumption is correct, and that members were accountable to the country as far as supply was concerned. Taxation was, as we have seen, unpopular: Prof. MacCaffrey suggested that urban opposition may have stemmed from the fact that merchants had the bulk of their resources in stock-in-trade, with very little cash in hand, and unbudgeted outgoings could thus have occasioned real trading difficulties for them. The judiciousness of this estimate is confirmed by much surviving probate material. A part cause of this liquidity deficiency, and probably a major factor in the growing reluctance to pay taxes, was the accelerating silver shortage of the period, a constant theme of parliamentary complaints, which must have made any new attempt to take what little there was left in the localities still more resented.[41] Accordingly, opposition was rural as well as urban, and parliamentary subsidies, just as distraint for Ship Money, could provoke riot. The bargain element inherent in a subsidy proposal by the early 17th century was certainly recognised in the localities, and attempts to sound out opinion in Norfolk and Suffolk in 1618 on what size of subsidy should be given in parliament to avert a Spanish Match provoked an irate governmental reaction.[42]

Perhaps the most telling instance of this sense of a bargain, to which the intermediary had to be bound, is provided by the fate of Sir Edwin Sandys at the Kent election of 1626. He had been one of the members in 1625 who had been most anxious to involve England in a naval war with Spain for the recovery of the Palatinate, and had supported a proposal for immediate supply made even before the Court had formulated its request. By this he had contravened the canons that told that supply should succeed the treatment of grievances, and he paid the penalty. A cousin of his successful rival wrote that all those who had supported Sandys for the 1625 election would have done the same in 1626, 'if he had not, at the Parliament deserted, and even betrayed us, and our freehould, contrarie to his owne ingagement and handwriting'. It is possible that Sir Robert Phelips, one of those who had sided with Buckingham in the attempt to drag James into a Spanish war in 1624, encountered a similar backlash at the 1625 Somerset election.[43] The implication of the Sandys affair is that he had, as an unsuccessful candidate in 1625, given certain explicit undertakings, even if only to his neighbours, before the poll on the subject of taxation (and hence the reference to the betrayal of freehold, or property), and that while he had not actually been sitting for the county, he was later taken to task by the electors for leading the move to give supply despite his promises.

There are other cases which bear out this contention. After the passing of the subsidy in mid-1621, which had filled members with so much unease at the prospect of retribution at home, Sir Thomas Wentworth made a long speech to the Yorkshire commissioners at Rotherham in extenuation of the House's decision to grant supply. He observed that 'it may be obiected that we have giuen away your money and made noe lawes, which are the true sure and parlamintary means whirby to redeme and secure the subiect . . . Neuerthelesse that itt may appeare unto you we have not been idle in performance of our duties ... I will shortly declaire unto you sum of the lawes which are allready past our howse.' He then went on to make a straight electoral plea in defence of his partner, Secretary Calvert, against whom opposition had concentrated at the election, and in defence of those (himself) who had made light of his Privy Councillorship. After recounting what Calvert had achieved, the general measure of the bill against informers, he concluded, 'which I dare say, as itt is more then any your neibours could haue been able to doe for you, soe is itt better seruice then hath been dun by any of your knights in Parlament thes twenty yeares'. The context of this elaborate self-vindication must be stressed: the election had to be defended to a presumably disenchanted audience in the county because supply had been granted. Moreover, the defence offered was not service to Yorkshire, but service of national relevance – the measure against informers, and the campaign which was under way against monopolists and corruption. Similarly, Heneage Finch, announcing the same subsidy to the London commissioners, felt compelled to make a long justificatory recital of the proceedings in train against the monopolists and patentees, and to point out that such benefits warranted a return. He reminded his listeners though that effectively they had authorised this tax, and that therefore it was pointless to carp: 'they that gave yt had their power to give, given by yow'.[44]

Such apologies had a long pedigree. McKisack's account implies their existence for King's Lynn in the 14th and 15th centuries, and an Exeter member in 1563 had related to the chamberlain what he was doing for the city in parliament before reporting the bad news of the subsidy, and begged his reader to make his services as widely-known to the city fathers as possible. But in the course of the 17th century such reports become both more frequent and more general in content, rather than purely local. In 1621, immediately after the subsidy had been granted, one of Exeter's members was assuring the city that it had been necessary – it was to recover the Palatinate 'out of the Jawes of the princelie palatine's invertirable enemye', and it would undoubtedly also produce favours from the King.[45] Hull's representatives reported to the corporation in 1621 that although supply had been granted, they were now petitioners to the King 'for the advancement of godes trew religion', and assured their readers of their hopes 'that at our coming into the country we may bring downe somme good lawes and remedy somme grevances'. Even though York's members in 1624 were the relative political heavyweights Sir Arthur Ingram and Christopher Brooke, it was with evident trepidation that they announced to the city that supply had been given, taking great care to justify themselves in terms of both the international and domestic situation. 'Albeit (the povertie of the realme considered) this is a greate guift, yet the dainger both of our religion and, our Countrie also Considered, it was of necessitie to be given', and they went on to give a long and breathless recital of the Commons' other efforts. This listed firstly the attacks on the monopolists and the corrupt abusers of government, and only later went on to detail the trading measures which were being handled, which must have been of more direct interest to York.[46]

Tighter links were being forged between the House of Commons and the country, and those with the Crown were being weakened, as the fiscal demands of the latter rose. The increasing competition for seats probably drove gentry members to take greater care to please their constituencies in order to give themselves a better chance at the next election, but beyond that, the connection between taxation and representation is clearly close. The repeated attempts to gain the enfranchisement of Durham were partly justified on the grounds that the county palatine was now taxed, and ought to have a say in its affairs in consequence; and several people complained that the poor had nothing to do with parliament because they were not taxed.[47] Possibly the clearest pointer to the links between money and representation is the fact that it was revealed in the course of the Bridport, Chippenham and Exeter franchise disputes that when the commons were involved in an election, the governing body shuffled the burden of paying the members' wages from the corporation chamber onto a special tax of all the freemen.[48] Representation and the payment of money were evidently thought to be inseparable, and this perhaps explains the widespread nature of the rejection of the benevolence and forced loan of 1626–7, and of Ship Money. The belief that taxation had to do with parliament was not just the property of the parliamentary gentry.

It was primarily in the fiscal debates in the House that members explored the subject of their duty to the country. A tract of 1629 sarcastically reported that 'if they stand stiffely out in the deniall of Subsidies . . . then they are excellent Patriots, good Commonwealthsmen, they have well and faithfully discharg'd the trust reposed in them by their City or Country'.[49] The coupling of taxation and electoral accountability was so common that it could be held up as a truism. But the other side of the coin was that members genuinely were increasingly being held to account. The Crown's financial problems not only ensured that parliament survived as an institution, but also that significant developments took place in the relationship between the country and its representatives. Furthermore, Coke's concern for the response of 'the poore 5 li. man', Holle's report of the reaction of the 'plebs' of Nottinghamshire to the Great Contract, the outcry against billeting, all suggest that in the crucial matter of taxation, arguably the one parliamentary activity that really affected the localities, the political nation to which the parliament men were accountable was not a thoroughly closed one. And if co-operation between Crown and parliament broke down in the 1620s on the question of taxation, then the existence of an involved and wide political nation outside Westminster was of fundamental significance.

# 9

# Accountability and National Politics

*Reports*

The prerequisite for a representative system that continues to work after the election is that information should be available in the constituencies. Only then can constituents act effectively. Members felt the need to justify themselves at home when they had been involved in granting away their neighbours' money, but fiscal matters were not the only subject which occasioned reports home. Knowledge of parliament's activities was surprisingly common in the localities.

Again, it must be stressed that this was not wholly novel. We have seen Sir Thomas More telling his audience to inform their localities of the King's marital problems, and the Secretary, Sir Robert Cecil, complained in the monopolies debate of 1601 that 'Parliament matters are ordinarily talked of in the streets. I have heard myself, being in my coach, these words spoken aloud: "God prosper those that further the overthrow of these monopolies. God send the prerogative touch not our liberty."' He made much the same point a couple of weeks later when he alleged that the chief critics of the government 'have desired to be popular without the House for speaking against Monopolies'. James I's attacks on those who 'hasten after grievances' in the House as seekers of 'popularity' are equally founded on the assumption that parliament men were speaking outside the House as well as in it.[1]

Cursory analysis of the available evidence risks distortion, for it is undoubtedly merely as a result of chance that we can know much more about such communication between the House and the outside world in the 17th century than is possible for earlier periods. Further distortion is made likely by the existence of a bureaucracy of a sort in the boroughs, and its absence in the counties. Letters to towns had an official destination in the corporations, and might be filed and preserved, while the bulk of reports from knights of the shires on the progress of business were in the form of newsletters to neighbours, and these might or might not be retained: occasionally in the case of exceptionally well-documented counties like Yorkshire, Norfolk or Kent we can watch news being disseminated through the county through private correspondence. Sometimes, though, and especially over subsidies, reports were more formal. News clearly was travelling in the shires: a recent study of Cheshire has found references to news from London in every surviving set of gentry family correspondence in the years around 1640.[2] Definite statements that formal information increased can be made on the basis of the borough archives, but this is obviously more difficult for the counties, where there was a relative lack of formality. Nevertheless, there is sufficient evidence to show that no major group of members was immune from pressure to inform and explain to their constituencies. This 'feed-back' followed some of the same patterns as applied to its converse, instructions: its volume increased, and its character changed, over roughly the same period. Over a wide range of constituencies, then, two-way communication took place with their representatives, and, predictably, this communication became far more urgent from 1640.

Examination of borough archives produces abundant evidence of detailed information flowing from members in parliament outwards. Long series of letters and communications survive for several towns, most notably Exeter, Great Yarmouth, Hull and York. The corporations of London, Hull, Great Yarmouth and York, as well as those of towns as small as Rye and East Looe, all at one time or another made it quite clear that they *expected* such reports to be tendered.[3] Some of these reports were purely local: all one of Rye's members in 1624 wrote about was the progress of the bill for the Dungeness light – which was what the corporation had instructed him to procure, so here was a case where instructions were being acted on. He informed the town that the matter was being delayed by vitally important national concerns, but he did not see fit to enlighten his constituency as to the intricacies of these.[4] The concept of representation adumbrated here was very much a localist one, but it does indicate that pressure on the member had some effect.

Increasingly, however, reports became more overtly 'national' in their content. This was apparently the kind of subject which members thought their constituents wanted to hear about, even if, as we have seen in the case of York, the constituencies might disclaim any attempt to mandate on such affairs. While in 1606 Hull had merely been given the heads of bills, by the 1620s it was being told of bribery accusations against the government's servants and repeatedly of the business of the Huguenots and the Palatinate. York's reports are very similar, and Great Yarmouth received in 1626, amongst other things, copies of Turner's articles of impeachment against Buckingham, and Clement Coke's speech for which he incurred the King's wrath. By the mid-1620s, Exeter was also being sent separates of speeches, as well as very partisan reports of the proceedings in the House. It preserved the copy of the Petition of Right which it was sent, and Bristol did the same, along with all the accompanying arguments 'in six paper books'. Members were taking pains to keep their constituencies aware of the national issues as a matter of normal practice, and not just in the event of having to justify taxation. The House collectively was capable of doing the same thing, as when it took steps to ensure that the City preserved some of the 1628 arguments relating to the liberty of the subject in its archives. So prevalent had the practice of disseminating parliamentary information become by 1640 that Sir Thomas Peyton regarded it merely as a subject of matter-of-fact comment that the causes and details of the breakdown of the Short Parliament were being spread at large in the country by returning members.[5]

Counties were in all probability little different from boroughs in the amount of information they were fed from the centre. One of Sir Nathaniel Bacon's neighbours in Norfolk was thanking him as soon after the start of the 1604 parliament as April for his 'late friendly advertisements', and was anxious to hear of the outcome of the business of the Union with Scotland. The Marshland area of the county was apparently sufficiently informed of the contents of a bill for the relief of flooded parts of the Severn Estuary in 1608 to urge an extension of its provisions to itself.[6] Bacon's successor, Sir Roger Townsend, returned for the summer recess in 1628 to make a report of the proceedings against Buckingham, and Sir Robert Phelips expected to be questioned on the fate of the unpopular following of the Spanish ambassador, Gondomar, when he returned into Somerset in 1624. Likewise, Phelips's colleague and hated rival in the county's representation, John Poulett, was alleged in 1628 to have made 'his report att his retourn from the Parliament' that Phelips 'had forsaken the country and was turned Courtyer', by his reported co-operation with Buckingham, with a view 'to withdrawe the good opinion of the country' from him.[7] It is significant that Poulett thought it worth his while to make such a charge, suggesting again that at this stage the county was interested in the political position of its knights rather than merely in the local service they were able to give.[8] The alleged fate of Sandys in Kent in 1626 for the same cause that Phelips was maligned for indicates that Poulett's calculations may have been correct, and that a constituency was prepared to apply electoral sanctions to an unsatisfactory member.

Men had obviously been elected for 'political' reasons before the 1620s, but these had centred primarily on local matters. The rebellious freemen of Sandwich in 1621 wanted someone to act against the local threat of the East India Company for them; Dr Hassell Smith's outline of Norfolk elections in the late Elizabethan period certainly shows that antipathy to local patentees underlay the divisions – but it was the disruption of traditional county government which was resented. But what we find by the 1620s is occasional instances of performances in *parliament* on national issues being used as electoral ammunition in the localities. Wentworth's plea to the Yorkshire subsidy commissioners in the summer of 1621 was patently an electoral appeal, and his defence of Calvert was on the basis of what had been done for the country, not the county. Again, it seems to have been Sandys's and Phelips's actions in parliament on issues that were not specifically local which created difficulties for them. Clearest of all was the Worcestershire election to the Long Parliament, where, while the description of Sir Thomas Littleton's past record was ambiguous (he 'had in former Parliaments done noe service for the cuntrie', which could mean Worcestershire or England), the allegation about his potential (he 'was fitter to breake Parliaments then to serve in Parliament') makes it probable that it was his activities as a courtier, rather than his local inadequacy, which were being held against him.[9] Candidates were calculating that the electorate wanted something more than just local service from its representatives.

An increasing amount and variety of information was being placed at the disposal of the constituencies, and this made it possible for more sophisticated political judgements to be made. The members evidently felt bound by their position to provide this information, but this inexorably subjected them to new forms of electoral constraint.[10] Even if direct communications from the parliament men back into the localities went only to an elite few, we must presume a gradual dissemination of the news, for information apparently became sufficiently widespread for defaulting members to be made to suffer electorally. In elections in the 1620s and 1640, choices were sometimes made for national as well as local reasons: it is clear that there was increasingly a basis of information available on which such choices could be made. The representative process was patently a continuing one. The early decades of the century, with rising taxation and accelerating political crisis, saw instructions and reports multiply and develop, as the constituencies began to ask more of their representatives, and to select them consciously with a new end in view.

## The quest for support, 1640-2

Outside interest in, and expectations of, parliament as a salve for the nation's ills grew in the early 17th century. After the unhappy fiscal experiments and military misfortunes of the previous two years, the news of the summoning of the 1628 parliament was greeted with the ringing of church bells in Ipswich. Grass-roots awareness that national reformation, given royal hostility, could only come through parliament is indicated by several pieces of evidence: it has recently been suggested that the approach of the Short Parliament was heralded by a revival of petitioning to JPs on moral causes by Essex puritans in their parishes, petitioning which had lapsed after the angry dissolution of the last parliament in 1629. In

London, one of the godly industrious sort reported that on the opening day of the Short Parliament, 'so many of God's children did meet together in divers places in fasting and prayer', and the frustration of these hopes by dissolution provoked placarding in the City, a huge public meeting in St George's Fields, and the hunting of the Laudian fox by the apprentices and leatherworkers to his den in Lambeth Palace. There were said to have been over 10,000 signatures to a London petition of September demanding the recall of parliament, which was not backed by the corporation.[11] This concern was not confined solely to the metropolis and its environs, for the parish of Cheddar in Somerset spent 4*d*. on a book of parliamentary proceedings in 1640, and the county and peers' petitions of late summer 1640 demanding recourse to a parliament were to be met in various parts of the country.[12]

Elections held in this atmosphere were likely to be rather different from those of a generation earlier. Edward Bagshaw was apparently elected for Southwark in the autumn as a result of arousing puritan expectations in the borough by taking an anti-Laudian position in a legal exercise in one of the Inns of Court the previous year, and at the same time in Kent Sir Edward Dering was gaining votes for similar reasons. Candidates in those elections where we have seen national issues playing a part were obviously making identical calculations.[13] But as interesting as what happened at the hustings is what went on afterwards.

Even those boroughs which had shown themselves entirely localist in the 1620s were now extending their interests outside the town walls, as they realised that what they suffered from was being felt elsewhere, and could only be remedied by national measures. Localism obviously continued, and in such a society this could hardly have been otherwise. While we have seen that Northampton corporation was one of the most notoriously puritanical in the country, the instructions it planned to send its members early in the Long Parliament had to do with improving the navigation on the River Nene, obtaining further relief from the county for the victims of the disastrous plague in the town, and tightening the borough's electoral regulations. Nevertheless, Great Yarmouth was broadening its outlook: in former parliaments it had agitated for nothing more than might be 'requisite and fitting for the Townes good', but in May 1640 (too late) it was prepared to present its much more political 'grievances' to its representatives, and these included, besides multiple impositions, the suppression of 'preaching and other religious exercises'. Norwich's particularist instructions similarly gave place to a list of grievances, and King's Lynn became exercised over 'the Grevances of the Church', although these were those 'which Bishope Wrenn Caused to be done in our Towne', rather than any national wrongs.[14] These novel demonstrations of constituency anger and concern were evidently so common that the members for Bristol in April and East Looe in November were constrained to write home asking for complaints of grievances to be sent up, in order, presumably, to make their points more strongly at a time when all other parliament men were alleging the national hatred of their particular bogy. East Looe greeted the request 'with Joy and thankes'.[15]

Political instructions and statements of grievances in 1640 were not necessarily the products of the socially respectable groups. A body of freemen in Newcastle in March drew up a list of instructions for their members, and alleged dereliction of duty on the part of the corporation for not doing so itself, for such instructions were said to be customary. Their demands certainly included local and material measures, but their primary concerns were that their members were 'wholly to oppose any innovation' in religion, and 'to stand out' for the liberty and freedom of the subject, 'which is principally in the maintenance of Magna Charta [sic] and the other fundamental parliamentary laws'. London's grievances were presented at the election court 'by the multitude to the Sheriffe to be by him delivered over to the Knights', and while part of the official reluctance to do this was probably procedural, there was in all likelihood some fear of the radical demands being advanced, for many of those present argued that such demands should only be published under the privilege of parliament, in order to avoid governmental retaliation.[16] At the spring election for Middlesex, a petition to be presented to the candidates was read amongst the freeholders, and in the autumn 'the Countrey people' drew up their own petition, in which attacks on the Church courts featured prominently, 'requyring' the knights to present it to the House. The Northamptonshire members were entrusted at the March hustings with the county's grievances over ship and coat and conduct monies, monopolies, Church courts, and the 'molestations of our most Godly and learned ministers', and these were presumably read out and assented to by the assembled freeholders in the open court, for this is what happened in Dorset in October, and as we have seen earlier, the Northamptonshire voters certainly knew what they wanted at that election.[17] The number of electors who believed that their members had a political programme was expanding.

Member after member rose from their seats in the early stages of both Short and Long Parliaments to announce that they had had petitions delivered into their hands by those for whom they served, and then begged the House to take these very political complaints into consideration. When interrogated by the Privy Council after the failure of the Short Parliament, Sir William Savile testified that the Yorkshire freeholders told him before he left the county that 'they did not care howe many subsidies were given soe that greivance of the shipp mony were taken awaye'.[18]

Even such conservative 'Country' figures as Sir John Colpepper and Lord Digby felt able to regard themselves as the instruments of their counties, delegated at the county court, and accordingly produced long and national lists of grievances which they had been entrusted to see redressed.[19] While 'entrustment' is not the same as 'instruction', it seems probable that understandings were being formed locally that members would do their best to effect what was being given into their charge. If so, attempts were being made in 1640 to guide members not only on local and tax matters, but on national affairs in general.

As alienation from the Court increased, particularly as a result of the events of the 1630s, the need for a larger role for parliament was recognised in the country, just as it had been recognised rather earlier by the parliament men themselves, when they insisted on trespassing on royal prerogatives. The country, or the politically vocal parts of it, felt themselves to be just as concerned in this larger role as they were in the matter of taxation or local goods, and in consequence the scope of instructions, or pressure on members, expanded. Not only then did members feel compelled to venture consciously into previously forbidden areas – their electors were sometimes ready to urge them to do so.

This new relationship, of the Long Parliament man with his politically-aroused constituents, can be traced most clearly in the case of Sir Edward Dering, one of the knights for Kent. He was understood to have given his supporters certain undertakings at the election as to his future behaviour in the House, and pressure was applied by those who elected him to conform to those undertakings. The justification explicitly advanced by his lobbyists was that as they had elected him he was their servant, bound to them by their votes. And the courses that were urged on him were by no means purely local ones, but had to do with the abolition of episcopacy.[20] By the end of 1641, the conservative faction in the county was hinting at a refusal to be bound by the House's votes, on the grounds that the members had been elected to act according to a purpose which the country, not the House, determined.[21] Kent is a uniquely fully documented county, and reveals a considerable degree of political excitement, but evidence survives elsewhere to suggest that other members were experiencing similar pressures. The religious complexion of Edward Bagshaw's election for Southwark has been noted, and the inhabitants of the borough lost little time in attempting to pressurise him into fulfilling his apparent promise; and members for Yorkshire and Herefordshire were being kept informed of the wishes of the godly in the country on religious matters. Dr Pearl has demonstrated the part played by London ministers and their minions, the apprentices and tradesmen, in co-ordinating the activities of the City and its members, but while for obvious reasons of geography and sophistication, this co-ordination was of a different order from elsewhere, the distinction was perhaps often one of degree rather than kind.[22]

The divisions of these months introduced a much more peremptory note, as one side or other felt themselves to be no longer effectively represented by a member whom they now found to be of an opposed party. Various Herefordshire JPs wrote to their knights in March 1642 demanding that a bill be introduced that members 'may bee enioyned more dilligentlie hereafter' to perform their duties, testifying to their disenchantment with their own present representatives, and hoped that they would not offend 'in this *not unusuall* or unlawfull manner of recommendinge our desires'. A month later, while disclaiming any attempt 'as private men' to dictate to the House, they equally denied that the House had any authorisation from them for its present course. The strength of the concept of electoral responsibility is illustrated by Sir Robert Harley's reply: while he deplored the contents of the JPs' letter, he was willing to do his duty and present it to the House. Many in Kent, as we have seen, were following a similarly intransigent line to that of the Herefordshire JPs, and a number of Nottinghamshire gentry ordered their knights not to vote to engage the county in a civil war. They reproved them for involving their constituents by the arbitrary ordinances of the two Houses, and suggested that it was no part of the members' function to tell the country what to do, for they were rather its servants than its masters: 'we hope you will not be unwilling to follow our sence, so far as you conceive it to be the sence of your County whose you are and for whom you serve'.[23]

The opposite attitude was certainly visible, as members subjected to unwelcome pressure protested their superiority to popular fancies. It was common for members in 1642 to stress that voting was an act of assent to the representative's future actions, and therefore that the electors had obliged themselves. Alternatively, sheer prejudice could come out, as when Lord Digby in 1641 realised that popular pressure was going farther than had seemed likely at the heady Dorset freeholders' election a few months before, and demanded, 'What can there bee of greater presumption, then for Petitioners ... to prescribe to a Parliament, what, and how it shall doe', or when Dering, by now equally at odds with the voices from below, abhorred 'this descension from a Parliament to a People'.[24] But pressure from the localities on the centre coincided with what many members were trying to achieve, for these were of course the months of the first real propaganda campaign. Just as many erstwhile electors were trying to bind their members closer to them, so the reverse process was in full swing, as public opinion for the first time became a major political factor. The activities of the House as a whole in encouraging petitions, or of the opposition leadership in concocting and manipulating this aspect of the *vox populi*, is well known, but what is not so obvious is that many members were adding their own efforts in their constituencies.

Again, the best documented instance of this process is provided by Dering's activities in Kent. Before his dramatic turn of coat in mid-1641, Dering was encouraging those pressures on himself which he was later to attack as improper 'descension'. He seems to have met constituents frequently, fed them with arguments to use against unpopular clerics, advised them how to proceed with petitioning campaigns, and perhaps most important, to have seen to it that his speeches were distributed in the countryside. His activities were matched elsewhere. Sir Robert Harley was engaged in similar endeavours on the Welsh borders in 1641, and one of Hythe's members seems to have been following suit at the end of the year.[25]

The two most important parliamentary documents of 1641, the Protestation of 3 May and the Grand Remonstrance, were avowedly ingredients in this determined campaign to whip up support in the constituencies for the policy and persons of the majority group in the House. In fear of a dissolution in the spring designed to engineer Strafford's reprieve, even the conservative Colpepper could urge the drawing up of the Protestation as a justification to the country, 'that if we should be dissolved, that we might be found doing the service we were hither sent for'. Cromwell and Lowry sent it to Cambridge to be subscribed, telling it, 'You shall herebie as the Bodie represented avow the practice of the Representative, the conformitie is in itself praiseworthy and will be by them approved...Combination carryes strength with it.' Members of very different political persuasions, Cromwell and Colpepper, evidently felt a need to defend their intransigence over Strafford to the country, and to associate the country in it. Apparently the Protestation produced similar letters from D'Ewes to Sudbury in its support, and similar epistles arrived at Tewkesbury and Newcastle-under-Lyme from their members.[26] The minister at Tewkesbury, John Geree, saw the practical consequences of the Protestation (which he depicted as a national covenant) as enormous: if godly ministers or people were in future unjustly oppressed, or 'if any shall now come upon thee with unlawfull taxes, ... thou mayst goe to any Peere or Parliament-man, and by vertue of this, require assistance'.[27] The Protestation was an open invitation to the populace to involve itself in the doings of parliament. And that it did have such tangible effects in the country is evidenced by the experiences of Dering's correspondent Robert Abbot in Kent, who was subjected to harassment in his ministry by those citing the Protestation and allied broadsides in their defence.[28] Not only was a general propaganda and pamphleteering campaign developing nationally, but individual members were taking steps to arouse their constituencies.

This populism was even more obviously at the root of the decision to publish the Grand Remonstrance. The radical William Purefoy pointed to the great need for money in order to pay off the commitments incurred in opposing the Scots, and 'conceived ther was [no] readier meanes to bring in monie then to cause our declaration [the Remonstrance] to be printed that soe wee might satisfie the whole kingdome'.[29] Glynne, the Recorder of London, and Pym had earlier used exactly the same argument, Pym urging that 'This declaration will binde the peoples hearts to us, when they see how we have been used'.[30] The fear of disaffection in the country, as the people began to make their own political judgements, is manifest, and those pamphleteers who attacked the withdrawal of the electors' allegiance from their representatives were clearly addressing a real problem. Lord Fairfax's agent in the North welcomed the appearance of the Remonstrance in terms which its promoters had presumably hoped for: it 'comes forth very seasonably, because the Anti-parliamentarian faction begin to extenuate the fruits of their long session ... And I think it were necessary to print a bill of the names of all those who voted for the printing and publishing of the Remonstrance or Declaration, and also of those who voted against the publishing of it, that the country may take notice of their friends, and know how to elect better patriots hereafter.'[31] The document was clearly and correctly seen as an attempt to win friends and influence people in the country, and, furthermore, as having a real electoral significance too.

To many in both parliament and country by 1641, the people were no longer merely to be governed, but they were to act in partnership with their representatives in the House. It was just this which frightened Dering when he protested over the Grand Remonstrance that it was unknown for a parliament 'to remonstrate downwards, tell stories to the people', and to look for a cure at the hands of the people[32] – conveniently forgetting that such dangerous populism had characterised his own actions only six months earlier. But Dering was, as has been indicated, not the only member to be concerned about public opinion, even if he was trying to manufacture it more blatantly than were many others.

The propaganda campaigns of 1641–2, however unprecedented they were in their intensity and content, were not wholly novel in their implications. A fairly wide social spectrum had expectations of parliament at this stage, and not only in London. The summoning of the Short Parliament and the anticipation that prerogative abuses would be downed, provoked pre-emptive action against enclosures in the Lincolnshire Fens; the frustration of the hopes held by the meaner sort that the parliamentary abolition of the forest courts would bring a better world for the forest dwellers led to widespread riots in Windsor Forest in the late summer and autumn of 1641.[33] These people at least evidently believed that the parliament should be responsive to their wishes. The electorate, or some varying part of it, had a history of being consulted and informed by its representatives. In yet another area, Leveller demands for a representative and responsive assembly could be seen as in some ways a systematisation of existing practice. Even their plea for annual parliaments had been made by the Northamptonshire freeholders in their petition to the Short Parliament.[34] While what was feared then was irresponsibility by the Crown rather than by parliament men, distrust of the representative arose in some quarters in the next two years, and is most clearly visible in the invigilatory bill proposed by the Herefordshire gentry in 1642.

There was developed two-way communication between member and constituency before the outbreak of civil war, and cries in parliament about responsibility to those who elected them were by no means a charade. Members felt they had to keep their constituencies both informed and satisfied, and increasingly from the mid-1620s the part of this satisfaction which had to do with national politics grew. As early as mid-1621, in fear of a dissolution, Sir Dudley Digges had claimed that the country was more interested in, and wanted satisfaction on, national grievances not local ones: 'we feare (as I understand) least the bills that we shall imbrace, not being of sufficient generall valew, the Country will not be so well pleased with them'.[35] By 1640-1, many constituents felt they could comment forcefully on such issues to their representatives, and expect some response. It seems clear that a House which was growing more representative numerically was also becoming more representative in the other way that mattered.[36]

# Conclusion

# 10

# Conclusion

England on the eve of the Civil War cannot be classed as politically closed for several important reasons. The King's government and Court certainly formed an extremely restricted world, but there were avenues of expression through parliament open to those outside, and those avenues were becoming broader. The spectacle of men like Sexby and Allen rising from the ranks to become senior officers in the New Model Army was not to be matched before the war – although perhaps six yeomen did sit in the Long Parliament House of Commons[1] – but such people did have some outlet for their political aspirations, and some means of gaining a political education before that assembly of saints on the march known as the New Model Army came into being. The Privy Council felt that elections were in themselves dangerously likely to disturb the tranquillity of the lower depths of society. After the disputed Buckinghamshire election of 1604 necessitated a second election, the Council warned the local JPs to take care, 'respectinge the Mean and inferior sorte of that Cuntrie whom this busines by severall elleccions hath afflicted and troubled'.[2] If even personal disputes risked arousing the meaner sort, the potential of more and more excited campaigns in later years cannot be underestimated. The high levels of turn-out in Wigan and Tewkesbury in 1640, the occurrence of rioting in London in the spring of 1640 and Windsor Forest in 1641 geared to the frustration of parliamentary hopes, all indicate that the common people had a very real interest in their representative.

Only the Crown seems to have viewed this state of affairs with unease, for the gentry were prepared to encourage its emergence. While it is arguable that many may not have been aware of the implications of the actions of their fellows, the gentry in their collective political capacity in the House, and individuals in the localities, were endeavouring to expand the electorate in the franchise disputes. Whether obstructing a suspected threat from the Crown at a national level, or for their own local advantage, they were prepared to employ the commons for their own ends. In this, they acted in much the same way as they did in the other main field where the commons were able to express themselves, in riots. There too, the gentry were prepared to encourage the commons to act in order to resist Crown exploitation, in the Fens and the South-West, and equally they often stirred up popular action against local gentry rivals.[3]

But the decisive factor here is the strength of the relative threats. Before the war, the propertied classes, with occasional exceptions, do not seem to have been excessively frightened of the threat from below, whereas there was often considerable disquiet about the activities of the Crown. The events of the years 1642–60 reversed that estimate, and a toughening of the attitude of the gentry became visible. The horror at the idea of any constitutional change,[4] the establishment of the game laws and the Act of Settlement, are symptomatic, and the Cavalier Parliament proceeded to overturn previous expansionist principles on the franchise. The very different prejudices of the Restoration parliamentary gentry from those of a generation earlier are revealed by the House's decision on the Windsor case in 1661. The franchise there had been opened by the Long Parliament, but having considered 'the whole Matter', the Cavalier House resolved that despite the involvement of the commons in '*Anno* 1640', the precedents told in favour of the oligarchy. In one of the few cases where the commons were supported, at Preston, it was almost certainly merely in order to outflank a presbyterian corporation.[5] The horrors of the revolutionary decades were only overlooked when in the Exclusion Crisis at the end of Charles II's reign the danger from above once again appeared to outweigh that from below and the Commons returned, if briefly, to their pre-war position of espousing the rights of the meaner sort in order to defend their own liberties and privileges.[6] The commons were in effect being politically exploited by the gentry in parliament.

The outcome of this was to differentiate England markedly from the rest of Europe where power was devolving upon smaller numbers, and opportunities for political consultation through representative assemblies were being eliminated as the Estates fell. In England, parliament increased in strength while assemblies abroad became debilitated; but more singular was the expansion of the political nation, which abroad was everywhere contracting. Urban oligarchies in England, backed up by the Crown, were tightening their grips in many fields just as was happening abroad, but the self-interested intervention of the parliamentary gentry prevented them extending their hold to the electoral franchise. The representatives of the third estate in England were thus possessed of a rather wider social base, not only than their 18th-century successors, but also than similar representatives abroad, both in the 17th century and later.

Although in one sense the relationship of the Commons to the meaner sort was one-sided and exploitative, this was not true overall. While the gentry, aided by inflation, helped to create a larger political nation, they were not always able to control it, and they had to take account of its wishes. The divergent electoral histories of large, populous constituencies and small ones show that popular involvement was not a stream that could be channelled at will by the gentry. And the gentry in parliament needed the commons, not just in the obvious ways, for their votes, for their physical support in 1641–2 – Prof. Underdown's description of the early stages of the war in Somerset shows just how important the adherence of the weavers and the countrymen could be[7] – but more generally to make sense of their claims.

Perhaps the major theme of Parliament's polemical defence against the King was its assertion that it represented England. We have seen that it was attacked on this score, but these attacks must have been far more damaging had its electoral base been narrower. The desperate quest for arguments by Parliament's propagandists in the summer and autumn of 1642 reveals the urgent need to develop a respectable legitimation for resistance to an anointed king. Part of Parliament's representative defence obviously looked back to the traditional vague, semi-mystical belief, subscribed to by Sir Thomas Smith and by Hooker, that all men were somehow present in parliament. But the task of its critics would have been easier had it been self-evident that this was factually incorrect, for the contention that Parliament was merely a narrow clique, and that the King really represented the people, would then have been more persuasive. Dr Hill has lately given weight to the royalist case by agreeing that 'we no longer swallow the claim of 17th-century Parliaments to represent the people of England; they represented the propertied class, the gentry and merchants'.[8] But I would argue that those claims cannot be so easily dismissed. Both in the numbers of people voting, in the relative freedom with which they voted and the kind of issues they voted on, and the responsiveness of members of the House to outside pressures, there was some justification for Parliament's claims to be representative. Before the reaction consequent on the mid-century troubles set in, and when under the early Stuarts the political consensus and the workings of patronage broke down, genuine consultations took place with large numbers of ordinary people.

# Constituencies Experiencing Franchise Disputes 1604–41

Where the events are discussed in the text, or in Appendix II, below, no further details are given here.

SP=Short Parliament; LP=Long Parliament.

Abingdon. SP. Not decided.

Bedford. SP and LP.

Bewdley. LP. Attempts by freemen to break corporation franchise: not decided by House of Commons.[1]

Bletchingley. 1624.

Bossiney. LP.

Boston. 1628.

Bridgnorth. 1610. Attempt to extend franchise to inhabitants at large on grounds of phrasing of charter? Not decided.[2]

Bridport. 1625? 1628.

Bristol. 1625. LP. There is little contextual evidence for the disputes here. The freemen pressed for the vote in 1625 in the midst of depression; they appear to have gained it as a result of their pressure in October 1640. The wordings of the indentures then and for the by-election of 1642 (the corporation 'cum multis aliis', 'et multi alii', made the elections) imply as much; they were certainly enfranchised by the Restoration, and apparently in 1654. The absence of any reference in the corporation archives to disorder at the intervening elections, such as that which was made in 1625 and 1640, indicates that the freemen's success was in 1640.[3]

Cambridge. 1621–5. LP?

Cambridge University. 1614. 1625. The Heads of Houses interpreted the Elizabethan statutes to mean that members should be chosen in the same manner as the Vice-Chancellor, which would effectively have destroyed the role of the MAs—it was a specious argument, for the University had not been represented at the time of the statutes, so parliamentary elections could not have been intended then. The attempts probably failed because of the continuing efforts by gentry other than the official nominees to gain the prestigious seats, for they were prepared to fight the cause in the House.[4]

Chester. 1621.

Chippenham. 1604? 1624.

Cirencester. 1624.

Clitheroe. 1640? Apparently owners of burgage tenures voted in 1628, but these were supplemented by tenants of non-resident owners in the Long Parliament election.[5]

Colchester. 1625? 1628.

Dover. 1624.

East Grinstead. SP.

Exeter. 1626. 1628.

Gatton. 1621. 1628. 1641.

Gloucester. 1624. The details are unclear, but it appears that the inhabitants of the
'inshire', two hundreds attached to the city, akin to the Ainsty at York (q.v.),
may have pressed for representation.[6]

Great Bedwin. SP. The franchise was remitted by the Committee of Privileges to
the scot-and-lot men from the burgage tenants.[7]

Great Yarmouth. 1625?

Hertford. SP.

Higham Ferrers. SP.

Hythe. 1624–6.

King's Lynn. LP. The port anciently possessed an indirect, committee-based form
of election, but this was broken by the freemen in 1640. The corporation re-
acted, as did that of Exeter earlier, by refusing to pay the members' wages.
The franchise remained in dispute for some time.[8]

Marlow. LP.

Mitchell. SP.

Monmouth. LP. Apparently the out-boroughs petitioned for the vote, a specifically Welsh electoral custom.[9]

Newcastle-under-Lyme. 1624.

Newport (Cornwall). 1626. 1628. SP? 1641?

Northampton. LP.

Oxford. 1621.

Oxford University. 1626. Similar to the Cambridge University disputes.[10]

Pembroke. 1621. The out-boroughs of Pembroke petitioned to be allowed the
vote: not decided by the House.[11]

Peterborough. LP. No details are known of this dispute, save that D'Ewes asserted
that the franchise was in question.[12]

Reading. SP and LP.

St Germans. LP.

Salisbury. LP.

Sandwich. 1621.

Tamworth. SP. The petitioners, the 'commonalty', claimed that charter had over-
ridden a prescriptive right to vote, and limited it to the chief burgesses; but
no details are known.[13]

Tewkesbury. 1625? LP.

Wallingford. LP. Again, no details are known of this dispute, over which the
House eventually extended the vote to the 'commonalty'.[14]

Warwick. 1621. 1626. 1628. 1641.

Wigan. LP. As in Bristol, there were two categories of freemen in Wigan: those
free of the corporation and those free to trade within the town. The corporation asserted in their petition to the House that the vote was confined to the
former, who were responsible for keeping the courts leet. But 'divers inferior
persons, inhabitants, laborers, and handicraftsmen, being Free only to trade
within the said Towne of Wigan, and no enrouled or sworne Burgesses of the
said Corporation, by the instigacion and incyteinge of others of uncivill
government, have combyned, confederated, and complotted together' to
overthrow the election.[15] No further details are known; but it is plain from
probate evidence that the 'burgesses of the corporation' also included 'divers
inferior persons'.

Windsor. LP.

Chipping Wycombe. SP.

York. LP. The Ainsty, an area within the liberties of York, petitioned for the
vote.[16]

# Case Studies of Disputes

*1. Chester*

The 1621 franchise dispute was not, as were so many other cases, occasioned by the clothing depression of the 1620s. Although the Dee was silting up and the city increasingly affected by the competition of Liverpool merchants, Chester had not yet become an economic backwater. After a depression at the start of the century, its cloth trade was recovering in the later 1610s, largely in response to the demands of the Irish market, and it was therefore not overly affected by the European slump. Trade generally was probably increasing around 1620, particularly that geared to the provisioning of Ireland, but much of this was not in the hands of Chester merchants, and thus failed to raise the town's prosperity proportionally. This perhaps accounts for some of the unusually strong hostility to 'foreigners' in the town. A further possible cause of disruption was that the leather trades bulked large in the city's economy, possibly related to the Irish cattle connection, and yet were considerably under-represented in the city's government. But militating most strongly against a purely economic interpretation of the 1620–1 troubles was the fact that the local harvest of 1620 was particularly good.[1]

Despite the relative economic stability of the city, its internal affairs were thoroughly disordered in the years before 1621. The freemen divided from, and were over-ruled by, the corporation in the mayoral election for 1619–20, and at the end of 1620 a major riot occurred, arising from a bull-baiting, in which the mayor's authority was completely flouted. Even more ominous was the situation within the governing body, which required interventions by an assize judge and by the Privy Council in the years 1619–20. The then mayor had in mid-1619 led a bid to oust the Recorder, Edward Whitby, and three of his allies were put off the corporation for various offences, which, it was said, stemmed from wider controversies within the city: 'the Cittizens beinge devyded all these Contentions did arise'. Conversely, the Whitby interest alleged that their enemies in the corporation were labouring the commons in the alehouses against them. At the same time, a long feud was reverberating through the courts between the former town clerk, another Whitby, extruded in 1617 on a technicality, and a fellow-alderman, 'a man towardes the law'.[2] It was little wonder that the magistrates' authority should have been so disregarded at the end of 1620.

Recorder Whitby sought to avenge his affronts when the parliamentary election of 1621 offered an occasion—although the differences between himself and his fellows had been officially composed a year earlier. He and his ally John Ratcliffe dissociated themselves from the choice of outsiders made by their fellow-magistrates, and stood on their own account. To this end, they echoed the alehouse tactics of their municipal opponents, and canvassed among the poor of the city, allegedly going below the ranks of the enfranchised freemen and furnishing themselves with mere 'inhabitantes and (for the most parte) those of the suburbs, of the basest sort, as labourers and hyred workemen and even beggars, and not with theise only but also with divers apprentices and forreigners, such as were not capable of voyces', and particularly such as were their own tenants.[3] There may have been a further ingredient in a religious divide within the city. There had been outbursts of iconoclasm earlier, involving Ratcliffe, and he was noted by a hostile witness in 1621, in a deleted passage in the account, as being 'the cheife Countenancer of the secte of Purytans and hath ben convented for his irregularity'. The corporation blamed the pressure to which it was subject in 1620–1 on the machinations of the pair of oligarchs, but it is manifest that the position of the magistrates was not very strong.[4]

The controversies did not die down after this ostensible popular victory, confirming that the position of the commons in parliamentary elections was not what the troubles were about. The relative positions in the corporation had been reversed by the later 1620s, and the new establishment was taking revenge, purging those by whom they themselves had been purged, and creating new disturbances. Both sides were heavily censured by the Privy Council, especially for taking their quarrels outside the council chamber. The success the new opposition had had in emulating Whitby's and Ratcliffe's tactics of 1620–1 was shown in the mayoral election for 1627–8 when the commons overthrew the official choice, Ratcliffe, the populist of earlier years. The freemen also refused to tolerate the presence of strangers in the hall, using violence on gentry as respected as Sir Richard Grosvenor and his son, and Peter Warburton (for Ratcliffe was now backed by the Earl of Derby). Subsequent attempts at intimidation of voters by the gentry in the 1628 parliamentary election almost produced a similarly violent reaction by the commons: as an observer testified, 'a Citty more devided in faction was never seene', and indeed, the remnant of the same factional alignment appears to have surfaced in the Short Parliament election for the city.[5] The franchise dispute was wholly rooted in these divisions, rather than specifically geared to the parliamentary election.

## 2. Chippenham

The affairs of Chippenham, a manorial clothing town struggling for independence from its lord, were complicated by a long-drawn and bitter dispute over the profits of the town lands. The benefits of these were restricted to the inhabitant freemen, and people could be excluded for such offences as drunkenness, contumacy, or contravention of the local farming practices, by the self-selecting bailiff and burgesses. Controversy was therefore inevitable, and spread throughout the early 17th century, requiring a Chancery decree in 1604, but this failed to institute peace.[6] As a fairly typical order of 1608 warned, in order to 'settle perfect peace and amitye betweene the saied Bayliffe Burgesses and Inhabitants which for longe time have remained at variance and unreconciled by meanes of some few persones haveing Turbulente and workinge spiritts and beinge of frowarde dispositon', if any challenged the corporation over the town lands, or 'consortes' with any that did so, then he would lose the benefit of the lands. It is probably significant that the freemen first became involved in the elections in 1604, when the land dispute was at its fiercest.[7]

The 1620s depression hit the Wiltshire woollen industry badly, and created substantial unemployment in Chippenham, the worst period being the autumn of 1623, that is, immediately before the decisive election. In this context, the question of the profit from the town lands must have weighed very heavily, exacerbating divisions. Matters could hardly have been helped when in 1623 the Crown started to enclose and disafforest Pewsham, or Chippenham, Forest.[8] Pym, the corporation's candidate in 1624, was royal receiver in the area, and was very deeply involved in a venture to which the commons were so sensitive, and which subsequently provoked extensive disorder. It may be significant that a neighbouring member who was angered at the House's decision to open the franchise construed the term 'Inhabytantes' in the House's discussions as not meaning that 'every hedge breaker, or Inmate' should vote, for this could suggest that opponents of enclosure were among those antagonistic to Pym. Certainly, the underprivileged were solidly against Pym, all 32 of the commons who attempted to vote siding with his and the corporation's opponent, Sir Francis Popham. Popham was furthermore a benefactor of the town, and responsible for the establishment of the town's alms-houses, a particularly important consideration in a period of hardship.[9] The franchise dispute here seems to owe far more to this most important of all causes of commons' concern than to any desire for a parliamentary role.

### 3. Colchester

Turbulence had for some time been evident in Colchester's internal affairs, possibly in consequence of its character as a sea-port close to the Netherlands, giving rise to a greater religious forwardness, possibly also as a result of its economic situation. It was in one of those areas with the highest concentration of labour almost totally dependent on cloth earnings, so any temporary textile depression, even when food prices might be low, caused disproportionate hardship.[10] The chronology of the disorders cannot be exactly linked to economic disruption, for they broke out before the cloth industry went into deep depression from 1620, but their continuation in that troubled decade, and the issue they focused on, suggests that there was a connection.

The disturbances first became marked in 1612, when a new constitution drawn up by the corporation was overwhelmingly rejected on the next municipal election day following. In the preamble to the new orders, the oligarchy justified themselves on the grounds that 'some disorders and inconveniences have increased within this Towne by the meanes of smalle estates and abilityes about the Choice of . . . the Bailiffes maiestrates and other officers of this Towne'. It appears that in the years leading up to these orders, all forms of municipal election had been under challenge. The corporation proposed to rectify matters by curtailing the powers of poor freemen in town government. A system of rigid property qualifications was laid down for participation in any election (for example, 40s. freehold land, or 100 marks in personal estate, was demanded for the right to vote for headman of the ward), and this was reinforced by a complex scheme of indirect election for other offices, all with the intention of curbing the prevailing 'greate disquiettnes of the good and peaceable government of this Towne'. Perhaps not surprisingly, the body of the freemen repudiated these orders at the first available opportunity.[11]

The matter could not be left in limbo, for the borough was compelled to revert to the old constitution of 29 Eliz., which had been powerless to prevent the pre-1612 disorders. Accordingly, the freemen challenged the corporation's powers in the municipal elections of 1615, driving the magistrates to assert their sole right in such matters in no uncertain terms and to brief counsel. Amidst a higher level of absenteeism than usual among the junior members of the corporation, suggesting that some of this body were opposed to the select group, the corporation approached the Attorney-General, Bacon, and the Chief Justice, Coke. But the attack which the magistrates alleged was under way, stirred up by an outside gentleman, on their general position and powers[12] was unsuccessful: Bacon managed to achieve a compromise solution (in the corporation's favour) of the municipal election dispute, and threatened that if the commons did not abide peaceably by it, he himself would lead an attack in King's Bench on their 'pretended Liberties'.[13]

The intervention of the judiciary brought some imperfect peace to the town.

There were complaints in 1623 that the commons were attacking all preachers of
whom they disapproved, and two years later, Thomas Darcy, Viscount Colchester,
attempting to persuade the town to elect Sir Francis Barrington and Sir Thomas
Cheeke, the candidates for the county endorsed by Buckingham, inveighed against
the 'base and leawd' opposition to him in the town: the apparent inclusion of the
freemen in the borough election in some capacity that year gives some colour to
his complaint of turbulence.[14] But there was little serious trouble until the old
disturbances broke out again in the extraordinary conditions of 1627–8, when the
corporation was decisively defeated.

Colchester was a main assembly point for the troops being sent overseas to the
King of Denmark, and was consequently troubled by the tumults of deserting
soldiers, and by men returning from the Ile de Ré disaster. Given its proximity to
the port of embarkation, Harwich, Colchester was also highly cessed to supply
provisions of all kinds. This inevitably induced an unsettled atmosphere, at a time
when food prices were certainly not low, and when unemployment was rising
again. The county trained bands refused to march to suppress the Harwich mutiny
of April 1627, indicating the extent of disaffection in the area. The corporation's
problems were mounting, and increasing absenteeism among its members suggests
that as in the earlier bout of troubles, it was no longer united.[15]

The local politics of the period were also complicated by the Earl of Warwick's
attempts to establish hegemony over the county. In Colchester, he had succeeded
in having his younger brother, the Earl of Holland, appointed Recorder in 1627,
and, by judicious use of his admiralty jurisdiction, he was slowly bringing all three
parliamentary boroughs in the county to heel. The corporation's love for him
could not have been increased by the fact that he was the most active of the county's
two Lords Lieutenant, and represented the military establishment, whose measures,
such as levying excessive amounts of powder for external use, were seen as undermining the independence of the town.[16]

To the same end of establishing his control over the town, Warwick was attempting to insinuate himself as ecclesiastical patron in 1627–8, persuading several of the
local gentry to write in support of his candidate for lecturer. The corporation
successfully resisted both Warwick and Laud, and seem to have been able to do this
partly because of the turbulence of the xenophobic freemen, who threatened to
make the position of a new stranger as 'uncomfortable as they did the life of the
good man deceased'. The man eventually appointed carried on the tradition of
'marked puritans' as town lecturers, suggesting that this dispute with Warwick was
over political control, not religion.[17] There was ample opportunity for friction
within the town in 1628, without the added challenge of a parliamentary election.
Although the corporation won the ecclesiastical clash with Warwick, the ousting of
the corporation's choice as burgess, Edward Alford, and Warwick's subsequent
domination of the representation of the town, suggests that the Earl was involved
in the 1628 dispute, the result of which must have gratified him. There is, however,
little positive evidence surviving to support this contention.

A central participant in the dispute testified that the far-reaching controversy
which developed was not solely related to the election. Sir William Masham,
Warwick's ally, wrote to the corporation towards the end of 1628, some time after
the election dispute had been settled by the House, telling them that he 'should be
glad to heare of a friendly end of that controversye betwixt you and the rest of the
Burgesses', and hoping that it would not come to a 'publike contest'—which of
course rules out the election, for that already had. He seems to have been too late
for the freemen's grievances had produced a general attack on the town's charter
The cause of the ultimate breach of relations, which involved the election dispute.

seems to have been very similar to the troubles in Chippenham, Coventry or Warwick. In a period of economic disruption, the magistrates appeared to be behaving
in a self-interested fashion. Friction had become evident some six months before
the arrival of the election writ, over the issue of grazing rights on the town commons, when the corporation attempted to limit the keeping of cattle on one of them
to themselves, and to exclude the freemen's beasts entirely. When trade was bad,
the relief brought by such privileges was valuable, and the freemen resolved to
challenge the magistrates' particularism, petitioning parliament not only against the
election, but also against the corporation's power to issue the grazing order.[18]
Edward Alford, despite his labours against the Court in the parliaments of the early
1620s, and despite 'his longe and loveinge service to this corporacion' was unseated
by the Commons, and replaced by Masham.[19] It was probably Alford's long and
loving service which defeated him, for his previous efforts against the Court were
outweighed by his association with the resented corporation.

The Colchester dispute illustrates the main themes which can be observed elsewhere. The challenge which the corporation was facing was long-term, and was
not specifically related to the election; its impact was intensified by the onset of
economic disruption, when the magistrates appeared to be more concerned with
their own salvation than with that of the town. And while outside agitation did
take place, both in 1627–8 and in the earlier confrontation of 1615, it was by no
means the sole determinant.

### 4. Dover

Dover's strategic importance, and the presence of its castle and garrison, meant that
outside forces affected its internal affairs more than in most towns of comparable
size. It is therefore possible that the initial rejection in 1624 by the freemen of the
candidates backed by the Court and the Lord Warden, Sir Edward Cecil and Sir
Richard Younge, who had been accepted by the corporation, owes much to that
hostility of the freemen to outside interference that was visible in Colchester and
Chester.

The same indigenous troubles were evident here as elsewhere. Earlier in James's
reign, two of the magistrates of the town were alleged to have been going the rounds
of the town's alehouses blackening each other as 'the spawne of a dogge', and
'pispott scowrer', and such behaviour must have served to discredit the corporation. A feud blew up over a lecturer in 1621–2, in which the commons, 'opposers
of all good government' split from the corporation, who were backing a minister
favoured by the Lord Warden. There were also allegations that the freemen
'faction' loved 'neither the government nor the ministers' of the Church.[20] But
much of the ensuing trouble was clearly fomented by the gentry. The corporation
feared the outbreak of a franchise dispute in 1624 before the election took place, at
a time when the candidates were still confining their appeals to the select group:
before they made their choice, the magistrates referred to 'some Question [that] of
late hath Risen', over the election, whether it should be by 'the whole Commonaltie
of Freemen', and answered by aggressively asserting the decree of 20. Eliz. vesting
the franchise in the Common Council. If the gentry were at this stage limiting their
activities to the Council chamber, then the freemen were pushing their claims
independently of external manipulation, and this conclusion is emphasized by the
corporation's decision soon after to imprison certain 'base fellows' for actions held
'to tend to the defamacion of Justice'.[21] The corporation was divided: the Common
Council only decided to maintain the restricted franchise 'by plurallity of voyces',
and when the question was taken before the Committee of Privileges, one of the

corporation's candidates reported disgustedly that 'the mayor spoke hesitatingly as to whether the elections should be general or not, thus implying the right of the freemen'.[22]

There was, then, some local uncertainty and division, providing ideal circumstances for a disappointed candidate to exploit. The petition against the exclusion of the freemen was signed by a local gentleman and an impeccably puritan minister, amongst others, and another participant referred to it as 'Captain Mainwaring's petition' (Mainwaring being the interested candidate), and all this suggests something less than total commons' responsibility for the dispute.[23] Sir Henry Mainwaring had apparently first directed his appeal to the corporation—there is no complaint by the touchy corporation about his early behaviour, but when rejected he evidently espoused what freemen discontent there was for his own ends. Mainwaring had until recently been Lieutenant of Dover Castle, and had sat for the port previously, but had been dismissed by the Lord Warden, Lord Zouch, and his candidature thus lost its official backing. One of his opponents alluded to his thoroughly self-interested aims in standing by the commons: 'Mainwaring's desire is to prove that, though his Lordship does not respect him, he has the love of the people, and may be restored some day to his place.'[24]

The case of Mainwaring was something of a *cause célèbre* of the 1620s, resulting eventually in Zouch's resignation of his office of Warden to Buckingham.[25] Mainwaring, an ex-pirate, had been appointed to his office by Zouch, but his behaviour did not improve, and he was finally dismissed for keeping low company and various other forms of dereliction of duty (including, probably most importantly, playing Court faction politics). He used every kind of influence to have himself reinstated, not stopping short of direct approaches to Prince Charles, and his parliamentary campaign, as Younge observed, was merely another form of pressure, in which his drinking habits seem to have stood him in good stead in gaining him a popular following. His agitation at Court and in parliament, to which Sir Edward Cecil also testified, were apparently crucial in the success of the freemen's petition—Cecil attributed the result not to the freemen's pressure, but to the 'malice' of Mainwaring.[26]

After the House's voiding of the first election, Mainwaring and another local gentleman, Sir Thomas Wilsford, son-in-law of the disturber of Sandwich, Sir Edwin Sandys, lost no time in canvassing again. Wilsford had previously been at loggerheads with the corporation, and he probably relished the prospect of joining Mainwaring in confronting the magistrates: judging by the 1624 encounter, and his willingness to rebuke the King personally in 1639, his character was turbulent.[27] In 1624 he was clearly paying off old scores with the corporation: at a dinner for Count Mansfeld in Dover during the course of the campaign, he denounced the mayor before the assembled company as a 'Knave, an Arrant Knave, Rascall', and continued the diatribe out into the streets of the town, 'to the disgrace and discreditt of the Incorporacion'. The corporation prepared to take his contempt before the Privy Council, but pleas by Sandys and another friend, and a recantation, got him off.[28] But eventually Younge and Cecil were elected again on the wider franchise.

At Dover, then, there were some stirrings among the freemen, which were rapidly taken over by strong outside forces, largely for self-interested reasons. But the dominance of these forces was not total, for as elsewhere, the urban struggle continued. In 1628, 'for the full setling and finall deciding' of 'diverse differences' arising from the exclusion of the commons from municipal elections, the freemen were granted the final choice from a list of official nominations. It seems that a more general struggle for control of the town was taking place, both for ecclesiastical appointments, and municipal offices, as well as parliamentary seats. The campaign for the elimination of corporation nominations in municipal elections finally merged with the wider political struggle of the 1640s, the insurgents relying upon parliament to break the hold of a royalist-favouring select group.[29] Here, as at Cambridge and elsewhere, the parliamentary dispute was part of a much wider confrontation, although unlike Cambridge, the aid of outside forces was necessary to give the insurgents victory in the parliamentary field.

## 5. Exeter

Exeter was encumbered with an electoral system like the later municipal form at Dover, whereby the corporation nominated a panel from which the commons selected two. Controversy was virtually inherent in this, for it gave the freemen of the city[30] the appearance of participation without the substance. Until the 1580s, the decisive stage appears to have been the Chamber, but the corporation was subsequently challenged, for by 1593 it was adding the rider that if the commons 'like better of any other persons nevertheless they may choose the same who they like better', and a similar declaration was made in the quarrel of 1628. That the corporation should be conciliatory in 1593 may have owed something to the economic difficulties and heavy fiscal burdens under which the city was suffering. In the 1604 election, some of the freemen increased their pressure and nominated two of their own candidates against those of the corporation, although they lost at the poll—and as was pointed out in 1628, the fact that a poll was administered demonstrated that the magistrates were prepared to accept the legality of the challenge. By the new charter of 1627, freemen participation was officially recognised.[31]

Popular activity seems to have declined after 1604, coinciding with the signing of peace and the recovery of the cloth trade. But the 1620s brought new and greater problems. In the cloth trades there was an increasing tendency towards oligarchy, with the larger merchants becoming more isolated from the craft freemen and, from the mid-20s, a deep depression set in.[32] Dislocation caused by levies, billeting and increased war taxation was increased by the disruption of the city's main overseas markets caused by war with Spain and the unofficial war with France. As at Salisbury, divisions arose within the city over the consequent poverty,[33] and these were almost certainly compounded by, or illustrative of, significant religious friction within the corporation, again as at Salisbury.[34]

But the major cause of unrest seems to have been the plague outbreak of 1625. Besides the inevitable dislocation of trade that this brought, it also occasioned a crisis of confidence in the municipal government, for almost all the corporation fled, leaving the poor to their fate. The Privy Council, abandoning for once its usual preference for seniority, fulminated against those responsible for entrusting power to such a clique of timorous old men. It ordered the newly-elected mayor to take up his responsibilities and return to his post, and criticised severely the four captains of the trained bands and their subordinate officers, both bailiffs, the aldermen, all the city constables, the church-wardens and overseers of the poor, for their flight and desertion of their duties. Not only did such dereliction mean that essential relief collapsed, but also, that no attention could be paid to the ensuing problems of security. Three months later, on the eve of the disordered 1626 election, the mayor complained bitterly that while he had returned, nobody else had, and the city was, 'through the exceeding poverty of multitudes in danger to fall into distemper and mutinie . . . [and because of the absence of the magistrates] there have happened manie dangerous tumults and the poorer sorte have assembled themselves in a bodie, resisted the officers and threatned by violence to relieve themselves'. Significantly, almost the only magistrate to remain at his post, and the one who took over the administration when the mayor fled, was the arch-puritan Ignatius Jourdain—and he was the candidate the commons insisted on electing, despite his absence from the official list, in 1626 and again in 1628. The repetition of the commons' intransigence in the latter year, which confirmed them in their role, is underlined by a plea by the corporation to the Privy Council in October 1627, a couple of months before the election, that the sickness was still in the town, trading was still stopped, and that most of the inhabitants of ability were still absent. Poor-rate yields were therefore insufficient, and the poor were threatening violence. When the better sort had such a history of irresponsibility, the forlorn attempt of the corporation to restore the restricted franchise—'if anie opposicion' occurred, the sheriff 'is desired to doe his best' to enforce it—was doomed; though opposed by a unanimous corporation, Jourdain and the commons' cause triumphed.[35] The Exeter dispute, perhaps above all others, was a reaction by the dissatisfied commons against a self-interested oligarchy, and Jourdain reaped the electoral benefits on that score, rather than as a result of his puritanism.

### 6. Newcastle-under-Lyme

The same chronology of disorder, again with little evidence of outside disruption, is visible at Newcastle-under-Lyme. A gradual tendency towards oligarchy throughout the 16th century was confirmed by the new charter of 1590, which established a closed corporation. This apparently provoked a wave of resistance, for the corporation complained frequently about disorders at municipal elections in the following decade. This trouble was obviously intensified by oligarchic disloyalty, for steps were taken in 1592 to prevent dissident members of the corporation from collaborating with the commons. At the same time, admission to freedom to trade was being limited: in 1591, an order set the price of purchased freedom at £5, and in 1607 this was increased to the prohibitive figure of £13 6s. 8d., although it fell back to 'vli. at the leaste, and all in hande' in 1620. The town was suffering from pressure on its economic resources, and as in Coventry, urban control was passing firmly into fewer hands. In April 1620, the participation of the commons in municipal politics was eliminated entirely.[36]

There also seems to have been a running feud with the minister of the town, perhaps understandably in view of the fact that his stipend (which was in 1618 a year in arrears) was less than that of the schoolmaster. Details of the franchise dispute which broke out in 1624 do not survive, beyond the fact that a local-boy-made-good (John Keeling of the Inner Temple, son of the 1612 mayor and brother of another mayor) agitated for votes among the commons when he found himself not favoured by the corporation. The town's minister probably had a hand in the affair, for his stipend was stopped immediately afterwards for obstructing the corporation. Possibly he was playing the same role as scourge of a narrow and unresponsive corporation which ministers at Hull, Lincoln and Warwick can be seen in.[37] The House upheld Keeling's petition for the freemen, but this failed to bring peace, for the new election ordered by the House apparently produced a repetition of the original conflict. And the increasing tax load of the later 1620s provoked continuing obstreperousness against the corporation.[38] This was probably another case where the parliamentary franchise dispute was merely an episode in a longer-term history of indigenous friction.

## 7. Oxford

In addition to its formal franchise dispute, Oxford also experienced a more peaceful expansion of its electorate, having probably some 400 freemen in the 1580s and perhaps 700 in the 1620s. This may have imposed some strain on the political structure of the city; and its internal affairs were further complicated by the presence of the University—the hostilities stemming from this were partly responsible for the 1621 troubles. The relationship between the two bodies was illustrated by the way in which the city became more puritan in the 1620s as the University became more High Church: friction was far more apparent than in Cambridge.[39] But a more important factor was the increasing assertiveness of the freemen.

Municipal elections in Oxford had traditionally been formally made by the freemen, but in the course of 1618 divisions within the corporation may have allowed this to become a reality. For the first time, two pairs of names were recorded as being sent down to the commons to choose between for alderman and chamberlain, rather than one pair to be approved, as formerly. Predictably, an attempt on the part of some of the corporation to insert a clause in the projected new charter excluding them seems to have taken place immediately afterwards.[40] In 1619, the commons extended their role, and 'with greate acclamation mayde choyce' of mayor and bailiffs, and in the following year, common councillors, as well. The terms of the charter providing for the participation of freemen came under heavy attack in 1620, possibly from the University, and the corporation was driven to defend them expressly, arguing that the custom of the city was for the freemen to vote.[41] Unlike other corporations, Oxford's was not apparently trying to engross all power to itself, but, if it was the University that was questioning it, this may have been because the threat from the gown was seen as greater that that from below.

The trouble in 1620–1 was provoked by a divided corporation's decision to discontinue the practice of electing the Recorder (who was now Thomas Wentworth) as one of its members. And unfortunately for it, Wentworth was sufficiently assertive to take exception to this. Unlike the municipal elections, the parliamentary election was made 'in the house', and there the voting was said to have gone 26 to 22 against Wentworth for the second seat.[42] It must be presumed that Wentworth exploited the increasing restiveness of the commons, who over the last three years had gained a more potent say in municipal elections, to have himself reinstated. He had been called upon to defend their role, and outline a case for them, in the charter controversy only three months earlier, so the basis for an alliance had been laid. The cases were similar, for the custom in parliamentary elections was identical to that in pre-1618 municipal elections, with the magistrates propounding their choice to the freemen for approval. The franchise dispute was again clearly a part of the general initiative being taken by the commons, this time helped along by a frustrated oligarch (as at Chester) against the corporation. There was a further major clash in the 1621 mayoral election, which required Privy Council intervention and a ban on canvassing and the use of disreputable votes,[43] and this clash itself evidently provoked another attempt to exclude the freemen, for a second resolution was taken by the corporation against such a move at the end of the year.[44] The decision not to elect the Recorder was taken at a bad time, when the commons were becoming increasingly and successfully restive, and when the Recorder was already co-operating with them over their municipal votes.

## 8. Salisbury

The unsuccessful franchise dispute at Salisbury seems as closely related to the economic plight of the town as was that at Exeter. The city's representation had earlier been affected by purely material pressures: in 1626 it was resolved to reject the Earl of Pembroke's nominee, and to elect only local men, for '( . . . having 2700 pore people that are to have relief of the Citty, and not 160 Subsidymen in the whole Cittie to relieve them) . . . [we] could not but see, that if we made choyce of Strangers . . . , we should neyther in the syght of god nor the world dischardge any parte of our dueties'.[45] The collapse of the Wiltshire cloth trade necessitated relief measures, and in particular a scheme for a municipal brewhouse,[46] which it was thought only a local man could support effectively.

The city's economy did not improve markedly in the course of the ensuing decade, and poor relief continued to occupy the attentions of the corporation. But increasingly, as the problem was realised to be a long-term one, rather than one of immediate crisis relief, it began to open divisions among the magistrates, and a group of puritans, most notably John Ivie and the Dove brothers became, like the puritan Jourdain at Exeter, identified with the cause of the poor. Against these were ranged a group within the corporation, and the Cathedral Close. The continuation of the economic difficulties throughout the 1630s is emphasised by the corporation's attempt in late 1639 to enforce the guild regulations more strictly, which led to the unprecedented creation of 116 freemen in one day, and which may have added to the friction within the city.[47]

The divisions were fully apparent in 1640. A resolution in February to reverse the earlier ban on the election of outsiders, at Pembroke's request, was only passed by a narrow majority, and there was a strong move to drop the Laudian Recorder, Robert Hyde, at the ensuing election, on the grounds of his opposition to education and to preaching, and his active support for Ship Money. The rejection by other towns of their Recorders in that election was cited in defence of the attempt. Hyde retrospectively justified this bid by having those who led it punished. A more wideranging and intense struggle came in October, when another move against him developed, this time with the added charge of his support for monopolies thrown in. This confrontation offers the unusual spectacle of a franchise dispute along national alignments, and as might be expected, the freemen who challenged the corporation's selection of Hyde and Pembroke's secretary, Oldsworth, were not acting alone, but were led by a group of eight magistrates, all of whom became active supporters of Parliament. But the origins of the dispute did not lie entirely in these national concerns. There was deep animosity within the city between the secular and ecclesiastical authorities, and one of the most damaging charges against Hyde was that of 'joyneinge the cleargy within the towne in power, which is most preiudiciall to the towne'.[48]

But other roots of the confrontation were probably even more localist than that. A further charge against the Recorder was 'for beinge against the breedinge of poore mens children to learninge', and this sets the dispute firmly within the context of the 1620s and 30s. For as Dr Slack observes, it identifies Hyde with the punitive attitude to the poor of the Chapter and its allies, which contrasts with the alleviatory position of the puritan magistrates. Furthermore, the freemen's candidates were just those magistrates who had been most conscientious over the problem of the poor, a problem which directly affected many of the freemen themselves.[49] This pair, John Ivie and John Dove, and their magisterial allies, almost certainly felt impelled to move against Hyde because of their religious and political opposition to his policies. But it seems likely that much of their support was owed, like Jourdain's, to their identification with the interests of the commons in the years of hardship. This is one of the clearest instances of the way in which in 1640 indigenous issues were being merged with national ones.

### 9. Sandwich

The port trade of Sandwich was declining steadily in the early 17th century as its harbour silted up: any increase in its population was probably accounted for solely by the settlement of European protestant refugees, which brought in some compensatory prosperity with their new draperies. By 1640, possibly one-quarter of the town's population was composed of Flemings. Its diminishing prosperity, and the large influx of strangers, may be related to the fact that it became one of the most disordered towns in the country.[50]

The commons had been debarred from voting in municipal elections 'by reason of somme dyscention and controversy which happened in the Reigne of Kinge Henry the Seaventh', but had apparently regained their rights in 1593. Continuing disorder broke out in the 1590s, so great in 1595 over elections to the sensitive revenue office of treasurers that no election of common councillors could be made, and this resulted in the renewed exclusion of the commons by an order of the Lord Warden in 1596. Agitation against alleged peculation by the corporation regained them their votes in 1599, under the leadership of a disaffected ex-mayor. But continued discord, and an outright split between the corporation and 'the mutinous opposition . . . sailors and others of the meaner sort' in the 1603 election, with accusations of self-interest on the part of the magistrates, who allegedly 'continuously choose their Kyndred', led to a renewal of the exclusion order, and the summoning of the malignants before the Privy Council. The Earl of Northampton thought that the disorders had become so bad as to put 'one of the strongest lockes of this state in great perrill and iopardie'.[51]

The 1603 disorders and their outcome, and the return of a degree of prosperity with peace and better harvests, appear to have brought some tranquillity, for there is little evidence of further disruption until about 1620. There was evidently some antipathy to the Lord Warden—very clear in the 1603 disturbances—and this was manifested in the 1614 parliamentary election: a minor undercurrent flowed through these years, of feuding between the Warden and the port, primarily the commons, but some of the officers were also involved. By the summer of 1620, the future Herald, John Philpott, was reporting to Zouch's secretary Edward Nicholas that 'my Lords presence was never so necessary in any place as this', so strong had the 'adverse parte' grown. It was being said in the town that nobody in England was as oppressed as the Portsmen were by the Lord Warden. The summoning of parliament provided an opportunity for displaying this resentment: the mayor, who pushed for the Warden's nominee, Sir Robert Hatton, was roundly abused in the corporation for sacrificing the town's liberties. The conflict with Zouch was a long-standing one, not merely related to a desire for parliamentary independence, and his nominee for town clerk was rejected in 1623.[52]

Eight candidates stood in 1621, and the corporation split in face of such an *embarras de richesse*. The election procedure was that the mayor and jurats should nominate candidates for approval to the common council, and the then mayor attempted to manipulate this process in order to get in Hatton and a jurat, but a majority over-ruled him, and chose Sir Edwin Sandys, a local gentleman who had been canvassing hard, and, eventually, Hatton, who was also a client of the Archbishop of Canterbury. This last stage was not passed through 'without some tumult',

and some of his colleagues told the mayor that they would petition parliament
against him for his chicaneries.[53] As might have been expected, this division in the
corporation did not develop in a vacuum, and the commons became involved: this
was the peg on which the mayor's opponents hung their petition against him.

Although Sandys received a majority of the magistrates' votes, he had apparently
not relied on his chances there, but had appealed to the commons as well. He
exploited the old tensions by promising to restore them to their former liberties
(presumably their municipal votes), concern for which still moved them; and one of
his allies in the corporation actually proposed there that the freemen should be
admitted, but this was 'easely cleered'. Sandys focused on a more concrete grievance afflicting the port, the trade of the London monopoly companies – although
an enemy testified to his hypocrisy, alleging that he himself was an adventurer.
Opposition to the London companies, and particularly to the East India Company,
had been growing locally in the years preceding the election, and in the early stages
of the session the Cinque Ports collectively presented a free trade bill, directed
primarily against the Merchant Adventurers, and urging the deleterious effects on
the outports of the proclamation of 15.Jac.[54] Sandys was skilfully playing on a real
grievance, and he was helped by a religious division within the town. 'A Precyse
Preacher' was agitating against Hatton's ties to Canterbury, and while Sandys was
himself no puritan, such developments obviously benefited him.[55] By this combination of possibly self-interested, possibly principled, exploitation of internal divisions,
economic fears and religious disagreement, Sandys had the vote extended to the
commons. A wider local concern for parliament was probably not responsible: it is
significant that Sandys seems to have campaigned for the freemen's parliamentary
support by promising to help them to their municipal votes again. Equally, the
election of Bacon's secretary Boroughs rather than Hatton to the second seat
suggests that opposition to the local power, the Lord Warden, and not to the
central government, was evident.

And as the struggle seems to have been primarily local, so it was not resolved by
the parliamentary outcome of 1621. The freemen tried to use the 1621 resolution by
the House in a petition to it in 1624 for the restoration of their votes in municipal
elections, but this was rejected by the House, which observed that only parliamentary elections were immune to restrictions by charter and ordinance. This move
reveals just how much the freemen saw the parliamentary development in a local
context. Probably in 1626 a petition was sent by the freemen to, amongst others, the
Lieutenant of Dover Castle, couched in very similar terms to that of 1603, to the
effect that magisterial nepotism and corruption was rife, and 'Jarres contencions
harte burninge and suites have ensued', and the town's economy was collapsing.
With increasing oligarchy, and increasing oligarchic selfishness, the only remedy
was said to be the restoration of the freemen's votes. In the succeeding year,
controversy developed over the mode of appointment of one of the town's preachers,
which the commoners eventually won,[56] but the story is lost from there (apart from
the modicum of trouble which was said to have occurred in the 1628 election) until
1640, when the two elections provided an occasion and a stimulus for a renewed
outburst.

There were probably six candidates in the spring, three official nominees and
three local gentry.[57] The corporation was driven to warn one of the courtiers,
Edward Nicholas, that reports of his alleged papist affections were being circulated
and must blight his chances; a correspondent advised him that these were put about
by his opponents, which seems plausible, but among the circulators of the rumours
were a saddler and a tanner.[58] It appears that the puritan feelings which had been
evident in James's reign were still present, and still a factor at election time, when

there was someone there to stir them. The damage that they worked was evidently great, for at one stage it was reported that Nicholas had withdrawn, and this was said to have given one of the local gentry, Sir Thomas Peyton, the confidence to move; and he echoed Sandys's tactics in 1621 by appealing to the commons in their own right, as well as to the corporation, believing that in the 'probable confusion' of the election he would gain some of the former's support.[59] His perception of the need to try the commons' favour was borne out by the corporation's tactics in only permitting the official nominees to go forward to the election: as the town clerk observed, this produced a near mutiny from 'the greate parte of the Cominalty'. The resentment of the freemen, 'dayly strengthening themselves against us', inspired real fear amongst the magistrates. The latter begged various parties not to send messengers, but rather private letters, for them to come up to justify the election, apparently in order to avoid humiliation in the commons' sight; and they put a double check on all their letters, because 'we doubt our posts loyalty'. Their reactions accorded ill with their claim that a single agitator was stirring up all the trouble, and were more in keeping with their response to the disorders. The freemen activists found themselves levied for Scotland (as in Hastings), and even the town clerk expressed surprise at the dubious manner in which this was done, the men being locked up overnight and not given press money.[60] Although there were reports of anti-papist rumours against Nicholas, the likelihood of which is given substance by the succession of puritanical clerics which Sandwich had enjoyed,[61] it seems that the bad relations between freemen and magistrates were as much at the root of the troubles as was gentry intervention.

For disorder continued: in the October election, the corporation complained angrily about the 'refractory cariages of the Commons', although they espoused the conspiracy theory as usual, alleging that they were stirred up by agitators from out of town. But this contention was belied by the 'great disorder and tumult' erupting two months later over the election of a new town clerk. And the absence of consistent national alignments was emphasised by the arrest and imprisonment in Newgate in 1642 of the chief anti-corporation, and therefore anti-courtier, activist of 1640, by this time a leading jurat – and a delinquent.[62] In Sandwich as elsewhere, the expansion of the parliamentary franchise settled little, and was indeed used as an instrument in municipal politics in 1624. Its political impact in 1621 and 1624 was minimal, and as late as 1640 its effect was confused, although it was certainly making elections more turbulent, and more prone to the agitation of larger issues.

### 10. Tewkesbury

The prosperity of the town had been founded on the cloth and leather trades, but, in the course of the years before 1640, the balance seems to have shifted away from the former, and may have been hit by Gloucester's competition.[63] In 1625 there were said to be 900 poor in the town, and by 1638 the numbers were rising again. In face of this problem, the corporation became increasingly restrictive, both towards outsiders in 1639, and towards the commons with new orders for government in March 1640 which laid great stress on the need to avert differences within the town. The difficulties may have been increased by an unprecedentedly high turn-over amongst the town's magistrates in the late 1630s.[64]

The freemen of the town, probably stimulated by gentry competition and economic upheaval, appear to have gained some electoral role in 1625.[65] Similar circumstances, depression and a surfeit of gentry, produced the final extension of the vote to the freemen. The new orders of the spring showed that there were already difficulties in the town, and a multiplicity of candidates, mainly local

land-owners, ensured the destruction of the magistrates' monopoly of power.
Indeed, one of the candidates in the second election of 1641 almost succeeded in
involving the inhabitants at large, including the almsmen. The political colour
of the choices made, the bailiffs trying to return future royalists, the inhabitants
future parliamentarians, may be related to the impact of two very staunch puritan
preachers, but lately suspended, on the town.[66]

## 11. Warwick

Warwick had two separate disputes over the franchise, one in 1586, and a prolonged one in the 1620s. That of 1586 has the added interest of having been ascribed
to sophisticated puritan electioneering, but on examination it proves to conform
more to the common pattern of borough disputes than to any scheme of puritan
populism.[67]

An unclear charter to the borough in 1554 had led to more than a decade of
jockeying for power between the principal burgesses and the lower ranks, and in
the early 1570s the former confirmed themselves in authority by abolishing their
assistants. The focus of the disputes was control over the town's properties and
revenues, the commons demanding that the self-selecting governing body should
not have unchecked power in this crucial matter. As a barrier to the selfish exploitation of the town's common assets by the oligarchs, the commons demanded some
form of at least indirect popular participation in the borough's affairs: the extent
of the distrust was revealed by the protest of the disappointed commons' leaders in
1573 that the worst of them was as honest as the best of the principal burgesses.[68]
This concern about misuse of the town's revenues by the tight corporation led to
prolonged troubles, including at least one sizeable riot, in the 1570s; a new outbreak
at the end of the decade, with placarding of the market cross and the county assizes
against the self-interest of the corporation, eventually prodded the Earl of Warwick
into intervening. His attempt at peacekeeping failed, and he, his brother Leicester,
and other local gentlemen, were repeatedly drawn in in the early 1580s, even
attending a public disputation in the shire hall between the corporation and the
commons' spokesmen. Significantly, in 1583 and again in 1585 the Earls and the
gentry came down on the side of the commons in the dispute, urging that they
should be given some say in municipal affairs.[69]

The parliamentary dispute was, to the commons at least, clearly a continuation of
the municipal battle. The leader of the popular candidate Job Throckmorton's
supporters, Richard Brooks, had been for years the commons' leader against the
corporation. More specifically, there had been yet another disputed municipal
election on the very day the parliamentary dispute broke out, and the division
within the corporation gave the puritan gentleman Throckmorton the chance to
intervene, being 'newely encouraged to thrust in when he saw that the baliff and
his company were devidid'. The dispute was set firmly in its local context when he
told the oligarchy that 'he woold not have this matter huddled upp in a corner as
the most of your matters bee amongs your selfs and not in publik'[70] – which was
exactly the complaint of the commons about the town affairs and accounts. The
parallels with the municipal confrontation are further emphasised by the way in
which the intervention of the neighbouring gentry against the corporation to which
Sir John Neale points was merely echoing what they had been doing for the last
three years in municipal disputes, where they had also been defending the claims of
the commons. And just as in disputes elsewhere, the parliamentary outcome (the
corporation defused the issue by allowing Throckmorton in) resolved little, for the
election of Recorder in the following year produced some further clash.[71] Neale's

verdict that Throckmorton and puritanism were the cause of the franchise dispute seems insufficient: it was merely one more round in the battle against an entrenched oligarchy from which a local gentleman determined to profit, as local gentlemen would. The role of puritanism is questionable: the other neighbouring gentry were doing nothing new in coming in; and Richard Brooks, Throckmorton's ally, whom Neale suggests may have been 'the leader of the local Puritans' against the backsliding oligarchs, was himself castigated by those same oligarchs for failing to come to church or attend the sermon, and keeping 'such company as have not resortid to the church, nor come at sermons nor recevid the sacrament in many yeres together wherby some doubtes have and doo rise of his Religion'. Absenteeism from church could have meant extreme protestantism, but absenteeism from sermons was hardly the mark of the convinced puritan.[72] The 1586 dispute looks like the archetypal case of particularist friction over urban power and exploitation.

The town's problems did not end there, for increasing poverty produced a worse crop in the early 17th century. The wages of one of the town's members in the 1604–10 parliament could only be paid at a half-rate two years later; there followed in the mid-1610s a spate of refusals to take office, and compensation had to be paid to the bailiffs for accepting office, for 'they are not so well able to bear it as in tymes past'. We should not be surprised to find that a major quarrel with the commons blew up centring on the charge that the magistrates were misusing the town's revenues for their own ends, particularly in regard to the gratuity to the bailiffs, and even more, that they were exploiting the change in the style and title of the corporation by the 1554 charter to appropriate town lands to themselves.[73] The depth of alienation of many of the commons from the magistrates was shown in the midst of the land dispute in 1615, when 'in derision and disgrace' of the authority of the corporation, the commons, allegedly angered by the suppression of an alehouse, established a counter-court. They appointed their own officers and town crier, and, with 'very many in number' present, proceeded to summon every magistrate and officer of the town, along with their few supporters. These they appointed to the jury, which was to 'bee and Consist all of Whoremongers'. In this classic charivari, every member of the corporation was stigmatised as guilty of a variety of sins: one was 'a greedy Cormorant', another 'an old gowetie whoremaister' that 'owed more then hee was worth', another 'a bankrupt and would bee a begger within these two yeares', and the majority were branded as sexual deviants. The 'court' was said to have applauded the proceedings hugely, with a common intent 'to bringe the very Magistracy itt selfe into Contempt and scorne and utterly to subvert all manner of order and government'. The minister of St Mary's, like other ministers elsewhere, was joining the attack on the actions of the corporation from the pulpit.[74] The tension which was evidenced by the franchise troubles of the following decade was part of a very much wider division than one focusing merely on parliamentary rights.

Into this charged atmosphere intruded neighbouring gentry, entirely selfishly, alleged the town clerk, for 'gentlemen were naturaly enemies to a corporation'. One was anxious for revenge for being passed over for the town's Recordership, others wanted to take over the town's ecclesiastical patronage, another, Sir Thomas Puckering, desired 'to overtop the corporation', and to bully them into electing him for parliament. To these ends, and like Throckmorton before them, they encouraged the commons in their opposition to the magistracy, 'countenancinge the meaner sort of inhabitance to disregard and contem the government of the corporation'. The town clerk feelingly warned all towns to beware the gentry, 'who make no other use of them but as they doe of their stirops to mount to their horse'. We have here the same situation as in several other boroughs: economic pressure stimulating opposition within the town, as the oligarchs were seen to be profiteering from their position; the gentry then moved in to profit. As was said of Puckering, he achieved his ends by taking 'advantages of the presant weaknesse of the Corporation beinge much indebted by there many sutes and troubles'.[75]

The parliamentary elections of the period gave an occasion for these 'troubles' to manifest themselves. The turbulence of the late 1610s was followed by an election at the end of 1620, and at this the 'freeholders and inhabitants' of the borough challenged the common council's power of election, demanding the election of two local gentry, as opposed to the Court-linked figures supported by a majority in the corporation. There was a double return in 1624, testifying either to a division amongst the magistrates, or to a continuation of that between them and their inferiors,[76] but the real trouble broke out two years later, with the renewed intervention of Puckering. The corporation rejected his appeal for a seat, the main reasons being his 'natural malignancy', the fact that he was a stranger, and, significantly reflecting the state of the town's economy, the fact that he 'not so commodious by sendinge corne to the market for the generall good of the peopell'. In reply, Puckering pressed the claims of the commons, arguing that the election 'ought to be populer'. But despite his efforts, the Committee of Privileges was allegedly on the point of confirming the corporation in its position when the parliament was dissolved.[77]

Renewed disorder in the town, and a more pressing problem of the poor, in the ensuing months evidently convinced the corporation of the need to play safe in the next election and to head off further trouble by electing Puckering on their own initiative, 'to obtaine the favor of the said Sir Thomas Puckrenge'. But Puckering 'playes fast and loose with the Corporation', and resolved to continue the battle as a matter of principle, or revenge, having chosen to sit elsewhere. The town clerk claimed that the Committee was squared by the enemy, but whatever the case, the commons' petition was upheld, with the result that almsmen and 'evry mecanick and . . . all sortes of ill conditioned peopell' were enfranchised.[78] But although the commons obtained their immediate goal, the divisions within the town continued. The late 1630s saw another wave of refusals of office, and the town clerk, now deputy-recorder, in a reluctant welcome to the 2nd Lord Brooke on the latter's appointment as Recorder in 1641, emphasised the town's troubles: he was 'not ignorant how many are redy to cast contempt upon the magistracy of this place . . . I need not perticuerlise the sinns of this place they are but two [sic] publicke and pregnant'. Yet again, the 'sinns' were flaunted in the 1641 by-election, when the inhabitants at large, encouraged by the deputy-recorder, attempted to join in the election in opposition to the candidate of Lord Brooke, who was supported by the magistrates and 'many of the better sorte of the towne'. Some at least of this initiative must be laid at the door of the personal, localist antipathy of the deputy-recorder for Lord Brooke, who was held to have cost the town money and lands, rather than to any political animosities.[79] The episode provides another instance of the wider group supporting a more local, and less opposition, figure than the opposition-supporting select group. But as interesting is the way in which the deputy-recorder, who as town clerk had been bitterly opposed to the 1628 widening of the franchise, was now prepared to extend it even further for his own ends.

# The Borough Franchises in 1641

These identifications, except in the cases of those marked with an asterisk, are taken from W. Taffs, 'The Borough Franchise in the First Half of the Seventeenth Century' (unpublished London MA thesis, 1926). Those so marked are identified from my own work, and the sources for the conclusions are normally discussed in the text.

Many of the identifications can only be described as at best tentative, for Taffs was forced to draw much of her evidence from the statements of 18th-century antiquarians as to what they remembered particular franchises as. For many boroughs firm evidence will never be obtained, for they were never subject to contest, and thus were never forced to define the exact nature of their franchises (as was shown at Cirencester in 1624); and for others, the evidence has disappeared, and the historian is forced to rely on the frequently misleading data provided by their indentures, which were often thoroughly formalised, as the magistrates of Bridport asserted in 1628.

Abingdon. ? Inhabitant/? householder*
Aldeburgh. Freemen.
Aldborough. Burgage holders.*¹
Amersham. Scot and lot.*
Andover. Governing body.
Appleby. Freemen.
Arundel. Inhabitants.
Ashburton. ? Inhabitant freeholders/ householders.
Aylesbury. Freemen.
Banbury. Governing body.
Barnstaple. Freemen.
Bath. Governing body.
Bedford. Inhabitants.*
Gt Bedwin. Burgage tenants.*²
Berealston. ?
Berwick. Freemen.
Beverley. Freemen.
Bewdley. Governing body.
Bishop's Castle. Freemen.
Bletchingley. Burgage tenants.
Bodmin. ?³
Boroughbridge. Burgage tenants.⁴
Bossiney. ? Inhabitants.*
Boston. Freemen.*
Brackley. Governing body.
Bramber. ? Inhabitants.*⁵

Bridgnorth. Freemen.
Bridgwater. Governing body.
Bridport. Freemen.
Bristol. ? Freemen.*
Buckingham. Governing body.
Bury St Edmunds. Governing body.
Callington. ?
Calne. Governing body.*⁶
Cambridge. Freemen.*
Cambridge University. Chancellor, masters and scholars.
Camelford. ? Burgage tenants.
Canterbury. Freemen.
Carlisle. Freemen.
Castle Rising. Burgage tenants.
Chester. ? Inhabitants.*
Chichester. ? Freemen.
Chippenham. Burgage tenants.*
Chipping Wycombe. Freemen.
Christchurch. ?
Cirencester. Householders.
Clitheroe. Burgage tenants.*
Cockermouth. Scot and lot.
Colchester. Freemen.
Corfe Castle. ? Governing body.
Coventry. Freemen.
Cricklade. ? Householders.

Dartmouth. ? Freemen.
Derby. ? Freemen.
Devizes. ? Freemen.
Dorchester. Freemen.
Dover. Freemen.
Downton. Burgage tenants.
Droitwich. Ownership of salt pans.
Dunwich. Freemen.*[7]
Evesham. Governing body.
Exeter. Freemen.
Eye. ? Scot and lot.
Fowey. ?
Gatton. Inhabitants.*
Gloucester. Freemen.
Grampound. ? Freemen.
Grantham. ? Freemen.
Grimsby. ? Freemen.
E. Grinstead. Inhabitants.
Guildford. ? Scot and lot.
Harwich. Governing body.
Haslemere. Burgage tenants.
Hastings. Freemen.
Hedon. Freemen.*[8]
Helston. Freemen.
Hereford. ? Freemen.
Hertford. ? Inhabitants.*
Heytesbury. ? Freemen.
Higham Ferrers. Freemen.
Hindon. ? Freemen.
Honiton. ? Inhabitant freeholders/
    householders.
Horsham. ? Burgage tenure.
Hull. Freemen.
Huntingdon. ? Freemen.
Hythe. Freemen*
Ilchester. ? Scot and lot.
Ipswich. Freemen.
King's Lynn. Freemen.
Knaresborough. Burgage tenure.
Lancaster. ? Freemen.
Launceston. ? Freemen.
Leicester. Governing body.
Leominster. ?
Lewes. Inhabitants.
Lincoln. ? Freemen.
Liskeard. Freemen.
Litchfield. ? Freemen.
Liverpool. ? Freemen.
E. Looe. ? Freemen.
W. Looe. ? Governing body.
Lostwithiel. ? Freemen.
Ludgershall. ? Burgage tenure.

Ludlow. ? Governing body.
Lyme Regis. Freemen.
New Lymington. Scot and lot*[9]
Maidstone. Freemen.
Maldon. Freemen.*
Malton. Burgage tenure.
Marlborough. Burgage tenure.
Marlow. Inhabitants.
Midhurst. Burgage tenure.
Milborne Port. ? Inhabitants.
Minehead. ? Scot and lot.
Mitchell. Inhabitants.
Monmouth. Freemen of Monmouth,
    Usk and Newport.
Morpeth. ? Freemen.
Newcastle-under-Lyme. Freemen.
Newcastle-upon-Tyne. Freemen.
Newport (Cornwall). ? Freeholders.[10]
Newport (I. of W.). ? Governing body.
Newton (Lancs.). ?
Newtown (I. of W.). ?
Northallerton. Burgage tenure.
Northampton. ? Governing body.*
Norwich. Freemen.
Nottingham. Governing body.[11]
Okehampton. ?*[12]
Orford. ?
Oxford. Freemen.
Oxford University. Chancellor, masters
    and scholars.
Penryn. ? Scot and lot.
Peterborough. ?
Petersfield. ? Freemen.
Plymouth. ? Governing body.
Plympton Erle. ?
Pontefract. Inhabitant householders.
Preston. ? Governing body.
Queenborough. ?
Reading. ? Scot and lot/ ? freemen/ ?
    inhabitants.*
Reigate. ? Freemen.
E. Retford. Freemen.
Ripon. ? Freemen.
Richmond. ? Governing body.
Rochester. ? Freemen.
New Romney. ? Freemen.
Rye. ? Freemen.
St Albans. Inhabitants.*
St Ives. Governing body.
St Mawes. ? Freemen.
Salisbury. Governing body.
Saltash. ? Freemen.

Sandwich. ? Freemen.
Old Sarum. Burgage tenure.
Scarborough. Governing body.
Seaford. ? Freemen.
Shaftesbury. ? Governing body.
Shoreham. 'Principal inhabitants.'
Southwark. Scot and lot.
Southampton. ? Governing body.
Shrewsbury. Freemen.
Stafford. Freemen.*[13]
Stamford. ? Freemen.
Steyning. ? Burgage tenure.
Stockbridge. ?
Sudbury. Governing body.
Tamworth. Governing body.
Taunton. ? Householder.
Tavistock. ? Burgage tenure.
Tewkesbury. Freemen.*
Thetford. ? Governing body.
Thirsk. ? Burgage tenure.
Tiverton. Governing body.*[14]
Totnes. Governing body.
Truro. ? Governing body.

Wallingford. ? Freemen.*
Wareham. ? Inhabitants.*[15]
Warwick. ? Inhabitants.*
Wells. ? Freemen.
Wendover. ? Scot and lot.
Wenlock. ? Freemen.
Weobley. ? Inhabitants.*
Westbury. ? Burgage tenure.
Westminster. ? Scot and lot.
Weymouth & Melcombe Regis. ?
   Burgage tenure.
Whitchurch. ? Burgage tenant.*
Wigan. Freemen.
Wilton. ? Freemen.
Winchelsea. Freemen.
Winchester. Governing body.
Windsor. Inhabitants.
Woodstock. ? Freemen.
Wootton Bassett. 'Principal inhabitants.'
Worcester. ? Freemen.
Gt Yarmouth. Governing body.
Yarmouth (I. of W.). ? Freemen.
York. Committee.*

The boundaries between ? scot and lot, ? householder, and ? inhabitant in such a scheme are clearly very narrow, and the attributions are in many cases very tenuous. Nevertheless, the important conclusion emerges that the freemen boroughs were by far the most numerous, and that they included most of the large towns. The approximate totals are:

|  |  |
|---|---|
| Governing body | 34 |
| Freemen | 83 |
| Burgage tenure | 24 |
| Scot and lot | 11 |
| Householder and inhabitant | 26 |
| Unknown | 12 |
| Undefined (Shoreham and Wootton Bassett) | 2 |
| Committee (York) | 1 |
| Universities | 2 |
| Oddity (Droitwich) | 1 |

# Contested Elections

---

The occurrence of a contest is sometimes self-evident – when there is a local record of a poll, or a description of the event, or when there was an involved dispute in the House, there can be no doubt. But the records are not always so helpful, and often assumptions have to be made. I have assumed that when there was a petition or a protest in the House a contest had taken place, for nobody was likely to undertake the costly process of petitioning unless they had an interest in doing so. A further fairly safe assumption is when reference is made somewhere to the choice having been made by 'the greater number of voices' or some such phrase, albeit there is nothing else to substantiate the presumption. Additionally, where there is evidence of a franchise dispute in small towns, but no other data, I have concluded that a contest probably occurred, for a dispute there was less likely to be self-generated.

The definition of a contest can, unfortunately, be rather difficult, especially in closed franchises. When several gentlemen made approaches for a seat, or had requests made for them, and yet the only subsequent record is that two had been elected, often with the addition '*unanimis assensis*', there is nothing to show that there was a contest. But presumably the gentlemen or their agents canvassed the governing body, and that body then proceeded to vote on their fate. Thus, even when the corporation records do not show a majority vote, we can suspect that what passed when there was an abundance of candidates was a contest, though, thanks to the reluctance of magistrates to admit that their communities were divided, there is no evidence to confirm it. Such situations have not, however, been included, for there is no way of determining the intensity of local activity, and the members may have effectively selected themselves, with no division amongst their electors. But when there is no statement that 'the greater number of voices' chose, and yet more gentlemen than the two who were finally to emerge victorious were admitted to the borough freedom (an almost universal requirement for membership) immediately before the election, then it seems possible to assume that there was a contest.

The totals of contest can only give a minimum indicator for the arousal of the voters. Evidence for many has probably perished totally; as was suggested in Chapter 6, candidates sometimes withdrew at the last minute, having canvassed extensively, to avoid the humiliation of imminent defeat. Similarly, the Short Parliament election for Salisbury was technically not contested, yet it betrays intense political excitement.[1] Additionally, we have seen that the Committee of Privileges reported in February 1641 that there were still about 85 cases outstanding, and some of these must have been contests for which no other evidence survives: there must therefore have been more contests for the Long Parliament than I have record of.

A line through a constituency's columns indicates that its representation had lapsed during that time.

When two contests are shown for one election a contested by-election, or new election in place of one that had been voided, occurred.

| | 1604 | 1614 | 1621 | 1624 | 1625 | 1626 | 1628 | Short Parlt. | Long Parlt. |
|---|---|---|---|---|---|---|---|---|---|
| *Bedfordshire*[2] | | | | | | | | ? × | × × |
| Bedford[3] | | | | | | | × | × | × |
| *Berkshire* | | | | | | | | ? × | |
| Abingdon | | | | | | | | × | |
| Reading[4] | | | | × | | × | × | × | × |
| Wallingford | | | | | | | | | × |
| Windsor[5] | | | | | | | | × | × × ? |
| *Buckinghamshire*[6] | | | | | | | | ? × | × |
| Amersham | | | | | | | | | |
| Aylesbury[7] | | | | | | | | × | |
| Buckingham | | | | | | | | | |
| Marlow[8] | | | | | | | | ? × | × |
| Wendover | | | | | | | | | |
| Wycombe | | | | | | | | × | × |
| *Cambridgeshire*[9] | | × | | × | | | | | |
| Cambridge | | | | | | | | | × |
| Cambridge University[10] | | | | | × | | | × | × |
| *Cheshire*[11] | | | | × | | × | × | | × |
| Chester[12] | | | × | | | | × | | |
| *Cornwall* | | | | | | | × | | |
| Bodmin | | | | | | | | | × |
| Bossiney | | | | | | | | | × |
| Callington | | | | | | | | | |
| Camelford | | | | | | | | | |
| Fowey | | | | | | | | | |
| Grampound[13] | | | | | | × | | × | |
| Helston | | | | | | | | | |
| Launceston[14] | | | | × | | | | | |
| Liskeard | | | | | | | | | |
| East Looe | | | | | | | | | ? × |
| West Looe | | | | | | | | | |
| Lostwithiel[15] | | | | | × | | | | |
| Mitchell[16] | | | | | | | × | × | |
| Newport | | | | | | × | × | × | × (by-election) |
| Penryn | | | | | | | | | |
| St Germans | | | | | | | | | × |
| St Ives[17] | | | | × | | | | | |
| St Mawes | | | | | | | | | |
| Saltash[18] | | | | | | | × | | |
| Tregony[19] | | | | | | | | × | |
| Truro | | | | | | | | | |

| | 1604 | 1614 | 1621 | 1624 | 1625 | 1626 | 1628 | Short Parlt. | Long Parlt. |
|---|---|---|---|---|---|---|---|---|---|
| *Cumberland* [20] | | | | × | | | | | |
| Carlisle | | | | | | | | | |
| Cockermouth[21] | | | | | | | | | × |
| *Derbyshire* | | | | | | | | | × |
| Derby[22] | | | | | | | | | × |
| *Devon* | | | | | | | | | |
| Ashburton | | | | | | | | | |
| Barnstaple | | | | | | | | × | × |
| Berealston[23] | | | | | | | | × | × |
| Dartmouth | | | | | | | | | |
| Exeter[24] | × | | | | | × | × | × | |
| Honiton | | | | | | | | | |
| Okehampton[25] | | | | | | | | | × |
| Plymouth | | | | | | | | | |
| Plympton Erle[26] | | | | | | | | × | × |
| Tavistock | | | | | | | | | |
| Tiverton | | | | | | | | | |
| Totnes | | | | | | | | | |
| *Dorset*[27] | | | | × | | × | | | |
| Bridport | | | | | | ?× | × | | |
| Corfe Castle | | | | | | | | | |
| Dorchester | | | | | | | | | |
| Lyme Regis[28] | | | | | | | | × | |
| Poole[29] | | | | × | | | | | |
| Shaftesbury | | | | | | | | | |
| Wareham[30] | × | | | | | | | ?× | × |
| Weymouth and Melcombe Regis[31] | | | | | | ?× | | | |
| *Essex*[32] | × | | | × | ?× | | × | × | |
| Colchester | | | | | ?× | | × | | |
| Harwich[33] | | | | × | | | | | |
| Maldon[34] | | | | × | × | ?× | | | |
| *Gloucestershire*[35] | | | | × × | | | | × | × |
| Bristol | | | | | | | | | |
| Cirencester[36] | | | | × | × | | | | |
| Gloucester[37] | × | | | | | | | × | × |
| Tewkesbury | | | | | × | | | | × × |
| *Hampshire*[38] | | × | | | | | | | |
| Andover[39] | | | | × | | | | | × (by-election) |
| Christchurch[40] | | | | | | | | | × |
| New Lymington[41] | | | | | × | | | | |
| Newport I.o.W. | | | | | | | | | |

| | 1604 | 1614 | 1621 | 1624 | 1625 | 1626 | 1628 | Short Parlt. | Long Parlt. |
|---|---|---|---|---|---|---|---|---|---|
| Newtown I.o.W. | | | | | | | | | |
| Petersfield | | | | | | | | | |
| Portsmouth | | | | | | | | | |
| Southampton[42] | | | | | | | | × | |
| Stockbridge[43] | | × | | × | | | | | |
| Whitchurch[44] | | × | | | | | | | |
| Winchester | | | | | | | | | |
| Yarmouth[45] | | | | | | | | × | |
| *Herefordshire* | | | | | | | | × | |
| Hereford | | | | | | | | | |
| Leominster | | | | | | | | | |
| Weobley | | | | | | | | | |
| *Hertfordshire* | | | | | | | | | × |
| Hertford | | | | × | | | × | × | × |
| St Albans[46] | | | | | | | | | × |
| *Huntingdonshire*[47] | | × | × | | × | | | | × |
| Huntingdon | | | | | | | | | |
| *Kent*[48] | | × | | × | × | × | | × | × |
| Canterbury[49] | | | | × | × | × | | × | |
| Maidstone[50] | | | | | × | | | | × |
| Queen-borough[51] | | | | | × | | | | |
| Rochester[52] | | | × | | | | | | |
| *Lancashire* | | | | | | | | | |
| Clitheroe[53] | | | ?× | | | | × | | × |
| Lancaster | | | | | | | | | |
| Liverpool | | | | | | | | | |
| Newton-in-Makerfield | | | | | | | | | |
| Preston | | | | | | | | | |
| Wigan | | | | | | | × | × | × |
| *Leicestershire*[54] | | × | | | | × | | | ?× |
| Leicester[55] | | | | | | | | | × |
| *Lincolnshire*[56] | | × | | | | | | × | |
| Boston[57] | | | | ?× | ?× | | × | | |
| Grantham | | | | | | | | | |
| Grimsby[58] | | | ?× | | | | | × | ?× |
| Lincoln | | | | | | | | | |
| Stamford | | | | | | | | | |
| *Middlesex*[59] | | × | ?× | × | × | | | | × |
| London[60] | × | × | | | | | × | | |
| Westminster[61] | | | × | | × | | × | × | |
| *Monmouthshire*[62] | | | | | × | | | | |
| Monmouth[63] | | | | | | | | | × |
| *Norfolk*[64] | | × | × | × | × | | | × | |
| Castle Rising | | | | | | | | | |
| King's Lynn | | | | | | | | | × |

| | 1604 | 1614 | 1621 | 1624 | 1625 | 1626 | 1628 | Short Parlt. | Long Parlt. |
|---|---|---|---|---|---|---|---|---|---|
| Norwich | | | | | | | | | × |
| Thetford[65] | | | | | | | ?× | | |
| Great Yarmouth[66] | | | × | | × | × | | | |
| *Northampton-shire*[67] | × | | | | | × | | × | |
| Brackley | | | | | | | | | |
| Higham Ferrers[68] | | | | | | | | × | ?× |
| Northampton | | | | | | | | × | × |
| Peterborough | | | | | | | | | × |
| *Northumberland*[69] | × | | | | | | | | |
| Berwick[70] | | | | | | | | | × |
| Morpeth[71] | | | ?× | | | | | | |
| Newcastle | | | | | | | | × | × |
| *Nottinghamshire*[72] | | | | | | | | × | |
| East Retford | | | | × | | | | | |
| Nottingham[73] | | | | | | × | | | |
| *Oxfordshire*[74] | | | | × | | | | | |
| Banbury | | | | | | | | | |
| Oxford | | | × | | | | × | × | × |
| Oxford University[75] | | | | × | | × | × | | ?× |
| Woodstock[76] | | | | | | | | | × |
| *Rutland* | | | | | | | | | |
| *Shropshire*[77] | | | | | | | | × | |
| Bishops Castle | | | | | | | | | |
| Bridgnorth[78] | × (by-election) | | | × | | | | | |
| Ludlow[79] | | | | | | | | × | |
| Shrewsbury[80] | × | | | | | | | | |
| Great Wenlock | | | | | | | | | |
| *Somerset*[81] | | × | | × | × | × | | × | × |
| Bath | | | | | | | | | |
| Bridgwater[82] | | | | | | | | | × |
| Ilchester[83] | | | | | | | | | × |
| Milborne Port | | | | | | | | | |
| Minehead[84] | | | | | | | | × | |
| Taunton | | | | | | | | | |
| Wells[85] | | | | × | | | | | |
| *Staffordshire* | | | | | | | | | |
| Newcastle-under-Lyme | | | | × × | | | | | |
| Stafford[86] | | | | × | | | | | |
| Tamworth | | | | | | | | × | |

| | 1604 | 1614 | 1621 | 1624 | 1625 | 1626 | 1628 | Short Parlt. | Long Parlt. |
|---|---|---|---|---|---|---|---|---|---|
| *Suffolk*[87] | | | × | | | | | | × |
| Aldeburgh[88] | × | | | | | | | | |
| Bury St Edmunds | | | | | | | | | |
| Dunwich[89] | | | | | | | × | | × |
| Eye | | | | | | | | | |
| Ipswich[90] | | | | | | | | × | ?× |
| Orford | | | | | | | | | |
| Sudbury | | | | | | | | | × |
| *Surrey* | | | | | | | | | |
| Bletchingley | | | | × | | | | | |
| Gatton | | | × | | | × | | | × |
| Guildford[91] | | | | | | × | | | |
| Haslemere[92] | | | | | | | | | × |
| Reigate[93] | | | | | | | | × | × |
| Southwark[94] | | | | × | | | | × | |
| *Sussex* | | | | | | | | | |
| Arundel[95] | | | | × | | | | | × × |
| Bramber[96] | | | | | | | | × | × |
| Chichester[97] | | | | | | × | | | |
| East Grinstead[98] | | | | | | | | × | × |
| Horsham | | | | | | | | | |
| Lewes | | | | | | × | | × | |
| Midhurst[99] | | | | | | | | | × |
| Shoreham | | | | | | | | | |
| Steyning[100] | | | × | × | | | | | × |
| *Warwickshire*[101] | | | | | | | | ?× | × × |
| Coventry[102] | | | × | × | | | × | | × |
| Warwick[103] | | | × | × | | × | × | | × |
| *Westmorland* | | | | | | | | | |
| Appleby | | | | | | | | | |
| *Wiltshire* | | | | | | | | | |
| Great Bedwin | | | | | | | | × | |
| Calne | | | | | | | | | |
| Chippenham[104] | × | ?× | | × | | | | × | × |
| Cricklade | | | | | | | | | |
| Devizes | | | | | | | | | |
| Downton | | | | | | | | | × × |
| Heytesbury | | | | | | | | | |
| Hindon[105] | | | × | | | | | | |
| Ludgershall[106] | | | | | | × | | | |
| Malmesbury[107] | | | | | × | | | | |
| Marlborough[108] | | | × | | | | | | × (by-election) |
| Old Sarum[109] | | | ?× | | × | ?× | | | |

| | 1604 | 1614 | 1621 | 1624 | 1625 | 1626 | 1628 | Short Parlt. | Long Parlt. |
|---|---|---|---|---|---|---|---|---|---|
| Salisbury | | | | | | | | | × |
| Westbury | | | | | | | | | |
| Wilton | | | | | | | | | |
| Wootton Bassett | | | | | | | | | |
| *Worcestershire*[110] | × | | | × | | | | | × |
| Bewdley[111] | | | | | | | | × | × |
| Droitwich | | | | | | | | | |
| Evesham[112] | | | | | | | | | × |
| Worcester | | | | | | | | | |
| *Yorkshire*[113] | | × | × | | × | × | × × | | × |
| Aldborough[114] | | | × | | | | | | |
| Beverley[115] | | | | | | | | × | × |
| Borough-bridge[116] | | | | | | × | | | |
| Hedon | | | | | | | | | |
| Hull[117] | × | | | × | | | | | |
| Knares-borough[118] | ?× | × | | | | ?× | × | × | × × |
| New Malton | | | | | | | | | |
| Northallerton | | | | | | | | | |
| Pontefract | | | | × | | | | | |
| Richmond[119] | | | ?× | | | ?× | × | | |
| Ripon | | | | | | | | | |
| Scarborough[120] | | | | | | | | × | |
| Thirsk | | | | | | | | | |
| York[121] | × | | | ?× | | × | | | × |
| (*Cinque Ports*) | | | | | | | | | |
| Dover | | | | × | | ?× | | | ?× |
| Hastings | | | | | | | | × | × |
| Hythe | | | | | | | | | |
| New Romney | | | | | | | | | |
| Rye[122] | | | | | × | × | | | × |
| Sandwich | | | × | | × | × | × | × | × |
| Seaford | | | | | | | | | |
| Winchelsea[123] | | | | × | | | | ?× | |

# Numbers of Voters

Any totals of voters for this period are inevitably rudimentary and haphazard, given the state of the evidence. All that this list can hope to do is convey some idea of how many people polled, or were estimated to have turned out (an extremely unreliable figure, in view of the statistical innocence of the day) in various constituencies at various times; in some cases, totals of those eligible to vote are given. These last are obviously most available for corporation franchise boroughs, so not many from this source have been included, in order to avoid the creation of too distorted an impression. Actual voting figures are minima for, as the treatment of Hertford and Clitheroe showed, many voters cast only one vote, and the totals were gained by taking the sum of votes cast and dividing by two, on the assumption that everybody cast two votes.

    *   indicates a contemporary estimate of turn-out.
  SP  Short Parliament
  LP  Long Parliament
Borough Constituencies for which there is no evidence have not been entered.

|  | Actual | Potential |
|---|---|---|
| *Bedfordshire* |  |  |
| Bedford[1] | 191 SP | |
|  | 600+ LP | |
| *Berkshire* |  |  |
| Reading[2] | c. 900, 1640s | |
| Windsor[3] | 179+, 1641 | |
| *Buckinghamshire* |  |  |
| Amersham[4] |  | ?173 |
| Aylesbury[5] | 100+, SP | |
| Marlow[6] | 245, LP | |
| *Cambridgeshire* |  |  |
| Cambridge University[7] | 247, LP | |
| *Cheshire* |  |  |
| Chester[8] | c. 1000, 1628 | |
| *Cornwall* |  |  |
| Mitchell[9] | 44+, SP | |
|  | 50+, LP | |
| Newport[10] | c. 20, 1628 | |
| Tregony[11] | 51+, SP | |
| *Cumberland* |  |  |
| *Derbyshire* |  |  |
| *Devon* |  |  |
| Barnstaple[12] | 156, LP | 160, 1640 |

| | Actual | Potential |
|---|---|---|
| *Dorset*[13] | c. 1,200, 1626 | |
| Bridport[14] | 100+, 1628 | |
| Shaftesbury[15] | 13, LP | |
| *Essex*[16] | 10–15,000*, 1628 | |
| Harwich[17] | | 32 |
| Maldon[18] | 89, 1624 | 131, 1624 |
| | (48 in-burgesses, 1624) | (61 in-burgesses, 1624) |
| *Gloucestershire*[19] | c. 5,000?, SP | |
| Bristol[20] | | c. 3000?, 1640 |
| Gloucester[21] | | c. 4–500? |
| Tewkesbury[22] | 310–360, 1641 | 360, 1641 |
| *Hampshire*[23] | 2,179+, 1614 | |
| Christchurch[24] | 16, LP | |
| New Lymington[25] | | c. 40 |
| Stockbridge[26] | 39, 1614 | |
| | 28, 1624 | |
| *Herefordshire*[27] | 3,475+, 1646 | |
| *Hertfordshire* | | |
| Hertford[28] | 244, 1624 | |
| | c. 170, 1628 | |
| St Albans[29] | 600+* | |
| *Huntingdonshire* | | |
| *Kent*[30] | 2,325, 10,000*, SP | |
| Canterbury[31] | | c. 200 ? |
| Maidstone[32] | | c. 200 ? |
| Queenborough[33] | | 26 |
| Rochester[34] | | c. 200 ? |
| *Lancashire* | | |
| Clitheroe[35] | 25, 1628 | |
| | 78, LP | |
| Liverpool[36] | | 240, 1620 |
| | | 454, 1644 |
| Wigan[37] | 75 (70 in-burgesses, | 138 (90 in-burgesses, |
| | 5 out-) 1628 | 48 out-) |
| | 148 (110 in-burgesses, | 296 (134 in-burgesses, |
| | 38 out-) SP | 162 out-) |
| | 163 (109 in-burgesses, | 296 (127 in-burgesses, |
| | 54 out-) LP | 169 out-) |
| *Leicestershire* | | |
| *Lincolnshire* | | |
| Boston[38] | 106, 1628 | c. 200 ? |
| Grimsby[39] | 55, SP | c. 55 ? |
| *Middlesex* | | |
| London[40] | | 4000 |
| *Monmouthshire* | | |
| *Norfolk*[41] | 3,000*, 1586 | |
| | 7,000*, 1593 | |
| | 4,000+*, 1614 | |
| | 3,000+, 1625 | |

|  | Actual | Potential |
|---|---|---|
| Castle Rising[42] | 14?, LP | c. 49 |
| Norwich[43] | c. 1,200, LP | c. 2,000 |
| Great Yarmouth[44] | 58, SP | 72 |
| *Northamptonshire* | | |
| Brackley[45] | 25+, LP | |
| Higham Ferrers[46] | 35, SP | |
| *Northumberland* | | |
| *Nottinghamshire* | | |
| East Retford[47] | 83, 1624 | |
| Nottingham[48] | | 56 |
| *Oxfordshire* | | |
| Oxford[49] | 310, 1628 | c. 700, 1620s |
| | 760, LP | |
| Woodstock[50] | 52+, LP | |
| *Rutland* | | |
| *Shropshire* | | |
| Ludlow[51] | | 37 |
| Shrewsbury[52] | c. 420, 1584 | |
| *Somerset* | | |
| Ilchester[53] | | 80 |
| *Staffordshire* | | |
| Newcastle-under-Lyme[54] | 155, 1624 | |
| | 116, 1626 | |
| | 91, 1628 | |
| Stafford[55] | 96, 1624 | 120, 1624 |
| *Suffolk*[56] | c. 3,500+, LP | |
| Dunwich[57] | 30, SP | |
| | 47, LP | |
| Ipswich[58] | 199, SP | |
| *Surrey* | | |
| Bletchingley[59] | 23, SP | 23?, 1640 |
| Gatton[60] | c. 7, 1621 | |
| | 15+, SP | |
| *Sussex* | | |
| Arundel[61] | 66, 1624 | |
| Horsham[62] | | 54 |
| Lewes[63] | 150, 1628 | |
| Steyning[64] | 100+, LP | |
| *Warwickshire*[65] | c. 1,750, LP by-election | |
| Coventry[66] | 600, 1628 | |
| *Westmorland* | | |
| *Wiltshire* | | |
| Calne[67] | 17, LP | 18 |
| Chippenham[68] | | c. 127 |
| Downton[69] | c. 80, LP by-election | 99? |
| Ludgershall[70] | 30, 1626 | |
| | 55+, LP | |
| Malmesbury[71] | | 84 |
| Marlborough[72] | | 93, temp. James I |

|  | Actual | Potential |
|---|---|---|
| Old Sarum[73] |  | 6, 1620 |
|  |  | 11, 1626 |
| Salisbury[74] |  | 76 |
| Wootton Bassett[75] |  | 250 |
| *Worcestershire*[76] | c. 750+, LP |  |
| Bewdley[77] | 150–200, 1647 |  |
| Droitwich[78] | 28, SP |  |
| *Yorkshire*[79] | c. 6,000*, 1597 |  |
|  | 7–10,000*, 1628 |  |
| Aldborough[80] |  | 9 |
| Hedon[81] |  | c. 100? |
| Hull[82] |  | c. 5–600? |
| Knaresborough[83] | 46 (59 try), 1628 | 88 |
| New Malton[84] |  | c. 100 |
| Pontefract[85] |  | c. 100 |
| Richmond[86] |  | 14 |
| Scarborough[87] |  | 44 |
| (*Cinque Ports*) |  |  |
| Dover[88] |  | 252, 1624 |
| Hastings[89] | 35, SP | 37, 1640 |
| Hythe[90] | 35, SP |  |
|  | 32, LP |  |
| Rye[91] |  | c. 30 |
| Sandwich[92] | c. 250, LP |  |

# Voting and Occupations in Hertford

### Key

| | | | | |
|---|---|---|---|---|
| AF | = Ashton and Fanshawe | | H | = Harrington alone |
| AH | = Ashton and Harrington | | WF | = Willowes and Fanshawe |
| FH | = Fanshawe and Harrington | | HW | = Harrington and Willowes |
| A | = Ashton alone | | WH | = Willowes and Harrington |
| F | = Fanshawe alone | | W | = Willowes alone |
| AW | = Ashton and Willowes | | B | = Barbor |

(For sources, see Chapter 5 section 2, and Chapter 6 section 2.)

| Occupation | 1624 | | | | | | | | | | | 1628 | |
|---|---|---|---|---|---|---|---|---|---|---|---|---|---|
| | AF | AH | FH | A | F | AW | H | WF | HW | WH | W | F | B |
| Gentry and Corporation | 12 | 2 | | 2 | | | | | | | | 12 | |
| Gentleman-grocer | | 1 | | | | | | | | | | 1 | 1 |
| Gentleman-tanner | | | | | | | | | | | 1 | 1 | 1 |
| Gentleman-baker | 1 | | | | | | | | | | | 1 | |
| Gentleman-draper | | | | | | 1 | | | | | | 1 | |
| Minister | | | | | | | | | | | | | 1 |
| Doctor | | | | | | | 1 | | | | | | |
| Brewer | 1 | | | | | | | | | | | 1 | |
| Baker | 3 | | | | 1 | | | | 1 | | | 2 | 1 |
| Innkeeper | | 3 | | | | | | | | | | 1 | 1 |
| Tanner | 3 | | | | | | | | 2 | | 1 | 2 | 3 |
| Yeoman | 2 | | | 1 | | | | | | | | 1 | |
| Grocer | | 1 | | 1 | | | | | | 1 | | | |
| Tailor | 2 | 1 | | | | | | | | | 1 | 3 | 1 |
| Locksmith | | 1 | | | | | | | 1 | 1 | | 2 | 1 |
| Bellfounder | | | | | | | | | | | | 1 | |
| Ironmonger | 2 | | | | | | | | | | | 2 | |
| Blacksmith | | | | | | | | | 2 | | | | |
| Carpenter | 2 | | | | | | | | 1 | | | 2 | 1 |
| Shoemaker | 1 | | | | | | | | 1 | | | 1 | 1 |
| Glover | 1 | | | | | 1 | | | 2 | | 1 | 1 | 2 |
| Maltgrinder | | | | | | | | | | | 1 | 1 | |
| Cook | 1 | | | | | | | | | | | 1 | |
| Glazier | | 1 | | | | | | | | | | | 1 |
| Brazier | 1 | | 1 | | | | | | | | | | 1 |
| Cooper | | | | | | | | | | | 1 | 1 | |

| Occupation | 1624 | | | | | | | | | | | 1628 | |
|---|---|---|---|---|---|---|---|---|---|---|---|---|---|
|  | AF | AH | FH | A | F | AW | H | WF | HW | WH | W | F | B |
| Barber |  | 1 |  |  |  |  |  |  |  |  |  |  | 1 |
| Wheeler |  |  |  |  |  |  |  |  |  |  |  | 1 |  |
| Butcher |  | 1 |  |  |  |  |  |  | 1 |  | 1 |  | 2 |
| Basketmaker |  | 1 |  |  |  |  |  |  |  |  |  | 1 |  |
| Cordwainer | 1 |  | 1 | 1 |  |  | 1 |  | 1 |  |  | 1 | 4 |
| Turner | 2 |  |  |  |  |  |  |  |  |  |  | 2 |  |
| Joiner |  |  |  |  |  |  |  | 1 |  |  |  | 1 |  |
| Tilemaker | 1 |  |  |  |  |  |  |  |  |  |  | 1 |  |
| Dyer | 1 | 1 |  |  |  |  |  |  |  |  |  | 1 |  |
| Fuller |  |  | 1 |  |  |  |  |  |  |  |  | 1 |  |
| Currier | 1 |  |  |  |  |  |  |  |  |  |  | 1 |  |
| Fishmonger |  |  |  |  |  |  |  |  |  | 1 |  |  | 1 |
| Woolcomber |  |  |  |  |  |  |  |  |  |  | 1 | 1 |  |
| Candlemaker |  |  |  |  |  |  |  |  | 1 |  |  |  | 1 |
| Gardener | 1 |  |  |  |  |  |  | 1 |  |  |  | 1 |  |
| Labourer | 1 |  |  |  |  |  |  |  |  |  |  |  | 1 |
| Poor non-householder |  |  |  |  |  |  |  |  |  |  | 1 |  |  |

There is a perceptible tendency to scatter, although certainly not a strong current of opposition, among those occupations further away from the 'respectable' levels.

# The Provisions of Bills to Regulate Elections

---

There were recurrent attempts to enforce residence requirements for members, but this account is not concerned with those, but only with efforts to reform elections and the electorate. These focused primarily on resisting influence from above – although this could also be seen as the aim of residence measures.

1606: Introduced by Christopher Brooke: no clients of noblemen or other parliament men to be chosen; none to be chosen 'upon any letters Mandatory or of Request, nor for Money or other Gift'. Willson, *Parliamentary Diary of Robert Bowyer*, 100.

1614: the details are unrecorded, but its concern was clearly the same as that of 1606, to prevent influence. Sir Henry Anderson protested against carpet-baggers, and Serjeant Montague demanded that none 'should come in by Letter, for the only Way to bring in Servitude'. This was evidently a common demand, for Sir Edwin Sandys had earlier drawn a distinction between nobles' letters 'to whom they bound in Love' which was not packing, whereas 'to press with Letters, or by Fear, etc.' was. Sir Francis Goodwin protested against the frequency of disputes, and that mayors and bailiffs were returning themselves, and demanded 'a plain Law' to clarify elections. Hakewill was concerned with the bill also, which clearly arose from the Stockbridge affair: as Montague said, 'This a fit Subject for a necessary Law'. *C.J.*, I, 463, 468, 478, 494.

1621: a major concern was with fairly traditional matters such as shrieval manipulation of the time and place of the election, but for the first time there was an attempt to produce an environment in which it would be more difficult to 'fix' elections, rather than just to ban influence. The situation is confused by the fact that there were clearly two separate bills, one in the spring and one in November; but besides that, the accounts differ:

A fixed procedure for the delivery of the writ, and the timing and place of election to be laid down.

No requests by great men for seats to be allowed.

Members to be resident, to avoid the King placing 'those that may serve his turn'.

Customary borough franchises to be continued, but no cottagers to vote, only householders and freeholders (? freemen).

No recusants or husbands of recusants to be chosen. *C.D. 1621*, II, 277–8.

Resident freemen only to vote, and no almsmen; if there are fewer than 24 inhabitants, then the majority to vote. *C.D. 1621*, IV, 422.

If election by voice or view leaves uncertainty, the poll is to be taken; the procedure and place of elections to be fixed.

Only residents of the county of six months' standing to vote.

Those possessed of £4 per annum freehold or £10 per annum copyhold to vote.

Invalid voters to receive one month's gaol and to be perpetually disfranchised [opposed by Sir George More: *C.J.*, I, 649].

Freemen to vote in towns, except where charters provide otherwise; and only householders to vote.

No mandatory letters from lords to be allowed, and no intimidation of voters.
  *C.D. 1621*, III, 411–12.
Sir Henry Poole appears to have initiated business this year, showing great concern about pressure from above: he later pronounced his opposition to solicitations or letters for places: 'Men should not stand to be Knights. – They to be chosen, whom the Country chuseth of themselves; and not they that desire it. This Competition bringeth a great Charge'. [*C.J.*, I, 513, 649] He did, however, pick up slightly less reactionary support: Sir Dudley Digges proposed the detailed bill, Edward Alford suggested Hakewill draw it up, and Hakewill seems to have chaired the committee; Sir Edward Coke was noted as being active on it, and Sir Edwin Sandys saw the matter as being so important that work should continue in the recess on the bill. The debates yielded one idiosyncrasy: Coke opposed the proposal that knights of the shires should have estates of at least £100 per annum in their counties, on the ground that this would ensure that they were rated at that for tax. *C.D. 1621*, II, 380; *ibid.*, v, 269, 286; *C.J.*, I, 572, 649.

1624: Edward Alford seems to have proposed the reviving of the 1621 bill (in response to his demand for a bill, 'The Clerk to look it up'); but Sir Henry Poole apparently proposed a new one. Sir Henry Spiller also showed an interest. *C.J.*, I, 673, 686, 718.

1625: Alford and Sir Arthur Ingram demand a bill. *C.J.*, I, 800.

1626: Seen as 'for the due Election and free Choice' of members: it again sought to tighten up the procedure for the delivery of writs, and while some of its provisions seem borrowed from the 1621 bill, in other respects it was even more unrealistic:
    No copyholders to vote.
    All that have votes to be present, on pain of 40s. fine.
    All elections 'procured by canvasing, void'.
    The proposal that knights should have £100 per annum freehold in their counties was also revived, as was that to ensure that they were not recusants.
      *C.J.*, I, 818; C.U.L. Mss., Dd. 12.20, 21, f. 87 v.

1628: Concern for fixing the timing of the election recurred; other proposals were:
    Only residents, or people rated for the subsidy, to vote in urban elections.
    No townsmen to vote in county elections.
    If any reward promised to an elector, the election to be void. B.M. Add. 36825, f. 216 v.
    The bill was rejected by the House.

Short Parliament. Two bills were evidently afoot, and a sub-committee of the Committee of Privileges was ordered to frame these, along with matter culled from previous bills and disputes, into a single bill. Judging by what little evidence is left of their provisions, both bills seem to have been more concerned with great men, rather than the franchise. One was to enforce residency requirements, the other decreed, 'No letter must be sent by any peer or privy councillor for or in the behalf of any man to be elected, upon pain of censure of the house and Star chamber'. *C.J.*, II, 16; Willis Bund, *Diary of Henry Townshend*, I, 13–14.
    Sir William Masham may have been the first to raise the matter, demanding that peers and justices should not intermeddle in elections. B.M. Harl. 4391, f. 47.

Long Parliament. Again, more than one bill was introduced: one was read in mid-December 1640, and at the same time, the complexities of the Tewkesbury franchise dispute drove the House to order the Committee of Privileges to draw up a bill to prevent such 'inconveniencies'. One bill had a second reading at the end of March, and yet another was introduced in April. B.M. Add. 11045, f. 138; *C.J.*, II, 49; B. M. Harl. 162, f. 377; Harl. 476, f. 178.

The bill which received its second reading in March proposed that:
No almsmen should vote.
'Undue expence' at elections should be checked.
Members should receive wages from their constituencies. B.M. Harl. 162, f. 377;
Bodl. Ms. Film 39, p. 107.

D'Ewes demanded that all inhabitants of urban constituencies should vote,
and that an end be put to 'monopolising elections'; that all votes should be polled
together (rather than separately for first and second seat); that the procedure for
taking the poll, and the checks on voters, be tightened up; and that steps be
taken to curb violence at elections. B.M. Harl. 162, f. 377.

The perennial concern about aristocratic interference (this time by the Earl
of Arundel at Arundel) seems to have produced an attempt to draw up a new bill
outlawing requests from above for seats at the end of 1641. Most active in this
were Cromwell, Pym and (said he) D'Ewes: Pym was, of course, reverting to his
constant theme here. *D'Ewes* (C), 236.

Additionally in 1640 there were local demands, by interested parties at elections,
that recusants, excommunicate persons, madmen and criminals be disfranchised.
[Longleat, Marquis of Bath's Mss., Whitelocke Papers, vol. VIII, ff. 30, 32; P.R.O.,
C.219/43. Pt. 1 (Bedford indenture).] Furthermore, the Herefordshire members,
Harley and Coningsby, were subject to pressure from various JPs in their constituency to introduce a bill 'for the future more orderlie, and Free elleccion of
Knights and burgesses, and to provide such meanes whereby they may bee enioyned
more dilligentlie hereafter to attend that service, in dischardge of that great trust
reposed in them'. Shropshire R.O., 212/364, f. 1.

# The Arguments for a Wider Franchise

An analysis of the arguments for expanding the franchise reveals again just how novel the issue was, in the speed with which sophistication and confidence was acquired from uncertain beginnings. But it also demonstrates how, in this period of reverence for the ancient constitution,[1] the House could elaborate a novel constitutional doctrine in a mere twenty years.

The first two decisions to widen, over Oxford and Sandwich in 1621, did not raise particularly great problems. The Oxford debate centred on the terms of its charter, and a decision was facilitated by the fact that one of its clauses stipulated that its constitution was to be as in its parent, London, where a wider group than the corporation was involved. Accordingly, there were apparently no dissentient voices to the proposal for widening.[2] Sandwich was dissimilar, and a pointer to later developments, in that it focused on custom as against executive fiat. The matter was fairly straightforward, however, for the exclusion of the freemen was recent, having taken place within living memory, orders from the end of Elizabeth's and the beginning of James's reigns being cited, and the mayor admitted that the commons had only been 'debard . . . in two or three former elections of Burgesses'. The House was thus introduced gently to electoral reform, and the precedents for later intervention laid down fairly inconspicuously. There was already some support for the idea of general franchise reform, as can be seen in the provisions of the 1621 election bill.[3] But such a wide gaze was rare, and the whole matter was conceived piecemeal and uncontroversially at the start.

The tempo speeded up in 1624, when Glanville's Committee began to construct its doctrine that parliamentary elections were above all conventional regulations, 'the commonwealth being interested in the freedom and consequence of such elections'. From this blanket assertion that the common good necessitated the overriding of the normal forms of local control (derived from bye-laws), and an undermining of often ancient powers derived from the Privy Council, the Committee of Privileges, and subsequently the House, denied the ability of local officials or Privy Council to regulate elections in five boroughs. This was not merely an assertion that recent orders could not negate ancient custom, as was the case in Sandwich, but that electoral rights, being of a higher order, were inalienable. The most obvious instance of this doctrine was over the lapsed parliamentary boroughs restored that session, where it was successfully argued that electoral rights could not be lost for non-user, however long they had been discontinued, for these were rather a service to the commonwealth than a privilege.[4] This extension of the Committee's competence was noticed, and inevitably aroused more disquiet than did the 1621 decisions. One member commenting on the Committee's refusal to allow the Winchelsea corporation to define a freeman for the purpose of an election thought 'it were dangerous to let men question the right of officers in poss[ession]'. The Committee clearly met similar disquiet over its decision on Dover, where it had denied the validity of the conditions imposed by a municipal ordinance of 1561, which had been continued ever since (that is, for longer than the 60 years normally ensuring the forfeiture of a right to the Crown). Glanville had to argue against such unease, and reported that, 'notwithstanding the antiquity thereof, and the usage according to the same ever since', it could not affect the parliamentary rights of the freemen, 'nor ought the same to bind, or prejudice, the privilege, or interest of the commonwealth', although it was valid in local affairs.[5]

Over Chippenham the Committee went further back, refusing to accept the 'void' charter of 1 Queen Mary as a regulator of parliamentary elections. The 'precedents and indentures, passed in silence' on the unprotesting freemen's part ever since were declared null, and this led Pym to make his outburst that all electoral rights were threatened by the juggernaut of the Committee.[6] The issue was clearly not one of customary rights (as it had been at Sandwich), for these rights were no longer customary: it was now almost one of natural rights, and very much an innovation. A doctrine of the greater validity of an unspecified public good than the normal formulae of custom was not foreign: Coke had developed the concept of a 'common right' capable of over-riding precedent and charter in the course of his opposition to monopolies at the end of Elizabeth's reign.[7] But the determined use to which the 1624 Committee put it was novel, and some members jibbed. There was no obvious political division on the issue, as has been seen, but tempers became hot, a Privy Councillor, Sir Thomas Edmondes, accusing Glanville of insolence, at which the Committee excepted, and blows were struck. One or two members in the House's debate expressed concern at the long duration of the custom which was being over-thrown. More significantly, the recommendation for a wider franchise eventually only passed the Committee by 26 votes to 12, the decisive argument being that, as Hakewill admitted, the Marian charter was not a *'confirmamus'*, and thus its provisions were new (although the fact that the freemen had been invited to assent to a return once also helped).[8]

That the House and Committee were drawn into an acceptance of the doctrine of 'common right', and of their powers with regard to it, suggests that Glanville was not alone in his firm opinions. But once that acceptance was gained, the Committee proceeded apace. It attempted to disguise its audacity by saying that it was compelled to resort to 'common law, or common right' when fixing the franchise for the newly-restored borough of Pontefract where no precedent could guide, though common law had little to say to the matter (unless the Committee was being thoroughly radical and referring to the statutes of Henry VI as D'Ewes and Palmer were to do in 1640, which is unlikely). The fiction was immediately dropped, and the Committee ruled that 'of common right, all the inhabitants, householders, and residents within the borough', rather than freeholders alone, should vote; it then took the same position over Cirencester, where in the absence of contests, no rules had been worked out.[9] These statements of principle by the Committee, that if possible franchises should be wide, had immediate relevance for the restored boroughs, as is shown by the absence of dispute in the Marlow case in 1640 about whether the commons should vote, but merely about exactly who the commons were.

As a result of the elaboration of the 'common right' concept, the Committee could contemplate with equanimity the prospect of making abstract pronouncements about the optimum size of the electorate in the Bletchingley case (thus going contrary to its normal position that it was only a court, and could merely pronounce on the case before it). It held that 'more persons than in the case in question' should vote, where there was no clear prescription to the contrary, although such a prescription was found in this instance. But the difficulty of finding such a valid limiting prescription was pointed to by Hakewill over the Bridport case in 1628, where, as we have seen, he argued against the Bletchingley decision: he reported 'that Glanvill said [over Bletchingley] that the Common right of the eleccion ought

to come from the generalitie But the Common right may bee deprived by prescripcion but that prescripcion ought to bee cleerely proved, and a little proofe will
disprove it'. The smallness of the 'proof' requisite to counter a limiting prescription
was demonstrated over Colchester that year, where the Committee discounted a
prescription for limited elections cited by the corporation extending back at least to
Edward IV, possibly even to Richard I.[10] This conclusion confirmed Glanville's
response in the Dover case to the objection that the limiting custom was valid
because of its endurance since 3 Elizabeth: it was 'no good Custom, since the
Beginning of it did appear'. Colchester showed that an 'immemorial custom' had to
be truly immemorial – or rather, that there could be *no* counter-custom, as Maynard
suggested when he argued over Tewkesbury in 1640 that liberties by prescription,
by common right, could not be lost. The immediately political fear of packed
parliaments which occasioned the development of the doctrine of common right –
that 'the general liberty of the realm . . . favoureth . . . the greatest number of voices'
– had fathered a new orthodoxy.[11]

After this, there was no stopping the Committee, which became yet more ad-
venturous under Hakewill in 1628. Boston was opened on similar grounds to
Colchester, on the mere assumption that the commons *might* have voted before the
precedents cited began in Henry VIII's reign.[12] The inalienability of the franchise
was emphasised by the decisions, over both Warwick and Bridport, that attempts by
freemen to deny that they had ever voted would not be considered: 'if but One
Commoner appear to sue for his Right, they will hear him'. In the same vein,
Hakewill made a thoroughly political, rather than legal, plea for the restoration of
the lapsed boroughs of Weobley and Milborne Port that year: for 'though a
Franchise might bee lost by non-user, yet because this was not soe much a Franchise
as a service to the Common Weale . . . Therefore this could not bee lost', for otherwise the House might be gradually divested of its members.[13]

The confirmation that electoral rights were natural, not merely customary,
meant that the Committee could now make general statements on the franchise,
instead of limiting itself to particular constituencies, which contrasts with the
refusal to follow Glanville on pronouncing on the franchises of the restored
Buckinghamshire boroughs in 1624. The House resolved on the Committee's report
over Bridport in 1628 that 'the Commonalty in general ought to have Voices in the
Election of Burgesses for the Parliament', and the Committee followed this with a
more explicit conclusion over Boston, 'that the Election of Burgesses, in all
Boroughs, did, of common Right, belong to the Commoners; and that nothing
could take it from them, but a Prescription, and a constant Usage beyond all
Memory'.[14] There was no hint of a possible role for charter here, and those men
such as Pym, Selden or Maynard who allowed some power to charters in 1640
were not the heirs of 1628. Fiennes, Palmer and D'Ewes, talking in terms of statute,
more nearly provided continuity, but the latter two went even further than the 1628
Committee. Palmer argued that the statutes of 8 and 10 Henry VI limiting the
county electorates from all the freeholders to those with land worth 40s. per annum
had not affected the original common law of inhabitant election in cities and boroughs, 'And if the Charter was to the contrary in expressis verbis, yet it is not
sufficient to Restraine the libertie of generall and Free Election established by the
Comon lawe, without an act of Parliament'. Not only could a charter not affect the
franchise in prescriptive boroughs: Palmer clearly stated that limitations by 'use
prescription or Charter . . . are voide' (which he claimed, incorrectly, was the
House's position in the 1620s), and that the only valid restriction was by statute, 'as
in Northampton, Leicester, etc.'[15] D'Ewes echoed this radical but unrealistic
proposition. Over Salisbury he talked of 'the hereditarie right' of Englishmen to

vote, and argued on the basis of Henry VI's statutes against prescriptive limitations. That he realised one of the implications of his position, that if it were implemented, all limited franchises would disappear, was shown by his contribution to the debate on the 1641 election bill, when he demanded an end to all 'monopolising of elections' in boroughs. The seed sown in the 1620s, and evident in the Short Parliament Committee's report on the East Grinstead election, that 'the Right of Election [is] original', had taken root, and a truly radical position had been achieved before war broke out, not by D'Ewes and Palmer alone, but by the 1628 Committee, by Fiennes, and perhaps by some of D'Ewes's supporters over Marlow too.[16]

But such attitudes rarely percolated into the country. The inhabitants of Marlow used a variant of D'Ewes's wide position when they urged to Whitelocke in 1640 that 'bicause it being no corporation, all the inhabitants had their votes in the election', seeming to believe that no limitation at all was possible in non-incorporate boroughs by prescription. One of the candidates in the Long Parliament Gatton dispute argued in the House 'that of Comon right the eleccion ought to be by the Inhabitants', but elsewhere, more traditional forms of argument survived. The local participants continued to base claims on local precedents and customs, rather that to appeal to the kind of general principle elaborated by the House, as the Marlow inhabitants did, and nor did they cite precedents drawn from the widening of franchises in similar boroughs. Only the statute-quoting Bristol freemen, Sir Thomas Puckering at Warwick in 1628, and Grenville at Bossiney used the developments taking place outside the borough to apply pressure locally, Puckering informing the Warwick corporation 'that many presidents in the present parlement were to vote down such maner of election and to reduce them to popular voyces'.[17] Elsewhere, claims were couched in the language of local precedent and the formulae of past returns,[18] although Palmer in his far-reaching case for Higham Ferrers did justify his conclusion by the statement that 'it hath beene formerly determined upon the like question in parliament'. In the House itself, precedents of earlier decisions were certainly cited, as when Colchester was opened on the precedent of Oxford, and itself became a precedent for Boston in 1628 and Windsor in 1640, or when the Long Parliament Wareham dispute was used to help determine the Gatton case.[19] But apart from the few instances cited, the local contenders were ignorant of, or unwilling to use, such arguments, and kept their gaze firmly fixed on the purely local past.

Likewise in the House, concentration on denigrating the powers of particular limitations was not total. Despite D'Ewes's attempts to divert the Tewkesbury debate onto the subject of statute, it stayed rooted in the details of the charter and the meaning of the word '*communitas*' contained therein, and the problem of Windsor was conceived in similar terms.[20] And while Palmer argued radically over Higham Ferrers that charters were ineffective in this area anyway because they could not offset the common law, this was his last point, and earlier he had analysed the specific provisions of the borough's charter, exploiting its inclusion of the undefined group, the '*burgenses*', in the terms of the incorporation. Heath, more conservatively, concentrated solely on this in his opinion, but St John, like Palmer, used incompatible arguments: that the borough was such before the charter, and therefore could not be limited electorally; and anyway, the charter used the undifferentiated term 'burgesses', and therefore its intention was not to limit.[21] Participants were evidently not so confident in their powers of persuasion that they would limit their argument to common right alone.

Palmer used a third argument in his opinion, and this was drawn from the House's role as a representative institution. He concluded that all inhabitants should vote 'because the Burgess of the Parliament is to serve for the whole Borough and his assent there concludes all the Inhabitants', and observed that as his wages were paid by the whole borough, therefore all were involved in his service.[22] This was the most fruitful line for later development, and was a practical application of the old maxim, '*quod omnes tangit ab omnibus tractetur*'. The arguments had indeed been used before in the context of electoral reform, although not so explicitly: as we have seen, in borough disputes, when the commons gained a say in the election, they were often roped in by the corporation to help pay the members' wages. The attempt to enfranchise the county palatine of Durham in 1621 had been justified 'in respect that they are charged and bound by Acts of Parliament', and after the failure of the attempts in the early 1620s, the commissioners for the 1627 loan reported strong feeling in the county that if it were to be taxed, then it should be represented. It seems to have been successfully argued in defence of a recusant in Gatton in the Long Parliament dispute that he should not be disfranchised, because he paid his taxes.[23] But predictably it was Glanville who phrased the argument most trenchantly in his report on the 1624 Gloucestershire dispute: it should be made possible for a maximum number of people to vote, 'for the choice of those, by whose voices in parliament, they and their heirs are to be bound for ever', and this principle, as much as the need to resist influence, may have occasioned the proposal of the 1625 election bill for compulsory voting. Apart from Coriton's abstract argument in c. 1629 that power since the Fall had lain with the heads of families, from whence it devolved upon the ruler, and that therefore all heads of families should vote, this argument from consent was the only justification of the extension of the franchise which was made in philosophical rather than political terms before the war.[24] The conclusion of Glanville's and Palmer's arguments was manhood suffrage, while the local acceptance of the connection between taxation and representation was perhaps part of the background for the army officers' moves towards a taxpayers' or rate-payers' suffrage that were to be formalised in the Officers' Agreement in the negotiations with the Levellers. But this in a sense more respectable argument from consent, whose long ancestry included most of the prominent English legal theorists, may have helped to quell the disquiet aroused by the pressure to extend the unrepresentative franchises.

# Notes

## 1. Introduction

1 J. H. Plumb, *The Growth of Political Stability in England 1675–1725* (London, 1967); J. E. Neale, *The Elizabethan House of Commons* (London, 1949).

2 See K. E. Wrightson, 'The Puritan Reformation of Manners, with special reference to the counties of Lancashire and Essex 1640–1660' (Cambridge Ph.D., 1974).

3 J. H. Hexter, 'The Myth of the Middle Class in Tudor England', and 'Storm over the Gentry', in *Reappraisals in History* (London, 1961).

4 For grand jury service and gentility, see a forthcoming article to be published in the Leicester University, Dept. of English Local History, Occasional Papers, by Dr J. S. Morrill, 'The Cheshire Grand Jury 1625–1659: a social and administrative study' (I am most grateful to Dr Morrill for permitting me to see an early draft of this article); for the elective gentility of aldermen, see the charge of a Hull minister in a Jacobean dispute that the mayor and aldermen 'were but Michaellmas gentlemen', or the more or less rigorous distinction maintained until 1608 in the Exeter records between gentlemen aldermen who had been mayors and non-gentlemen aldermen who had not. P.R.O., St. Ch. 8/79/5; City of Exeter R.O., Act Book VI.

5 See below, Chapter 2.

6 Wrightson, 'Reformation of Manners', 179–91; E. P. Thompson, 'The Moral Economy of the English Crowd in the Eighteenth Century', *Past and Present* l (1971), 76–120; C. S. L. Davies, 'Peasant Revolt in England and France', *Agricultural History Review* xxi (1973), 122–34; *C.S.P.D. 1637–1638*, 501; *C.S.P.D. 1640*, 190. We must await J. D. Walter's 1975 Cambridge Ph.D. thesis, 'Popular Disorder in England c. 1596–1660', for a fuller elucidation of this problem.

7 *Reliquiae Baxterianae*, ed. M. Sylvester (1696), 94; A. J. and R. H. Tawney, 'An Occupational Census of the Seventeenth Century', *Economic History Review* v (1934), 25–64; see below, Chapter 2, for a further development of this argument.

8 A similar process of the diminution of the electorate through the effect of economic polarisation on the property franchise is argued to have occurred over the same period, in the late 17th and early 18th centuries, in New England. K. Lockridge, 'Land, Population and the Evolution of New England Society 1630–1790', *Past and Present* xxxix (1968), esp. 75–6.

9 J. P. Cooper, 'The Differences between English and Continental Governments in the Early Seventeenth Century' in J. S. Bromley and E. H. Kossmann, eds., *Britain and the Netherlands* (London, 1960), 62–90; Phelips is quoted in P. Zagorin, *The Court and the Country* (London, 1969), 87.

10 *Ibid.*, 83, 87; Somerset R. O., DD/PH 227/16; S. R. Gardiner, *Constitutional Documents of the Puritan Revolution* (Oxford, 1906), 211.

11 See below, Chapters 8 and 9, for a development of this argument.

12 A. Hassell Smith, *County and Court* (Oxford, 1974), *passim*.

13 See below, Chapter 4 for this fear and some of its consequences; and T. L. Moir, *The Addled Parliament of 1614* (New York, 1958).

14 Neale, *House of Commons*, 158–61.

15 See my forthcoming article in the *Historical Journal*, 'Elections and the Privileges of the House of Commons in the early 17th century', for a discussion of the

election cases; I am most grateful to Mr Conrad Russell for discussions on the unpopularity of the Court, and for pointing to the possible impact of the Essex revolt.

16 Hassell Smith, *County and Court*, esp. Chap. VI.

17 Quoted in J. H. Plumb, 'The Growth of the Electorate in England from 1600 to 1715', *Past and Present* xlv (1969), 94; and see below, Chapters 6 and 7, for appeals to public opinion.

18 Neale, *House of Commons*, 255; and for numbers of contests, see below, Appendix IV.

19 J. S. Roskell, *The Commons in the Parliament of 1422* (Manchester, 1954), 24; P.R.O., S.P. 16/448/79: but the same account shows that concern for prestige might still cause people to be brought out even when there was no contest.

20 Quoted in W. Prynne, *Brevia Parliamentaria Rediviva* (1662), 186; A. Rogers, 'Parliamentary Elections in Grimsby in the Fifteenth Century', *Bulletin of the Institute of Historical Research* xlii (1969), 212–20.

21 Sir Goronwy Edwards, 'The Emergence of Majority Rule in English Parliamentary Elections', *Transactions of the Royal Historical Society*, 5th series, xiv (1964), 187–9 (I am grateful to Mr K. Thomas for emphasising this point to me). There were a variety of forms of election: by voice (the candidate winning whose supporters shouted his name loudest), by view (the voters being asked to raise their hands, or to separate into rival parties), and, if these proved indecisive, by poll.

22 B.M. Add. 26639, f. 41. A similar demand was made, though more weakly, in the 1624 Committee. J. Glanville, *Reports of Certain Cases* (London, 1775), 10.

23 P.R.O., St. Ch. 8/201/17, no. 9; J. T. Cliffe, *The Yorkshire Gentry* (London, 1969), 283; *H.M.C. 14th Report*, App. II, *Duke of Portland's Mss.*, vol. III, 147. Dering in Kent in the spring of 1640 was as concerned as Wentworth in 1625 to stress the status, rather than just the number, of his voters. Bodl. Ms. Top. Kent e.6.

24 B.M. Harl. 2313, f. 8v; Nottinghamshire R.O., DD. SR. 221/96/4.

25 *C.J.*, I, 749; D. B. Rutman, *Winthrop's Boston* (Chapel Hill, 1965), 170.

26 B.M. Add. 18016, f. 139v; York Public Library, House Book 30, f. 378v; *ibid.*, House Book 32, ff. 314v–315; Essex R.O., D/B3/1/19, ff. 176v, 207. Many indentures in the P.R.O. for constituencies where contests are known to have occurred echo this formula of unanimity.

27 J. P. Collier, ed., *The Egerton Papers* (Camden Soc., 1840), 384–5; for an instance of its effect in Gloucester, see P.R.O., St. Ch. 8/207/25.

28 For Chester corporation's hostility to canvassing in 1621, see below, Appendix II.

29 Bodl. Ms. Tanner 67, f. 176; *C.J.*, I, 649; Bodl. Ms. Tanner 321, f. 3; W. Knowler, ed., *The Earl of Strafforde's Letters and Dispatches* (London, 1739), I, 8. It was possibly this same modesty which prevented any candidate voting for himself: all the surviving records show votes being cast for opponents.

30 R. N. Dore, *The Civil Wars in Cheshire* (Chester, 1966), 3.

31 See below, Chapter 3.

32 E. de Villiers, 'The Parliamentary Boroughs Restored by the House of Commons 1621–1641', *E.H.R.* lxvii (1952), 175–202; and see below, pp. 132–3 (for Amersham and Malton) and Appendix I. The House, in restoring the boroughs, had refused to pronounce on the franchise because that would have been to elevate an order of one House into a law: all it could do was to adjudicate disputes when they were submitted to it.

33 Neale, *House of Commons*, 267–8; T. Kemp, ed., *The Black Book of Warwick* (Warwick, 1898), 410; Glanville, *Reports* 105–7. Similarly, the sheriff of Rutland

wreaked havoc among puzzled voters when he insisted on the precise franchise, a 40s. freehold above all charges, in 1601. Neale, *House of Commons*, 137.

34 *Ibid.*, 272–3; P.R.O., St. Ch. 8/228/30, no. 28.

35 G. D. Langdon, jnr, 'The Franchise and Political Democracy in Plymouth Colony', *William and Mary Quarterly* xx (1963), 516–17, 520; Rutman, *Winthrop's Boston*, 170, 223–4; R. E. Wall, 'The Massachusetts Bay Colony Franchise in 1647', *William and Mary Quarterly* xxvii (1970), 143; R. C. Simmons, 'Freemanship in Early Massachusetts', *ibid.*, xix (1962), 422–8; T. H. Breen, 'Who Governs: The Town Franchise in Seventeenth-Century Massachusetts', *ibid.*, xxvii (1970), 460–74; R. E. Wall, 'The Decline of the Massachusetts Franchise: 1647–1666', *Journal of American History* lix (1972–3), 307–8.

36 Roskell, *The Commons in 1422*, 11; Neale, *House of Commons*, 182–5; *C.D. 1621*, vi, 354; *D'Ewes* (N), 463; C. Hill, *The World Turned Upside Down* (London, 1972), 250–1; W. Atkinson, 'A Parliamentary Election in Knaresborough in 1628', *Yorkshire Archaeological Journal* xxxiv (1938–9), 213–14; R. T. Fieldhouse, 'Parliamentary Representation in the Borough of Richmond', *ibid.*, xliv (1972), 208.

37 B.M. Harl. 165, f. 8; Harl. 158, f. 285v; see below for his questions to the judges.

38 R. G. Marsden, 'A letter of William Bradford and Isaac Allerton, 1623', *American Historical Review* viii (1902–3), 299.

39 See below, Chapter 2, for further examination of this problem.

40 Anon., *The Priviledges and Practice of Parliaments in England* (—, 1640): but it was not much use on the franchise; M. G. Hobson and H. E. Salter, eds., *Oxford Council Acts 1626–1665* (Oxford Historical Society, xcv, 1933), 91–2; Shropshire R.O., Ludlow Corporation Minute Book 1590–1648, f. 214.

41 Lancashire R.O., DDKE/9/23/56; *D'Ewes* (N), 441; B.M. Loan 29/50, no. 76A; Lincolnshire R.O., Mm. vi/10/5 (I am grateful to Dr C. A. Holmes for this reference).

42 Leeds Public Library Mss., Mx 177/25; Hertford Borough Mss., vol. 23, ff. 13–14, 17; W. S. Weeks, *Clitheroe in the 17th Century* (Clitheroe, n.d.), 226–7, 229–30; *C.D. 1621*, vii, 568; M. F. Keeler, *The Long Parliament* (Philadelphia, 1954), 42.

43 *Ibid.*, 33; Hertford Borough Mss., vol. 23, f. 17; Sandwich had switched to totalling votes by 1640: see Keeler, *Long Parliament*, 77; B.M. Harl. 165, f. 6. But in the 1604 Somerset election, the crowd was divided into three parts, the two biggest winning – effectively depriving everybody of their second vote. Somerset R.O., DD/PH/224/8. See Appendix vii for the views of D'Ewes.

44 Sir Robert Filmer, *Patriarcha, and Other Political Works*, ed. P. Laslett (Oxford 1949), 133, 174, 183; Sir John Spelman, *A View of a Printed Book Intituled Observations* (Oxford, 1643), sig. D2.

45 A. S. P. Woodhouse, *Puritanism and Liberty* (London, 1938), 64; J. Lilburne, *Londons Liberty in Chains discovered* (—, 1646), 14 (this statement was contained in the *Citizens' Protestation* of 29 September, but Lilburne held he was the 'Contriver' of this: *ibid.*, 12).

46 Woodhouse, *Puritanism and Liberty*, 54, 57–8, 61, 73, 79; N.R.O., FH 3467/1; Inner Temple Mss., 511/23, f. 3. See below, Chapter 2, for a discussion of the definition of freeholds, and Appendix iii, for a list of the borough franchises.

47 This perceptive argument and counter-argument had in fact been met in disputes in Southwark in 1605. John Stow, *A Survey of the Cities of London and Westminster*, ed. J. Strype (London, 1720), Bk. iv, 10.

48 Although Rainborough was capable of arguing from the existing electoral system: he countered Ireton's argument that to innovate on the existing county

franchise would be to produce chaos by pointing out that the House had altered borough franchises. Woodhouse, *Puritanism and Liberty*, 64, 78.

49 K. Thomas, 'The Levellers and the Franchise', in G. E. Aylmer, ed., *The Interregnum* (London, 1972), 67–8.

50 See below, Chapter 6, for an expansion of this argument.

51 A. H. Dodd, *Studies in Stuart Wales* (Cardiff, 1952), 177; see also R. E. Ruigh, *The Parliament of 1624* (Cambridge, Mass., 1971), 95n; Neale, *House of Commons*, 102, 137–8; Somerset R.O., DD/SF 1076/21/36; Hampshire R.O., Jervoise Mss., 44M69/012; J. Ballinger, ed., *Calendar of Wynn (of Gwydir) Papers* (Cardiff, 1926), 145, 148, B. W. Quintrell, 'The Government of the County of Essex 1603–42' (London Ph.D., 1965), 32.

52 P.R.O., S.P. 16/79/38, S.P. 16/366/48.

53 Lilburne, *Londons Liberty in Chains*, 56.

54 The fact that it was a parliamentary borough was cited in the sale documents. 'Shardeloes Muniments – III', *Records of Buckinghamshire* xiv, pt. 5 (1945), 283.

55 Neale, *House of Commons*, 257; P. R. Seddon, 'A Parliamentary Election at East Retford, 1624', *Transactions of the Thoroton Society of Nottinghamshire* lxxvi (1972), 30–1; at Maldon, the unusually high number of five freemen were admitted immediately before the election, and all but one voted with the corporation, thus ensuring it victory: there were complaints later from the freemen about the oligarchy's manipulation of the freedom. Essex R.O., D/B3/3/392/53/3, and *ibid.*, D/B3/392/18; and C. A. Holmes, 'The 1640 Elections in East Anglia' (unpublished paper deposited at Essex R.O.), 20. Extensive manipulation of this sort was unlikely, for, in contrast with the 18th century, the economic aspects of freedom of a corporate borough were still of great significance, and corporations would have risked rebellion had they behaved in such a 'political' fashion.

56 L. Stone, 'The Electoral Influence of the second Earl of Salisbury, 1614–1668', *E.H.R.* lxxi (1956), 398; B. Boothroyd, *History of Pontefract* (Pontefract, 1807), 462; N.R.O., FH 50, f. 37; B.M. Add. 36827, f. 40v.

57 Atkinson, 'Parliamentary Election in Knaresborough', 213–15; B. Jennings, *A History of Harrogate and Knaresborough* (Huddersfield, 1970), 138–9; Yorkshire Archaeological Society Mss., DD 56/B1: unnumbered: list of 'Single Borrow men and heres without devideing. 66'. This list shows Thomas Stockdale now in possession of several tenures formerly belonging to his and Fairfax's enemies, the Bensons. He was just succeeding in replacing them as member at the time.

58 N.N.R.O., 349X/How. 633/1; compare this with *ibid.*, 10–14; Keeler, *Long Parliament*, 70–1; Sir R. C. Hoare, *History of Modern Wiltshire* (London, 1822–1844), IV, *Hundred of Downton*, 19. M. G. Rathbone, *Wiltshire Borough Records before 1836* (Wiltshire Archaeological and Natural History Soc., v, 1949), 21. The gentry names were not present in the 1640 Downton indentures. P.R.O., C219/43. Pt. 3.

59 Fieldhouse, 'Parliamentary Representation of Richmond', 208–9.

## 2. *The County Electorate*

1 There was some dispute for example over whether the clergy should vote: the House resolved in 1624 that clergy possessed of lay freehold were eligible, but it was argued elsewhere that they were excluded by the doctrine of separation of powers, or because they themselves could not sit in the House. Nevertheless, they frequently did vote. Staffordshire R.O., D661/11/1/2, n.f. (entry for 28 May 1624); P.R.O., St. Ch. 8/288/9: the complaint of William Vaughan; *D'Ewes* (N), 470 n. 14.

2 Sir Edward Coke, *The Fourth Part of the Institutes* (1644), 48–9; Spelman, *A View of a Printed Book*, sig. D2.

3 'The State of England (1600). By Sir Thomas Wilson', ed. F. J. Fisher, in *Camden Miscellany* vol. XVI (Camden Soc., 1936), 19–20; the wealth of King's freeholder can best be understood by comparing his published figures of freeholder income with some of his unpublished thoughts which recognised the existence of freeholders worth less than 40s. per annum and with less than £5 in goods. [J. Thirsk and J. P. Cooper, eds., *17th Century Economic Documents* (Oxford, 1972), 780; P.R.O., T64/302, no. 19: I am indebted to Mr Cooper for this reference.] Some instances of the loose use of the term can be seen in *The Life of Adam Martindale*, ed. R. Parkinson (Chetham Soc., 1845), 6–7; *Reliquiae Baxterianae*, 1.

4 Roskell, *The Commons in 1422*, 27; A. Rogers, 'The Lincolnshire County Court in the Fifteenth Century', *Lincolnshire History and Archaeology* i (1966), 68; Plumb, 'Growth of the Electorate', 96. I am grateful to Mrs Christine Carpenter for her assistance on the 15th century.

It should be noted that these scholars of the 15th-century scene, to which the 1430 statute was directed, are of the opinion that the 40s. freehold was defined by its yield, rather than by its rent. The wording of the act, that the vote should lie with those having 'free tenement to the value of forty shillings by the year at the least above all charges' is conclusive, for rent is of course a charge. Had the 40s. freehold been valued as rent, then there would have been very few sufficient freeholders, given the extent to which freehold rents in the 17th century lagged economically, and this would have been incompatible with all the evidence about the social character of the electorate.

5 B. M. Harl. 38, f. 153; J. Nalson, *An Impartial Collection of the Great Affairs of State* (1682–3), I, 279–80: Woodhouse, *Puritanism and Liberty*, 64. See also the proposal of the 1621 election bill to increase the freehold requirement from £2 to £4. Plumb, 'Growth of the Electorate', 96.

6 P. Bowden, 'Agricultural Prices, Farm Profits and Rents', in J. Thirsk, ed., *The Agrarian History of England and Wales. IV. 1500–1640* (Cambridge, 1967), 652–4; A. Macfarlane, *The Family Life of Ralph Josselin* (Cambridge, 1970), 60–1; G. E. Fussell, ed., *Robert Loder's Farm Accounts 1610–1620* (Camden Soc., 1936), pp. x, xxii, xxv–xxviii; *C.S.P.D. 1629–1631*, 247–8; E. H. Bates Harbin, ed., *Quarter Sessions Records for the County of Somerset. II. 1625–1639* (Somerset Record Soc., xxiv, 1908), 278–9; J. Bankes and E. Kerridge, eds., *The Early Records of the Bankes Family at Winstanley* (Chetham Soc., 1973), 26, 29–31, 38–40. The Windsor Forest and the Bankes family examples demonstrate that it was possible to construct a valuation of land based on yield, as does much of Dr Thirsk's work: see J. Thirsk, 'Seventeenth-Century Agriculture and Social Change', in J. Thirsk, ed., *Land, Church and People: Agricultural History Review Supplement* (1970), 160–3. In relation to the Bankes case, it must be observed, however, that the Lancashire customary acre was larger than the statute one: I am grateful to Mr J. P. Cooper for this point.

7 Neale, *House of Commons*, 137.

8 A. M. Everitt, 'Farm Labourers', in Thirsk, *Agrarian History. IV*, 400; Neale, *House of Commons*, 137; *C.D. 1621*, II, 277–8; B.M. Harl. 159, f. 126; M. Spufford, 'People, Land and Literacy in Cambridgeshire in the Sixteenth and Seventeenth Centuries' (Leicester Ph.D., 1970), 7 n.1.

9 R. H. Tawney, *The Agrarian Problem in the Sixteenth Century* (London, 1912); H. J. Habakkuk, 'La Disparition du Paysan Anglais', *Annales* xx (1965), 649–63; Thirsk, 'Agriculture and Social Change', 148, 156–7: Dr Thirsk also stresses that the forest regions did not undergo the same changes, *ibid.*, 172–3.

10 A similar process of the diminution of an electorate by the operation of economic factors on a property franchise can be observed in late 17th- and 18th-century New England. Lockridge, 'Land, Population and the Evolution of New England Society', 75–6.

11 Tawney, *Agrarian Problem*, 25; D. G. Hey, *An English Rural Community: Myddle under the Tudors and Stuarts* (Leicester, 1974), 70–1; V. H. T. Skipp, 'Economic and Social Change in the Forest of Arden', in Thirsk, *Land, Church and People*, 103; see also E. Kerridge, *Agrarian Problems in the Sixteenth Century and After* (London, 1969), 33–5.

12 Tawney, *Agrarian Problem*, 32–3; C. S. and C. S. Orwin, *The Open Fields* (Oxford, 1967), 106–23; W. G. Hoskins, *The Midland Peasant* (London, 1957), 105–30, 188; F. Hull, 'Agriculture and rural society in Essex, 1560–1640' (London Ph.D., 1950), 471 (I am grateful to Mr J. D. Walter for this reference). These were all the kind of people who were likely to be squeezed off the land in time.

13 Hatfield Mss., Cecil Family and Estate Papers, Box E/3, 'List of freeholders 1640', ff. 5v–7v. I am grateful to Lord Salisbury for permission to use these papers.

14 Woodhouse, *Puritanism and Liberty*, 54; Plumb, 'Growth of the Electorate', 107.

15 Tawney, *Agrarian Problem*, 25–6; Spelman, *View of a Printed Book*, sig. D2.

16 Kerridge, *Agrarian Problems*, 32–64. All the reviews of this work have disputed Kerridge's conclusions on the factual side of the question of security of tenure (i.e. economic pressures), but not his legal propositions: see M. A. Havinden, in *Agricultural History Review* xix (1971), 181–2; *Times Literary Supplement* 1970, pp. 1135–6; and the legal historian John Barton, in *E.H.R.* lxxxvi (1971), 618–19. I am grateful to Dr Thirsk for directing me to the last two references.

17 Sir Edward Coke, *The Compleate Copy-Holder* (1641), 14; Inner Temple Ms. 511/23, f. 3, *C.D. 1621*, VI, 22; W. Taffs, 'The Borough Franchise in the First Half of the Seventeenth Century' (London M.A., 1926), Appendix, 86–7. The same definition of a freehold, as an estate for life or greater, held in the New World. R. E. and B. K. Brown, *Virginia 1705–1786: Democracy or Aristocracy?* (East Lansing, 1964), 126.

18 Which was the sense used in the first section of this chapter.

19 Tawney, *Agrarian Problems*, 25, 300.

20 W. G. Hoskins, *Provincial England* (London, 1963), 139, 141; Skipp, 'Economic and Social Change in Arden', 106; L. Stone, *Family and Fortune* (Oxford, 1973), 136; Hey, *English Rural Community*, 70–5. Thus, all the Wollavington voters on the 1614 Somerset poll list held leases for lives, as did the others connected tenurially with Pym. Somerset R.O., DD/PH/216/102. I am grateful to Conrad Russell for the identifications.

21 P.R.O., St. Ch. 8/201/17, 8/293/11; M, Campbell, *The English Yeoman* (New Haven, 1942), 355; C.U.L. Mss., Dd. 12.20, 21, f. 87v. Candidates in the 1624 Cambridgeshire election were said to have gone round the inns the night before, trying to find as many copyholders as they could. *C.J.*, 1, 485.

22 *H.M.C. 14th Report Appdx. Pt. II (Duke of Portland's MSS. Vol. III)*, 61.

23 See above, p. 19; Hatfield Mss., Cecil Family and Estate Papers, Box E/3, 'Freeholders list', ff. 1–4v. Likewise, the careful survey of the manor executed by John Norden in 1621 was supposedly primarily concerned with the freeholders, but throughout it showed great uncertainty as to who these were: 'Freeholders of the Borough of Hertford. By John Norden', transcribed, with annotations, by H. C. Andrews, in Hertford Borough Museum; Stone, *Family and Fortune*, 130–2.

24 Hatfield Mss., Cecil Family and Estate Papers, Box E/3, 'Freeholders list', f. 7v.

25 See J. P. Cooper, 'The Social Distribution of Land and Men in England, 1436–1700', *Economic History Review* xx (1967), 428, for details of some freeholders' lists which were mainly compiled for jury service; for an instance of the disparity between wealth and taxation assessment, see Hoskins, *Midland Peasant*, 177, or the assertion that there were less than 200 subsidy-men in Southwark in 1605: Stow, *A Survey of the Cities of London and Westminster*, Bk. iv, 10.

26 Bodl. MS. Rawl. D. 1098, ff. 95–95v; Neale, *House of Commons*, 96, 109.

27 P.R.O., S.P. 14/31/57; Roskell, *The Commons in 1422*, 20; on the requirements for jury service generally, see Morrill, 'The Cheshire Grand Jury 1625–59'.

28 P.R.O., S.P. 14/31/57, S.P. 14/120/24; J. S. Cockburn, ed., *Somerset Assize Orders 1640–1659* (Somerset Record Soc., lxxi, 1971), 27; M. Campbell, *The English Yeoman* (New Haven, 1942), 343; W. L. Hardy, ed., *Hertfordshire County Records. V. Sessions Books 1619–1657* (Hertford, 1928), 501. It has been argued that the reaction to the breakdown of government at mid-century produced a concern to compile more accurate lists of substantial freeholders for jury service after the Restoration. If this was the case, then it may have facilitated the elimination of dubious voters. J. S. Cockburn, *A History of English Assizes 1558–1714* (Cambridge, 1972), 112.

29 Guildford Museum, Loseley Mss., LM 1331/25; Bodl, Ms. Rawl. D. 1098, ff. 95–95v. The efficacy of the threat of jury service is testified to by a Somerset candidate in 1614: he had 'taken order that as many as present themselves theare [at the hustings] for freeholders shall have theare names booked and by that meanes be subiecte to be returned in all Juryes and yf this be knowen before hand I know a great many will step back'. Somerset R.O., D.D./SF. 1076/21/36.

30 *C.D. 1621*, iv, 23.

31 Private communication from Dr Spufford, to whom I am indebted; an example of pressure to enclose putting a high premium on freehold can be seen at P.R.O., S.P. 14/37/107.

32 Tawney, *Agrarian Problem*, 86; Richard Gough, *History of Myddle*, ed. W. G. Hoskins (Fontwell, Sussex, 1968), 85; see also Hey, *English Rural Community*, 83.

33 Guildford Museum, Loseley Mss., LM 1331/25. As Noy said in this context, 'Elections ought to be free' [*C.J.*, 1, 570]. One of Wentworth's supporters warned him correctly before the poll that the House would object to his tactics, and Secretary Calvert tried to dissociate himself from them afterwards. Sheffield City Library Mss., Str. 2, p. 63; *ibid.*, Wentworth Woodhouse Muniments, WWM. phot. 2/C. I am grateful to the Earl Fitzwilliam, the Trustees of the Wentworth Woodhouse Estate, and the City Librarian for permission to consult these Mss.

34 B.M. Harl. 1601, f. 27v; Add. 36825, f. 196v. (The same point, that a list was necessary to prevent perjury, was made in the 1614 Hampshire dispute. Hampshire R.O., Jervoise Mss., 44 M 69/012, articles of complaint against the sheriff.) However, by 1641, the House was prepared to welcome poll lists, as an aid to judging disputes; moreover, the proposal in the 1626 election bill that voting should be compulsory for those qualified would have necessitated the compilation of lists – though the proponent of the measure may not have realised that. *D'Ewes* (N), 306, 463; CUL. Mss., Dd. 12.20, 21, f. 87v.

35 *C.J.*, 1, 884; B.M. Add. 36825, ff. 196–196v; Harl. 2313, f. 50; Harl. 2240.

36 C.U.L. Mss., Mm.6.62, ff. 62–3; B.M. Harl. 374, f. 160; Add. 26639, ff. 48–48v.

37 Hampshire R.O., Jervoise Mss., 44 M69/012, articles of complaint against the sheriff.

38 Neale, *House of Commons*, 88; P.R.O., St. Ch. 8/288/9: complaint of William

Vaughan; B.M. Add. 26639, f. 41. But Dering's account of the spring 1640 Kent election shows the oath was not necessarily administered to all voters even in the event of a poll. Bodl. Ms. Top. Kent e.6.

39 Nalson, *Impartial Collection*, I, 279; Neale, *House of Commons*, 91; P.R.O., S.P. 16/95/35; B.M. Harl. 378, f. 29v; N.N.R.O., City Revenue and Letters, f. 8; Maidstone's votes were also judged likely to control the 1628 county election, as the time for canvassing was so short. Kent A.O., U350, c/2/17.

40 B.M. Add. 36825, f. 216v; N.N.R.O., Norwich Assembly Book 1613–42, f. 564v; *D'Ewes* (N), 441.

41 Huntingdonshire R.O., Godmanchester Borough Records, Box 3, Bundle 15 (I am indebted to Prof. Plumb for this reference); *ibid.*, Borough Records, Box 10, unsorted; the probate evidence (of admittedly doubtful reliability because of problems of identification and the possibility of transfer of property) relates to those Godmanchester voters whose wills or inventories survive among the Archdeaconry of Huntingdon wills in the Record Office. A £15 personal estate is taken by Prof. Everitt as marking the ordinary poor labourer in this period. Everitt, 'Farm Labourers', 413 n. 1.

42 Bodl. Ms. Top. Kent e.6; Kent A.O., Consistory Court of Canterbury, original wills, C61, C249; *C.S.P.D. 1637–1638*, 224; Bodl. Ms. Top. Kent e.6, p.60. There are remnants of other county lists, but these, and the supporting evidence for them, are too fragmentary to be of any use. *H.M.C. Report, Duke of Buccleuch's MSS.*, III, 172 (originals of the 1604 Northants list are in the N.R.O.); and the 1614 Somerset list, at Somerset R.O., DD/PH/214/94–104, DD/PH/225/5.

43 For numbers of voters, see below, Appendix v; for the poll as a deterrent, and for entertaining in Derbyshire, see below, Chapter 6, pp. 116–18.

44 And hence the efforts of the 1624 and 1625 Committees of Privileges to encourage the taking of the poll: see above, p. 14. But this stress on selectivity might be unlikely to endear itself to all, for the exclusion of unqualified votes was a novelty, and a rarity, given the normal absence of the poll – as Sir Goronwy Edwards has pointed out, 'the *de facto* participation of all and sundry after 1430 ... was no more than a continuation of ancient usage'. See also the violent reception that greeted the attempt to establish the new order at the 1461 Norfolk election. Edwards, 'The Emergence of Majority Rule', 193; C. H. Williams, 'A Norfolk Parliamentary Election, 1461', *E.H.R.* xl (1925), 81–6.

45 Kent A.O., U115, 015/1; D. Parsons, ed., *The Diary of Sir Henry Slingsby* (London, 1836), 77; see also the sustained battle imagery used of the Norfolk 1624 election. H. W. Saunders, ed., *The Official Papers of Sir Nathaniel Bacon of Stiffkey, Norfolk* (Camden Soc., 1915), 41.

46 N.N.R.O., Norwich Assembly Book 1613–42, f. 223v; S.P. 16/366/48.

47 Kent A.O., U1115, 015/1; B.M. Harl. 2313, f. 8v; Gough, *History of Myddle*, 67.

48 B.M. Add. 36825, f. 196.

### 3. The Borough Franchise Disputes

1 See Appendix I.

2 M. McKisack, *The Parliamentary Representation of the English Boroughs during the Middle Ages* (Oxford, 1932), 35, 38, 65; M. Weinbaum, *The Incorporation of Boroughs* (Manchester, 1937), esp. 11, 97, 107, 123–4.

3 A. B. Hibbert, 'The Economic Policies of Towns', in M. M. Postan, E. E. Rich, E. Miller, eds., *The Cambridge Economic History of Europe. III* (Cambridge, 1963), 183–4, 195–7, 199–202, 206, 211–13, 220–3.

4 S. L. Thrupp, 'The Gilds', *ibid.*, 243–4.

5 B. E. Supple, *Commercial Crisis and Change in England 1600–1642* (Cambridge, 1959), *passim*.

6 See, for example, G. C. F. Forster, 'The English Local Community and Local Government 1603–1625', in A. G. R. Smith, ed., *The Reign of James VI and I* (London, 1973), 204. A good example of the increasing attempts at regulation of these years is the Norwich Craft Ordinances of 1622. W. L. Sachse, ed., *Minutes of the Norwich Court of Mayoralty 1630–1631* (Norfolk Record Soc. xv, 1942), 13.

7 A. D. Dyer, *The City of Worcester in the sixteenth century* (Leicester, 1973), 221–3; P. Clark and P. Slack, eds., *Crisis and Order in English Towns 1500–1700* (London, 1972), 19–22.

8 Even London, which might have been presumed unique, appears to have witnessed the same chronology of trouble. V. Pearl, *London and the Outbreak of the Puritan Revolution* (Oxford, 1961), 61. See below for the other towns.

9 Weinbaum, *Incorporation of Boroughs*, 97, 107, 123 and *passim*.

10 J. P. Cooper, 'Economic Regulation in the Cloth Industry in seventeenth-century England', *Transactions of the Royal Historical Society* xx (1970), 73–87.

11 Hoskins, *Provincial England*, 78; for migration, see especially P. Clark 'The migrant in Kentish towns 1580–1640', in Clark and Slack, *Crisis and Order*, 117–63.

12 *A.P.C. 1627*, 157; *A.P.C. 1627–1628*, 140–1; *C.S.P.D. 1639–1640*, 516.

13 L. Stone, *The Causes of the English Revolution 1529–1642* (London, 1972), 125–6.

14 *A.P.C. 1597*, 329–30; *A.P.C. 1597–1598*, 168, 451–2, 507. A rigidly closed oligarchy had been established at Totnes by a charter of 1596, and this must have intensified suspicions. M. Weinbaum, *British Borough Charters 1307–1660* (Cambridge, 1943), 28.

15 *A.P.C. 1597–1598*, 627–8; also, *A.P.C. 1598–1599*, 181–2. For the dispute generally, see R. Howell, *Newcastle upon Tyne and the Puritan Revolution* (Oxford, 1967), 35–62.

16 *A.P.C. 1597*, 329.

17 P.R.O., P.C. 2/47 (Privy Council Register 1636–7), f. 235v. I am grateful to Mr J. D. Walter for this reference.

18 B.M. Add. 18016, ff. 131–187v; and see above, p. 15.

19 N.N.R.O., Norwich City Records, Shelf 17b, Book of Charters, f. 27. See also *ibid.*, Norwich Assembly Book 1613–42, for the period 1619–1628; and *A.P.C. 1617–1619*, 484.

20 *A.P.C. 1627–1628*, 114, 140–1; P.R.O., S.P. 16/79/38.

21 *A.P.C. 1619–1621*, 147–9; see also similar centralisation in Bristol, *ibid.*, 244.

22 *A.P.C. 1627–1628*, 164–5; Pearl, *London and the Puritan Revolution*, 97; *C.S.P.D. 1628–1629*, 555; *C.S.P.D. 1637*, 194; *Privy Council Registers Preserved in the P.R.O.: Reproduced in Facsimile*, vol. 1, 1 June–31 October 1637 (London, 1967), 213–14. I am grateful to Mr J. D. Walter for this reference.

23 *C.S.P.D. 1641–1643*, 177. In the light of all this evidence, Prof. MacCaffrey's suggestion that Privy Council pressure on towns diminished after 1600, as the problem of order receded and habits of good behaviour formed, seems dubious. W. T. MacCaffrey, *Exeter, 1540–1640* (Cambridge, Mass., 1958), 231.

24 D. Underdown, *Pride's Purge* (Oxford, 1971), 91.

25 *A.P.C. 1625–1626*, 217–18, 312–15, 422–3; *C.S.P.D. 1631–1633*, 199–200; *A.P.C. 1630–1631*, 304.

26 P.R.O., S.P. 16/366/48.

27 McKisack, *Representation of Boroughs*, 38. A similar 'natural' development of

oligarchy was evident in the early New England towns. K. A. Lockridge and A. Kreider, 'The Evolution of Massachusetts Town Government, 1640 to 1740', *William and Mary Quarterly* xxiii (1966), 551.

28 Zagorin, *Court and Country*, 147.

29 Much of the information for this paragraph is derived from an unpublished paper, 'The Metamorphosis of Medieval Community: Coventry, 1480–1620', delivered by Dr C. Phythian-Adams to the Conference of Anglo-American Historians at the Senate House, London University, on 7 July 1972. I am greatly indebted to Dr Phythian-Adams for permission to use some of his findings.

30 Coventry City Mss., Court Leet Book II (1588–1834), 117, 127; Clark and Slack, *Crisis and Order*, 16.

31 This situation is paralleled by the dominance exerted by the Hostmen and Merchant Adventurers of Newcastle (Howell, *Newcastle upon Tyne*, 44–62); the charge of dynasticism is also met at Sandwich: see Appendix II.

32 Coventry City Mss., Minute Book 1554–1640, f. 282v.

33 *Ibid.*, Acc. 4, City Annals F, ff. 33–34v, 35v, 39v; Court Leet Book II, 124; F. Bliss Burbidge, *Old Coventry and Lady Godiva* (Birmingham, n.d.), 242; P.R.O., St. Ch. 8/144/24; *C.S.P.D. 1635–1636*, 22. Evidence for the increase of poverty in the middle and later 1620s can be seen in the City Minute Book, ff. 278v, 279, 282v.

34 *A.P.C. 1627*, 80, 297, 363; *C.S.P.D. 1627–1628*, 203; Coventry City Mss., Court Leet Book II, 87–8, 124, 127; City Annals F, ff. 38v, 39v; Bliss Burbidge, *Old Coventry*, 242; Keeler, *Long Parliament*, 316.

35 *V.C.H. Warwickshire* viii, 218–19; *C.S.P.D. 1635–1636*, 22; C. Bridenbaugh, *Vexed and Troubled Englishmen* (Oxford, 1968), 135; *C.J.*, II, 78.

36 See Appendix II for these disputes.

37 C. H. and J. W. Cooper, *Annals of Cambridge* (Cambridge, 1842–1908), III, 31; Cambridge Guildhall Mss., Corporation Common Day Book 1610–1646, f. 12.

38 *Ibid.*, Corporation Common Day Book, ff. 100–200 *passim*; *A.P.C. 1623–1625*, 318–19; Cooper, *Annals of Cambridge*, III, 218–19. See Appendix II for similar developments in Oxford and Sandwich.

39 Taffs, 'Borough Franchise', Appendix, 52–3, 55, 57; Corporation Common Day Book, ff. 102, 125, 137v.

40 Keeler, *Long Parliament*, 36–7. However, the form of the 'official' group's indenture for the Long Parliament election makes it plain that they were claiming the support of the majority of the freemen. This is therefore unlikely to have been an attempt to reverse the result of the 1620s disputes. P.R.O., C. 219/43/ Part I.

41 G. Wilks, *The Barons of the Cinque Ports and the Parliamentary Representation of Hythe* (Folkestone, n.d.), 71–2, 74–8. The election of Heyman and Dixwell, in which the freemen participated from the start, occurred in 1626, and not 1625 as Wilks stated.

42 The indenture in 1621, similar to that of 1624, was 'by the greater number of Freeburgesses'; the indenture of 1626 was made by the corporation, and adds 'and likewise the Burgesses' also elected them, suggesting an alteration. The Short Parliament indenture was made very assertively by the corporation only. While indentures are formalised, and therefore unreliable, their evidence is supported by a letter brushing off an aspiring patron in 1624, 'the Choice ... consisting in the brests of so many'. Gt Yarmouth Guildhall, Corporation Mss., C. 18/6 (Entry Book I), ff. 199, 203, 210v, 220, and C. 18/7 (Entry Book II), f. 30v; P.R.O., C219/42. Pt. I, no. 156.

43 *A.P.C. 1623–1625*, 457–8; P.R.O., S.P. 16/147/56, and S.P. 16/157/57–8; Gt Yar-

mouth Corporation Mss., C19/6 (Assembly Book 1625–42), ff. 33–33v, 98. There was also trouble in 1631 over the new charter, *ibid.*, C18/6, f. 288v.

44 The prosperity came with an increase in the fish harvest, but the town's mono-culture economy may also have resulted in the abnormally low total of freemen. I am grateful to Mr A. R. Michell for discussions on this subject, and for allowing me to see his calculations of urban freemen in a draft copy of his forthcoming Cambridge Ph.D. thesis on the economy of Gt Yarmouth.

45 *C.S.P.D. 1628–1629*, 353; Corporation of London R.O., City Remembrancia vi, f. 159; G. W. Johnson, ed., *The Fairfax Correspondence* (London, 1848), i, 89.

46 Corporation of London R.O., Journals of Common Council no. 33 f. 245v, no. 35 f. 269v, no. 36 f. 82, no. 38 ff. 271v and 274, no. 39 f. 95v. And as Dr Keeler points out, it was the mayoral rather than the parliamentary elections, which caused trouble in 1640. Keeler, *Long Parliament*, 55–6.

47 *C.S.P.D. 1639–1640*, 601–2; Howell, *Newcastle upon Tyne*, 35–62; Zagorin, *Court and Country*, 151.

48 N.R.O., FH 3501; Leicester City Museum, Leicester Hall Papers xi (1640–45), f. 24; McKisack, *Parliamentary Representation of Boroughs*, 36–7; Northampton Corporation Mss., Assembly and Order Book 1627–1744, p. 62.

49 P.R.O., S.P. 16/366/48.

50 P. Gregg, *Free-born John* (London, 1961), 150.

51 *A.P.C. 1597–1598*, 451–2; P.R.O., St. Ch. 8/115/14; St. Ch. 8/121/12; Stow, *Survey of the Cities of London and Westminster*, Bk. iv, 9–10; *A.P.C. 1596–1597*, 488–9.

52 P.R.O., S.P. 16/204/36–7; S.P. 16/366/48; P. Slack, 'Poverty and Politics in Salisbury 1597–1666', in Clark and Slack, *Crisis and Order*, 164–203.

53 *A.P.C. 1597*, 329–30; P.R.O., St. Ch. 8/79/5; St. Ch. 8/290/22; St. Ch. 8/130/2–3; St. Ch. 8/138/8; *C.S.P.D. 1631–1633*, 567, 590; P.R.O., S.P. 16/245/34.1; *C.S.P.D. 1628–1629*, 560; *A.P.C. 1630–1631*, 333; the common lands were also at issue in Huntingdon's disputes around 1630. C. H. Firth, *Oliver Cromwell* (London, 1900), 31–2.

54 Hoskins, *Provincial England*, 100–1; P.R.O., St. Ch. 8/164/10, 8/168/23, 8/181/6; Dyer, *City of Worcester*, 226.

55 The longevity of the oral memory is suggested by the precise testimony about the 1586 election provided by an old man for the Long Parliament Gatton dispute. Longleat House, Marquis of Bath's Mss., Whitelocke Papers, vol. viii, f. 30.

56 For Exeter, see Appendix ii; for Newcastle, see above. And even London, as has been seen, suggests similar developments.

57 N.N.R.O., Norwich Assembly Book 1613–42, ff. 118v–120; P.R.O., S.P. 16/79/38; Sachse, *Minutes of Norwich Court of Mayoralty*, 19. Although in the very bitter troubles in Lynn at the start of the 15th century, when the House of Commons had not been taken over by gentry, the *inferiores* succeeded in having members of their own number elected more than once. I am indebted to Miss L. Woodger for this information.

58 See Appendix ii.

59 Pearl, *London and the Puritan Revolution, passim.*

60 J. K. Gruenfelder, 'The Spring Parliamentary Election at Hastings, 1640', *Sussex Archaeological Collections* cv (1967), 49–55 and see below, Chapter vii, p. 135; L. J. Ashford, *The History of the Borough of High Wycombe from its Origins to 1880* (London, 1960), 126–34; *D'Ewes* (N), 513.

61 It should be noted that of those cited, only Salisbury's was a franchise dispute; but the others display similar configurations.

62 *V.C.H. Berkshire*, iii, 356; *C.S.P.D. 1631–1633*, 406; *H.M.C. 11th Report, App.*

*VII* (Reading Corporation Mss.), 213–14; and information kindly communicated to me by Mr Kneebone, the corporation archivist. See also the continuity of concern for the poor and the state of trade in J. M. Guilding, *Reading Records* (London, 1896), III, *passim.*

63 *V.C.H. Berkshire*, III, 356; *C.S.P.D. 1638–1639*, 163; information about mortality kindly supplied by Mr Kneebone. The fact that about 1000 were voting in the Interregnum elections, while the Register of Freemen is unlikely to give more than c. 400 freemen, indicates how thoroughly the electorate was widened. *H.M.C. 11th Report, App. VII*, 189, 193; Reading Corporation Records, R/RF/1.

64 Taffs, 'Borough Franchise', App. 225–33; *H.M.C. 11th Report, App. VII*, 189: thus, the Chippenham freemen claimed in 1624 that they had only refrained from protesting against earlier closed elections because they agreed with the corporation's choice. Glanville, *Reports*, 50.

65 *C.S.P.D. 1636–1637*, 439; *C.S.P.D. 1637–1638*, 518, 535; *C.S.P.D. 1638–1639*, 588; *C.S.P.D. 1640*, 108; Northampton Corporation Mss., Assembly and Order Book 1627–1744, 57; *H.M.C. 9th Report, App. Pt. II* (Woodforde Mss.), 498.

66 C. A. Markham and J. C. Cox, eds., *Records of the Borough of Northampton* (Northampton, 1898), II, 496; N.R.O., FH 3501. There is, however, the possibility of a moderate reaction in October to a militant corporation: see below, p. 135.

67 *C.S.P.D. 1637–1638*, 518; the disintegration of control which plague might bring is illustrated by the problems of Exeter in the 1620s, and by Leicester corporation's order in the midst of an outbreak 'that everye shoppkeeper shall have readye ... or neare his shopp one woodden clubb at the least ...': for Exeter, see Appendix II; Leicester Museum, Hall Papers x, f. 495v.

68 M. R. Frear, 'The election at Great Marlow in 1640', *Journal of Modern History* xiv (1942), 433–48; for evidence of voting support, see the successive indentures, which have very many signatures. P.R.O., C. 219/43. Pt. I.

69 Pearl, *London and the Puritan Revolution*, 249. The same lack of commitment to democratic principle, and the same tendency to view the franchise as a means to a political end, has been alleged for early Massachusetts: see, for example, Lockridge, and Kreider, 'Evolution of Massachusetts Town Government', 561, 570–3; R. E. Wall jnr, 'The Decline of the Massachusetts Franchise', *Journal of American History* lix (1972–3), 307.

70 See, for example, the role of Puckering at Warwick in the 1620s: Appendix II.

71 B.M. Add. 42711, ff. 37–37v. The franchise here seems to have been asserted as scot and lot, although Grenville's references to the fact that a freehold conveyed a title to a voice in the town's affairs seems to have imported confusing considerations of a burgage tenure or freedom franchise. *Ibid.*, f. 34.

72 *C.J.*, II, 10; B.M. Harl. 6799, f. 335v; Taffs, 'Borough Franchise', App., 173. About 50 people seem to have participated in both 1640 elections, judging by the indentures. P.R.O., C. 219/42. Pt. I, nos. 23–5; C. 219/43. Pt. I, nos. 44–5.

73 The first indenture was signed by the bailiff and 18 select burgesses: those for the subsequent contested by-election had some 80 names to them; there were adjudged to be 99 burgage tenants in the 18th century, *ibid.*, C. 219/43. Pt. 3, nos. 43, 45–6; Rathbone, *Wiltshire Borough Records*, 21.

74 B.M. Add. 36825, ff. 171–171v; Harl. 6799, f. 335v; P.R.O., C. 219/41B.

75 *C.J.*, I, 837; C.U.L. Mss., Dd. 12. 20, 21. ff. vib, 23. The fact that one of the candidates 'deserted the cause' absolved the Committee of the necessity of deciding on the franchise.

76 There was a double return for the Short Parliament (P.R.O., C. 219/42 Pt. I), and Newport was one of the cases which was still to be reported from the Com-

mittee of Privileges in July 1641 (*C.J.*, II, 212). Miss Keeler's criticism of Carlyle's suggestion that Prynne was elected for Newport may be affected by the fact that in 1641, when preparing his brief for Tewkesbury, he had notes on the wholly irrelevant Newport case of 1628, which he tried to use in his argument. He may have had these as a result of being counsel, and not realised their inapplicability; or he may have had an electoral link with the town, and used them because they were to hand. Keeler, *Long Parliament*, 39 n. 81; Inner Temple Ms. 511/23, ff. 5–6.

77 Neale, *House of Commons*, 250–5, 261–72; Plumb, 'Growth of the Electorate', 94; for Sandwich, see Appendix II; A. N. Groome, 'The Higham Ferrers Elections in 1640', *Northamptonshire Past and Present*, ii, no. 5 (1958), 243–50.

78 See below, p. 80; J. Bruce, ed., *Verney Papers: Notes of Proceedings in the Long Parliament* (Camden Soc., 1845), 33. Very similar were some of the campaigns for the restoration of boroughs to representation: Sir Samuel Rolle resolved in 1640 only 'to trouble the house' over Lidford or Torrington if he could not 'obtaine a place anie where' else. Cornwall R.O., Carew-Pole Mss., BC/24/2, letter of 7 Dec. 1640.

79 According to the carefully annotated and argued indentures, the freemen gained the vote in the spring, and the inhabitants at large in the autumn. P.R.O., C. 219/42. Pt. 1, no. 46; C. 219/43. Pt. 1; and see below, Chapter 5, for a fuller discussion of the Bedford electorate.

80 N.R.O., FH 50, ff. 6, 55; B.M. Add. 36825, ff. 297–297v; Add. 36827, f. 40v; *C.J.*, II, 10; B.M. Add. 42711, f. 37.

81 The exceptions were possibly Sir Walter Earle's otherwise inexplicable involvement in the Long Parliament Salisbury dispute, and Sir Edwin Sandys's activities in Sandwich, Dover and Virginia. See below, Chapter 4, pp. 81–2.

82 See Appendix I.

## 4. The Support of the House of Commons

1 G. Wilson, ed., *The Reports of Sir Edward Coke* (London, 1777), II, pt. iv, ff. 77v–78; B.M. Add. 37343, f. 209v; Add. 42711, ff. 34, 37; N.R.O., FH 3467; J. Latimer, *Annals of Bristol in the Seventeenth Century* (Bristol, 1900), 148.

2 Stow, *Survey of the Cities of London and Westminster*, IV, 10; *C.D. 1621*, II, 277; Alford is quoted in Zagorin, *Court and Country*, 87; *C.J.*, I, 939.

3 Moir, *Addled Parliament*, 20; *C.J.*, I, 456–7, 478. Sandys was echoed by the lawyer Thomas Mallett in 1621, in response to Wentworth's abuses at the 1621 Yorkshire election: 'If eleccions not free, wee shall have packt Parliaments. Free eleccions the foundacon of our parliament libertye'. *C.D. 1621*, v, 66.

4 *C.S.P.D. 1623–1625*, 162; for election bills, see Appendix VII, and R. L. Bushman, 'English Franchise Reform in the Seventeenth Century', *Journal of British Studies* iii (1963), appdx., 53–6. I am grateful to Prof. Plumb for emphasising the longevity of such futile purgative measures.

5 B. Worden, *The Rump Parliament* (Cambridge, 1974), 154; for the attitudes of Pym, etc., see below, pp. 83–4, 231, and Keeler, *Long Parliament*, 66; Strode's and Pym's vehemence can be best seen at Bodl. Ms. Rawl. C: 956, ff. 46v–47.

6 Plumb, 'Growth of the Electorate', 90–116; Glanville, *Reports*, 55; C.U.L. Mss., Dd. 12.20, 21, f. 87v; Bodl. Ms. Film 39, p. 45.

7 C. Hill, *The Century of Revolution* (Edinburgh, 1961), 120; *H.M.C. Report, Earl of Denbigh's Mss.*, Pt. v, 70; Thomas Hobbes, *Behemoth*, ed. F. Tonnies (London, 1969), 121; Spelman, *View of a Printed Book*, sig. Fv; Lord Braybrooke, ed. *The Autobiography of Sir John Bramston* (Camden Soc., 1845), 160–1; John

Bramhall, *The Serpent Salve* (—, 1643), 131: I am grateful to Mr R. Tuck for this reference; *D'Ewes* (N), 3 n. 4.

8 See above, p. 15; Prynne, *Brevia Parliamentaria*, 186–7, 323–5.

9 *H.M.C. 10th Report, Appdx. Pt. IV* (Corporation of Bishop's Castle Mss.), 406; *ibid*. (Boycott's Mss.), 210–11; *C.S.P.D. 1631–1633*, 468.

10 de Villiers, 'Parliamentary Boroughs Restored by the House of Commons', 176–8, 181–2; Prynne, *Brevia Parliamentaria*, 186; D. Gardiner, *Historic Haven* (Derby, 1954), 157.

11 B.M. Eg. 2723, f. 104. The Crown, as has been suggested, was ready to assert itself over the restoration of boroughs.

12 M.B. Rex, *University Representation in England 1604–1690* (London, 1954), 60; J. R. Jones, *The Revolution of 1688 in England* (London, 1972), 128–75.

13 N.R.O., FH 3467/2; Warwickshire R.O., Warwick Borough Mss., W.21/6, 270–1.

14 Wilson, *Coke's Reports*, II, iv. ff. 77v–78; *C.D. 1621*, VII, 571–2; B.M. Add. 18597, ff. 64–64v.

15 See my forthcoming article in the *Historical Journal*, 'Elections and the Privileges of the House of Commons'.

16 Glanville, *Reports*, 54–5, 59–60; *C.J.*, I, 684, 686; *D'Ewes* (N), 137–8, 138 n. 7.

17 Glanville, *Reports*, 29–46. Mr Thomas is incorrect in stating that the House resolved that 'all the inhabitants' should vote here: the House resolved that in principle this might be so, but that prescription told for a limited franchise. Thomas, 'The Levellers and the Franchise', 62.

18 Glanville, *Reports*, 34–6; B.M. Add. 18597, f. 91v; Inner Temple Ms. 511/23, f. 6; C.U.L. Mss., Dd. 12.20, 21, f. 12; B.M. Add. 36825, ff. 165v–166.

19 See above, p. 39.

20 *C.D. 1621*, IV, 24–5; *ibid.*, VI, 359–60; *C.S.P.D. 1619–1623*, 221–2; *C.J.*, I, 511–12, 875; Glanville, *Reports*, 107, 142; B.M. Add. 33468, f. 45; *C.J.*, II, 303. It was claimed in 1641 that neither in 1621 nor 1628 had the House pronounced on the question of a non-resident freeholder franchise, but this seems fallacious. Longleat, Marquis of Bath's Mss., Whitelocke Papers, vol. VIII, ff. 31v–32.

21 *C.S.P.D. 1623–1625*, 199, 201; *C.J.*, I, 748; Bodl. Ms. Rawl. C.956, f. 46; *D'Ewes* (N), 362; B.M. Harl. 541, f. 109v. In the 1624 Bletchingley case, the House had also countenanced the re-election going through unconventional channels, in order to prevent abuse. Glanville, *Reports*, 37–8.

22 B.M. Add. 56103, (no foliation) entry for 30 Nov.; Hoare, *History of Modern Wiltshire*, VI, 391; Plumb, 'Growth of the Electorate', 103; *D'Ewes* (N), 432 n. 11.

23 Plumb, 'Growth of the Electorate', 101–3; Hill, *Century of Revolution*, 120; *D'Ewes* (N), 222–3; Keeler, *Long Parliament*, 58; Inner Temple Ms. 511/23, f. 3.

24 Plumb, 'Growth of the Electorate', 103; Hill, *Century of Revolution*, 120.

25 The Committee lists for the 1620s are to be found at *C.J.*, I, 507–8, 671, 799, 816, 873. At least Sir Thomas Edmondes and Sir Edward Hoby, neither of whom had been listed, were present and active; see also Bacon's statement in 1614 that he was present at the committee on the elections bill, although not named. B.M. Add. 18597, f. 63v; *C.J.*, I, 478.

26 Staffordshire R.O., D661/11/1/2, entry for 4 May. The House was a court competent to deal with cases of disputed elections submitted to it, but alone it was not a legislature.

27 See Appendix VIII. The boroughs opened were Chippenham, Cirencester, Dover, Newcastle-under-Lyme; and a statement of principle was also made over Bletchingley.

28 Warwickshire R.O., W.21/6, 269–70; C.U.L. Ms. Dd. 12.20, 21, ff. 23, 32v,

23–20v (reverse foliation); *C.J.*, 1, 837. The franchise was also involved in the 1626 Newport, Cornwall, dispute, but the case was withdrawn, see above, p. 62n.75.

29 For the Boston decision, see *C.J.*, 1, 893. In 1626, the Committee was taken up with bad-tempered disputes, *inter alia*, about the rectitude of hearing Sir Edward Coke plead in person, after he had attempted to sit while sheriff elsewhere. C.U.L. Mss., Dd. 12.20, 21 *passim*.

30 *C.J.*, 11, 15. Here we have a statement of principle, and perhaps a clarification of (or a retreat from?) the 1628 Committee's Boston position: when there was no agreed limitation, the House was prepared to make a general statement in favour of expansion, but not to all the householders.

31 Harvard Ms. Eng. 982, ff. 30v, 58–58v; *C.J.*, 11, 10. Joncs was presumably appointed to the chair as a result of his prominence in the legal and constitutional battles of the late 1620s. A. H. Dodd, 'Welsh Opposition Lawyers in the Short Parliament', *Bulletin of the Board of Celtic Studies* xii (1948), 106.

32 *C.J.*, 11, 303; Bodl. Ms. Film 39, p. 38; B.M. Add. 37343, f. 210; Hoare, *History of Modern Wiltshire*, vi, 391; *D'Ewes* (N), 43, 99, 248.

33 *Ibid.*, 69 n. 5, 137–8, 138 n. 7; Bodl. Ms. Film 39, p. 45; Bodl. Ms. Rawl. C956, f. 95v; B.M. Harl. 541, f. 81.

34 Bodl. Ms. Rawl. C956, f. 46; Cornwall R.O., Carew-Pole Mss., BO/25/59, p. 154; and see above, p. 74n.21.

35 Plumb, 'Growth of the Electorate', 102; *C.J.*, 1, 513; *H.M.C. Report, Hastings Mss.*, iv, 286. He was a personal friend of the new owner of Amersham, one of the boroughs, in 1624. 'The Shardeloes Muniments – 1', *Records of Buckinghamshire* xiv, pt. 5 (1945), 173 n. 15.

36 C.U.L. Ms., Dd. 12.20, 21, f. 22v; B.M. Add. 18597, ff. 64–64v; *C.J.*, 1, 893; Plumb, 'Growth of the Electorate', 102: contrary to Prof. Plumb's suggestion, Hakewill's brother John and Ignatius Jourdain, the member elected by the freemen, were bitterly at odds over the crucial 1628 election. City of Exeter R.O., Act Book vii, pp. 710–11.

37 B.M. Add. 37343, ff. 197v–202, 209–211v.

38 Wilson, *Coke's Reports*, 11, iv, f. 78; Coke, *Fourth Part of the Institutes*, 48–9; *C.D. 1621*, iv, 87. The emptiness of some of these claims to lost rights can best be seen in the petition of the Marlow inhabitants in 1640 that the borough had sent, and they had elected, members 'time out of mind' – when the borough had only been restored in 1624 after a lapse of centuries! Longleat, Marquis of Bath's Mss., Whitelocke Papers, viii, f. 34.

39 B.M. Add. 18597, f. 65.

40 See Appendix 11 for Sandwich and Dover; Thomas, 'Levellers and the Franchise', 65; W. F. Craven, *The Dissolution of the Virginia Company* (New York, 1932), 277–8. A similar instance of local concern for a wider franchise is provided by Sir Thomas Puckering, the freemen's candidate in the 1626 Warwick election: although seated elsewhere, he successfully agitated the cause again for reasons of 'honour'. Not unnaturally, the corporation suspected vindictiveness. Warwickshire R.O., W.21/6, 270.

41 B.M. Harl. 159, f. 106v; *D'Ewes* (N), 43, 69, 137, 431; Thomas, 'Levellers and the Franchise', 63.

42 *C.J.*, 1, 684; B.M. Add. 18597, ff. 65–65v; Add. 56103 (n.f.), 30 Nov.; Keeler, *Long Parliament*, 165–7; *D'Ewes* (N), 69, 98–9; B.M. Harl. 541, f. 111v. He also opposed the restoration of Seaford to representation in 1641, on the grounds of the papist danger there. *D'Ewes* (N), 322.

43 N.R.O., FH 3467/1; B.M. Add. 37343, f. 210; Bodl. Ms. Film 39, p. 85; for Palmer's career generally, see the *Dictionary of National Biography*.

44 N.R.O., FH 3467; *C.J.*, 1, 684, 686; *C.S.P.D. 1623–1625*, 200; Harvard Ms. Eng. 980, p. 21 (I am grateful to Mr Conrad Russell for this reference).

45 Wiltshire R.O., Charles Hayward's Parliamentary Note Book, f. 191; Bodl. Ms. Rawl. C956, ff. 47, 96; *D'Ewes* (N), 69, 69 n. 6, 120, 137–8, 138 n. 7, 362; Bodl. Ms. Film 39, p. 38; Harvard Ms. Eng. 982, f. 30v; C.U.L. Mss., Kk. 6. 38, f. 8; 'Certain select Observations on the several Offices, and Officers, in the Militia of *England* . . .', *Harleian Miscellany* (London 1745), vi, 274–8 (I am grateful to Mr Richard Tuck for this reference).

46 B.M. Add. 18597, f. 65; *C.J.*, 1, 673, 717; Harvard Ms. Eng. 980, pp. 21–2; B.M. Harl. 6806, ff. 262–262v (I am grateful to Mr Russell for bringing this to my notice). While the positions taken here as elsewhere probably owed more to attitudes to the protagonists than to principles, it remains the case that for reasons of political expediency, members were broadening the franchise.

47 *D'Ewes* (N), 120; Keeler, *Long Parliament*, 49; but the lack of clear 'political' alignments in an allied field is demonstrated by the House's readiness to be driven by precedents into restoring Seaford, whose lord was a papist. *D'Ewes* (N), 322.

48 B.M. Add. 42711, f. 37; *D'Ewes* (N), 69, 137–8, 138 n. 7; B.M. Harl. 541, f. 81; Bodl. Ms. Rawl. C956, f. 96v; Inner Temple Ms. 511/23, ff. 2–3; Prynne, *Brevia Parliamentaria*, 320–2.

49 *D'Ewes* (N), 99, 431–2; Hoare, *History of Modern Wiltshire*, vi, 391; *C.J.*, ii, 95 (the tellers are clearly the wrong way round); for Earle, see above. D'Ewes made a similar distinction suggesting a party line over the Windsor vote, between 'All the honester men' and the rest. *D'Ewes* (N), 121 n. 8.

50 *Ibid.*, 98–9, 430, 432; *C.J.*, ii, 39, 95; A. H. A. Hamilton, ed., *The Notebook of Sir John Northcote* (London, 1877), 26.

51 *D'Ewes* (N), 43; B.M. Add. 37343, f. 210.

52 *Ibid.*, f. 210; *D'Ewes* (N), 42–3; *C.J.*, 1, 697; Bruce, *Verney Papers*, 2–3.

53 But then consistency is not necessarily to be expected in politics: Coriton had apparently argued an intellectual position for a householder franchise at the end of the 1620s, but that hardly accords with his actions as Mayor of Bossiney in 1640. P.R.O., S.P. 14/205/36.

54 *D'Ewes* (N), 69 n. 4, 138 n. 7, 430–2. In the Salisbury debate, D'Ewes was to be found arguing against the 'immemorial constitution' position taken by Selden, and he effectively denied the immemoriality of parliament. He concluded that he was 'confident ther never was any returne sent from New Sarum before the . . . 11th yeare of H.3 of burgesses elected ther to the Parliament. Such a monument weere well worth the seeing'. *Ibid.*, 430–1.

55 Apart from the consistently expansionist position taken by Palmer, and possibly those of Bagshaw and Whistler over Marlow, there seems little justification for the second half of Dr Hill's statement that while on the whole royalists were opposed to any extension of the franchise, on certain occasions they pressed for an even wider franchise than did the opposition. In any case, in the 1620s such party labels are inapplicable. Hill, *Century of Revolution*, 120.

56 Prof. Plumb suggested this in 'Growth of the Electorate', 102.

57 His book, *Europae Speculum*, published without his permission in 1605, revealed his dabblings with all religions and none.

58 For Jourdain, see F. Nicolls, *The Life and Death of M. Ignatius Jurdain* (1654).

59 Clarendon, *History of the Rebellion*, ed. W. D. Macray (Oxford, 1888), iii, 526; Cliffe, *Yorkshire Gentry*, 345–6, 349.

60 For these cases, see below, Chapter 7, pp. 133–6, and Appendix ii.

61 *Reliquiae Baxterianae*, 30–3, 89; C. Hill, *Society and Puritanism in Pre-Revolu-*

*tionary England* (London, 1964), 124–44; Zagorin, *Court and Country*, 119–55.

62 The apparent inconsistency is not necessarily at odds with the general belief of the 1620s that to expand the franchise was to defeat unwanted influence. The analysis above has been of members' responses to their experience of those decisions, and to the politics of candidates on various franchises in 1640, in relation to the sides they took for war, which is a rather different problem.

### 5. The Urban Voters

1 For a list of the various franchises, see Appendix III.

2 *Reliquiae Baxterianae*, 94.

3 Gt Yarmouth Corporation Mss., C 18/7, f. 31; N.N.R.O., Norwich Consistory Wills, 39 Houchin (will of John Symondes); and see Consistory Wills index for wills of John Warryn snr, John Smith, Robert Hewes, Thomas Bransby and John Ingram. Probate evidence is unreliable as a guide to the wealth of the testator (even setting aside problems of identification), because of the likelihood that property may have been granted away beforehand. But where the deceased was clearly in possession of more than his retirement chamber, the available evidence has been taken as providing at least a useful indicator.

4 W. B. Stephens, *Seventeenth-Century Exeter* (Exeter, 1958), 43; T. Pape, *Newcastle-under-Lyme in Tudor and Early Stuart Times* (Manchester, 1938), 265–6, 270–1, 275–6, gives voting lists for 1624, 1626 and 1628, and from these can be identified at Lichfield Joint R.O. the wills of John Fernihaugh, Richard Ward, Thomas Jenyns and Richard Harrison.

5 See above, Chapter 3; and Nottingham had evidently been opened by the Recruiter election: Lucy Hutchinson, *Memoirs of the life of Colonel Hutchinson* (Oxford, 1973), 164.

6 Glanville, *Reports*, 107, 142; for Glanville's personal position, see above, Chapter 4, p. 77.

7 B.M. Add. 42711, f. 37; B.M. Lansdowne 491, f. 56; *C.J.*, II, 15; for the divisions caused by Tewkesbury and Marlow, see above, Chapter 4, pp. 84–5.

8 For the campaigns in these boroughs, see above, Chapter 3, and Appendix II.

9 Bodl. Ms. Film 39, p. 44; *C.D. 1621*, III, 412, *ibid.*, IV, 422; Woodhouse, *Puritanism and Liberty*, 54, 57–8, 79; the argument over Warwick is at C.U.L. Ms. Dd. 12.20, 21, f. 12, and Prynne's notes at Inner Temple Ms. 511/23, ff. 1–8.

10 B.M. Add. 36825, ff. 297–297v; Harl. 5324, f. 26v; about 10–15 freemen were admitted yearly in the early 17th century: Boston Town Hall, Borough Records, 5/B/1/1.

11 Hill, *Society and Puritanism*, 133–4.

12 D. M. Woodward, 'Sources for Urban History. Freemen's Rolls', *Local Historian* IX (1970), 91; I am most grateful to Mr A. R. Michell for the Great Yarmouth and King's Lynn figures, and for allowing me to see his draft list of freemen totals in various boroughs, part of his forthcoming thesis on Great Yarmouth.

13 Zagorin, *Court and Country*, 128; W. S. Prideaux, ed., *Memorials of the Goldsmiths' Company* (London, n.d.), I, 342; B. P. Johnson, 'The Gilds of York', in A. Stacpoole, ed., *Noble City of York* (York, 1972), 526, 533; Woodward, 'Sources for Urban History. Freemen's Rolls', 91.

14 For mortality, see E. A. Wrigley, 'Mortality in Pre-industrial England', *Daedalus* XCVII (1968), 546–80, esp. 560; I am indebted to Mr Peter Laslett and Dr Roger Schofield for providing me with estimates of the proportion of adult males in the population – although they do stress that this figure will vary with time and place.

15 John Pound, *Poverty and Vagrancy in Tudor England* (London, 1971), 25-6.

16 Bristol A.O., 04359(2)a; Clark and Slack, *Crisis and Order*, 32; P. Millican, *The Register of the Freemen of Norwich 1548-1713* (Norwich, 1934); P. Corfield, 'A provincial capital in the late seventeenth century: the case of Norwich', in Clark and Slack, *Crisis and Order*, 266.

17. Howell, *Newcastle Upon Tyne*, 125n; G. Chandler, *Liverpool under Charles I* (Liverpool, 1965), 37; Hull Guildhall, Corporation Mss., Freemen's Registers; R. Carroll, 'Yorkshire Parliamentary Boroughs in the 17th century', *Northern History* iii (1968), 91; Clark and Slack, *Crisis and Order*, 31-2.

18 At Coventry, c. 600 freemen voted in 1628, out of a total population of c. 6000 (*C.J.*, 1, 880; Phythian-Adams, 'Metamorphosis of Mediaeval Community'); transcripts of the Dover admissions lists are at B.M. Add. 29625, ff. 36-60, and estimates of Dover's population set it at 2500-3000 (M. V. Jones, 'The Political History of the Parliamentary Boroughs of Kent 1642-1662' (London Ph.D., 1967), 13, and C. W. Chalklin, *Seventeenth Century Kent* (London, 1965), 30); Tewkesbury had c. 360 freemen in 1640 out of a total adult male population of not much more than double that (Inner Temple Ms. 511/23, f. 1; *V.C.H. Gloucestershire*, VIII, 120).

19 An assize judge ordered in 1621 that only freemen rated for scot and lot should vote in Oxford's municipal elections; the Wigan court leet jury list contained 117 names in 1640, whereas there were about 130 inhabitant freemen; the 1640 Bedford election papers contain a list of 18 'Burgisses and Freemen Inhabitants that pay noe Scott nor lott'. H. E. Salter, ed., *Oxford Council Acts 1583-1626* (Oxford Historical Society, lxxxvii, 1928), 299; D. Sinclair, *History of Wigan* (Wigan, 1882), II, 3-9, 11; Bedfordshire R.O., TW 891.

20 Bristol A.O., 04264 (2), ff. 92, 111, 118, 122v, 124v; *ibid.*, 04264 (3), f. 2v; P. Slack, 'Poverty and Politics in Salisbury 1597-1666', in Clark and Slack, *Crisis and Order*, 164-203; P.R.O., S.P. 16/366/48; Bedfordshire R.O., T.W. 891.

21 B.M. Add. 29625, ff. 36-60; for the prosperity of Dover mariners, see Kent A.O., Consistory Court of Canterbury wills 1600-1640, Liber 46/70 (Robert Fleming jnr), Liber 46/72 (Robert Foster), Liber 47/54 (William Tiddeyman), Liber 47/136 (Henry Stone), Liber 48/293 (George Fagg), Liber 49/173 (Christopher Bulger). Thomas Perkin was admitted 'fisherman', but died as a very substantial 'mariner', Liber 47/56.

22 Hertford Borough Mss., vol. XXIII, ff. 13-14; Hertford Borough Museum, 'Freeholders of the Borough of Hertford, By John Norden', transcribed and annotated by H. C. Andrews, ff. 94-108; Borough Mss., vol. XLVI, ff. 925-6, 934-940v.

23 The occupations of the voters are obtained from a somewhat later (c. 1648) list of freemen, on which some of the 1620s names are still to be found, at the top of the list of precedence now, instead of at the bottom; from the few surviving wills and from the county quarter session records. *Ibid.*, vol. XXV. ff. 6-6v; Hertfordshire R.O., Archdeaconry of Huntingdon wills; Hardy, *Hertfordshire Sessions Books, 1619-1657*; Sir Henry Chauncy, *The Historical Antiquities of Hertfordshire* (London, 1700), 241, 252.

24 R. E. Wall, 'The Massachusetts Bay Colony Franchise in 1647', *William and Mary Quarterly* xxvii (1970), 136-44, T. B. Lewis and L. M. Webb, 'Voting for the Massachusetts Council of Assistants, 1674-1686', *ibid.*, xxx (1973), 628-9.

25 It should be noted that the freemen total may also have provided a minimum figure, for often, as in county elections, there was little effective check on those turning out, especially in the larger communities. Pearl, *London and the Puritan Revolution*, 50-1; *C.S.P.D. 1631-1633*, 440-1.

26 Hampshire R.O., Jervoise Mss., 44M69/012; Weeks, *Clitheroe*, 223; *V.C.H.*

*Lancashire*, vi, 368; Fieldhouse, 'Parliamentary Representation in the Borough of Richmond', 208; F. H. Goldney, *Records of Chippenham* (London, 1889), 26–8; Chippenham Borough Records, Minute Book, ff. 76–77v, 116.

27 See above, Chapter 1, pp. 24–5.

28 Fieldhouse, 'Parliamentary Representation of Richmond', 208, and information privately communicated to me by Mr Fieldhouse, to whom I am extremely grateful.

29 N.N.R.O., 349x/How.633/1; for the wills of those listed on the burgage rental, see *ibid.*, Castle Rising Wills 1639–1692; for Marlborough, see Taffs, 'Borough Franchise', App., 170.

30 Atkinson, 'Parliamentary Election in Knaresborough', 215, 217; Weeks, *Clitheroe*, 5–6, 227, 229–30; B.M. Harl. 6806, f. 259; Carroll, 'Yorkshire Parliamentary Boroughs', 96; B.M. Harl. 1327, f. 11.

31 A. M. Johnson, 'Buckinghamshire 1640 to 1660. A Study in County Politics' (University of Wales, Swansea, M.A., 1963), 4, 52; 'The Shardeloes Muniments – III', 283; Buckinghamshire R.O., D/DR.12/37.

32 Bruce, *Verney Papers* 3; *D'Ewes* (N), 248. Marlow was of course not a scot-and-lot borough; and see below for D'Ewes's doubts about the almsmen status of some of the voters.

33 Bedfordshire R.O., T.W. 891.

34 For Arundel, see B.M. Harl. 159, f. 98v; for Bedford, see below; for Bramber, see the allegations that inmates (i.e. lodgers) voted, Bruce, *Verney Papers*, 4; in Chester, almost 1000 voted in 1628, when the total population of the city was about 4500–5000 in 1640: B.M. Harl. 2125, f. 59v, and J. S. Morrill, *Cheshire 1630–1660* (Oxford, 1974), 7; for Marlow, see above, and for St Albans, see below, p. 102; for St Germans, see below.

35 See the closely annotated indentures for both Short and Long Parliament elections; the poll list for the October election is clearly not complete, for it gives Luke 269 votes and Boteler 301, and yet Boteler, who was responsible for its compilation, admitted that Luke had the majority. P.R.O., C. 219/42. Pt. 1, no. 46, and *ibid.*, C. 219/43 Pt. 1; Bedfordshire R.O., T.W. 890–891.

36 *Ibid.*, T.W. 891–893; Woodhouse, *Puritanism and Liberty*, 83; conclusions as to the similarity, socially, of the two groups of voters are derived from the numerous wills of those voting which can be found through the index to the Bedfordshire wills in Bedfordshire R.O.

37 Thomas, 'Levellers and the Franchise', 57–78; S. E. Morison *et al.*, eds., *The Winthrop Papers* (Massachusetts Historical Society, 1929), III, 296; Brown, *Virginia 1705–1786*, 125; *C.D. 1621*, II, 277; Wiltshire R.O., Charles Hayward's Parliamentary Note Book, p. 192; Gloucestershire R.O., D 2688, entry for 1640; Inner Temple Ms. 511/23, f. 3; *D'Ewes* (N), 43: alternatively, the assertion that all freeholders voted in counties could have meant that D'Ewes doubted the effect of the 40s. requirement.

38 Thomas, 'Levellers and the Franchise', 62–3.

39 Keeler, *Long Parliament*, 77; Jones, 'Political History of the Parliamentary Boroughs of Kent', 11; Chalklin, *Seventeenth Century Kent*, 30.

40 Warwickshire R.O., W. 21/6, pp. 270, 277; Inner Temple Ms. 511/23, f. 3; Chauncy, in his 1700 account of the Hertford troubles, made an identical point about the consequences of the term 'communitas': Chauncy, *Historical Antiquities of Hertfordshire*, 241, 252; *C.J.*, I, 697.

41 *D'Ewes* (N), 248; Bruce, *Verney Papers*, 3–4.

42 Cornwall R.O., Carew-Pole Mss., BC/24/2, letter of John Moyle to Sir Richard Buller, 1640 Dec. 18; Bruce, *Verney Papers*, 4; *C.J.* VIII, 351.

43 *D'Ewes* (N), 248; B.M. Harl. 162, f. 377; *C.D. 1621*, IV, 422; Bodl. Ms. Film 39, p. 107. Such confusion in D'Ewes, while perhaps unsurprising, was approached by the uncertainty of men such as Gerrard on similar issues: see above, Chapter 4.

44. For the ultimate refusal of all concerned to come to terms with the issues at Tewkesbury, see *C.J.*, III, 352, 378–9; Gloucestershire R.O., D. 2688, entry for 1640; for Gatton, see *C.J.*, II, 303, and B.M. Add. 33468, f. 35v.

45 Thirsk and Cooper, *17th Century Economic Documents*, 766, 780. The figures were scarcely likely to have been lower in the early part of the century, given that the elimination of the peasantry had not yet proceeded as far as it was soon to do.

46 Plumb, *Growth of Stability*, 29; see above, pp. 94–5 for the basis for these proportional calculations. The figure was perhaps towards the higher end of this range, for it was in the second half of the century that the proportion of adults in the population started to rise as mortality fell. I am grateful to Dr Schofield for this point.

## 6. Control and Independence in Voting

1 P.R.O., S.P., 16/79/38; *ibid.*, S.P. 16/366/48; see above, pp. 54–5.

2 Pearl, *London and the Puritan Revolution*, 163–5; P.R.O., S.P. 16/366/48; Hutchinson, *Memoirs of Col. Hutchinson*, 106.

3 Hoskins, *Midland Peasant*, *passim*; W. O. Ault, 'Open-Field Husbandry and the Village Community', *Transactions of the American Philosophical Society*, n.s., lv, pt. 7 (1965), *passim*; Bridenbaugh, *Vexed and Troubled Englishmen*, 242–7. The use to which the parish meeting could be put is revealed by the way in which a 1618 Cambridgeshire enclosure riot developed from one. P.R.O., St. Ch. 8/27/8.

4 Thompson, 'Moral Economy of the English Crowd', 76–120; *C.S.P.D. 1631–1633*, 501; Hill, *World Turned Upside Down*, 49; for an account of Clubmen activity in this area, see D. Underdown, *Somerset in the Civil War and Interregnum* (Newton Abbot, 1973), 98–135: I am most grateful to Prof. Underdown for discussions on this subject.

5 See B. Manning, 'The Outbreak of the English Civil War', in R. H. Parry, ed., *The English Civil War and After* (London, 1970), 16.

6 Bedford Corporation Archives, Box 8, no. 5, pp. 43–8; *C.S.P.D. 1625–1626*, 414; J. Rushworth, *Historical Collections* (1659–1701), III, 8 (I am grateful to Mr J. D. Walter for this reference); *C.S.P.D. 1627–1628*, 65; Pearl, *London and the Puritan Revolution*, 74.

7 *C.S.P.D. 1619–1623*, 233; P.R.O., St. Ch. 8/175/19; Cockburn, *History of English Assizes*, 234; *C.S.P.D. 1640–1641*, 13.

8 For lists of contests, see Appendix IV; *D'Ewes* (N), 321; B.M. Add. 37343, f. 206v.

9 B.M. Harl. 162, f. 377; *H.M.C. 13th Report, Appdx. IV* (Dovaston Mss.), 260; Ballinger, *Calendar of the Wynn (of Gwydir) Papers*, 199–200.

10 B.M. Harl. 378, f. 29v; see also *C.J.*, I, 649, for the rather similar, but more mundane, attitude of Sir Henry Poole.

11 St Albans City Library, City of St Albans Muniments, no. 159 (Mayor's accounts 1620–1); see also, for example, *C.J.*, I, 161 (Buckinghamshire 1604). It is plain from the account of the 1624 Norfolk election that the election crowds were gathered outside the court, so the possibility of control was even less. Saunders, *Official Papers of Sir Nathaniel Bacon*, 39–41.

12 Plumb, *Growth of Stability*, esp. Chapter VI.

13 There were also hopes of beating up the leading rebel. B.M. Eg. 2722, ff. 90–90v.
14 R. Yarlott, 'The Long Parliament and the Fear of Popular Pressure, 1640–1646' (Leeds M.A., 1963), 231; Hampshire R.O., Jervoise Mss., 44M69/012, Anthony Knott to Sir Richard Paulett, 1 March 1613/14; Longleat House, Marquis of Bath's Mss., Whitelocke Papers, VIII, f. 35v.
15 Neale, *House of Commons*, 267; *H.M.C. 10th Report, Appdx. Pt. II* (Gawdy Papers), 176; N.N.R.O., Norwich City Records, shelf 17b, City Revenue and Letters, f. 23; Longleat, Marquis of Bath's Mss., Whitelocke Papers, VIII, f. 43v; P.R.O., SP. 16/451/44 (Hastings); Kent A.O., Sa./Ac.7, f. 368 (Sandwich).
16 P.R.O., S.P. 16/366/48; Kerridge, *Agrarian Problems*, 65–93; *Reliquiae Baxterianae*, 89.
17 B. Manning, 'Neutrals and Neutralism in the English Civil War 1642–1646' (Oxford D.Phil., 1957), 106; *V.C.H. Lancashire*, IV, 70, 72; *C.S.P.D. 1633–1634*, 339–40; Wigan Public Library, Bishop Bridgeman's Account Book, pp. 172–3; G. T. O. Bridgeman, *History of the Church and Manor of Wigan*, II (Chetham Soc., 1889), 308–19; and for the Wigan voters' independence, see below, pp. 125–7.
18 Longleat, Marquis of Bath's Mss., Whitelocke Papers, VIII, f. 35v; see above, Chapter 2, for a discussion of the Hertfordshire listing.
19 Bristol Archives Office, AC/C58/1/3–5 (I am grateful to Prof. D. Underdown for this reference); Guildford Museum, LM 1331/25; Hassell Smith, *County and Court*, 326–7.
20 R. W. Ketton-Cremer, *Norfolk in the Civil War* (London, 1969), 110; C.U.L. Mss., Dd. 12.20, 21, f. 87v.
21 Somerset R.O., DD/SF 1076/21/36; Stone, 'Electoral Influence of second Earl of Salisbury', 385–6; A. M. Everitt, *The Community of Kent and the Great Rebellion* (Leicester, 1966), 69–83; B.M. Eg. 2722, f. 90.
22 B. G. Blackwood, 'Social and Religious Aspects of the History of Lancashire 1635–1655' (Oxford B.Litt., 1956), 42–4; B. G. Blackwood, 'The Lancashire Cavaliers and their Tenants', *Transactions of the Historic Society of Lancashire and Cheshire* cxvii (1965), 21, 31; Underdown, *Somerset in the Civil War*, 31, 38–9; B.M. Harl. 2125, f.59v.
23 Everitt, *Community of Kent*, 69–83; Bodl. Ms. Top. Kent e. 6; *C.S.P.D. 1639–1640*, 162; B.M. Add. 26639, f. 45v; B.M. Harl. 2125, f. 59v (I am grateful to Dr J. S. Morrill for this reference).
24 Sheffield City Library Mss., Str. 2, pp. 63–4; Gloucestershire R.O., D 2510/10; Bodl. Ms. Top. Kent e.6; B.M. Harl. 158, f. 287v. The sheriff at the 1656 Somerset election gave the voters an hour after names had been propounded 'to retire and looke over your lists': the canvassing then must have been intense. Cockburn, *Somerset Assize Orders 1640–1659*, 76.
25 Bodl. Ms. Rawl. D. 1098, f. 95v; B.M. Harl. 165, f. 5; *ibid.*, Harl. 158, ff. 287–288; N.N.R.O., Walsingham Mss., xvii/2, Sir William de Grey to (Sir Drew) Drury, 2 Dec. 1620; W. B. Willcox, *Gloucestershire: A Study in Local Government 1590–1640* (New Haven, 1940), 34; Kent A.O., U1115, 015/1.
26 See, for example, Knowler, *Strafforde's Letters and Dispatches*, I, 8, 13; Bradford City Library, Spencer Stanhope Mss., 10/4.
27 F. P. and M. M. Verney, *Memoirs of the Verney Family* (London, 1904), 203; B.M. Add. 37343, f. 198v; Bodl. Ms. Top. Kent e.6; B.M. Add. 34163, f. 108v.
28 J. P. Cooper, 'The Fortune of Thomas Wentworth, Earl of Strafford', *Economic History Review* xi (1958–9), 231 n; *H.M.C. 12th Report, Appdx. (Earl Cowper's Mss.)*, III, 138–41; Stone, 'Electoral Influence of second Earl of Salisbury' 387 (Prof. Stone comes to the rather different total of £193 1s. 8d. for Derbyshire); M. E. Bohannon, 'The Essex election of 1604', *E.H.R.* xlviii (1933), 402; *H.M.C.*

*14th Report, Appdx. II, Duke of Portland's Mss., vol. III,* 147 (there were possibly c. 3500 Harley supporters in 1646).

29 Quoted in Neale, *House of Commons,* 78.

30 R. F. Williams, ed., *The Court and Times of Charles I* (London, 1848), i, 19; P.R.O., S.P. 16/450/39; Stone, 'Electoral Influence of second Earl of Salisbury', 393–4; *Verney Papers,* 3; Nottingham U.L., Cl.L.P. 51; Hampshire R.O. Jervoise Mss., 44 M69/012, 'A note of the Expence at Whitchurch'; Wigan Public Library, Bishop Bridgeman's Account Book, p. 228; B.M. Loan, 29/50, no. 76A; N.R.O., FH 3468.

31 *D'Ewes* (N), 160; P.R.O., S.P. 16/448/45; Cornwall R.O., Carew-Pole Mss., BO/23/73, Francis Buller to —.

32 H. T. Weyman, 'The Members of Parliament for Ludlow', *Transactions of the Shropshire Archaeological and Natural History Society,* 2nd series, vii (1895), 23; Taffs, 'Borough Franchise', Appdx., 196; C.U.L. Mss., Dd. 12.20, 21, f. 76v; N.R.O., FH 50, f. 37v; Nottingham U.L., Cl.L.P. 51; Willcox, *Gloucestershire,* 31; Gloucestershire R.O., D 760/36.

33 B.M. Cotton Julius C. iii, ff. 402–402v; Ruigh, *Parliament of 1624,* 80 n. 64; C.U.L. Mss., Dd. 12.20, 21, f. 76v; *D'Ewes* (N), 160; Longleat, Marquis of Bath's Mss., Whitelocke's Papers, viii, f. 35v; Nottingham U.L., Cl.L.P. 51; BM. Harl. 6806, f. 254.

34 *C.S.P.D. 1627–1628,* 566; B.M. Add. 29974, f. 319; N. Rogers, 'Aristocratic Clientage, Trade and Independency: Popular Politics in Pre-Radical Westminster', *Past and Present* lxi (1973), 78–94; *C.J.,* i, 749; B.M. Add. 37343, f. 198v; *ibid.,* Add. 29974, f. 319. A steward of the Gawdy family did not feel bound to vote with his master in the Norfolk Short Parliament election – though he suffered for it. *H.M.C. 10th Report, Appdx. Pt. II,* 176.

35 B.M. Add. 36825, ff. 322–322v; B.M. Harl. 2313, f. 8v; *C.J.,* i, 806; J. K. Gruenfelder, 'The Election to the Short Parliament', in H. S. Reinmuth, jnr, ed., *Early Stuart Studies* (Minneapolis, 1970), 214; P.R.O., S.P. 16/451/44; for Sandwich, see Appendix ii; Bodl. Ms. Bankes 18/5; and see also the case of Berwick: *C.S.P.D. 1640–1641,* 404.

36 W. Scott, ed., *The Somers Collection of Tracts* (London, 1810), iv, 105; see also Williams, *Court and Times of Charles I,* i, 332; *H.M.C. 12th Report, Appdx. (Earl Cowper's Mss.),* i, 356; *C.S.P.D. 1628–1629,* 24.

37 Bodl. Ms. Top. Kent e.6; Nalson, *Impartial Collection,* i, 279; *D'Ewes* (N), 440–1; Bradford City Library, Spencer Stanhope Mss., 10A/8.

38 *Ibid.,* 10/4; Johnson, *Fairfax Correspondence,* i, lx; Knowler, *Strafforde's Letters and Dispatches,* i, 11–13; Bodl. Ms. Tanner 290, f. 28; *ibid.,* Tanner 283, f. 174; *C.S.P.D. 1628–1629,* 24.

39 *H.M.C. 11th Report, Appdx. IV* (Townshend Papers), 21; B.M. Add. 37343, f. 198v; B.M. Harl. 165, f. 5; Nottinghamshire R.O., DD. SR. 221/96/4. Canvassing on horseback may also have occurred in the 1624 Norfolk election crowd. Saunders, *Official Papers of Sir Nathaniel Bacon,* 40.

40 Johnson, *Fairfax Correspondence,* ii, 375.

41 Cornwall R.O., Carew-Pole Mss., BC/24/2, letter of Sir Samuel Rolle to Thomas Wyse, 7 Dec. 1640.

42 Poll lists could be compiled for a variety of purposes: in towns, they were often official tallies of votes; in counties, the surviving fragments were often compiled after the event in furtherance of a projected complaint to the House. In Yorkshire in 1621 and Huntingdonshire in 1625, lists of prospective supporters were kept.

43 Bodl. Ms. Top. Kent e.6; for Godmanchester, see above, pp. 40–1.

44 This conclusion is derived from a comparison of the clergy in Dering's list with those given in A. G. Matthews, ed., *Walker Revised* (Oxford, 1948), and A. G. Matthews, ed., *Calamy Revised* (Oxford, 1934).

45 Keeler, *Long Parliament*, 33, 261–2; *C.S.P.D. 1640–1641*, 147; the Bedford poll list is at Bedfordshire R.O., T.W. 890, and the Bunyan congregation can be identified from G. B. Harrison, ed., *The Church Book of Bunyan Meeting* (London, 1928). The Luke voters were: Edward Coventon, Richard Cooper, John Grue, Anthony Harrington, Richard Spencely, William Whitbread, John Wilson; the sole Boteler voter was John Gifford.

46 C.U.L. Mss., Kk. 6. 38, f.8; Zagorin, *Court and Country*, 154; Ketton-Cremer, *Norfolk in the Civil War*, 173–5, 177, 332–4; P.R.O., C 219/43. Pt. 2, 61 and 62; Keeler, *Long Parliament*, 57; Bodl. Ms. Tanner 68, ff. 153–5.

47 F. R. Beecheno, 'The Norwich Subscription for the Regaining of Newcastle, 1643', *Norfolk Archaeology* xviii (1914), 149–60; N.N.R.O., Norwich Assembly Book 1613–1642, f. 565; Zagorin, *Court and Country*, 131–55. A list of the 55 voters in the Grimsby spring election also survives, and here again there does not appear to be a division of royalists and parliamentarians (staunch future members of both sides were standing, in Gervase Holles and Sir Christopher Wray), but the evidence is far too scanty to allow of any firm conclusions. Grimsby Corporation Mss., Court Book, 24 March 1640. I am indebted to Mr P. J. Shaw and Mr E. Gillett for their help here.

48 Sinclair, *Wigan*, 1, 196–9, 215–21; *ibid.*, 11, 3–9; rising turn-outs elsewhere can be observed at Appendix v.

49 The distinction between first and second seat was not inconsequential: some of the candidates in the 1624 Norfolk election refused to consider the second place. B.M. Add. 18597, ff. 31, 65v–66.

50 W. E. Gregson, 'Recusant Roll for West Derby Hundred, 1641', *Transactions of the Historic Society of Lancashire and Cheshire*, l, new series vol. xiv (1898), 239; the wills and inventories of Wigan voters can be found in the Lancashire R.O., Consistory Court of Chester wills, etc.; these are indexed in publications of the *Lancashire and Cheshire Record Society*, vols. IV, XV, XLIII, LII.

51 Weeks, *Clitheroe*, 135–40, 226–30. It might be thought that the casting of only one vote was that sophisticated political action known as 'plumping', which is found later when one candidate stood against a pair, and his supporters were reluctant to give votes to either of the challengers. But in view of the evident absence of pairing here, or in Wigan, and of the confusion which existed, this is unlikely. Indeed where a candidate (Sir Robert Phelips) was standing against a pair in Somerset in 1614, he was advised by his experienced father that his supporters 'must be instructed to name any other Gentleman, or other whatsoever', rather than either of the pair, for their second choice – but not to plump. Somerset R.O., DD/PH/224/9.

52 Hertford Borough Mss., vol. 23, ff. 13–14, 17; Stone, 'Electoral Influence of second Earl of Salisbury', 391–3. Willowes (Richard Willis) was a local gentleman with property in the town, as had Harrington: Hertford Borough Mss., vol. 46, pp. 896, 904.

53 F. M. Page, *History of Hertford* (Hertford, 1959), 79, 83; for wills of voters, see Hertfordshire R.O., Archdeaconry of Huntingdon wills; and for Fanshawe, see L. M. Munby, 'Sir Richard Fanshawe (1608–66) and his Family', *Hertfordshire Past and Present* iii (1962–3), 6–9.

54 See Appendix vi.

55 For the identities of the freemen, see P.R.O., S.P. 16/448/45; *ibid.*, 450/39. 11 and 40. I am indebted to the kindness of J. Manwaring Baines, Curator of Hastings

Public Museum, for supplying me with the fruits of his labours in identification of the port's inhabitants.

56 The total of votes also contrasts with the mere 310 in 1628. Hobson and Salter, *Oxford Council Acts 1626–1665*, 9–10, 97.

57 Hampshire R.O., Jervoise Mss., 44M69/012, 'A Bill of the Free Eleccion'. While it is clear from the Grimsby Short Parliament poll list that everybody there cast two votes, the frequent inability to cast the correct number of votes must throw grave doubts on the conclusions of those who have calculated the totals of early New England voters by dividing the numbers of votes cast by the number of votes possessed by each voter: for example, R. C. Simmons, 'Godliness, Property and the Franchise', *Journal of American History* lv (1968–9), 502.

58 N.R.O., FH 3466, FH 3468.

59 That awareness went with experience might be inferred from the records of the repeated contests at Grimsby in the later 15th century: in 1455 there were seven candidates and no pattern at all to the voting; later on, pairing became visible, and votes were cast in order. Rogers, 'Parliamentary Elections in Grimsby in the Fifteenth Century', 217–20.

## 7. The Electorate and Politics

1 Carroll, 'Yorkshire Parliamentary Boroughs', 100–1; Keeler, *Long Parliament*, 35, 66; Buckinghamshire R.O., D/DR12/38.

2 *C.S.P.D. 1625–1626*, 217, 218, 221; Wilks, *Barons of the Cinque Ports*, 74–8, and see above, p. 53; *C.S.P.D. 1627–1628*, 583.

3 Keeler, *Long Parliament*, 76–7; L. B. Larking, ed., *Proceedings in Kent in 1640* (Camden Soc., 1862), 24.

4 *C.D. 1621*, vii, 568; *C.S.P.D. 1619–1623*, 212–13; B.M. Add. 37819, f. 11v; N. E. McClure, ed., *The Letters of John Chamberlain* (Philadelphia, 1939), ii, 617; Gardiner, *Historic Haven*, 230; Ruigh, *Parliament of 1624*, 135. I am most grateful to Mrs V. Millenson for discussions on influence in the Cinque Ports and elsewhere.

5 *C.S.P.D. 1625–1626*, 230; B.M. Add. 37819, f. 19v; J. D. Thomas, 'Survey of Parliamentary Elections, 1625–1628' (London M.A., 1952), 55, 65; Gardiner, *Historic Haven*, 227; *C.D. 1621*, vii, 568.

6 *C.S.P.D. 1628–1629*, 13; Keeler, *Long Parliament*, 77; and see Appendix ii.

7 Salter, *Oxford Council Acts 1583–1626*, lxi; Hobson and Salter, *Oxford Council Acts 1626–1665*, 9–10, 91–2, 97; Cooper, *Annals of Cambridge*, iii, 176, 183, 200; Keeler, *Long Parliament*, 36; for Colchester, see Appendix ii.

8 At Newcastle-under-Lyme, the influence of the Earl of Essex and other local figures replaced the Duchy's after 1624. After the defeat of Sir Thomas Edmondes at Chester in 1621, courtiers were absent – although resentment against outsiders was also a characteristic of the already enfranchised freemen, so the change may not have been solely the result of the expansion of the franchise. Pape, *Newcastle-under-Lyme*, 33, 133, 139; Ruigh, *Parliament of 1624*, 52, 66; Keeler, *Long Parliament*, 37, 63; J. K. Gruenfelder, 'The Parliamentary Election at Chester, 1621', *Transactions of the Historic Society of Lancashire and Cheshire* cxx (1968), 40–1; B.M. Harl. 2105, f. 271; and see Appendix ii.

9 At Boston, Bishop Williams' influence is evident in the 1620s, in the cases of Boswell and Oakley (the defeated candidate in 1628), although this is not strictly Court: this influence was defeated in 1628, and was clearly absent in 1640. Ruigh, *Parliament of 1624*, 144; Keeler, *Long Parliament*, 55; again, I am grateful to Mrs Millenson for the identification of Oakley: Mrs Millenson, of Colum-

bia University, is working on the general problem of electoral influence in this period.

10 Keeler, *Long Parliament*, 47, 54–5 (Secretary Coke's son was accepted at the instance of the local power, the Countess of Devonshire, not at the Duchy's); *C.S.P.D. 1627–1628*, 562; Morison, *Winthrop Papers*, I, 326; Ruigh, *Parliament of 1624*, 62 n. 29.

11 Gruenfelder, 'Election at Hastings, 1640', 49–55; Richard Culmer, *Cathedrall Newes from Canterbury* (1644), 18–19; Anon., *Antidotum Culmerianum* (Oxford, 1644), 28–9; Williams, *Court and Times of Charles I*, I, 327; P.R.O., 31/3/72, f. 59 (I am grateful to Mr Conrad Russell for this reference).

12 P.R.O., SP. 16/450/6, 39, 52.

13 Jones, 'Parliamentary Boroughs of Kent', 29–30, 59–60.

14 Some 200 freemen tried to return John Barnard instead of the puritan Richard Knightley: the identity of Barnard is uncertain, but the staff of the N.R.O. are of the opinion that it could only have been John Barnard of Abington, an arch-neutral of the war, who was knighted at the Restoration. I am indebted to the staff of the Record Office for their assistance in this point, as in many others. N.R.O., FH 3501; Mrs Napier-Higgins, *The Bernards of Abington and Nether Winchendon* (London, 1903), I, 55–66.

15 Keeler, *Long Parliament*, 34–5; Groome, 'Higham Ferrers Elections', 245–7.

16 B.M. Add. 34601, ff. 26–8, 30–6. I am extremely grateful to Mr C. W. Crawley, of Trinity Hall, for allowing me to use his biographical notes of those involved.

17 For Salisbury, see Appendix II; W. H. D. Longstaffe, ed., *Memoirs of the Life of Ambrose Barnes* (Surtees Soc., 1867), 329–30; R. Welford, *History of New-castle and Gateshead* (London, 1884–7), III, 368–71, 381–6; B.M. Add. 34373 ff. 209–209v, 211v.

18 Thompson, 'Moral Economy of the English Crowd', esp. 76–120; for Warwick, see Appendix II, and for Coventry, see above, Chapter 3.

19 See Appendix II.

20 See above, Chapter 4.

21 B.M. Add. 37343, f. 198. This was of course an open borough, though a small one.

22 We must await the forthcoming Columbia University Ph.D. thesis of Vivienne Millenson for clarification of these matters.

23 It also indicates a willingness on the part of the gentry to consult or profit from the political opinions or prejudices of the common people.

24 See Thomas, 'Parliamentary Elections, 1625–1628', for a discussion of Gardiner's claim.

25 Hassell Smith, *County and Court*, 314–32.

26 Cliffe, *Yorkshire Gentry*, 282–308; Ruigh, *Parliament of 1624*, 93 n. 4.

27 See below, Chapter 8, for further development of this theme.

28 Morison, *Winthrop Papers*, I, 326; Great Yarmouth Corporation Mss., C19/5, f. 323v; *C.S.P.D. 1619–1623*, 200; Stone, 'Electoral Influence of second Earl of Salisbury', 389 (Salisbury was not quite a courtier, but the reasons expressed are identical); Clark and Slack, *Crisis and Order*, 187. The xenophobia of the Chester and Colchester freemen (see Appendix II) shows that the corporations were not alone in disliking strangers.

29 W. Notestein, *The House of Commons 1604–1610* (New Haven and London, 1971), 394; H.M.C. Report, *Duke of Buccleuch's Mss.*, I, 256.

30 Jennings, *History of Harrogate and Knaresborough*, 130–2; C.J., I, 485; *C.S.P.D. 1619–1623*, 212–13.

31 Birch, *Court and Times of James I*, I, 302; Johnson, *Fairfax Correspondence*, I,

89; Williams, *Court and Times of Charles I*, I, 130–1, 151, 153–4, 157, 327; Pearl, *London and the Puritan Revolution*, 74.

32 For a list of contests, see Appendix IV; and for the 1597 contest in Yorkshire, see Neale, *House of Commons*, 83; I am grateful to Dr Hassell Smith for details of the Elizabethan Norfolk contests.

33 Thirsk, *Agrarian History* IV, 29, 45; Neale, *House of Commons*, 91.

34 Bradford City Library, Spencer Stanhope Mss., 10A/9; Knowler, *Strafforde's Letters and Dispatches*, I, 10–11; Johnson, *Fairfax Correspondence*, I, 7; also, Sheffield City Library Mss., Str. 2, p. 60.

35 Bradford City Library, Spencer Stanhope Mss., 10A/9.

36 Knowler, *Strafforde's Letters and Dispatches*, I, 11; Bodl. Ms. Add. D. 109, f. 307; H. Heaton, *The Yorkshire Woollen and Worsted Industries* (Oxford, 1965), 82–3; P.R.O., S.P. 16/439/6. The clothing industry was also a major factor in the by-election to the 1628 parliament. Sheffield City Library Mss., Str. 12, no. 53.

37 Saunders, *Official Papers of Sir Nathaniel Bacon*, 39–41; B. Schofield, ed., *The Knyvett Letters 1620–1644* (Norfolk Record Soc., 1949), 69; C. A. Holmes, 'The Eastern Association' (Cambridge Ph.D., 1967), 48.

38 *C.S.P.D. 1623–1625*, 150; Bodl. Ms. Rawl. A346, f. 233v. Sandys probably also made a dangerous harangue at the 1625 Kent election, when he found himself losing it. McClure, *Letters of John Chamberlain*, II, 615.

39 Cheshire R.O., Grosvenor Mss., Sir Richard Grosvenor's speech, 2 Feb., 1623/4; B.M. Harl. 2125, f. 59v; 'Family Memoranda of the Stanleys of Alderley', *Journal of the Chester and North Wales Archaeological and Historic Society*, xxiv (1921), 99. I am most grateful to Dr J. S. Morrill for directing me to these references.

40 B.M. Cotton Julius CIII, f. 168.

41 Sheffield City Library Mss., Str. 16, no. 245. These gentry opportunists apparently included Wentworth, who in 1624 had wished to have the 1624 Pontefract election voided on the grounds that it was 'procured by a Popish faction'. N.R.O., FH 50, f. 37.

42 Knowler, *Strafforde's Letters and Dispatches*, I, 27, 32; *C.J.*, I, 801; Johnson, *Fairfax Correspondence*, I, 9.

43 For example, at the Rutland election of 1601: Neale, *House of Commons*, 135.

44 Birch, *Court and Times of James I*, II, 232; Bodl. Tanner Ms. 321, ff. 3–3v; for the 1624 Norfolk election, see above, p. 144; Bedfordshire R.O., J. 1369.

45 P.R.O., St. Ch. 8/201/17; Hampshire R.O., Kingsmill Mss., no. 1317; *ibid.*, Jervoise Mss., 44M69/012, Anthony Knott to Sir Richard Paulett, 1 March 1614.

46 Bedfordshire: *D'Ewes* (N), 480; Kent: Plumb, 'Growth of the Electorate', 106; Hastings: *C.S.P.D. 1640–1641*, 160–1, 198; Knaresborough: Johnson, *Fairfax Correspondence*, II, 227–8, 290; Sandwich: *C.S.P.D. 1639–1640*, 561; Warwickshire: Maxstoke Castle, Fetherstone-Dilke Mss., dining-room, in wooden chest by door, bundle 25, no. 29: draft petition to House of Commons (this is the National Register of Archives reference: the chest is now by the window in the ground floor drawing-room, and the numbering of the bundle is now confused. A substantially complete transcript is in my possession). I am most grateful to Capt. C. B. Fetherstone-Dilke for permission to consult this Ms.

47 Kent: *C.S.P.D. 1623–1625*, 150; Canterbury: *ibid.*, 155; Ludlow: Weyman, 'Members of Parliament for Ludlow', 22; Winchelsea: B.M. Harl. 159, f. 87; Pontefract: N.R.O., FH 50, f. 37; Yorkshire: Sheffield City Library Mss., Str. 2, p. 123.

48 Nalson, *Impartial Collection*, I, 279; *C.S.P.D. 1639–1640*, 582; B.M. Add. 37343, f. 198 (though Whitelocke's testimony is weakened by the fact that he was

Recorder of the town: his candidature was to be expected); P. Slack, 'An Election to the Short Parliament', *Bulletin of the Institute of Historical Research* xlvi (1973), 112, 114; *C.S.P.D. 1640–1641*, 198; *D'Ewes* (N), 441.

49 Keeler, *Long Parliament*, 54; Culmer, *Cathedrall Newes*, 19; for Salisbury, see Appendix II; Longleat, Marquis of Bath's Mss., Whitelocke Papers, VIII, f. 25.

50 Pearl, *London and the Puritan Revolution*, 107–8; N. Wallington, *Historical Notices*, ed. R. Webb (London, 1869) I, 138–9.

51 Quoted in Holmes, 'Eastern Association', 45; B.M. Harl. 158, f. 293v; Plumb, 'Growth of the Electorate', 107; Nalson, *Impartial Collection*, I, 279. A bevy of aristocrats also met a very rude reception at the spring election in Northampton-shire. Bedfordshire R.O., J. 1369.

52 Edward Bagshaw, *A Just Vindication of the Questioned Part of the Reading* (1660) 3; Plumb, 'Growth of the Electorate', 99 n., 105–6; Hirst, 'Defection of Dering', 198–202, 208.

53 B.M. Eg. 2722, ff. 90–90v; P.R.O., S.P. 16/448/79.

54 Although the Dorset and Middlesex petitions to the Long Parliament appear to have been widely aired at the election meetings: see below, p. 183.

55 And even if these challenges were manufactured by the gentry, they were still contriving to open politics to the people.

56 Barnes, *Somerset 1625–1640*, 211; Hirst, 'Defection of Dering', 198; Plumb, 'Growth of the Electorate', 106; Keeler, *Long Parliament*, 54; Slack, 'Election to the Short Parliament', 113; P.R.O., S.P. 16/448/79; Bodl. Ms. Tanner 65, f. 164; Cornwall R.O., Carew-Pole Mss., BO/25/59, p. 143; *D'Ewes* (N), 513, 539. The corporation's allegedly corrupt levying of Ship Money was also an issue at Hastings in the spring. P.R.O., S.P. 16/450/39.

57 *C.S.P.D. 1639–1640*, 321; Middlesex: *D'Ewes* (N), 539, and Cornwall R.O., Carew-Pole Mss., BO/25/59, p. 143; Kent: B.M. Add. 34163, f. 108v; Bucking-hamshire: Bodl. Ms. Bankes 44/13; Norfolk: B.M. Eg. 2722, f. 90; Northampton-shire: Bedfordshire R.O., J1369, also Bodl. Ms. Bankes 18/5, 13/23, 42/55, 44/13.

58 Bedfordshire: *D'Ewes* (N), 480; Lincolnshire: Keeler, *Long Parliament*, 54; Essex: Nalson, *Impartial Collection*, I, 279; Gloucester and Gloucestershire: P.R.O., S.P. 16/448/79; Lewes: *C.S.P.D. 1639–1640*, 387; Newcastle: Welford, *Newcastle and Gateshead*, III, 381–6; Southwark: Bagshaw, *Just Vindication*, 3; Kent: Hirst, 'Defection of Dering', 197–9. For the rest, see the discussions of anti-papistry and anti-laudianism above.

59 Bletchingley: Staffordshire R.O., D661/11/1/2, endpaper; Yarmouth: *C.S.P.D. 1625–1626*, 232; for Cheshire and Kent, see above.

60 Bedford 1628: Bedford Corporation Archives, Box 8, no. 5, pp. 53–4; Bletchingley 1624: see above; Cheshire 1624 and 1626: see above; East Retford 1624: Notting-ham U.L., Cl.L.P.51; Kent 1624 and 1625: see above; Knaresborough 1614: Yorkshire Archaeological Society, Slingsby papers, DD 56/B2, Henry Thompson to Sir Henry Slingsby, 5 May 1614; Middlesex 1614: Birch, *Court and Times of James I*, I, 235; Norfolk 1604: N.N.R.O., Raynham Temporary Deposit, 252 (I am grateful to Lord Townshend for permission to use these Mss., and to Dr Hassell Smith for reference to the collection); Somerset 1625: Somerset R.O., DD/PH/216/12; Suffolk 1621: Birch, *Court and Times of James I*, II, 232; Yar-mouth 1626: see above; ? Yorkshire 1625: B.M. Add. 26639, f. 45v. Speeches and sermons were also sometimes made at municipal elections: H.M.C. *Report, Earl of Verulam's Mss.*, 198–203; Jones, 'Parliamentary Boroughs of Kent', 37–9.

61 Cornwall: R. N. Worth, ed., *The Buller Papers* (—, 1895), 33; Cheshire: *C.S.P.D. 1639–1640*, 565; Canterbury: Culmer, *Cathedrall Newes*, 19; Dunwich: H.M.C. *Report, Various Vol. VII* (Dunwich Corporation Mss.), 99; Essex: Nal-

son, *Impartial Collection*, I, 279; Gloucestershire: *C.S.P.D. 1639–1640*, 582; Hastings: P.R.O., S.P. 16/450/52; Kent: Plumb, 'Growth of the Electorate', 106; Lincolnshire: Keeler, *Long Parliament*, 54; Norfolk: *D'Ewes* (N), 364; Northamptonshire: Bodl. Ms. Bankes 44/13; Sandwich: *C.S.P.D. 1639–1640*, 561–2; Worcestershire: *D'Ewes* (N), 440–1; Warwickshire: Maxstoke Castle, Fetherstone-Dilke Mss., Wooden chest by door in dining-room, bundle 25, no. 29 (and see above, n.46).

62 Neale, *House of Commons*, 251; P. Collinson, *The Elizabethan Puritan Movement* (London, 1967), 278; Plumb, 'Growth of the Electorate', 94.

63 Neale, *House of Commons*, 251–4; Plumb, 'Growth of the Electorate', 94; and see Appendix II.

## 8. Local Benefits, and Taxes

1 Thomas Hobbes, *Behemoth*, ed. F. Tonnies (London, 1969), 120; Bodl. Ms. Rawl. A123, f. 9; Henry Parker, *Observations upon some of his Majesties late Answers and Expresses* (1642): this work provoked more replies than did any other single tract (I am most grateful to Mr Richard Tuck for this information); *C.J.*, II, 330.

2 Miss Judson identified the tendency to appeal to a responsibility to the country, but she saw this as 'almost mystical'. M. A. Judson, *The Crisis of the Constitution* (New Brunswick, 1949), 304.

3 S. R. Gardiner, *History of England* (London, 1883), I, 353; Gardiner, *Constitutional Documents*, 93.

4 Sir Simonds D'Ewes, *A Compleat Journal of the Votes, Speeches and Debates, both of the House of Lords and House of Commons throughout the whole Reign of Queen Elizabeth* (London, 1693), 631; Bodl. Ms. Ashmole 822, f. 265v; Bramhall, *Serpent Salve*, 148.

5 Barnes, *Somerset 1625–1640*, 87; McKisack, *Representation of Boroughs*, 134–9.

6 D'Ewes, *Compleat Journal*, 175; Coke is quoted in Ruigh, *Parliament of 1624*, 94.

7 D'Ewes, *Compleat Journal*, 169–70; *The Diary of Henry Townshend of Elmley Lovett*, ed. J. W. Willis Bund (Worcestershire Historical Society, 1920), I, 13; private communication from Mr A. R. Michell.

8 Neale, *House of Commons*, especially Chapters VII, IX and X; Hastings corporation wished to elect the Court Official Robert Read to the Short Parliament, 'well knowing that of himselfe and by his Relacions he is able to be more beneficiall to ower Towne in other kinds'. P.R.O., S.P. 16/450/39.II; Gruenfelder, 'Election to the Short Parliament', 221.

9 Quoted in Thomas, 'Survey of Parliamentary Elections', 194; N.N.R.O., Aylsham Hall Mss., bundle 16, January 13, 1592/3 (I am grateful to Dr Hassell Smith for directing me to this correspondence); Knowler; *Strafforde's Letters and Dispatches*, I, 26; Gloucestershire R.O., D 760/36; *V.C.H. Wiltshire*, v, 128; B.M. Harl. 159, f. 119v.

10 N.N.R.O., Raynham Temporary Deposit, 253; B.M. Eg. 2715, ff. 250, 286, 290; *H.M.C. Report, Hatfield Mss.*, XVI, 264; Jones, 'Parliamentary Boroughs', 289; B.M. Harl. 160, f. 153.

11 I am grateful to Dr J. R. Pole for discussions on this point: thus, while Rye at one stage in the 1620s was promising to give instructions to one of its members, it urged him also to come 'to view our ruins'. East Sussex R.O., Rye Corporation Mss., 47/98/8.

12 D'Ewes, *Compleat Journal*, 169; E. Sussex R.O., Rye Corporation Mss., 47/98/7; York Public Library, House Book 33, f. 282v; Kent A.O., Sa./C1, f. 13.

13 J. Scott, *Berwick-Upon-Tweed* (London, 1888), 474; Bristol A.O., 04264(2), f. 137;

Cooper, *Annals of Cambridge*, III, 137, 142; *H.M.C. Report, City of Exeter Mss.*, 41, 90, 113; Gloucester City Library Mss., no. 1451, ff. 497–8; *ibid.*, no. 1452, ff. 170v–171; Great Yarmouth Corporation Mss., C 19/5, ff. 293, 323v; *ibid.*, C 19/6, f. 460v; P.R.O., S.P. 16/450/52; Hull Guildhall Mss., Corporation Minute Book 1609–1650, 183–4; King's Lynn Corporation Mss., Assembly Book 1637–58, ff. 54v, 81v; N.N.R.O., Raynham Temp. Deposit, 253; Pearl, *London and the Puritan Revolution*, 195; *C.S.P.D. 1639–1640*, 600; N.N.R.O., Norwich Assembly Book 1585–1613, f. 330v; *ibid.*, Assembly Book 1613–1642, f. 26v; *ibid.*, Mayor's Court Book 1624–34, ff. 82v–83v; *ibid.*, Mayor's Court Book 1634–46, ff. 278, 301; Salter, *Oxford Council Acts 1583–1626*, 298; E. Sussex R.O., Rye Corporation Mss., 47/98/7, 8, 16; Kent A.O., Sa./C1, f. 30; B.M. Add. 44846, f. 6v; *V.C.H. Yorkshire: The City of York* (1961), 195.

14 Gt. Yarmouth Corporation Mss., C19/5, f. 231v; Bristol A.O., 04264(2), f. 137; Jennings, *Harrogate and Knaresborough*, 132; York Public Library, House Book 33, ff. 290v, 287v. Edward Alford seems to have drawn general conclusions about the strength of local materialism from this reticence: he warned the House in 1621 that England 'must be satisfied. Wee must not leave England miserable and looke onelie to the palatinate': quoted in Judson, *Crisis of the Constitution*, 303.

15 D'Ewes, *Compleat Journal*, 169; *H.M.C. Reports, Various*, IV, (Corporation of Orford Mss.), 276; S.R. Gardiner, ed., *Reports of Cases in the Courts of Star Chamber and High Commission* (Camden Soc., 1886), 147: I am grateful to Mr J. D. Walter for this reference.

16 N.N.R.O., Raynham Temp. Deposit, 252–4; *H.M.C. 10th Report, Appendix, Pt. II*, 92; P.R.O., S.P. 14/57/96, 14/76/53; Nottingham U.L., Cl.C.360; Sheffield City Library Mss., Str. 20, no. 241.

17 For Nottinghamshire, see above; Morrill, *Cheshire 1630–1660*, 29–30; Ruigh, *Parliament of 1624*, 57 n. 23.

18 Parsons, *Diary of Sir Henry Slingsby*, 56; *C.S.P.D. 1639–1640*, 312; *H.M.C. 9th Report, Appdx. Pt. II* (Chandos–Pole–Gell Mss.), 390.

19 Neale, *House of Commons*, 381, and *passim*.

20 Pearl, *London and the Puritan Revolution*, 195; Corporation of London R.O., Repertory 31, pt. ii, f. 290; *ibid.*, Repertory 38, f. 61; *ibid.*, Repertory 40, ff. 94v–95; City of Exeter R.O., Act Book VIII, 202, 222.

21 *H.M.C. Report, Duke of Buccleuch's Mss.*, III, 91; Cheshire R.O., Grosvenor Mss., speech of 2 Feb., 1623/4; Zagorin, *Court and Country*, 86.

22 McKisack, *Representation of Boroughs*, 130–45; R. S. Schofield, 'Parliamentary Lay Taxation 1485–1547' (Cambridge Ph.D., 1963), 463–70; F. C. Dietz, *English Public Finance, 1558–1641* (London, 1932), esp. 72, 78–80, 382–93.

23 Schofield, 'Parliamentary Lay Taxation', 463–70.

24 S. E. Lehmberg, *The Reformation Parliament 1529–1536* (Cambridge, 1970), 129–30. Similarly, in 1604 the House ordered all shire knights to take copies of the King's message waiving any subsidy, and to publish them in the country. *C.J.*, I, 247.

25 L. F. Brown, 'Ideas of Representation from Elizabeth to Charles I', *Journal of Modern History* XI (1939), 28; Richard Hooker, *Ecclesiastical Polity Book VIII*, ed. R. A. Houk (New York, 1931), 241–2; D'Ewes, *Compleat Journal*, 175, 241.

26 *Ibid.*, 484, 490, 497, 645–6.

27 *H.M.C. Report, Hatfield Mss.*, XVI, 132 (although this report was made to the Lord Treasurer of Scotland, a circumstance hardly encouraging objectivity); D. H. Willson, ed., *The Parliamentary Diary of Robert Bowyer* (Minneapolis, 1931), 46; Birch, *Court and Times of James I*, I, 60.

28 Notestein, *House of Commons 1604–1610*, 134; E. R. Foster, ed., *Proceedings in Parliament 1610* (New Haven, 1966), II, 76, 147. Ironically, the wage-conscious member was then engaged in sueing his constituency for his pay. *Ibid.*, II, 373.

29 *Ibid.*, II, 138–9, 301–2.

30 *Ibid.*, II, 75, 292, 318; *C.J.*, I, 453; *C.S.P.D. 1606–1610*, 630, 633; Notestein, *House of Commons 1604–1610*, 393–4.

31 *C.S.P.D. 1606–1610*, 630; Notestein, *House of Commons 1604–1610*, 393. Similar consultation over tax may have taken place in Norfolk a few years earlier over composition for purveyance: the county also had a long record of discussion of new rates. Hassell Smith, *County and Court*, 300–2, 335.

32 Bodl. Ms. Rawl. A 123, f. 12v; Notestein, *House of Commons 1604–1610*, 280; *H.M.C. Report, Hastings Mss.*, IV, 234. A newsletter writer reported that 'by his majesty's own method, they were first to provide for the subjects' ease, before they entered into the consideration of the king's relief'. Birch, *Court and Times of James I*, I, 315.

33 N.R.O., FH 50, f. 30v.

34 *C.D. 1621*, II, 23; *ibid.*, III, 347, 379. Sir Nathaniel Bacon had certainly told the Norfolk freeholders in 1604 that he would strive to satisfy them. N.N.R.O., Raynham Temp. Deposit, 252.

35 *C.D. 1621*, III, 334, 353; see also *ibid.*, II, 410, 413; *ibid.*, III, 362, 370; *ibid.*, V, 212.

36 The relationship between member and elector was often thought of as almost a contractual one. One correspondent told Sir Edward Dering early in 1642 that 'because I, and all my friends are engaged in our votes for your worship, I could not but intimate my heart unto yow'; and a correspondent of Sir Roger Twysden just before the Short Parliament had written that he 'doubt[ed] not but as your Contrey shewed their loves to you [at the election], so you will shew your care for them'. Hirst, 'Defection of Dering', 208; B.M. Add. 34173, f. 18.

37 Morison, *Winthrop Papers*, I, 326; B.M. Harl. 159, f. 94; Harvard Ms. Eng. 980, f. 120 (I am most grateful to Mr Conrad Russell for this reference); Sir John Eliot, *An Apology for Socrates and Negotium Posterorum*, ed. A. B. Grosart (—, 1881), II, 82.

38 T. Fuller, *Ephemeria Parliamentaria* (1654), 18; B.M. Harl. 6445, f. 32v; J. H. Hexter, *The Reign of King Pym* (New Haven, 1941), 33 n; Bodl. Ms. Rawl. A.78, f. 195v. See also Digges's fairly specific report about the complaints from the farmers of east Kent about billeting, cited in Judson, *Crisis of the Constitution*, 303; and L. Boynton, 'Billeting: The Example of the Isle of Wight', *E.H.R.* lxxiv (1959), 23–40.

39 Huntingdonshire R.O., dd. M. 36, n.f. (April 22); N.R.O., FH 50, p. 56; Nalson, *Impartial Collection*, I, 326–9; B.M. Add. 44846, f. 2v; Harvard Ms. Eng. 982, ff. 26–26v. When resentment at taxation was directed at the House, members could react angrily: the courtier Henry Killigrew was reproved at the Bar in the Long Parliament for warning that 'before wee imposed the militia uppon the people, or layd a tax on them, a knight and a burgesse should doe well to goe into the country to see if they would consent and obay'. Bruce, *Verney Papers*, 171.

40 A rare instance of express concern for the satisfaction of the electors' grievances on Rich's part occurred in the parliament of 1628–9, when he, typically, urged the expedition of action against Arminians, rather than any gut grievances. B.M. Harl. 4264, f. 224v. I am most grateful to Mr Conrad Russell for discussions on this point.

41 McCaffrey, *Exeter, 1540–1640*, 267; Supple, *Commercial Crisis and Change*, 164–78.

42 P.R.O., St. Ch. 8/255/14; *C.S.P.D. 1611-1618*, 525.
43 S. R. Gardiner, ed., *Debates in the House of Commons in 1625* (Camden Soc., 1873), 32; Bodl. Ms. Rawl. A. 346, f. 233v; Somerset R.O., DD/PH/216/12 and 228/26; *A.P.C. 1623-1625*, 458; *A.P.C. 1625-1626*, 103-4. Lord Poulett, Phelips's opponent, pointed to the strength of such sentiments when he complained that 'the common people' supported all who refused supply. Barnes, *Somerset 1625-1640*, 294.
44 J. P. Cooper, ed., *Wentworth Papers 1597-1628* (Camden Soc., 1973), 153-5; B.M. Add. 18016, ff. 134-134v.
45 McKisack, *Representation of Boroughs*, 130-1, 140-4; *H.M.C. Report, City of Exeter Mss.*, 51-2, 111. Similarly, the first significant recorded contacts during session between Boston and its members occurred over subsidies in 1604 and 1624. Boston Corporation Mss., Minute Book, vol. I, f. 413; *ibid.*, vol. II, f. 193.
46 Hull Guildhall, Corporation Letters, L, 179; York Public Library, House Book 33, ff. 286v-287v.
47 *D'Ewes* (N), 76 n; *C.S.P.D. 1639-1640*, 609; Johnson, *Fairfax Correspondence*, II, 261, 292. It was of course around this concept that many of the reapportionment proposals of the later 1640s centred. J. Cannon, *Parliamentary Reform 1640-1832* (Cambridge, 1973), 5-23.
48 B.M. Add. 36825, f. 165v; Glanville, *Reports*, 50; *H.M.C. Report, City of Exeter Mss.*, 188-9.
49 Quoted in Zagorin, *Court and Country*, 37. I am grateful to Mr Henry Procter for bringing this to my notice.

### 9. *Accountability and National Politics*

1 See above, pp. 166-7; J. E. Neale, *Elizabeth I and her Parliaments* (London 1957), II, 386; D'Ewes, *Compleat Journal*, 675; J. R. Tanner, *Constitutional Documents of the Reign of James I* (Cambridge, 1930), 266; *C.D. 1621*, v, 425.
2 Morrill, *Cheshire 1630-1660*, 39-42.
3 For instances of reports over tax and allied matters, see above, Chapter 8; for expectations of reports, see: Corporation of London R.O., Repertory 38, ff. 61-61v; Hull Corporation Mss., L 178; Gt Yarmouth Corporation Mss., C 19/6, f. 470v; York Public Library, House Book 33, f. 283; E. Sussex R.O., Rye Corporation Mss., 47/98/16; Cornwall R.O., Carew-Pole Mss., BC/24/2, Philip Hickes to Francis Buller, 3 Dec. 1640.
4 E. Sussex R.O., Rye Corporation Mss., 47/98/22. Similarly, Sir Thomas Peyton's reply to Sandwich in January 1641 was in answer to instructions he had received. B.M. Add. 44846, f. 6v.
5 Hull Corporation Mss., L 159, L 168-171; York Public Library, House Book 33, ff. 283, 286v; Gt Yarmouth Corporation Mss., C 19/6, f. 20; *H.M.C. Report, City of Exeter Mss.*, 111-14, 184-8; P. McGrath, *Merchants and Merchandise in Seventeenth-Century Bristol* (Bristol Record Soc., 1955), 144; Corporation of London R.O., Repertory 42, f. 303v; D. Gardiner, ed., *Oxinden Letters 1607-42* (London, 1933), 173. Later, Tewkesbury, for example, was very well-informed of the events of 1640-1: Tewkesbury Corporation Mss., A1/1, ff. 57v-58v.
6 N.N.R.O., Raynham Temp. Deposit, 254; *ibid.*, Bradfer-Lawrence Bacon Mss., Box VII. b. (1), folder '50 Bacon Letters', letter of Thomas Hanston *et al.*, to Sir Nathaniel Bacon, 1 March 1607/8: I am grateful to Dr Hassell Smith for directing me to this correspondence; equally, the Nottinghamshire JPs who were concerned about the clerk of the market knew just what they wanted altering in the bill then before the House. Nottingham U.L., Cl.C. 360.

7 M. A. Everett Green, ed., *The Diary of John Rous* (Camden Soc., 1856), 16–17; N.R.O., FH 50, f. 44v; Somerset R.O., DD/PH/222/53.

8 Thus, some inhabitants of Colchester wrote to Sir John Suckling as a parliament-man and as 'a good common weal's man' to give him notice of the illegal export of gunpowder from the town – but Suckling was not Colchester's member. *C.S.P.D. 1625–1626*, 275.

9 *D'Ewes* (N), 440–1.

10 Although when Sir Thomas Savile was told that an account would be required of his care of Yorkshire's interests in 1624, his contemptuous response almost provoked a duel. B.M. Add. 24470, ff. 30–30v.

11 *East Anglian*, n.s. iii (1889–90), 356 (I am grateful to Mr J. D. Walter for this reference); Wrightson, 'The Puritan Reformation of Manners', 175–6; Wallington, *Historical Notices*, I, 132; Pearl, *London and the Puritan Revolution*, 107–8, 174–5.

12 *H.M.C. 3rd Report, Appdx.*, 330; Everett Green, *Diary of John Rous*, 91–2; J. O. Halliwell, ed., *Autobiography and Correspondence of Sir Simonds D'Ewes* (London, 1845), II, 242. An extremely well-informed pamphlet testified con-temptuously to the expectations generated by the summoning of the Long Parliament: 'The Countrey people generally phansied that a Parliament would free them from paying of Tyths...All sorts of Trades and Companies in Lon-don hoped for some encrease of their Trading, if a Parliament were called... And all sorts of people dreamed of an Utopia, and infinite liberty, especially in matters of Religion'. Anon., *Persecutio Undecima* (—, 1648), 7–8.

13 Bagshaw, *Just Vindication*, 3; Hirst, 'Defection of Dering', 199; and see above, Chapter 7.

14 See above, p. 59; Northampton Corporation Mss., Assembly and Order Book 1627–1744, p. 62; Great Yarmouth Corporation Mss., C 19/5. ff. 39, 231v, 293, 323v; *ibid.*, C 19/6, f. 460v; N.N.R.O., Mayor's Court Book 1636–46, f. 278; King's Lynn Corporation Mss., Assembly Book 1637–58, f. 54v.

15 McGrath, *Merchants and Merchandise in 17th-century Bristol*, 146; Cornwall R.O., Carew-Pole Mss., BC/24/2, letter of Philip Hickes to Francis Buller, 3 Dec. 1640.

16 *C.S.P.D. 1639–1640*, 601; B.M. Add. 11045, f. 128v; Pearl, *London and the Puritan Revolution*, 113.

17 *C.S.P.D. 1640*, 164; B.M. Add. 11045, ff. 128–128v; *C.S.P.D. 1640*, 7; *The Speeches of the Lord Digby...Concerning Grievances and the Triennial Parlia-ment* (1641), 2–3; for the Northamptonshire election, see above, p. 151. It was probably this same Northamptonshire petition's demands which Sir Gilbert Pickering defended to another local gentleman: 'there are some things com-playned of as the greivances of this county others as nationall greivances, whearin this county hath her share as well as others and thearfore it is added'. There was a clear distinction between local and national wrongs – but national wrongs were now a valid area of concern. Bedfordshire R.O., J. 1402.

18 Thus, Edward Seymour rose in November clutching 'This petition of Rig[ht] from the Freeholders of the County of Devon, which doth not only speak the general greeveances of this Kingdome but allso those particular ones under which the westerne partes doe suffer'. Cornwall R.O., BO/25/29, p. 182; see also *C.J.*, II, 6; Savile is quoted in Cliffe, *Yorkshire Gentry*, 317.

19 *Speeches of the Lord Digby . . . Concerning Grievances*, 2–3; *Speeches and Pas-sages of this Great and Happy Parliament* (1641), 342.

20 Hirst, 'Defection of Dering', *passim*; see also *C.S.P.D. 1641–1643*, 314 (I am grateful to Mr M. J. Mendle for this reference). Sir Roger Twysden, sitting for the same county in April, had also been given advice how to act in parliament,

'to sweeten all things . . . and not provoke his Majestie'. B.M. Add. 34173, ff. 18–18v.

21 Hirst, 'Defection of Dering', 207. A semi-official attack on the Militia Ordinance took the same line, that the country determined the purpose for which members were elected. A precedent for this position was to hand in James I's angry prorogation speech of 1604. *A Vindication of the King, with Some Observations upon the Two Houses* (1642), 7–8; Gardiner, *History of England*, I, 190–1.

22 Bagshaw, *Just Vindication*, 3; Johnson, *Fairfax Correspondence*, II, 104–7, 202–5, 207, 226–7, 289–90, 293–4, 375–7, 381–2,; *H.M.C. 14th Report, Appdx. II, Duke of Portland's Mss., vol. III*, 76, 79–80; Pearl, *London and the Puritan Revolution*, 210–36.

23 Shropshire R.O., 212/364, ff. 1–4 (my italics); the Nottinghamshire gentry are quoted in Hirst, 'Defection of Dering', 194. The questions of the binding nature of representation, of delegation and its withdrawal, are treated extensively by Prof. E. Sirluck, in D. Wolfe, ed., *The Complete Prose Works of John Milton* (New Haven, 1953 —), II, 1–51, but the debate is more wide-ranging than Prof. Sirluck indicated. Its prevalence in polemic in these years is testimony to the extent to which people were familiarised with representation and its implications. One tract argued very perceptively that such an emphasis on instructions and delegation would necessitate virtual referenda on every issue before the House. Anon., *Plain Fault in Plain-English. And the same in Dr. Fearne (1642)*, 6.

24 See, for example, Hirst, 'Defection of Dering', 194; *The Third Speech of the Lord George Digby* (1641), 10–11.

25 Hirst, 'Defection of Dering', 201–2; Shropshire R.O., 212/364, letters of Edward Martin to the Earl of Bridgewater, May 17 and Nov. 22, 1641; *H.M.C. 14th Report, Appdx. II, Duke of Portland's Mss. III*, 76; Wilks, *Barons of the Cinque Ports*, 81–2. It must be stressed that Dering's speeches were not just heard of, but *seen*, in Kent. Kent A.O., U350/C2/86.

26 B.M. Harl. 477, f. 28; Cooper, *Annals of Cambridge*, III, 311; B.M. Harl. 160, f. 153 (a local minister asked D'Ewes to write again about it); John Geree, *Iudahs Ioy at the Oath* (1641), sig. A2 (epistle dedicatory); Staffordshire R.O., D 868/2/30.

27 Geree, *Iudahs Ioy, passim*, and esp. sig. D; although he continued that in view of the country's relationship to the House of Commons, 'our entring into this Protestation, will not be much more than what already we are by consequent ingaged unto, save only for a more formall and actuall expression of that in our owne persons, which we have already vertually done in the persons of others'. *Ibid.*, sig. D3.

28 Hirst, 'Defection of Dering', 205.

29 *D'Ewes* (C), 294. Haslerig used the identical argument to justify the early proceedings against Laud. B.M. Add. 33468, f. 35v.

30 Bruce, *Verney Papers*, 123, 125.

31 Johnson, *Fairfax Correspondence*, II, 289–90.

32 Rushworth, *Historical Collections*, IV, 425–8.

33 *C.S.P.D. 1640*, 34; see the forthcoming exposition of John Denham's poem *Cooper's Hill* by Prof. J. M. Wallace: I am most grateful to Prof. Wallace for allowing me to see a draft of his work.

34 *C.S.P.D. 1640*, 7. Miss Judson's conclusion that nobody until the Levellers was concerned with making parliament truly responsible to the country seems mistaken. Judson, *Crisis of the Constitution*, 305.

35 *C.D. 1621*, III, 379.

36 However, the dictates of national emergency and divine inspiration in the ensuing struggles to some extent reversed this trend.

## 10. Conclusion

1 Keeler, *Long Parliament*, 22.
2 Bodl. Ms. Rawl. D.918, f. 35.
3 As in, for example, Cromwell's soubriquet, 'Lord of the Fens'; and see D. G. C. Allan, 'The Rising in the West, 1628–1631', *Economic History Review* v (1952), 82–3; E. Kerridge, 'The Revolts in Wiltshire against Charles I', *Wiltshire Archaeological and Natural History Magazine* lvii (1958), 65–72.
4 Cannon, *Parliamentary Reform*, 24–7.
5 *C.J.*, VIII, 292; D. Ogg, *England in the Reign of Charles II* (Oxford, 1955), II, 473.
6 Plumb, 'Growth of the Electorate', 109–10.
7 Underdown, *Somerset in the Civil War*, 31–48.
8 Christopher Hill, 'County Matters', *New Statesman* vol. 88, no. 2263 (2nd August, 1974), p. 159.

## Appendix I. Constituencies experiencing Franchise Disputes

1 Willis Bund, *Diary of Henry Townshend*, I, 6; Keeler, *Long Parliament*, 73.
2 *C.J.*, I, 407.
3 Latimer, *Annals of Bristol*, 93, 148, 250–1; Prynne, *Brevia Parliamentaria*, 367; P.R.O., C219/43, pt. I.
4 Cooper, *Annals of Cambridge*, III, 61; Williams, *Court and Times of Charles I*, I, 6.
5 The tenants, as opposed to the owners, had been urged by the bailiffs to pay heed to the borough's affairs earlier in the century, so their inclusion in the franchise may have been an almost natural development. Weeks, *Clitheroe*, 5–6, 223, 226–30.
6 Gloucester City Library Mss., no. 1451, ff. 497–498v; the matter was clarified in the city's charter of 1627: Taffs, 'Borough Franchise', Appdx., 114.
7 *C.J.*, II, 14–15.
8 *H.M.C. 11th Report, Appdx. III* (Corporation of King's Lynn Mss.), 179, 182–5.
9 *C.J.*, II, 36.
10 C.U.L. Mss., Dd. 12. 20, 21, ff. 23v–20v (reverse foliation).
11 *C.J.*, I, 624.
12 Keeler, *Long Parliament*, 58.
13 Taffs, 'Borough Franchise', Appdx., 274–5.
14 Keeler, *Long Parliament*, 34.
15 Sinclair, *History of Wigan*, I, 222–3; *ibid.*, II, 10–11.
16 York Public Library, House Book 36, f. 53.

## Appendix II. Case Studies of Disputes

1 W. B. Stephens, 'The Overseas Trade of Chester in the early seventeenth century', *Transactions of the Historic Society of Lancashire and Cheshire* cxx (1968), 24–34; D. M. Woodward, 'The Overseas Trade of Chester, 1600–1650', *ibid.* cxxii (1970), 40–2; D. M. Woodward, 'The Chester Leather Industry 1558–1625', *ibid.* cxix (1967), 66–7, 100. A chronicle complained that 'foreigners' trading had 'brought a greate confusion in the comon wealth of this Cittye'. Chester Public Library Mss., 94.3, ff. 21v, 36v.
2 *Ibid.*, ff. 30v, 33–33v, 34v, 35v–36, P.R.O., St.Ch.8/297/15; *ibid.*, S.P.16/98/111.
3 Chester Public Library Mss., 94.3, f. 33 v; Gruenfelder, 'Parliamentary Election

at Chester, 1621', 40–2; B.M. Harl. 2105, ff. 277–277v. The reference to hired labourers could mean that journeymen and labourers were unable to become freemen (although this was not the case in, for example, Bedford or Hertford); or alternatively it could mean merely that suburban workers were no freemen.

4 P.R.O., St.Ch. 8/21/6; Chester Public Library Mss., 94.3, f. 23v; B.M. Harl. 2105, ff. 277–277v; Gruenfelder, 'Election at Chester', 42.

5 *C.S.P.D. 1627–1628*, 94, 117, 420; *C.S.P.D. 1625–1649*, 201; P.R.O., St.Ch. 8/297/15; *A.P.C. 1627–1628*, 164–5; B.M. Harl. 2125, ff. 59–59v; *C.S.P.D. 1639–1640*, 564, 590.

6 *V.C.H. Wiltshire*, v, 121; Rathbone, *Wiltshire Borough Records*, 5; Goldney, *Records of Chippenham*, 25–56; Wiltshire R.O., 473/399.

7 Goldney, *Records of Chippenham*, 35–6; Glanville, *Reports*, 50.

8 G. D. Ramsay, *The Wiltshire Woollen Industry in the Sixteenth and Seventeenth Centuries* (London, 1943), 76–9; Kerridge, 'Revolts in Wiltshire', 66.

9 Wiltshire R.O., Charles Hayward's Parliamentary Note Book, 192; Glanville, *Reports*, 52–3. I am very grateful to Mr Conrad Russell for the information about the almshouses and about the extent of Pym's involvement in the enclosure, and for discussions on the Chippenham situation; for further evidence of Popham as benefactor, see Goldney, *Records of Chippenham*, 18, 58.

10 Supple, *Commercial Crisis and Change*, 12, and *passim*.

11 Colchester Corporation Archives, Assembly Book 1600–20, entries for 18 Dec. 1612 and 8 Dec. 1615.

12 *Ibid.*, 5 Oct. and 15 Nov. 1615; Essex R.O., Morant Mss., vol. 46, p. 241, and vol. 48, p. 191. The corporation blamed Sir John Sammes, a neighbouring landowner and active JP, who had sat for Maldon in James's first parliament, but appears to have been edged out by the growing influence of the Mildmay and Herrys families, and was now transferring his attentions to Colchester.

13 *Ibid.*, vol. 46, pp. 23–4.

14 *Ibid.*, vol. 46, pp. 19, 271, 277, and vol. 43, p. 23. Buckingham's co-operation with the Barrington connection in this election indicates that his rupture with the 'opposition' after 1624 was not total.

15 *Ibid.*, vol. 44, p. 93, vol. 46, pp. 245 and 285, and vol. 47, pp. 3, 259 and 312; *C.S.P.D. 1627–1628*, 140.

16 Quintrell, 'The Government of the County of Essex 1603–42', 32 ff; Essex R.O., Morant Mss., vol. 46, p. 243.

17 *Ibid.*, vol. 43, pp. 119, 139, 183, vol. 47, pp. 19, 27; Colchester Corporation Archives, Assembly Book 1620–46, f. 71v; H. Smith, *The Ecclesiastical History of Essex* (Colchester, 1932), 24. Richard Ward, the minister appointed, was probably a St Antholin's and St Benet's, Gracechurch St, lecturer in the 1630s: P. S. Seaver, *The Puritan Lectureships* (Stanford, 1970), 252.

18 Essex R.O., Morant Mss., vol. 47, p. 233; Colchester Assembly Book 1620–46, ff. 62v, 68v, 73, 81.

19 Essex R.O., Morant Mss., vol. 43, p. 23.

20 P.R.O., St.Ch. 8/291/1; *C.S.P.D. 1619–1623*, 246; *C.S.P.D. 1625–1626*, 18; B.M. Eg. 2584, ff 305–305v, 307–307v

21 Dover Public Library, Corporation Mss., Acts and Decrees of the Reigns of James I and Charles I, ff. 115v–116; *ibid.*, Records of the Reigns of James I and Charles I (reverse foliation), f. 192v.

22 N.R.O., FH 50, f. 40; *C.S.P.D. 1623–1625*, 198.

23 Corporation Mss., Acts and Decrees, f. 116; for the character of the incumbent, see R. Griffin, 'Monumental Brasses in East Kent', *Archaeologia Cantiana* xxxii (1917), 33–4; *C.S.P.D. 1623–1625*, 192: Younge complained of the likelihood that

the House would accept the petition, for 'the House is violent for free elections', but this is hardly surprising, given that Younge wanted 'more time to falsify the witnesses to the petition'.

24 *Ibid.*, 200.

25 *Ibid.*, 279, 304, 333.

26 There are dozens of references to the dispute in *C.S.P.D. 1619–1623*, and *C.S.P.D. 1623–1625*.

27 *C.S.P.D. 1623–1625*, 198; *C.S.P.D. 1619–1623*, 581; Everitt, *Community of Kent*, 65–6.

28 Corporation Mss., Acts and Decrees, ff. 116v, 117v; *C.S.P.D. 1623–1625*, 245.

29 Corporation Mss., Acts and Decrees, f. 129; Jones, 'Parliamentary Boroughs of Kent', 29–30, 59–60.

30 This was, as at Bristol or Wigan, a less extensive group than those merely with the freedom to exercise their trade by doing piecework: it has been estimated that under Elizabeth only about one-third of those with guild freedom took out freedom of the city. J. Youings, *Tuckers Hall Exeter* (Exeter, 1968), 41–2.

31 MacCaffrey, *Exeter*, 222–4, 236–40; B.M. Harl. 2313, f. iv; see also Plumb, 'Growth of the Electorate', 102.

32 MacCaffrey, *Exeter*, 241; Youings, *Tuckers Hall*, 49–50; Stephens, *Seventeenth-Century Exeter*, 8–9, 17–21.

33 *Ibid.*, 13–16; MacCaffrey, *Exeter*, 242–3; *H.M.C. Report, City of Exeter Mss.*, 180–4; Nicolls, *Jurdain*, 14–16.

34 *Ibid.*, 13; P.R.O., St.Ch. 8/161/10; Williams, *Court and Times of Charles I*, 1, 276.

35 Stephens, *Seventeenth-Century Exeter*, 13–15; *A.P.C. 1625–1626*, 217–18, 312–15; Nicolls, *Jurdain*, 14–15; *C.S.P.D. 1627–1628*, 388; City of Exeter R.O., Act Book VII, 693, 710–11.

36 Pape, *Newcastle-under-Lyme*, 34, 67–8, 71, 213–15, 228–9, 233–4, 257.

37 *Ibid.*, 118, 141, 255, 261; P.R.O., St.Ch. 8/79/5, St.Ch. 8/121/12; for Warwick, see below.

38 Pape, *Newcastle-under-Lyme*, 132–3, 156–8.

39 Salter, *Oxford Council Acts 1583–1626*, xi, xxxi–xxxii, xlvi; Hobson and Salter, *Oxford Council Acts 1626–1665*, xi. The city's Recorder, Thomas Wentworth, as well as being the main defender of the freemen, was the leading opponent of the University, and was discommoned as a result.

40 Salter, *Oxford Council Acts 1583–1626*, xvi–xvii, 276–7. The bid to exclude the freemen was explicitly resolved against.

41 *Ibid.*, 284, 294–5. The University was clearly opposed to the charter, although on what grounds is unclear. *Ibid.*, 278, 290.

42 *Ibid.*, 297; *C.D. 1621*, v, 444.

43 Salter, *Oxford Council Acts 1583–1626*, 294, 299. The orders were directed against non-scot-and-lot men, but only freemen of the city were liable to scot and lot. *Ibid.*, ix.

44 *Ibid.*, 306.

45 Salisbury Corporation Archives, Mayor's Official Correspondence, letter to William, Earl of Pembroke, 16 Jan. 1625–6. This crisis coincided with a possible attempt by the aldermen to curb the role of the common council: Corporation Archives, Ledger Book C (1571–1640), f. 299.

46 Slack, 'Poverty and Politics in Salisbury', 164–203.

47 *Ibid.*, esp. 184–5, 191; Corporation Archives, Ledger Book C, ff. 410, 411.

48 See Slack, 'Election to the Short Parliament', 108, 114, for the city's spring election, and for some details of that in October; also, *D'Ewes* (N), 98–9, 545–6; Hoare, *History of Modern Wiltshire*, vi, 377–82, 391; B.M. Harl. 541, f. 91v.

49 *Ibid.*, f. 91v; Slack, 'Poverty and Politics in Salisbury', 191; Slack, 'Election to the Short Parliament', 110.

50 Chalklin, *Seventeenth Century Kent*, 30, 115, 124, 169–70; Jones, 'Parliamentary Boroughs of Kent', 11.

51 B.M. Add. 33512, f. 19; Gardiner, *Historic Haven*, 157–9; *A.P.C. 1595–1596*, 97–8; *H.M.C. Report, Hatfield Mss.*, xv, 307–8.

52 *Ibid.*, 308; Gardiner, *Historic Haven*, 227, 233–4; B.M. Eg. 2584, ff. 279–279v; *C.S.P.D. 1619–1623*, 212–13, 288, 602; Kent A.O., Sa./Ac.7 (Sandwich Year Book 1608–42), f. 85v.

53 *C.D. 1621*, vii, 568–9.

54 *Ibid.*, vii, 567–9; *C.S.P.D. 1619–1623*, 212–13; Gardiner, *Historic Haven*, 222–3; B.M. Add. 34121, f. 106v.

55 *C.D. 1621*, vii, 569. The religious unrest possibly owed something to the presence of the many religious refugees in the port.

56 N.R.O., FH 50, f. 57; B.M. Add. 33512, ff. 18, 20–21v; Gardiner, *Historic Haven*, 160; *H.M.C. 5th Report, Appendix* (Corporation of Sandwich Mss.), 569.

57 They were Sir John Manwood, Lieutenant of Dover Castle; Nathaniel Finch, recommended by the Lord Keeper, and a neighbour; Edward Nicholas, recommended by the Lord Admiral; and Sir Thomas Palmer, Sir Thomas Peyton, and Edward Partridge. There was possibly initially a seventh, a Mr Cullen, apparently a puritan local gentleman, like Partridge. Kent A.O., Sa./Ac.7, f. 365v; *C.S.P.D. 1639–1640*, 561.

58 *Ibid.*, 561–2; M. V. Jones, 'Election Issues and the Borough Electorates in mid-seventeenth-century Kent', *Archaeologia Cantiana* lxxxv (1970), 21.

59 B.M. Add. 44846, ff. 2–2v. Where there was friction in a borough, a delicate path had to be trodden by the candidate: Peyton endorsed his copy of a letter to the magistrates, 'This superscription had an error that it was nott directed likewise to the Commons'. *Ibid.*, f. 2.

60 Kent A.O., Sa./Ac.7, ff. 366–366v, 368; B.M. Add. 33512, ff. 40–42.

61 Gardiner, *Historic Haven*, 280; Jones, 'Parliamentary Boroughs of Kent', 58.

62 Kent A.O., Sa./C.1, ff. 60–1; *ibid.*, Sa./Ac.7, f. 380; Gardiner, *Historic Haven*, 275.

63 *V.C.H. Gloucestershire*, viii, 142; *C.S.P.D. 1591–1594*, 420; the freemen lists show a decline in the numbers admitted in the clothing trades, with some increase in the supply and leather trades: Tewkesbury Corporation Mss., A1/2 (Book of Ordinances), ff. 27–99v, 101–2.

64 *Ibid.*, A1/1 (Minute Book and Accounts), f. 10v (reverse foliation); Gloucestershire R.O., D. 2688, n.f., entries for 1636 and 1638; *V.C.H. Gloucestershire*, viii, 148–9; Corporation Mss., A1/2, ff. 17–20.

65 The return was made 'with the whole assent and consent of the rest of the burgesses and communaltie': Corporation Mss., A1/1, f. 11; Gloucestershire R.O., D.760/36.

66 Keeler, *Long Parliament*, 47–8; Inner Temple Mss., 511/23, f. 1; *V.C.H. Gloucestershire*, viii, 132, 134, 136; *C.S.P.D. 1639–1640*, 581–2.

67 Neale, *House of Commons*, 251–2; Plumb, 'Growth of the Electorate', 94.

68 Neale, *House of Commons*, 250–1; T. Kemp, ed., *The Black Book of Warwick* (Warwick, 1898), 56–61, 104–17.

69 *Ibid.*, 227–343, 351–2, 358–9.

70 Neale, *House of Commons*, 252; Kemp, *Black Book*, 371–8, 385, 391, 393.

71 Neale, *House of Commons*, 252; Kemp, *Black Book*, 382, 397.

72 Neale, *House of Commons*, 251–2; Kemp, *Black Book*, 371.

73 Warwickshire R.O., Warwick Borough Mss., W.21/6 (Minute Book 1610–62), pp. 45, 52–7, 59, 259–65. The attack on the corporation was probably justified, for

its defence was based on a mere technicality: the opposition case was that the land was granted to the town and the burgesses thereof, but the corporation argued that this was a mere formula, and that it was really granted to the named burgesses of the first incorporation and their successors, that is, themselves. *Ibid.*, p. 260.

74 P.R.O., St.Ch. 8/282/29–30; Warwick Borough Mss., W.21/6, p. 62.
75 *Ibid.*, pp. 259, 262, 264–9, 271.
76 Kemp, *Black Book*, 409–11; N.R.O., FH 50, f. 4v.
77 Warwick Borough Mss., W.21/6, pp. 269–70; *V.C.H. Warwickshire*, VIII, 497.
78 Warwick Borough Mss., W.21/6, pp. 87, 93–4, 270.
79 *Ibid.*, pp. 127–34, 229, 275–7, 279.

### Appendix III. The Borough Franchises in 1641

1 Carroll, 'Yorkshire Parliamentary Boroughs', 80–1.
2 The 1628 indenture was made by the freeholders. P.R.O., C.219/41B, no. 64.
3 Taffs argued for Bodmin that it was a corporation borough, but Bramston's account of the Long Parliament election could be taken as suggesting that more than just the 'select number' voted. Taffs, 'Borough Franchise', Appdx., 37; Braybrooke, *Autobiography of Sir John Bramston*, 160.
4 Carroll, 'Yorkshire Parliamentary Boroughs', 96.
5 The fact that inmates voted in the Long Parliament election indicates that the franchise was probably an inhabitant one. Bruce, *Verney Papers*, 4.
6 A. E. W. Marsh, *History of the Borough and Town of Calne* (Calne, n.d.), 38.
7 Ipswich and East Suffolk R.O., EE6:1144/12 (Dunwich Borough Minute Book 1627–53), ff. 115v, 118v.
8 Carroll, 'Yorkshire Parliamentary Boroughs', 92.
9 E. King, *Old Times Revisited in the Borough and Parish of Lymington* (London, 1879), 181.
10 There had been many conflicting indentures in 1628, but that for the Short Parliament was made by '*Liberi Tenentes et Inhabitantes*'. P.R.O., C.219/42, pt. 1.
11 But as we have seen, soldiers came back from the siege of Newark for the Recruiter election, so the franchise was clearly open by then.
12 The Long Parliament indenture had over 30 signatures and marks to it, so it was unlikely, in a borough of this size, to have been a corporation franchise. P.R.O., C.219/43 pt. 1.
13 B.M. Add. 18597, f. 91. 24 of the c. 120 burgesses were said to have been absent from the 1624 election.
14 The corporation '*elegerunt et nominaverunt*' according to the Long Parliament indenture. P.R.O., C.219/43, pt. 1.
15 Pitt spoke of 'the Burgesses together with the Inhabitants' making choice of him in 1624. B.M. Add. 29974, f. 72.

### Appendix IV. Contested Elections

No identification is given for contests to which reference has already been made in the text.

1 Slack, 'Election to the Short Parliament', 108–14.
2 I am grateful to Mr Conrad Russell for the information that there was probably a contest for the Short Parliament; for the Long Parliament, see Keeler, *Long Parliament*, 33.

3 Bedford Corporation Archives, Box 8, no. 5, pp. 53–4 (1628).

4 Ruigh, *Parliament of 1624*, 116 (1624); Thomas, 'Parliamentary Elections 1625–1628', Appdx. II (1626, 1628).

5 R. R. Tighe and J. E. Davies, *Annals of Windsor* (London, 1858), II, 144–5 (Short Parliament); P.R.O., C.219/43 pt. I (the mayor, etc., were not parties to the 1641 by-election indenture).

6 Bodl. Ms. Bankes 44/13 (Short Parliament); *C.J.*, II, 47 (Long Parliament).

7 *Ibid.*, II, 17.

8 *Ibid.*, II, 14.

9 *Ibid.*, I, 677 (1624).

10 J. Crossley, ed., *The Diary and Correspondence of Dr John Worthington* (Chetham Soc., 1847), I, 7 (Short Parliament).

11 Morrill, *Cheshire 1630–1660*, 34 (Long Parliament).

12 *C.S.P.D. 1639–1640*, 590, reveals another instance of contention occurring when no contest took place: it was reported for the Short Parliament that 'There was no opposition as it fell out, but it was well stickled'.

13 C.U.L. Mss., Dd. 12.20, 21, f. 80v (1626); Nalson, *Impartial Collection*, I, 293 (Short Parliament).

14 Wiltshire R.O., Charles Hayward's Parliamentary Note Book, p. 145.

15 Thomas, 'Parliamentary elections 1625–1628', Appdx. II.

16 *Ibid.*

17 *C.S.P.D. 1623–1625*, 152.

18 Thomas, 'Parliamentary Elections 1625–1628', Appdx. II.

19 Nalson, *Impartial Collection*, I, 294.

20 Wiltshire R.O., Charles Hayward's Parliamentary Note Book, p. 302.

21 B.M. Add. 14827, f. 147.

22 Keeler, *Long Parliament*, 41.

23 P.R.O., C.219/42 pt. I, no. 85 (Short Parliament).

24 Harvard Ms. Eng. 982, f. 31 (Short Parliament).

25 Keeler, *Long Parliament*, 41.

26 B.M. Add. 36827, f. 22 (Short Parliament); Keeler, *Long Parliament*, 43 (Long Parliament).

27 Wiltshire R.O., Charles Hayward's Parliamentary Note Book, p. 145 (1624); C.U.L. Mss., Dd. 11.73 (reverse foliation), ff. 149–151 (1626).

28 Nalson, *Impartial Collection*, I, 295.

29 B.M. Add. 29974, ff. 72, 74, 76.

30 *C.S.P.D. 1603–1610*, 87 (1604); B.M. Add. 29974, f. 319 (Short and Long Parliaments).

31 C.U.L. Mss., Dd. 12.20, 21, f. 61.

32 Bohannon, 'Essex Election of 1604', 395–413 (1604); Wiltshire R.O., Charles Hayward's Parliamentary Note Book, p. 145 (1624); Essex R.O., D/B3/1/19, f. 197 (1625).

33 Wiltshire R.O., Charles Hayward's Parliamentary Note Book, p. 145.

34 Thomas, 'Parliamentary Elections 1625–1628', Appdx. II (1625); Essex R.O., D/B3/1/19, f. 207 (1626). Maldon had narrowly avoided a contest in the by-election of 1605: after all the canvassing had been done, one of the candidates was persuaded to withdraw by Salisbury's intervention. *H.M.C. Report, Hatfield Mss.*, xvii, 455.

35 B.M. Add. 18597, ff. 124v–125; Gloucester City Library Mss., Gloucestershire Collections, 16526(40).

36 C.U.L. Mss., Dd. 12.20, 21, f. 8 (1626).

37 Keeler, *Long Parliament*, 47 (Short and Long Parliaments).

38 P.R.O., St.Ch. 8/293/11.
39 Wiltshire R.O., Charles Hayward's Parliamentary Note Book, p. 194 (1624); Keeler, *Long Parliament*, 49 (1641 by-election).
40 *Ibid.*
41 Thomas, 'Parliamentary Elections 1625-1628', Appdx. II.
42 N.R.O., FH 50, f. 14.
43 B.M. Add. 18597, ff. 124-124v.
44 Hampshire R.O., Jervoise Mss., 44M69/012, letter of Anthony Knott to Sir Richard Paulett, 1 March, 1613/14.
45 Nalson, *Impartial Collection*, 1, 290.
46 Keeler, *Long Parliament*, 51.
47 B.M. Cotton Julius C.III, f. 115 (1614); P.R.O., St.Ch. 8/47/7 (1621); the existence of the long poll list for Godmanchester indicates that there was in all probability a contest in 1625; Bodl. Ms. Tanner 65, f. 164 (Long Parliament).
48 Birch, *Court and Times of James I*, 1, 236, 302 (1614); Bodl. Ms. Rawl. A346, ff. 224-234 (1626).
49 *C.S.P.D. 1623-1625*, 155 (1624); Thomas, 'Parliamentary Elections 1625-1628', Appdx. II (1626).
50 McClure, *Letters of John Chamberlain*, II, 617 (1625); Keeler, *Long Parliament*, 52-3 (Long Parliament).
51 C. E. Woodruff, 'Notes on the Municipal Records of Queenborough', *Archaeologia Cantiana* xxii (1897), 183.
52 Guildford Museum and Muniment Room, LM 1331/28.
53 Weeks, *Clitheroe*, 225.
54 *C.J.*, 1, 511, 513 (1621); C.U.L. Mss., Dd. 12.20, 21, f. 87 (1626); *C.J.*, II, 21, and *D'Ewes* (N), 95 n.8 (Long Parliament).
55 Keeler, *Long Parliament*, 54.
56 McClure, *Letters of John Chamberlain*, 1, 518.
57 Boston Corporation Minute Book, vol. II, ff. 188v, 199v.
58 The evidence submitted to the Committee of Privileges in the Recruiter election dispute makes it plain that there had been more than one contest recently; one of these was for the Short Parliament, but the space in the borough's Court Book where the account of the Long Parliament election should have been is left blank, making it appear likely that another contest occurred then. B.M. Loan 29/50, no. 76A; Grimsby Central Library, Borough Court Book VIII, ff. 85v-86: I am most grateful to Mr A. A. Garner for this reference. The 1621 return was questioned in the House. *C.J.*, 1, 513.
59 Birch, *Court and Times of James I*, 1, 235 (1614); Thomas, 'Parliamentary Elections 1625-1628', 18, and *H.M.C. Report, Duke of Buccleuch's Mss. at Montagu House*, 1, 256 (1621); McClure, *Letters of John Chamberlain*, II, 543 (1624); Williams, *Court and Times of Charles I*, 1, 18 (1625).
60 Birch, *Court and Times of James I*, 1, 302, and Somerset R.O., DD/PH/216/82 (1614); Johnson, *Fairfax Correspondence*, 1, 89 (1628).
61 *C.J.*, 1, 800 (1625); Williams, *Court and Times of Charles I*, 1, 327 (1628); *H.M.C. Report, De L'Isle and Dudley Mss.*, VI, 236 (Short Parliament).
62 *C.J.*, 1, 806.
63 Keeler, *Long Parliament*, 56.
64 *C.J.*, 1, 468 (1614); N.N.R.O., Walsingham Mss., xvii/2, letters of Philip Calthorpe and Sir Anthony Drury, ?Nov. 1620 and [—, 1621], (1621); Thomas, 'Parliamentary Elections 1625-1628', Appdx. II (1625).
65 B.M. Add. 27395, ff. 196-8.

66 Great Yarmouth Corporation Mss., C18/6, f. 203 (1621); Thomas, 'Parliamentary Elections 1625–1628', Appdx. II (1625, 1626).

67 *H.M.C. Report, Duke of Buccleuch's Mss.*, III, 74–5, 77–8 (1604); Thomas, 'Parliamentary Elections 1625–1628', Appdx. II (1626).

68 There was clearly some difficulty over the Long Parliament election, although probably no contest. Groome, 'Higham Ferrers Elections', 250; N.R.O., FH 3469.

69 *C.J.*, I, 457–8; P.R.O., S.P. 14/76/52.

70 Keeler, *Long Parliament*, 58.

71 *C.J.*, I, 513.

72 Nottinghamshire U.L., Cl. C. 237, 294, 296, 344, 429.

73 Thomas, 'Parliamentary Elections 1625–1628', Appdx. II.

74 McClure, *Letters of John Chamberlain*, II, 543.

75 P.R.O., S.P. 14/177/7 (1624); Rex, *University Representation*, 115 (1628); Keeler, *Long Parliament*, 60.

76 *Ibid.*

77 T. T. Lewis, ed., *Letters of the Lady Brilliana Harley* (Camden Soc., 1854), 86.

78 Thomas, 'Parliamentary Elections 1625–1628', Appdx. II.

79 Penry Williams, 'Government and Politics in Ludlow 1590–1642', *Transactions of the Shropshire Archaeological Society* lvi (1957–60), 290. When dealing with claims arising from the will of one of its members throughout the 1620s (Richard Tomlyns), the corporation averred that they had resisted the advances of several 'persons of honour' in order to elect him, suggesting that some form of contest had taken place, and this hypothesis is supported by Tomlyns's willingness to bribe. Weyman, 'Members of Parliament for Ludlow', 24, and see above, p. 119.

80 *C.J.*, I, 201.

81 Keeler, *Long Parliament*, 62.

82 Bristol A.O., AC/C58/8.

83 Keeler, *Long Parliament*, 62.

84 P.R.O., C.219/42 pt. 2, nos. 7 and 8.

85 Thomas, 'Parliamentary Elections 1625–1628', Appdx. II.

86 B.M. Add. 18597, f. 91.

87 Birch, *Court and Times of James I*, II, 232 (1621). Suffolk was another constituency which experienced extensive disruption in years when there was possibly no contest (it is not clear whether there was any contest in the later 1620s or in the spring of 1640): Morison, *Winthrop Papers*, I, 324–6 (1626); B.M. Eg. 2644, f. 264v (1628: I am grateful to Mr Arthur Searle for this reference); B.M. Harl. 378, f. 29v (1628 by-election); Holmes, 'Eastern Association', 43–4 (Short Parliament, when there was a concerted attempt to prevent the election of Barnardiston and Parker, which possibly failed to come to a head when Sir William Playters apparently did not come forward to oppose them).

88 *H.M.C. Report, Various*, IV (Aldeburgh Corporation Mss.), 304.

89 B.M. Eg. 2715, f. 422 (1628); Ipswich and East Suffolk R.O., EE 6: 1144/12 Dunwich Borough Minute Book 1627–53), ff. 118–119.

90 Keeler, *Long Parliament*, 64.

91 Thomas, 'Parliamentary Elections 1625–1628', Appdx. II.

92 Keeler, *Long Parliament*, 65.

93 B.M. Add. 36827, ff. 21–21v (Short Parliament); Keeler, *Long Parliament*, 65–6 (Long Parliament).

94 *C.J.*, I, 724 (1624); B.M. Add. 11045, f. 101v (Short Parliament).

95 *C.J.*, I, 748 (1624); Keeler, *Long Parliament*, 66–7.

96 *H.M.C. 4th Report, Appdx.* (House of Lords Mss.), 25 (Short Parliament); Keeler, *Long Parliament*, 67.

97 *A.P.C. 1626*, 256.

98 Keeler, *Long Parliament*, 67.

99 *Ibid.*

100 H. A. Merewether and A. J. Stephens, *The History of Boroughs and Municipal Corporations* (London, 1835), III, 1513–14 (1621; and Arundel's nominees for 1624 also failed); Keeler, *Long Parliament*, 68.

101 *Ibid.*

102 Ruigh, *Parliament of 1624*, 93 n.4 (1621); Coventry City Mss., Minute Book 1554–1640, f. 268, and B. Poole, *Coventry: its History and Antiquities* (London, 1870), 387 (1624); Keeler, *Long Parliament*, 68–9.

103 N.R.O., FH 50, f. 4v (1624).

104 Goldney, *Records of Chippenham*, 59 (Short Parliament); Keeler, *Long Parliament*, 70.

105 *C.J.*, I, 580.

106 *Ibid.*, I, 834.

107 Thomas, 'Parliamentary Elections 1625–1628', Appdx. II.

108 B.M. Eg. 2651, f. 26v (1621); *C.J.*, II, 134 (1641 by-election).

109 Stone, 'Electoral Influence of the second Earl of Salisbury', 394–8 (on the 1620s generally).

110 P.R.O., St.Ch. 8/201/17 (1604); Wiltshire R.O., Charles Hayward's Parliamentary Note Book, p. 302 (1624).

111 P. Styles, 'The Corporation of Bewdley under the later Stuarts', *University of Birmingham Historical Journal* i (1947), 103 (Short and Long Parliaments).

112 Keeler, *Long Parliament*, 73.

113 *C.J.*, I, 468 (1614); Sheffield City Library Mss., Str. 12, no. 53 (1628–9 by-election).

114 J. J. Cartwright, *Chapters in the History of Yorkshire* (Wakefield, 1872), 202.

115 Keeler, *Long Parliament*, 74 (Short and Long Parliaments).

116 C.U.L. Mss., Dd. 12.20, 21, f. 8.

117 Hull Guildhall Mss., Corporation Minute Book 1555–1609, f. 357v (1604); *ibid.*, Minute Book 1609–1650, ff. 122, 123 (1624).

118 Yorkshire Archaeological Society Mss., DD56/M2, 1600–1620/1, letters of Sir Henry Slingsby to Lord President, Oct. 21, 1603 (1604); *ibid.*, DD56/B2, letter of Henry Thompson to Slingsby, 5 May 1614 (1614); Jennings, *History of Harrogate and Knaresborough*, 138–9 (1626).

119 A. Gooder, ed., *The Parliamentary Representation of the County of York*, II (Yorkshire Archaeological Soc., xcvi, 1937), 48 (1621); Sheffield City Library Mss., Str. 20, no. 262 (1626); Thomas, 'Parliamentary Elections 1625–1628', Appdx. II (1628).

120 *C.J.*, XXII, 692.

121 Wiltshire R.O., Charles Hayward's Parliamentary Note Book, p. 145 (1624); B.M. Add. 36825, ff. 221–221v (1628); Keeler, *Long Parliament*, 76.

122 *H.M.C. 13th Report, Appdx. IV* (Rye Corporation Mss.), 173, 176, 189 (1625 and 1626); Gruenfelder, 'Election to the Short Parliament', 199–200.

123 *C.J.*, I, 739–40 (1624); *ibid.*, II, 11 (Short Parliament).


## Appendix V. Numbers of Voters

1 P.R., C.219/42 pt. 1 no. 46 (Short Parliament); for the Long Parliament, see the discussion in Chapter 5 above, pp. 99–100.

2 *H.M.C. 11th Report, Appdx. Pt. VII* (Reading Corporation Mss.), 189, 193, 194.
3 There were 179 names, 'being the maior parte of the Burgesses and Inhabitants', to the indenture for the 1641 election. P.R.O., C.219/43 pt. 1.
4 See above, pp. 98–9.
5 There were about 80 names to the indenture, '*et multos alios*', and these were said to represent '*maior pars Burgenses*'. P.R.O., C.219/42 pt 1, no. 69.
6 See *ibid.*; many people were also said to have been absent from the borough's election at the county election: Longleat, Marquis of Bath's Mss., Whitelocke Papers, vol. VIII, f. 34.
7 A total of 493 votes was cast for four candidates: obviously, not everybody could have voted twice, but a minimum of 247 is obtained. Cooper, *Annals of Cambridge*, III, 304.
8 'Mr Recorder had 631 voyses Mr Ratliffe 570 Sir Ran [dall Mainwaring] and Sir Tho [mas Smyth] had ether 300 and od apeace'. B.M. Harl. 2125, f. 59v.
9 These were the approximate total of names to the respective indentures: P.R.O., C.219/42 pt. 1, nos. 23–5, and C.219/43 pt. 1.
10 B.M. Add. 36825, ff. 171–171v.
11 There were 51 signatures and marks to the Short Parliament indenture. P.R.O., C.219/42 pt 1, no. 13.
12 Keeler, *Long Parliament*, 42; J. R. Chanter and T. Wainwright, ed., *Barnstaple Records* (Barnstaple, 1900), II, 169.
13 C.U.L. Mss. Dd. 11.73, f. 151.
14 B.M. Add. 36825, ff. 164v–165.
15 Keeler, *Long Parliament*, 45.
16 Williams, *Court and Times of Charles I*, I, 329.
17 Taffs, 'Borough Franchise', Appdx., 118.
18 Essex R.O., D/B3/392/18; D/B3/1/19, ff. 171v–172.
19 The calculation here is a rather indirect one: it was reported that at the first day's polling, one of the candidates conveyed 800 of his second votes to his supposed partner, but received only 20 back; the polling lasted four days, and allowing for many desertions and single pollers, it seems possible to assume that at least 5000 turned out. *C.S.P.D. 1639–1640*, 581–2.
20 See above, p. 95.
21 Neale, *House of Commons*, 272.
22 Inner Temple Mss., 511/23, f. 1.
23 P.R.O., St.Ch. 8/293/11, Answer of Sir Richard Norton. Many voters were also said to have been excluded.
24 Keeler, *Long Parliament*, 48–9.
25 King, *Borough and Parish of Lymington*, 181.
26 Hampshire R.O., Jervoise Mss., 44M69/012, 'A Bill of the Free Eleccion' (1614); B.M. Add. 18597, ff. 124–124v (1628).
27 *H.M.C. 14th Report, Appdx. II, Duke of Portland's Mss.*, vol. III, 147.
28 See above, p. 96.
29 *H.M.C. Report, Earl of Verulam's Mss.*, 99.
30 See above, p. 117.
31 Jones, 'Election Issues and Borough Electorates in Kent', 19.
32 *Ibid.*
33 *Ibid.*
34 *Ibid.*
35 See above, p. 98.
36 Chandler, *Liverpool under Charles I*, 37.
37 See above, pp. 125–7.

38 B.M. Add. 36825, ff. 297–297v; Boston Corporation Mss., 5/B/1/1 (Admissions to freedom 1555–1704), where the average of admissions for the early 17th century is about 12 per annum, which might give a total of just over 200 at any one time. The low turn-out is explained by the fact that in a franchise dispute, notice would not be given to all the freemen.

39 Grimsby Corporation Mss., Court Book viii, 26 March 1640; I am indebted to Mr P. J. Shaw, the Assistant Archivist, for the conclusion that the total of free-men was unlikely to be any higher – and this is borne out by the material for the Recruiter election, at B.M. Loan 29/50, no. 76A.

40 See Zagorin, Court and Country, 128, for a discussion of this figure and its rela-tion to those with freedom to trade.

41 Hassell Smith, County and Court, 314 (1586 and 1593); McClure, Letters of John Chamberlain, i, 518 (1614); in the 1625 election, the four leading contenders each had totals falling between 1110 and 1610 votes, the fifth total not being given: R. Hughey, ed., Correspondence of Lady Katherine Paston 1603–1627 (Norfolk Record Soc., xiv, 1941), 82.

42 Keeler, Long Parliament, 56; and see above, p. 97. Evidence drawn from inden-tures, as Keeler's is here, probably does not give a full total, for even in as small a borough as this it is unlikely that all those present were made parties to the indenture.

43 Keeler, Long Parliament, 57 n. 264a; and see above, p. 95.

44 Great Yarmouth Corporation Mss., C18/7, f. 31; Neale, House of Commons, 250.

45 There were 25 names to the Long Parliament indenture, 'et ceteris Burgensibus Burgi'. P.R.O., C.219/43 pt. ii, no. 70.

46 N.R.O., FH 3468.

47 Nottingham U.L., Cl.L.P. 52.

48 W. H. Stevenson, ed., Records of the Borough of Nottingham. IV. 1547–1625 (London, 1889), xviii.

49 Hobson and Salter, Oxford Council Acts 1626–1665, 9–10, 97; Salter, Oxford Council Acts 1583–1626, xi.

50 There were 52 signatures and marks to the indenture, and they said they made the return 'as well for our whole number as our selves'. P.R.O., C.219/43 pt. ii, no. 107.

51 Keeler, Long Parliament, 61.

52 Neale, House of Commons, 248.

53 D. Underdown, 'The Ilchester Election, February 1646', Proceedings of the Somersetshire Archaeological and Natural History Society cx (1966), 46.

54 Pape, Newcastle-under-Lyme, 133. Only the 1624 election was contested, which probably explains the falling turn-out.

55 B.M. Add. 18597, f. 91.

56 Polling for the three candidates was 2240, 2140 and 1422: many were turned away or cast only one vote. B.M. Harl. 158, f. 285v; and see above, Chapter 1 pp. 18–19, 21, for some of the confusion at this election.

57 Ipswich and East Suffolk R.O., EE6: 1144/12, ff. 115v, 118v. Only the Long Parliament election was contested.

58 Keeler, Long Parliament, 64.

59 Harvard Ms. Eng. 982, f. 30v.

60 B.M. Eg. 2651, f. 26 (1621); there were 15 names to the Short Parliament inden-ture, 'et diversos alios Burgenses'. P.R.O., C.219/42 pt. ii.

61 Glanville, Reports, 72–3.

62 Keeler, Long Parliament, 67.

63 B.M. Harl. 2313, f. 8v.

64 There were over 100 names to the conflicting indentures. P.R.O., C.219/43 pt. II, nos. 210–12.
65 Maxstoke Castle, Fetherstone-Dilke Mss., wooden chest by door in dining-room, bundle, 25, no. 29 (and see above, p. 262, for a comment on this reference).
66 *C.J.*, I, 880.
67 Keeler, *Long Parliament*, 70; Marsh, *Borough and Town of Calne*, 38.
68 Chippenham Borough Records, Minute Book, ff. 76–77v, 116; Goldney, *Records of Chippenham*, 26–8. The total varied slightly, but it stayed around 127.
69 There were about 80 signatures and marks to the conflicting indentures. P.R.O., C.219/43 pt. II, nos. 45–6; Rathbone, *Wiltshire Borough Records*, 21.
70 C.U.L. Mss., Dd. 12.20, 21, f. 32v (1626); there were about 55 names to the Long Parliament indenture, who were said to be the 'Maior part *Burgenses Burgi*'. P.R.O., C.219/43 pt. III, no. 7.
71 Rathbone, *Wiltshire Borough Records*, 28.
72 Taffs, 'Borough Franchise', Appdx., 170.
73 Stone, 'Electoral Influence of second Earl of Salisbury', 395, 398.
74 Rathbone, *Wiltshire Borough Records*, 65.
75 *V.C.H. Wiltshire*, IX, 198.
76 The poll was broken off before it had been completed, and many were allegedly excluded: nevertheless, this figure and that for Warwickshire (although not the slightly later Herefordshire figure) contrasts markedly with county totals in other parts of the country. *D'Ewes* (N), 441, 463.
77 There were 171 names to the conflicting indentures. P.R.O., C.219/42 pt. III, nos. 70, 72.
78 There were 28 names to the indenture, over half of them gentry, which gives some idea of the social complexion resulting from the idiosyncratic franchise. P.R.O., C.219/42, pt. II.
79 Stanhope, with allegedly 3000 votes, lost in 1597: Neale, *House of Commons*, 83; B.M. Harl. 2313, f. 50, and B.M. Add. 36825, f. 196v (1628).
80 Carroll, 'Yorkshire Parliamentary Boroughs', 80–1.
81 *Ibid.*, 92.
82 *Ibid.*, 91; and see also Hull Guildhall Mss., Freemen's Register, which gives an average of about 35 admissions per annum in the later 1620s and 30s.
83 Atkinson, 'Election in Knaresborough', 213–15.
84 Carroll, 'Yorkshire Parliamentary Boroughs', 96.
85 *Ibid.*, 95.
86 *Ibid.*, 81.
87 *Ibid.*
88 See above, pp. 95–6.
89 P.R.O., S.P. 16/450/39. II.
90 Wilks, *Barons of the Cinque Ports*, 80, 82.
91 East Sussex R.O., Rye Corporation Mss., 1/12, f. 349.
92 Keeler, *Long Parliament*, 77.

## Appendix VIII. *The Arguments for a Wider Franchise*

1 J. G. A. Pocock, *The Ancient Constitution and the Feudal Law* (Cambridge, 1957), *passim*.
2 *C.D. 1621*, v, 444; *C.J.*, I, 515.
3 Guildford Museum and Muniment Room, LM 1331/24; *C.J.*, I, 568; *C.D. 1621*, VII, 567–72; see above Appendix VII, for the election bill.
4 Glanville, *Reports*, 17–18; B.M. Eg. 2723, f. 104. The motive force for the restora-

tion of the boroughs appears to have been just the same fear that parliament's status might be diminished that drove members to expand the franchises: 'for every Burgess so sent is a member of the great Councel of the Kingdom... and if such a neglect may be permitted in one Borough so may it be in more... and then it might follow that for want of Burgesses there should be no parliament'.

5 Staffordshire R.O., D.661/11/1/2, entry for 4 and 28 May; B.M. Add. 26639, ff. 29v–30; Glanville, *Reports*, 66–7.

6 *Ibid.*, 57; see above, p. 83, for Pym's position.

7 D. Little, *Religion, Order, and Law* (Oxford, 1970), 195–6.

8 B.M. Add. 18597, ff. 63v–65, 109v; *C.J.*, 1, 684, 686, 735.

9 Glanville, *Reports*, 107, 141–2.

10 *Ibid.*, 33–4; B.M. Add. 36825, ff. 165v–166; *C.J.*, 1, 876.

11 *Ibid.*, 748; *D'Ewes* (N), 138 n.7; Glanville, *Reports*, 55.

12 B.M. Add. 36825, ff. 297–297v. This 'assumption of guilt' by the Committee stands in contrast with the House's attitude to the Bletchingley franchise of 1624, where, because it was politically convenient, the House was prepared to recognise the alleged customary limitation. The fraudulent pleas that the problem and the attitude to history generated are best illustrated by the claim of the commons of Marlow (newly-restored to representation) in 1640 that they had voted for members 'time out of mind'. Glanville, *Reports*, 34–7; Longleat, Marquis of Bath's Mss., Whitelocke Papers, vol. VIII, f. 34.

13 *C.J.*, 1, 882, 907; B.M. Add. 8980, f. 23.

14 *C.J.*, 1, 882, 893. The Boston resolution is also quoted in Thomas, 'Levellers and the Franchise', 62.

15 N.R.O., FH 3467/1.

16 *D'Ewes* (N), 431, and see above, Appendix VII (D'Ewes also talked of the electoral 'birthrights' of Englishmen in the debate on whether to restore Seaford to representation in 1641, but he confused the issue by describing them as 'ancient', stemming from Edward I's time: *D'Ewes* (N), 322); for the East Grinstead decision, see *C.J.*, II, 10.

17 B.M. Add. 37343, f. 209v; Longleat, Marquis of Bath's Mss., Whitelocke Papers, vol. VIII, f. 30; for Bristol and Grenville, see above, pp. 65–66, and for Puckering, see Warwickshire R.O., W.21/6, p. 270.

18 Although in a sophisticated argument, Bridport corporation in 1628 dismissed these arguments from the wording of the returns as mere empty stylisations. B.M. Add. 36825, f. 165v.

19 N.R.O., FH 3467/2; Bodl. Ms. Rawl. A.78, ff. 190–190v; B.M. Add. 36825, f. 297v; B.M. Harl. 541, f. 111v; Longleat, Marquis of Bath's Mss., Whitelocke Papers, vol. VIII, f. 32; and see above, p. 73, for the difficulties caused in the Bridport case by the Bletchingley decision.

20 *D'Ewes* (N), 69, 69n., 138; *C.J.*, II, 47.

21 N.R.O., FH 3467.

22 *Ibid.* (in fact he placed the argument first). A peer in the Long Parliament adumbrated the theme of virtual representation in order to fill the gap left in this argument by the unprivileged: 'The House of Commons represents the meanest person, so did the Master his slave.' *Speeches and Passages of this Great and Happy Parliament* (1641), 306.

23 *C.D. 1621*, V, 28, 38; *D'Ewes* (N), 76 n.1; Longleat, Marquis of Bath's Mss., Whitelocke Papers, vol. VIII, f. 32.

24 Glanville, *Reports*, 102; P.R.O., S.P. 14/205/36.

# Bibliography

## MANUSCRIPT SOURCES

### *MANUSCRIPTS IN CENTRAL ARCHIVES*

#### BRITISH MUSEUM

Additional Manuscripts

| | |
|---|---|
| 8980, ff. 22–23 | Hakewill's report of the case for the 1628 restored boroughs. |
| 11045 | Newsletters to Lord Scudamore. |
| 14827 | Framlingham Gawdy's journal of the Long Parliament. |
| 18016 | Miscellaneous 17th-century parliamentary papers. |
| 18597 | ? Sir Walter Earle's journal of the 1624 parliament. |
| 24470 | Hunter collections. |
| 26639 | Anonymous journal of the 1624 parliament. |
| 29550 | Hatton correspondence. |
| 29625 | Transcripts of Dover court material. |
| 29974 | Pitt correspondence. |
| 33468 | Miscellaneous political and parliamentary proceedings, early 17th century. |
| 33512 | Sandwich corporation correspondence. |
| 34121 | John Smith of Nibley's journal of the 1621 parliament. |
| 34163 | Note-book of Sir Roger Twysden. |
| 34173 | Twysden's correspondence. |
| 34601 | Sir Henry Spelman's correspondence. |
| 36825 | Anonymous journal of the 1628 parliament. |
| 36827 | Anonymous journal of the Short Parliament. |
| 37343 | Whitelocke's annals. |
| 37819 | Nicholas correspondence relating to the Cinque Ports. |
| 42711 | Miscellaneous papers, including Grenville correspondence. |
| 44846 | Sir Thomas Peyton's letter-book. |
| 56103 | Framlingham Gawdy's journal of the Long Parliament. |

Egerton Manuscripts

| | |
|---|---|
| 2584 | Lord Warden's correspondence. |
| 2644, 2651 | Barrington correspondence. |
| 2715, 2722 | Gawdy correspondence. |
| 2723, f. 104 | 'A true relation' of the restoration of parliamentary boroughs. |

Harleian Manuscripts

| | |
|---|---|
| 38, f. 153 | A treatise on the privileges of yeomen. |
| 158, 159, 162, 163, 165, 374, 378 | Papers of Sir Simonds D'Ewes. |
| 541 | John Moore's diary of the Long Parliament. |
| 1601 | Parliamentary notes 1626–41. |
| 2105, 2125 | Randle Holme's Chester collections. |

2313                          ? Denzil Holles's notes of the 1628 parliament.
6799                          Notes of parliamentary proceedings in the 1620s.
6806                          Miscellaneous 17th-century parliamentary papers.
Cotton Julius C III          Miscellaneous correspondence of Sir Robert Cotton.
Lansdowne 491                Collection of parliamentary tracts.
Loan 29/50                   Sir Robert Harley's Committee of Privileges papers
                             relating to Recruiter elections.
Stowe 743                    Sir Edward Dering's correspondence.

                              PUBLIC RECORD OFFICE

C. 219                       Returns into Chancery of members of parliament.
P.C. 2/43                    Privy Council Register 1633–4.
S.P. 14                      State Papers, James I.
S.P. 16                      State Papers, Charles I.
Star Chamber 8               Star Chamber papers, James I and Charles I.
T. 64/302                    John Locke's notes for Treasury business.
31/3/72                      Transcripts of French Embassy correspondence.

                            BODLEIAN LIBRARY, OXFORD

Ashmole 822                  Miscellaneous 17th-century papers.
Bankes 13/23, 18/5,          Privy Council investigations into the Short Parliament
    42/55, 44/13             Northamptonshire election.
Rawl. A. 78, A. 346          Miscellaneous 17th-century tracts and papers relating to
                             parliament.
C. 956                       Anonymous journal of proceedings in parliament, Nov.
                             1640.
D. 918                       Miscellaneous papers relating to parliament.
D. 1098                      Notes of proceedings in parliament 1621.
Tanner 65, 67                Political papers, 1637–40.
283                          Miscellaneous papers, temp. Elizabeth and James I.
290                          Miscellaneous 17th-century papers.
321                          Speeches of Sir John Holland.
Top. Kent e. 6               Sir Edward Dering's poll list and account of the Short
                             Parliament Kent election.
Film 39                      Microfilm of Sir Thomas Peyton's journal of the Long
                             Parliament.

                          CAMBRIDGE UNIVERSITY LIBRARY

Dd. 11. 7. 73, ff. 149–51    Account of the 1626 Dorset election.
Dd. 12. 20, 21               ? Bulstrode Whitelocke's journal of the 1626 parliament.
Kk. 6. 38                    Geoffrey Palmer's journal of the Long Parliament.
Mm. 6. 62, ff. 62–3          D'Ewes's queries to the judges relating to elections,
                             1640.

                           HOUGHTON LIBRARY, HARVARD

Eng. 980                     Sir William Spring's parliamentary journal for 1624.
Eng. 982                     Anonymous journal of the Short Parliament.

                             INNER TEMPLE LIBRARY

511/23                       William Prynne's notes of certain cases.

## MANUSCRIPTS IN LOCAL ARCHIVES

The major, and invaluable, guide to such sources is the National Register of Archives county-by-county catalogue.

### BEDFORDSHIRE

Bedfordshire R.O.
Trevor-Wingfield Mss.: TW 887–894, Papers relating to the 1640 Bedford dispute.
St John Mss.: J. 1369, 1402, Northamptonshire correspondence, 1640.
Bedford Town Hall
Corporation Mss.: Box 8, no. 5, 17th-century papers.

### BERKSHIRE

Reading Public Library
Corporation Records: R./RF/1, Register of freemen 1603–1700.

### BUCKINGHAMSHIRE

Buckinghamshire R.O.
Tyrrwhit-Drake Mss.: D/DR. 12. 37–8, Parliamentary papers.

### CAMBRIDGESHIRE

Cambridge Guildhall
Corporation Mss.: Common Day Book 1610–46.

### CHESHIRE

Cheshire R.O.
Grosvenor Mss. Paper endorsed '2 febr. 1623. My speech at the election of Knights for the parliament'.
Chester Public Library
Corporation Mss.: 94/3, Edward Whitby's list of mayors.

### CORNWALL

Cornwall R.O.
BO/25/59, Sir Richard Buller's journal of the Long Parliament.
BC/24/2, BO/23/73, Buller correspondence, early 17th century.

### DEVON

City of Exeter R.O.
Corporation Mss.: City Act Books VI, VII, VIII.

### ESSEX

Essex R.O.
Maldon Borough Records: D/B3/3, Correspondence and miscellaneous papers; D/B3/1/19 and 20, Assembly and Quarter Sessions Books, 1606–31, 1631–64.
Morant Mss.: Vols. 43–48, Papers relating to Colchester.
Colchester Town Hall
Corporation Archives: Assembly Books 1600–20, 1620–46.

### GLOUCESTERSHIRE

Gloucestershire R.O.
D760/36, Letter of Sir Robert Tracy to Tewkesbury corporation, 1625; D2510/10

Letter of Sir Robert Cooke to John Smith of Nibley, 1640; D2688, Account Book of Giles Geaste Charity, Tewkesbury.

Bristol A.O.

Corporation Archives: 04264(2) & (3), Common Council proceedings 1608–27, 1627–42; 04359(2)a & b, Registers of admissions to freedom 1607–51.

Ashton Court Mss.: AC/C58/1–15, Correspondence of Edward Phelips in 1640.

Gloucester City Library

City Library Ms. 1451, Gloucester Corporation Minute Book 1565–1632.

Gloucester Collections: 16526(40), Petition of Sir Maurice Berkeley, 1624.

Tewkesbury Town Hall

Corporation Mss.: A1/1, Corporation Minute Book and Accounts; A1/2, Book of Ordinances.

### HAMPSHIRE

Hampshire R.O.

Jervoise Mss.: 44M69/012, Early 17th-century parliamentary papers.

### HERTFORDSHIRE

Hertfordshire R.O.

Archdeaconry of Huntingdon wills.

Hertford Castle

Borough Mss.: vol. 23, Correspondence, political papers, etc.; vol. 25, Trades, etc.; vol. 46, Taxation, rating, etc.

Hertford Borough Museum

'Freeholders of the Borough of Hertford. By John Norden', transcribed, with annotations, by H. C. Andrews.

Hatfield House

Cecil Family and Estate Papers: Box E/3, List of freeholders, 1640.

St Albans City Library

City of St Albans Muniments: no. 159, Mayor's accounts 1620–1.

### HUNTINGDONSHIRE

Huntingdonshire R.O.

Archdeaconry of Huntingdon wills and inventories.

Godmanchester Borough Records: Box 3, bundle 15, List of borough voters for the 1625 county election; Box 10, unsorted, Borough rentals.

Manchester Mss.: dd.M.36, Notes of the Short Parliament.

### KENT

Kent A.O.

U350, Dering correspondence.

U1115, c/22–4 and 015, Edward Scott's correspondence, 1625.

Queenborough Mss.: Qb/C1, Borough correspondence.

Sandwich Mss.: Sa./C1; Corporation Letter Book; Sa./Ac.7, Corporation Year Book 1608–42.

Consistory and Archdeaconry Courts of Canterbury, registers and original wills.

Dover Public Library

Corporation Mss.: Acts and Decrees of the Reigns of James I and Charles I; Records of James I and Charles I.

### LANCASHIRE

Kenyon Mss.: DD/KE/9/23, 24, and 56, Kenyon correspondence, 17th-century.

Consistory Court of Chester wills.
Wigan Public Library
Transcript of Bishop Bridgeman's Account Book.

### LEICESTERSHIRE

Leicester Museum
Leicester Hall Papers, vols. x (1637–40) and xi (1640–5).

### LINCOLNSHIRE

Lincolnshire R.O.
Massingberd-Munby Deposit: MM. vi/10/5, Voting papers for the 1656 election.
Boston Public Library
Corporation Mss.: Minute Book, vol. 1; 5/B/1/1, Admissions to freedom 1555–1704.
Grimsby Central Library
Borough Mss.: Court Book VIII.

### LONDON

Corporation of London R.O.
Journals of Common Council
Remembrancia VI
Repertories

### NORFOLK

Norfolk and Norwich R.O.
City Records: Assembly Books 1585–1613, 1613–42; Book of Charters; Mayor's Court Books 1624–34, 1634–46; Revenue and Letters.
Howard Mss.: 349x/How.633, Castle Rising papers.
Walsingham Mss.: xvii/2, de Grey correspondence.
Raynham Temporary Deposit. Papers of Sir Nathaniel Bacon.
Bradfer-Lawrence Bacon Mss. Papers of Sir Nathaniel Bacon.
Aylsham Hall Mss. Papers of Sir Nathaniel Bacon.
Norwich Consistory wills.
Castle Rising wills 1639–92.
Great Yarmouth Guildhall
Corporation Mss.: c. 18/6–7, Entry Books I and II; c. 19/5–6, Assembly Books 1598–1625, 1625–42.
King's Lynn Guildhall
Corporation Mss.: Assembly Book 1637–58.

### NORTHAMPTONSHIRE

Northamptonshire R.O.
Finch Hatton Mss.: FH 50, Journal of the 1624 and Short Parliaments; FH 2735, 3441, 3444, 3461, 3466–3469, Higham Ferrers material; FH 2790, 3501, Papers relating to Northampton, 1640.
Northampton Town Hall
Corporation Mss.: Assembly and Order Book 1627–1744.

### NOTTINGHAMSHIRE

Nottinghamshire R.O.
DD/SR.221/96/4, Letter about the Yorkshire election, 1658.
Nottingham University Library

Clifton Mss.: Cl.C, Clifton correspondence; Cl.LP. 51–2, Papers relating to the 1624 East Retford election.

SHROPSHIRE

Shropshire R.O.
Bridgwater Mss.: 212/364, Correspondence, 17th century.
Ludlow Corporation Mss.: Minute Book 1590–1648.

SOMERSET

Somerset R.O.
Phelips Mss.: DD/PH/216, 221, 224, Phelips correspondence.
Sanford Mss.: DD/SF/1076/21, Poulett correspondence.

STAFFORDSHIRE

Staffordshire R.O.
D661/11/1/2, Richard Dyott's journal of the 1624 parliament.
D868/2/30, Leveson correspondence, 1640s.
Lichfield Joint R.O.
Newcastle-under-Lyme wills.

SUFFOLK

Ipswich and East Suffolk R.O.
Dunwich Borough Mss.: EE.6:1144/12, Minute Book 1627–53.

SURREY

Guildford Museum and Muniment Room.
Loseley Mss.: LM 1331, Sir George More's Committee of Privileges papers, 1621.

SUSSEX

East Sussex R.O.
Rye Corporation Mss.: 1/12, Hundred, Sessions and Assembly Book; 47/98, Corporation letters.

WARWICKSHIRE

Warwickshire R.O.
Warwick Borough Mss.: W.21/6, Minute Book 1610–62.
Coughton Court
Throckmorton Mss.: Box 60, folder of 'Correspondence 1629–52'.
Coventry City A.O.
Corporation Mss.
Court Leet Book II (1588–1834).
Minute Book 1554–1640
Acc. 4, City Annals F.
Maxstoke Castle
Fetherstone-Dilke Mss.: Bundle 25, no. 29, Draft petition about the 1641 Warwickshire by-election.

WILTSHIRE

Wiltshire R.O.
Charles Hayward's parliamentary note-book for 1621 and 1624.
Chippenham Borough Material: 473/399, Transcript of details of the 1604 Chippenham case in Chancery.

Archdeaconry of Wiltshire wills.
Chippenham Borough Offices.
Corporation Mss.: Minute Book; CBW/264, List of voters 1624.
Longleat House
Marquis of Bath's Mss.: Whitelocke Papers, vol. VIII. Whitelocke's correspondence.
Salisbury City Archives
Corporation Mss.: Mayor's Official Correspondence; Ledger Book C (1571–1640).

### WORCESTERSHIRE

Worcester Town Hall
Corporation Mss.: Order Book II (1602–50).

### YORKSHIRE

Bradford City Library
Spencer-Stanhope Mss.: 10, Stanhope correspondence.
Hull Guildhall
Corporation Mss.: Corporation Letters; Minute Books 1555–1609, 1609–50; Freemen's Registers.
Leeds Public Library
MX 177/25, Letter about the Long Parliament Nottingham election.
Knaresborough wills.
Sheffield City Library
Wentworth Woodhouse Mss.; Str. 2 and 12, and WWM/phot.2, Sir Thomas Wentworth's correspondence in the 1620s.
York Public Library
Corporation Mss.: House Books 30–3, 36.
Yorkshire Archaeological Society
Slingsby Mss.: DD. 56/B1–2 and M2, Letters and Knaresborough estate material of Sir Henry Slingsby.

## THESES AND UNPUBLISHED PAPERS

Holmes, C. A. 'The Eastern Association.' (Cambridge Ph.D., 1967).
'The 1640 Elections in East Anglia' (Paper deposited at Essex R.O.).
Hull, F. 'Agriculture and Rural Society in Essex, 1560–1640.' (London Ph.D., 1950).
Johnson, A. M. 'Buckinghamshire 1640 to 1660. A study in county politics.' (University of Wales, Swansea, M.A., 1963).
Jones, M. V. 'The Political History of the Parliamentary Boroughs of Kent 1642–1662.' (London Ph.D., 1967).
Manning, B. 'Neutrals and Neutralism in the English Civil War 1642–1646.' (Oxford D.Phil., 1957).
Phythian-Adams, C. V. 'The Metamorphosis of Medieval Community: Coventry 1480–1620.' Paper delivered to the Conference of Anglo-American Historians at the Senate House, London University, 7 July, 1972.
Quintrell, B. W. 'The Government of the County of Essex 1603–42.' (London Ph.D., 1965).
Schofield, R. S. 'Parliamentary Lay Taxation 1485–1547.' (Cambridge Ph.D., 1963).
Spufford, M. 'People, Land and Literacy in Cambridgeshire in the Sixteenth and Seventeenth Centuries.' (Leicester Ph.D., 1970).

Taffs, W. 'The Borough Franchise in the First Half of the Seventeenth Century.' (London M.A., 1926).

Thomas, J. D. 'Survey of Parliamentary Elections, 1625–1628.' (London M.A., 1952).

Wrightson, K. E. 'The Puritan Reformation of Manners, with special reference to the counties of Lancashire and Essex 1640–1660.' (Cambridge Ph.D., 1974).

Yarlott, R. 'The Long Parliament and the Fear of Popular Pressure, 1640–1646.' (Leeds M.A., 1963).


## PRINTED WORKS – PRIMARY SOURCES

*Acts of the Privy Council.*

Anon. *Antidotum Culmerianum.* Oxford, 1644.

    *Persecutio Undecima.* —, 1648.

    *Plain Fault in Plain-English. And the same in Dr. Fearne.* 1642.

    *The Priviledges and Practice of Parliaments in England.* —, 1640.

*The Autobiography of Sir John Bramston.* Ed. Lord Braybrooke. Camden Soc., 1845.

*Autobiography and Correspondence of Sir Simonds D'Ewes.* Ed. J. O. Halliwell. London, 1845.

Bagshaw, Edward. *A Just Vindication of the Questioned Part of the Reading.* 1660.

*Barnstaple Records.* Ed. J. R. Chanter and T. Wainwright. Barnstaple, 1900.

*The Black Book of Warwick.* Ed. T. Kemp. Warwick, 1898.

Bramhall, John. *The Serpent Salve.* —, 1643.

*Calendar of State Papers, Domestic.*

*Calendar of Wynn (of Gwydir) Papers.* Ed. J. Ballinger. Cardiff, 1926.

'Certain select Observations on the several Offices, and Officers, in the Militia of England. . .'. *Harleian Miscellany.* VI. London, 1745.

*The Church Book of Bunyan Meeting.* Ed. G. B. Harrison. London, 1928.

Clarendon, Lord. *History of the Rebellion.* Ed. W. D. Macray. Oxford, 1888.

Coke, Sir Edward. *The Compleate Copy-Holder.* 1641.

    *The Fourth Part of the Institutes.* 1644.

    *The Reports,* Ed. G. Wilson, II. London, 1777.

*Commons Debates in 1621.* Ed. W. Notestein, F. H. Relf and H. Simpson. New Haven, 1935.

*The Complete Prose Works of John Milton.* Ed. D. Wolfe. II. New Haven, 1953.

*Constitutional Documents of the Puritan Revolution.* Ed. S. R. Gardiner. Oxford, 1906.

*Constitutional Documents of the Reign of James I.* Ed. J. R. Tanner. Cambridge, 1930.

*Correspondence of Lady Katherine Paston 1603–1627.* Ed. R. Hughey, Norfolk Record Soc., xiv. 1941.

*The Court and Times of Charles I.* Ed. R. F. Williams. London, 1848.

*The Court and Times of James I.* Ed. T. Birch. London, 1848.

Culmer, Richard. *Cathedrall Newes from Canterbury.* 1644.

*Debates in the House of Commons in 1625.* Ed. S. R. Gardiner. Camden Soc., 1873.

D'Ewes, Sir Simonds. *A Compleat Journal of the Votes, Speeches and Debates, both of the House of Lords and House of Commons throughout the whole Reign of Queen Elizabeth.* London, 1693.

*The Diary and Correspondence of Dr John Worthington.* ed. J. Crossley. Chetham Soc., 1847.

*The Diary of John Rous.* Ed. M. A. Everett Green. Camden Soc., 1856.

*The Diary of Sir Henry Slingsby.* Ed. D. Parsons. London, 1836.

*The Diary of Henry Townshend of Elmley Lovett.* Ed. J. W. Willis Bund. Worcestershire Historical Soc., 1920.

*The Earl of Strafforde's Letters and Dispatches.* Ed. W. Knowler. London, 1739.
Eliot, Sir John. *An Apology for Socrates and Negotium Posterorum.* Ed. A. B. Grosart.
 —, 1881.
*The Fairfax Correspondence.* Ed. G. W. Johnson. London, 1848.
'Family Memoranda of the Stanleys of Alderley', *Journal of the Chester and North Wales Archaeological and Historic Society,* xxiv (1921).
Filmer, Sir Robert. *Patriarcha, and Other Political Works.* Ed. P. Laslett. Oxford, 1949.
Fuller, Thomas. *Ephemeria Parliamentaria.* 1654.
Geree, John. *Iudahs Ioy at the Oath.* 1641.
Glanville, John. *Reports of Certain Cases.* London, 1775.
Gough, Richard. *History of Myddle.* Ed. W. G. Hoskins. Fontwell, Sussex, 1968.
*Hertfordshire County Records. V. Sessions Books 1619–1657.* Ed. W. L. Hardy. Hertford, 1928.
*Historical Manuscripts Commission, Reports.*
 *3rd Report, Appendix* (1872) Cheddar Mss.
 *4th Report, Appendix* (1874) House of Lords Mss.
 *5th Report, Appendix* (1876) Corporation of Sandwich Mss.
 *9th Report, Appendix Pt. II* (1884) Chandos-Pole-Gell and Woodforde Mss.
 *10th Report, Appendix Pt. II* (1885) Gawdy Mss.
 *10th Report, Appendix Pt. IV* (1885) Boycott's and Corporation of Bishop's Castle Mss.
 *11th Report, Appendix Pt. III* (1887) Corporation of King's Lynn Mss.
 *11th Report, Appendix Pt. IV* (1887) Townshend Mss.
 *11th Report, Appendix Pt. VII* (1888) Corporation of Reading Mss.
 *12th Report, Appendix (Earl Cowper's Mss.)* (1888–9).
 *13th Report, Appendix Pt. IV* (1892). Dovaston and Corporation of Rye Mss.
 *14th Report, Appendix II, Duke of Portland's Mss. vol. III* (1894).
 *Duke of Buccleuch's Mss.* (1897–1903).
 *Duke of Buccleuch's Mss. at Montagu House* (1899–1926).
 *De L'Isle and Dudley Mss.* VI (1966).
 *Earl of Denbigh's Mss.* V (1911).
 *City of Exeter Mss.* (1916).
 *Hastings Mss.* (1928–47).
 *Hatfield Mss.* (1883–1973).
 *Various Collections* IV (1907) Corporations of Aldeburgh and Orford Mss.
 *Various Collections* VII (1914) Dunwich Corporation Mss.
 *Earl of Verulam's Mss.* (1906).
Hobbes, Thomas. *Behemoth.* Ed. F. Tonnies, London, 1969.
Hooker, Richard. *Ecclesiastical Polity Book VIII.* Ed. R. A. Houk. New York, 1931.
Hutchinson, Lucy. *Memoirs of the life of Colonel Hutchinson.* Oxford, 1973.
*Journals of the House of Commons.*
*The Journal of Sir Simonds D'Ewes from the beginning of the Long Parliament to the trial of the Earl of Strafford.* Ed. W. Notestein. New Haven, 1923.
*The Journal of Sir Simonds D'Ewes from the first recess of the Long Parliament to the withdrawal of King Charles from London.* Ed. W. H. Coates. New Haven, 1942.
*The Knyvett Letters 1620–1644.* Ed. B. Schofield. Norfolk Record Soc., 1949.
*The Letters of John Chamberlain.* Ed. N. E. McClure. Philadelphia, 1939.
*Letters of the Lady Brilliana Harley.* Ed. T. T. Lewis. Camden Soc., 1854.
*The Life of Adam Martindale.* Ed. R. Parkinson. Chetham Soc., 1845.
Lilburne, John. *Londons Liberty in Chains discovered.* —, 1646.

*Memoirs of the Life of Ambrose Barnes.* Ed. W. H. D. Longstaffe. Surtees Soc., 1867.

*Memorials of the Goldsmith's Company.* Ed. W. S. Prideaux. London, n.d.

Nalson, John. *An Impartial Collection of the Great Affairs of State.* 1682–3.

Nicolls, F. *The Life and Death of M. Ignatius Jurdain.* 1654.

*The Notebook of Sir John Northcote.* Ed. A. H. A. Hamilton. London, 1877.

*The Official Papers of Sir Nathaniel Bacon of Stiffkey, Norfolk.* Ed. H. W. Saunders. Camden Soc., 1915.

*Oxford Council Acts 1583–1626.* Ed. H. E. Salter. Oxford Historical Soc., lxxxvii, 1928.

*Oxford Council Acts 1626–1665.* Ed. M. G. Hobson and H. E. Salter. Oxford Historical Soc., xcv, 1933.

*Oxinden Letters 1607–42.* Ed. D. Gardiner. London, 1933.

Parker, Henry. *Observations upon some of his Majesties late Answers and Expresses.* 1642.

*The Parliamentary Diary of Robert Bowyer.* Ed. D. H. Willson. Minneapolis, 1931.

*Privy Council Registers Preserved in the P.R.O.: Reproduced in Facsmile,* i. London, 1967.

*Proceedings in Kent in 1640.* Ed. L. B. Larking. Camden Soc., 1862.

*Proceedings in Parliament in 1610.* Ed. E. R. Foster. New Haven, 1966.

Prynne, William. *Brevia Parliamentaria Rediviva.* 1662.

*Quarter Sessions Records for the County of Somerset. II. 1625–1639.* Ed. E. H. Bates Harbin. Somerset Record Soc., xxiv, 1908.

*Reading Records.* Ed. J. M. Guilding. London, 1896.

*Records of the Borough of Northampton.* Ed. C. A. Markham and J. C. Cox. Northampton, 1898.

*Records of the Borough of Nottingham. IV. 1547–1625.* Ed. W. H. Stevenson. London, 1889.

*The Register of the Freemen of Norwich 1548–1713.* Ed. P. Millican. Norwich, 1934.

*Reliquiae Baxterianae.* Ed. M. Sylvester, 1696.

*A Remonstrance or Declaration of Parliament.* 1642. B.M. E.148/23.

*Reports of Cases in the Courts of Star Chamber and High Commission.* Ed. S. R. Gardiner. Camden Soc., 1886.

Rushworth, John. *Historical Collections.* 1659–1701.

*Mr St John his Speech in Parliament . . . Concerning the Charge of Treason then exhibited to the Bishops.* 1641.

'Shardeloes Muniments.' *Records of Buckinghamshire,* xiv, 1941–6.

*The Somers Collection of Tracts.* Ed. W. Scott. London, 1810.

*The Speeches of the Lord Digby . . . Concerning Grievances, and the Triennial Parliament.* 1641.

*Speeches and Passages of this Great and Happy Parliament.* 1641.

Spelman, Sir John. *A View of a Printed Book Intituled Observations.* Oxford, 1643.

'The State of England (1600). By Sir Thomas Wilson'. Ed. F. J. Fisher in *Camden Miscellany.* xvi. Camden Soc., 1936.

Stow, John. *A Survey of the Cities of London and Westminster.* Ed. J. Strype. London, 1720.

*The Third Speech of the Lord George Digby.* 1641.

Thirsk, J. and Cooper, J. P. *17th Century Economic Documents.* Oxford, 1972.

*Verney Papers: Notes of Proceedings in the Long Parliament.* Ed. J. Bruce. Camden Soc., 1845.

*A Vindication of the King, with Some Observations upon the Two Houses.* —, 1642.

Wallington, Nehemiah. *Historical Notices.* Ed. R. Webb. London, 1869.

*Wentworth Papers 1597–1628.* Ed. J. P. Cooper. Camden Soc., 1973.

*The Winthrop Papers.* Ed. S. E. Morison *et al.* Massachusetts Historical Society, 1929.

## PRINTED WORKS - SECONDARY SOURCES

Allan, D. G. C. 'The Rising in the West, 1628–1631', *Economic History Review*, v (1952).

Ashford, L. J. *The History of the Borough of High Wycombe from its Origins to 1880.* London, 1960.

Atkinson, W. 'A Parliamentary Election in Knaresborough in 1628', *Yorkshire Archaeological Journal*, xxxiv (1938–9).

Ault, W. O. 'Open-Field Husbandry and the Village Community', *Transactions of the American Philosophical Society*, n.s., lv, pt. 7 (1965).

Bankes, J. and Kerridge, E. (eds.). *The Early Records of the Bankes Family at Winstanley.* Chetham Soc., 1973.

Barnes, T. G. *Somerset 1625–1640.* Oxford, 1961.

Beecheno, F. R. 'The Norwich Subscription for the Regaining of Newcastle, 1643', *Norfolk Archaeology*, xviii (1914).

Blackwood, B. G. 'The Lancashire Cavaliers and their Tenants', *Transactions of the Historic Society of Lancashire and Cheshire*, cxvii (1965).

Bliss Burbidge, F. *Old Coventry and Lady Godiva.* Birmingham, n.d.

Bohannon, M. E. 'The Essex Election of 1604', *English Historical Review*, xlviii (1933).

Boothroyd, B. *History of Pontefract.* Pontefract, 1807.

Bowden, P. 'Agricultural Prices, Farm Profits and Rents', in J. Thirsk (ed.), *Agrarian History of England and Wales. IV. 1500–1640.* Cambridge, 1967.

Boynton, L. 'Billeting: The Example of the Isle of Wight', *English Historical Review*, lxxiv (1959).

Breen, T. H. 'Who Governs: The Town Franchise in Seventeenth-Century Massachusetts', *William and Mary Quarterly*, xxvii (1970).

Bridenbaugh, C. *Vexed and Troubled Englishmen.* Oxford, 1968.

Bridgeman, G. T. O. *History of the Church and Manor of Wigan.* II. Chetham Soc., 1889.

Brown, L. F. 'Ideas of Representation from Elizabeth to Charles I,' *Journal of Modern History*, xi (1939).

Brown, R. E. and B. K. *Virginia 1705–1786: Democracy or Aristocracy?* East Lansing, 1964.

Bushman, R. L. 'English Franchise Reform in the Seventeenth Century', *Journal of British Studies*, iii (1963).

Campbell, M. *The English Yeoman.* New Haven, 1942.

Cannon, J. *Parliamentary Reform 1640–1832.* Cambridge, 1973.

Carroll, R. 'Yorkshire Parliamentary Boroughs in the 17th Century', *Northern History*, iii (1968).

Cartwright, J. J. *Chapters in the History of Yorkshire.* Wakefield, 1872.

Chalklin, C. W. *Seventeenth Century Kent.* London, 1965.

Chandler, G. *Liverpool under Charles I.* Liverpool, 1965.

Chauncy, Sir Henry. *The Historical Antiquities of Hertfordshire.* London, 1700.

Clark, P. and Slack, P. (eds.). *Crisis and Order in English Towns 1500–1700.* London, 1972.

Clark, P. 'The Migrant in Kentish Towns 1580–1640', in Clark and Slack. *Crisis and Order.*

Cliffe, J. T. *The Yorkshire Gentry.* London, 1969.

Collier, J. P. (ed.). *The Egerton Papers.* Camden Soc., 1840.

Cockburn, J. S. *History of English Assizes 1558–1714.* Cambridge, 1972.

(ed.). *Somerset Assize Orders 1640–1659.* Somerset Record Soc. lxxi. 1971.

Collinson, P. *The Elizabethan Puritan Movement.* London, 1967.

Cooper, C. H. and J. W. *Annals of Cambridge*. Cambridge, 1842–1908.
Cooper, J. P. 'The Differences between English and Continental Government in the Early Seventeenth Century' in J. S. Bromley and E. H. Kossmann (eds.). *Britain and the Netherlands*. London, 1960.
  'Economic Regulation in the Cloth Industry in seventeenth-century England', *Transactions of the Royal Historical Society*, xx (1970).
  'The Fortune of Thomas Wentworth, Earl of Strafford', *Economic History Review*, xi (1958–9).
  'The Social Distribution of Land and Men in England, 1436–1700', *Economic History Review*, xx (1967).
Corfield, P. 'A provincial capital in the late seventeenth century: the case of Norwich' in Clark and Slack. *Crisis and Order*.
Craven, W. F. *The Dissolution of the Virginia Company*. New York, 1932.
Davies, C. S. L. 'Peasant Revolt in England and France', *Agricultural History Review*, xxi (1973).
de Villiers, E. 'The Parliamentary Boroughs Restored by the House of Commons 1621–1641', *English Historical Review*, lxvii (1952).
*Dictionary of National Biography*.
Dietz, F. C. *English Public Finance 1558–1641*. London, 1932.
Dodd, A. H. *Studies in Stuart Wales*. Cardiff, 1952.
  'Welsh Opposition Lawyers in the Short Parliament', *Bulletin of the Board of Celtic Studies*, xii (1948).
Dore, R. N. *The Civil Wars in Cheshire*. Chester, 1966.
Dyer, A. D. *The City of Worcester in the sixteenth century*. Leicester, 1973.
*East Anglian*. New series, iii (1889–90).
Edwards, G. 'The Emergence of Majority Rule in English Parliamentary Elections', *Transactions of the Royal Historical Society*, xiv (1964).
Everitt, A. M. *The Community of Kent and the Great Rebellion*. Leicester, 1966.
  'Farm Labourers' in Thirsk, *Agrarian History. IV*.
Fieldhouse, R. T. 'Parliamentary Representation in the Borough of Richmond', *Yorkshire Archaeological Journal*, xliv (1972).
Firth, C. H. *Oliver Cromwell*. London, 1900.
Forster, G. C. F. 'The English Local Community and Local Government 1603–1625' in A. G. R. Smith (ed.). *The Reign of James VI and I*. London, 1973.
Frear, M. R. 'The election at Great Marlow in 1640', *Journal of Modern History*, xiv (1942).
Fussell, G. E. (ed.). *Robert Loder's Farm Accounts 1610–1620*. Camden Soc., 1936.
Gardiner, D. *Historic Haven*. Derby, 1954.
Gardiner, S. R. *History of England*. London, 1883–4.
Goldney, F. H. *Records of Chippenham*. London, 1889.
Gooder, A. (ed.). *The Parliamentary Representation of the County of York*. II. Yorkshire Archaeological Soc., xcvi, 1937.
Gregg, P. *Free-born John*. London, 1961.
Gregson, W. E. 'Recusant Roll for West Derby Hundred, 1641', *Transactions of the Historic Society of Lancashire and Cheshire*, new series xiv (1898).
Griffin, R. 'Monumental Brasses in East Kent', *Archaeologia Cantiana*, xxxii (1917).
Groome, A. N. 'The Higham Ferrers Elections in 1640', *Northamptonshire Past and Present*, ii, no. 5 (1958).
Gruenfelder, J. K. 'The Election to the Short Parliament' in H. S. Reinmuth jnr, (ed.). *Early Stuart Studies*. Minneapolis, 1970.
  'The Parliamentary Election at Chester, 1621', *Transactions of the Historic Society of Lancashire and Cheshire*, cxx (1968).

'The Spring Parliamentary Election at Hastings, 1640', *Sussex Archaeological Collections*, cv (1967).

Habakkuk, H. J. 'La Disparition du Paysan Anglais', *Annales*, xx (1965).

Hassell Smith, A. *County and Court*. Oxford, 1974.

Heaton, H. *The Yorkshire Woollen and Worsted Industries*, Oxford, 1965.

Hexter, J. H. *The Reign of King Pym*. New Haven, 1941.

*Reappraisals in History*. London, 1961.

Hey, D. G. *An English Rural Community: Myddle under the Tudors and Stuarts*. Leicester, 1974.

Hibbert, A. 'The Economic Policies of Towns' in M. M. Postan, E. E. Rich and E. Miller (eds.). *The Cambridge Economic History of Europe*. III. Cambridge, 1963.

Hill, C. *The Century of Revolution*. Edinburgh, 1961.

*Society and Puritanism in Pre-Revolutionary England*. London, 1964.

*The World Turned Upside Down*. London, 1972.

'County Matters'. *New Statesman*, vol. 88, no. 2263 (2 Aug. 1974).

Hirst, D. M. 'The Defection of Sir Edward Dering, 1640–41,' *Historical Journal*, xv (1972).

'Elections and the Privileges of the House of Commons in the early seventeenth century', *Historical Journal*, forthcoming.

Hoare, Sir R. C. *History of Modern Wiltshire*. London, 1822–44.

Hoskins, W. G. *The Midland Peasant*. London, 1957.

*Provincial England*. London, 1963.

Howell, R. *Newcastle upon Tyne and the Puritan Revolution*. Oxford, 1967.

Jennings, B. *History of Harrogate and Knaresborough*. Huddersfield, 1970.

Johnson, B. P. 'The Gilds of York' in A. Stacpoole (ed.). *Noble City of York*. York, 1972.

Jones, M. V. 'Election Issues and the Borough Electorates in mid-seventeenth-century Kent', *Archaeologia Cantiana*, lxxxv (1970).

Jones, J. R. *The Revolution of 1688 in England*. London, 1972.

Judson, M. A. *The Crisis of the Constitution*. New Brunswick, 1949.

Keeler, M. F. *The Long Parliament*. Philadelphia, 1954.

Kerridge, E. *Agrarian Problems in the Sixteenth Century and After*. London, 1969.

'The Revolts in Wiltshire against Charles I', *Wiltshire Archaeological and Natural History Magazine*, lvii (1958).

Ketton-Cremer, R. W. *Norfolk in the Civil War*. London, 1969.

King, E. *Old Times Revisited in the Borough and Parish of Lymington*. London, 1879.

Langdon, G. D. jnr. 'The Franchise and Political Democracy in Plymouth Colony', *William and Mary Quarterly*, xx (1963).

Latimer, J. *Annals of Bristol in the Seventeenth Century*. Bristol, 1900.

Lehmberg, S. E. *The Reformation Parliament 1529–1536*. Cambridge, 1970.

Lewis, T. B., and Webb, L. M. 'Voting for the Massachusetts Council of Assistants, 1674–1686', *William and Mary Quarterly*, xxx (1973).

Little, D. *Religion, Order, and Law*. Oxford, 1970.

Lockridge, K. 'Land, Population and the Evolution of New England Society 1630–1790', *Past and Present*, xxxix (1968).

Lockridge, K. A. and Kreider, A. 'The Evolution of Massachusetts Town Government, 1640 to 1740', *William and Mary Quarterly*, xxiii (1966).

MacCaffrey, W. T. *Exeter 1540–1640*. Cambridge, Mass., 1958.

Macfarlane, A. *The Family Life of Ralph Josselin*. Cambridge, 1970.

McGrath, P. *Merchants and Merchandise in Seventeenth-Century Bristol*. Bristol Record Soc., 1955.

McKisack, M. *The Parliamentary Representation of the English Boroughs during the Middle Ages*. Oxford, 1932.

Manning, B. 'The Outbreak of the English Civil War' in R. H. Parry (ed.). *The English Civil War and After*. London, 1970.

Marsden, R. G. 'A Letter of William Bradford and Isaac Allerton, 1623', *American Historical Review*, viii (1902–3).

Marsh, A. E. W. *History of the Borough and Town of Calne*. Calne, n.d.

Matthews, A. G. (ed.). *Calamy Revised*. Oxford, 1934.

    *Walker Revised*. Oxford, 1948.

Merewether, H. A. and Stephens, A. J. *The History of Boroughs and Municipal Corporations*. London, 1835.

Moir, T. L. *The Addled Parliament of 1614*. New York, 1958.

Morrill, J. S. *Cheshire 1630–1660*. Oxford, 1974.

    'The Cheshire Grand Jury 1625–1659: a social and administrative study.' (Forthcoming in the Leicester University, Dept. of English Local History, Occasional Papers.)

Munby, L. M. 'Sir Richard Fanshawe (1608–66) and his Family', *Hertfordshire Past and Present*, iii (1962–3).

Napier-Higgins, Mrs. *The Bernards of Abington and Nether Winchendon*. London, 1903.

Neale, J. E. *The Elizabethan House of Commons*. London, 1949.

    *Elizabeth I and her Parliaments*. II. London, 1957.

Notestein, W. *The House of Commons 1604–1610*. New Haven, 1971.

Ogg, D. *England in the Reign of Charles II*. Oxford, 1955.

Orwin, C. S. and C. S. *The Open Fields*. Oxford, 1967.

Page, F. M. *History of Hertford*. Hertford, 1959.

Pape, T. *Newcastle-under-Lyme in Tudor and Early Stuart Times*. Manchester, 1938.

Pearl, V. *London and the Outbreak of the Puritan Revolution*. Oxford, 1961.

Plumb, J. H. *The Growth of Political Stability in England 1675–1725*. London, 1967.

    'The Growth of the Electorate in England from 1600 to 1715', *Past and Present*, xlv (1969).

Pocock, J. G. A. *The Ancient Constitution and the Feudal Law*. Cambridge, 1957.

Poole, B. *Coventry: its History and Antiquities*. London, 1870.

Pound, J. *Poverty and Vagrancy in Tudor England*. London, 1971.

Ramsay, G. D. *The Wiltshire Woollen Industry in the Sixteenth and Seventeenth Centuries*. London, 1943.

Rathbone, M. G. *Wiltshire Borough Records before 1836*. Wiltshire Archaeological and Natural History Soc., v. 1949.

Rex, M. B. *University Representation in England 1604–1690*. London, 1954.

Rogers, A. 'The Lincolnshire County Court in the Fifteenth Century', *Lincolnshire History and Archaeology*, i (1966).

    'Parliamentary Elections in Grimsby in the Fifteenth Century', *Bulletin of the Institute of Historical Research*, xlii (1969).

Rogers, N. 'Aristocratic Clientage, Trade and Independency: Popular Politics in Pre-Radical Westminster', *Past and Present*, lxi (1973).

Roskell, J. S. *The Commons in the Parliament of 1422*. Manchester, 1954.

Ruigh, R. E. *The Parliament of 1624*. Cambridge, Mass., 1971.

Rutman, D. B. *Winthrop's Boston*. Chapel Hill, 1965.

Sachse, W. L. (ed.). *Minutes of the Norwich Court of Mayoralty 1630–1631*. Norfolk Record Soc., xv. 1942.

Scott, J. *Berwick-upon-Tweed*. London, 1888.

Seaver, P. S. *The Puritan Lectureships*. Stanford, 1970.

Seddon, P. R. 'A Parliamentary Election at East Retford, 1624', *Transactions of the Thoroton Society of Nottinghamshire*, lxxvi (1972).

Simmons, R. C. 'Freemanship in Early Massachusetts', *William and Mary Quarterly*, xix (1962).

'Godliness, Property and the Franchise', *Journal of American History*, lv (1968–9).

Sinclair, D. *History of Wigan*. Wigan, 1882.

Skipp, V. H. T. 'Economic and Social Change in the Forest of Arden' in Thirsk, *Land, Church and People*.

Slack, P. 'An Election to the Short Parliament', *Bulletin of the Institute of Historical Research*, xlvi (1973).

'Poverty and Politics in Salisbury 1597–1666', in Clark and Slack, *Crisis and Order*.

Smith, H. *The Ecclesiastical History of Essex*. Colchester, 1932.

Stephens, W. B. 'The Overseas Trade of Chester in the early seventeenth century', *Transactions of the Historic Society of Lancashire and Cheshire*, cxx (1968).

*Seventeenth-Century Exeter*. Exeter, 1958.

Stone, L. *Causes of the English Revolution 1529–1642*. London, 1972.

*Family and Fortune*. Oxford, 1973.

'The Electoral Influence of the second Earl of Salisbury, 1614–1668', *English Historical Review*, lxxi (1956).

Styles, P. 'The Corporation of Bewdley under the later Stuarts', *University of Birmingham Historical Journal*, i (1947).

Supple, B. E. *Commercial Crisis and Change in England 1600–1642*. Cambridge, 1959.

Tawney, A. J. and R. H. 'An Occupational Census of the Seventeenth Century', *Economic History Review*, v (1934).

Tawney, R. H. *The Agrarian Problem in the Sixteenth Century*. London, 1912.

Thirsk, J. (ed.). *The Agrarian History of England and Wales. IV. 1500–1640*. Cambridge, 1967.

'Seventeenth-Century Agriculture and Social Change' in J. Thirsk (ed.). *Land, Church and People: Agricultural History Review Supplement* (1970).

Thomas, K. 'The Levellers and the Franchise' in G. E. Aylmer (ed.). *The Interregnum*. London, 1972.

Thompson, E. P. 'The Moral Economy of the English Crowd in the Eighteenth Century', *Past and Present*, l (1971).

Thrupp, S. L. 'The Gilds' in Postan, Rich, Miller, *Cambridge Economic History of Europe. III.*

Tighe, R. R. and Davies, J. E. *Annals of Windsor*. London, 1858.

Underdown, D. *Pride's Purge*. Oxford, 1971.

*Somerset in the Civil War and Interregnum*. Newton Abbot, 1973.

'The Ilchester Election, February 1646', *Proceedings of the Somersetshire Archaeological and Natural History Society*, cx (1966).

Verney, F. P. and M. M. *Memoirs of the Verney Family*. London, 1904.

*Victoria County Histories*

Berkshire, III (1923).

Gloucestershire, VIII (1968).

Lancashire, IV (1911)

Warwickshire, VIII (1969).

Wiltshire, v (1957) and IX (1970).

Yorkshire: the City of York (1961).

Wall, R. E. 'The Massachusetts Bay Colony Franchise in 1647', *William and Mary Quarterly*, xxvii (1970).

'The Decline of the Massachusetts Franchise: 1647–1666', *Journal of American History*, lix (1972–3).

Wedgwood, C. V. *Poetry and Politics under the Stuarts*. Cambridge, 1960.

Weeks, W. S. *Clitheroe in the 17th Century*. Clitheroe, n.d.

Weinbaum, M. *The Incorporation of Boroughs*. Manchester, 1937.
   *British Borough Charters 1307–1660*. Cambridge, 1943.

Welford, R. *History of Newcastle and Gateshead*. London, 1884–7.

Weyman, H. T. 'The Members of Parliament for Ludlow', *Transactions of the Shropshire Archaeological and Natural History Society*, 2nd ser. vii (1895).

Wilks, G. *The Barons of the Cinque Ports and the Parliamentary Representation of Hythe*. Folkestone, n.d.

Willcox, W. B. *Gloucestershire: A Study in Local Government 1590–1640*. New Haven, 1940.

Williams, C. H. 'A Norfolk Parliamentary Election, 1461', *English Historical Review*, xl (1925).

Williams, Penry, 'Government and Politics in Ludlow, 1590–1642', *Transactions of the Shropshire Archaeological Society*, lvi (1957–60).

Woodhouse, A. S. P. *Puritanism and Liberty*. London, 1938.

Woodruff, C. E. 'Notes on the Municipal Records of Queenborough', *Archaeologia Cantiana*, xxii (1897).

Woodward, D. M. 'The Chester Leather Industry 1558–1625', *Transactions of the Historic Society of Lancashire and Cheshire*, cxix (1967).
   'The Overseas Trade of Chester, 1600–1650', *ibid.*, cxxii (1970).
   'Sources for Urban History. Freemen's Rolls', *Local Historian*, ix (1970).

Worden, B., *The Rump Parliament*. Cambridge, 1974.

Wrigley, E. A., 'Mortality in Pre-industrial England', *Daedalus*, xcvii (1968).

Youings, J. *Tuckers Hall Exeter*. Exeter, 1968.

Zagorin, P. *The Court and the Country*. London, 1969.

# Index

Abbot, Robert, 186
Abingdon, 62, 80, 121, 138, 147
Agreement of the People, 3, 23
Aldborough, 132
Alford, Edward, 66, 84, 170–1, 200–1, 230, 265n.14
Allen, William, 191
almsmen, 87, 99–103, 229, 231
Amersham, 16, 24, 98–9, 132–3
Anderson, Sir Henry, 229
Arundel, 67, 74, 99, 132, 231
Arundel, Thomas Earl of, 67, 144, 146, 231
Ashburnham, John, 85
Aylesbury, 18
Ayscough, Sir Edward, 85, 88

Bacon, Francis, 67, 133, 199, 250n.25
Bacon, Sir Nathaniel, 180, 266n.34
Bagshaw, Edward, 86–7, 149, 182, 184
Barnard, John, 261n.14
Barnardiston, Sir Nathaniel, 18, 117, 277n.87
Barnes, T. G., 158
Barnstaple, 20, 48, 49
Barrington, Sir Francis, 200
Barrington, Sir Thomas, 118
Baxter, Richard, 6, 88–9, 91, 114
Bedford, 20, 22, 63, 95, 98–100, 123, 271n.3
Bedford, Francis Earl of, 24, 75, 84
Bedfordshire, 146, 151
Berealston, 122
Berkeley, Sir Maurice, 13
Berkshire, 40, 116
Berwick, 161–2
Bewdley, 195
Bishop's Castle, 69
Bletchingley, 56, 61, 132; debate on, 72–5, 79, 89, 233–4, 250n.21, 282n.12; electioneering in, 119, 152
Borlace, John, 59, 62–3
Boroughs, John, 133
Bossiney, 61, 63, 65–6, 74, 79, 82, 84, 121, 235
Boston, 63, 134, 280n.38; debate on, 78–

80, 93, 234, 235
Boteler, William, 63, 99–100, 123
Bowden, P., 30–1
Bramber, 99, 102
Bramhall, Bishop John, 68
Bramston, Sir John, 68, 75, 274n.3
bribery, see electioneering
Bridgeman, Edward, 126–7
Bridgeman, Bishop John, 114–15, 126–7
Bridgnorth, 195
Bridport, 77, 119, 176, 213, 233–4, 282n.18
Bristol, 50, 95, 272n.30; franchise dispute in, 66, 195, 235; and members, 161–2, 179, 183
Brooke, Christopher, 83, 175–6, 229
Brooke, Robert Lord, 88, 212
Brooks, Richard, 210–11
Buckingham, George Duke of, 53, 88, 133, 145, 174, 179, 180, 200, 271n.14
Buckinghamshire, 68, 151; 1604 election dispute, 9, 66, 69, 71, 191
Bunyan, John, 124
burgage tenure, see franchise
Bury St Edmunds, 134–5, 141

Cade, Jack, 13
Caernarvonshire, 23
Caesar, Sir Julius, 49
Cage, William, 84
Calvert, Sir George, 143, 175, 181, 243n.33
Cambridge, 53, 58, 60, 134, 161, 186, 203
Cambridge University, 118–19, 135–6, 195
Cambridgeshire, 142, 242n.21
Canterbury, 56, 135, 146, 148, 151, 152
canvassing, see electioneering
Carey, Sir George, 167
Cecil, Sir Edward, 201–2
Cecil, Sir Robert, see Salisbury, Earl of
chairing, see electioneering
Charles I, 158
charters, 65, 70–2, 79, 83–6, 232–5
Chaworth, Sir George, 74